CHARLES PEIRCE AND MODERN SCIENCE

In this book, T. L. Short places the notorious difficulties of Peirce's important writings in a more productive light, arguing that he wrote philosophy as a scientist, by framing conjectures intended to be refined or superseded in the inquiries they initiate. He argues also that Peirce held that the methods and metaphysics of modern science are amended as inquiry progresses, making metaphysics a branch of empirical knowledge. Additionally, Short shows that Peirce's scientific work expanded empiricism on empirical grounds, grounding his phenomenology and subverting the fact/value dichotomy, and that he understood statistical explanations in nineteenth-century science as reintroducing the idea of final causation, now made empirical. Those innovations underlie Peirce's late ideas of a normative science and of philosophy as a branch of science. Short's rich and original study shows us how to read Peirce's writings and why they are worth reading.

T. L. SHORT was President, Charles S. Peirce Society, 1990, Chairman, Board of Advisors to the Peirce Edition Project, 2001–2010, and President, Peirce Foundation, 2006–2014. His book, *Peirce's Theory of Signs*, was published by Cambridge University Press in 2007.

CHARLES PEIRCE AND MODERN SCIENCE

T. L. SHORT

CAMBRIDGE
UNIVERSITY PRESS

Shaftesbury Road, Cambridge CB2 8EA, United Kingdom

One Liberty Plaza, 20th Floor, New York, NY 10006, USA

477 Williamstown Road, Port Melbourne, VIC 3207, Australia

314–321, 3rd Floor, Plot 3, Splendor Forum, Jasola District Centre, New Delhi – 110025, India

103 Penang Road, #05–06/07, Visioncrest Commercial, Singapore 238467

Cambridge University Press is part of Cambridge University Press & Assessment, a department of the University of Cambridge.

We share the University's mission to contribute to society through the pursuit of education, learning and research at the highest international levels of excellence.

www.cambridge.org
Information on this title: www.cambridge.org/9781009223522

DOI: 10.1017/9781009223508

First published 2022
First paperback edition 2024

A catalogue record for this publication is available from the British Library

Library of Congress Cataloging-in-Publication data
NAMES: Short, T. L. (Thomas Lloyd), 1940– author.
TITLE: Charles Peirce and modern science / T.L. Short.
DESCRIPTION: Cambridge, United Kingdom ; New York, NY : Cambridge University Press, 2022. | Includes bibliographical references and index.
IDENTIFIERS: LCCN 2022024924 | ISBN 9781009223546 (hardback) | ISBN 9781009223508 (ebook)
SUBJECTS: LCSH: Peirce, Charles S. (Charles Sanders), 1839–1914. | Science – Philosophy. | Philosophy and science. | Civilization, Modern – 19th century. | Philosophy, American – 19th century. | BISAC: PHILOSOPHY / History & Surveys / Modern
CLASSIFICATION: LCC B945.P44 S4765 2022 | DDC 191–dc23/eng/20220714
LC record available at https://lccn.loc.gov/2022024924

ISBN   978-1-009-22354-6   Hardback
ISBN   978-1-009-22352-2   Paperback

In memoriam
George Raymond Geiger (1903–1988)
Frank Tannenbaum (1893–1969)
Sidney Hook (1902–1989)
Three of John Dewey's students who at turning points shaped my life

Contents

Preface

What is, or ought to be, the relation of philosophy to science? The study of nature, if theoretical rather than descriptive or practical, was not distinguished from philosophy until after the advent of modern science. Since then, philosophy has defined itself largely by its relation to science. In the stock phrases, it has sometimes seen itself as the queen of the sciences, laying the foundations for scientific inquiry and/or fitting scientific conclusions to a grand system, and sometimes as its handmaiden, clarifying its methods and purpose. Instead of or in addition to either queen or handmaiden, philosophy has been conceived of as specializing in all the questions which the sciences do not address; sometimes, as with Kant, as drawing boundaries around science to make room for another mode of knowledge. If science is conceived of as factual in contradistinction to normative, then normative questions are left for philosophy, including normative questions about what science is good for and how it should be pursued. The American scientist and philosopher, Charles Sanders Peirce (1839–1914), had conceptions of science, philosophy, and their relation that fit none of the preceding categories.

Peirce drew his definition of science from the historical fact of modern science, but not from its initial methods and metaphysics. He defined science by its 'spirit' of untrammeled discovery. Science, then, is not limited to any method or metaphysics established a priori. Its methods and their metaphysical presuppositions are tested empirically by their fruitfulness or lack thereof in guiding inquiry. Indeed, Peirce argued that nineteenth-century developments in physics and biology introduced nonmechanistic modes of explanation. So also, the limits of science – the possible topics of factual inquiry – are discovered as empirical methods are tried and prove either to have or to lack interesting results. In these ways, the philosophy of science is internal to science: cognitive norms are a product of empirical inquiry.

But then the alleged dichotomy of fact and value is thrown into question. In that and in other ways, Peirce held that modern science, properly understood, subverts the features of modernity – materialism, cynicism, and purposelessness – for which it has usually been blamed. But he also turned modernity's restlessness to good account, on the model of science. Toward the end of his career, he proposed that all of philosophy should become a branch of empirical inquiry: not a body of doctrine a priori but part of the endless enterprise of discovery, including normative discovery. This is an alternative to prevailing conceptions of philosophy, one which it may prove salutary to consider.

That is one theme of this book. The second concerns the notorious difficulties of Peirce's philosophical writings: their many contradictions and lacunae, which provide his exegetes so much frustrating labor and explain why philosophers who choose not to be specialists in Peirce find they must ignore him altogether. These seeming defects, I argue, acquire a different and more productive significance once it is perceived that Peirce wrote philosophy as a scientist, not as a philosopher in any of the usual senses. He made conjectures, extraordinarily bold, and developed them in some technical detail, first in one way and then in another not consistent with the first, and then again in third and fourth ways – all for the sake of trying them out, of pushing them as far as they can go, so as to find what works. Think of how the idea of atomism was developed over 2,000 years in such different, mutually incompatible ways, until finally it resulted in fruitful theories (chemistry and statistical mechanics): Peirce's leading ideas were like that – expressed incompletely and inconsistently, never completely nor finally. Just as he understood science to be inquiry rather than knowledge, so also his aim in philosophy was to open up lines of inquiry, not to state final truths. To read Peirce either as a system builder or as an analytic philosopher *avant la lettre*, engaged primarily in conceptual analysis, is to miss his meaning and mistake his strengths for weaknesses.

Combining these themes results in a complex book, but its parts hang together and cannot be thoroughly developed in separation. At the same time, the focus is narrow: I am not attempting an overview of Peirce's philosophical *oeuvre* nor even of all that he had to say about the methods of science. I shall, for example, touch only briefly on what he wrote about probability, statistical reasoning, and the three modes of inference that he distinguished; perhaps because these topics are technical, they have been relatively well treated in the literature. My aims, rather, are to establish Peirce's unique conception of science, to modify the way in which his philosophical writings are read, and to argue for the relevance of those writings to contemporary philosophy – not by fitting in with current discussions but as suggesting an alternative to them.

This book is addressed to anyone interested in philosophy and not to students of Peirce only: it presupposes some acquaintance with philosophy but no knowledge of Peirce's writings. Although not written as an introduction to his thought, it may nonetheless serve as one entrance, among many, to the labyrinth.

...

It may help to outline the chapters that follow, as they vary in kind yet are interdependent. Chapter 1 briefly reviews Peirce's life in science, emphasizing the variety of his researches in mathematical logic, chemistry, astronomy, geodesy, experimental psychology, and the history of science. Chapter 2 discusses in depth his conception of science, difficult precisely because it is not technical but turns on the nebulous idea of a scientific 'spirit': one which eventually expressed itself in specialist research and is now embodied in the institutions that support that research. He reversed the usual deprecation of specialization, portraying it as exemplary devotion to a transcendent cause. Chapter 3 defends this conception of science against a pair of current, mutually antagonistic ideas of the difference of modern science from classical and medieval philosophy; Peirce saw that difference more subtly as one in which the classical ideal of knowing is transformed rather than abandoned. That revolution in cognitive aim occurred, it is argued, in consequence of empirical discoveries: thus the history of science reviewed in Chapter 3 provides evidence for the argument of Chapter 9, that there is normative knowledge and that it is empirical.

Chapters 4–6 cover much of what is usually included in accounts of Peirce's philosophy, but their contrarian aim is to subvert the notion that he had 'a philosophy' in the usual sense. Chapter 4 examines what was most constant in his thought but constantly evolving: his early embrace of 'scholastic realism' deepened over time as did his so-called pragmatism. Eventually, he came to see that his 1878 'pragmatic' rule for clarifying ideas presupposes a modal realism the meaning of which it cannot clarify; this led to that rule's amendment in 1903. Chapters 5 and 6 examine mutually incompatible stages of Peirce's idealism, stressing their exploratory character and unresolved problems. The formal structures projected in writings of 1867 and 1868–1869 (Chapter 5) were in later years retained somewhat modified but transformed in meaning. Most importantly, the orders of relation that proved illuminating in an 1867 essay were later reestablished on an entirely different basis, the 'phenomenology' described in Chapter 8. The cosmological speculations of the 1890s (Chapter 6) were fascinating but unsuccessful. In their context, however, Peirce saw that the nonmechanistic modes of explanation aforementioned reintroduced, with one basic change, Aristotle's idea of what came to be named 'final causation'. This nontheistic teleology explains the possibility of normative science, the topic of Chapter 9.

The part played by Peirce's scientific work in the development of his philosophy has not heretofore been noticed. His measurements of small differences in the brightness of stars (their 'magnitudes') and in the force of the Earth's gravity prompted psychological experiments and related studies probing the limits of perception. Chapter 7 argues that Peirce extended the scope of empiricism on empirical grounds, by making putative observations, finding that they agree, and finding that their agreement can be explained by what is putatively observed; in that way, what is at first putative becomes established as genuine. Thus a theme underlying all of this book: that there is no empirical knowledge without metaphysical presuppositions and that these are tested empirically by the success of the observations they permit. Peirce expanded empiricism in two directions, both surprising. Ranking stars by order of magnitude requires careful attention to one's own sensations: interpersonal agreement in that ranking suggested the possibility of phenomenology – the observation and description of experience itself. And the impressionistic ranking of stars' magnitudes became the model on which Peirce developed his idea of normative science.

In consequence of these discoveries, Peirce in the early 1900s framed a taxonomy of the sciences in which is included philosophy, identified as a number of empirical inquiries, of which the most basic is phenomenology. Chapter 8 states that taxonomy briefly, stressing its anti-foundationalist conception, and then presents the science of phenomenology – or phaneroscopy, as Peirce later renamed it – systematically. Phaneroscopy depends not only on empiricism's expansion (Chapter 7) but also on a vocabulary of phaneroscopic description drawn from the algebra of relations, viz., the three orders of relation that had been discovered in 1867 to be illuminating (Chapter 5). This chapter concludes by illustrating the use of phaneroscopy in establishing the meaning, hence the meaningfulness, of metaphysical categories. That use was mandated by Peirce's 1903 reformulation of pragmatism (Chapter 4).

Peirce's concept of science entails that normative judgment in science, about which types of theory or explanation or evidence, etc., are good, must depend on the evidence provided by the experience of inquiring (Chapter 2), a thesis supported by the history of science (Chapter 3). This implies a method, at once empirical and normative, which his late sketch of a trio of 'normative sciences' generalizes and rationalizes. Its generalization is supported by the expansion of empiricism (Chapter 7) and its rationalization depends on the rediscovery of final causation (Chapter 6). On Peirce's account of them, however, the three strands of normative inquiry abstractly portrayed cannot in practice be disentangled from ongoing experience. Thus, they cannot have been intended to be new specializations. The importance of his idea is, rather, that its plausibility undermines that most pernicious of dichotomies, of fact and value. Chapter 9 explicates Peirce's idea of normative science, traces its method through Schiller's aesthetics to Kant (surprisingly), and suggests that the rediscovery of final causation corrects what is most problematic in Kant's metaphysics of morals, viz., its anti-naturalism.

The brief concluding chapter (Chapter 10) summarizes the preceding as an ironic opposition of modern science to modernity.

Acknowledgments

Many friends and colleagues have read versions of this book and related articles and given me the benefit of their criticism. The two who have read the whole book and who have done the most to save me from the error of my ways are Nathan Houser and David Rohr. Dr Rohr also kindly did the index. Cambridge University Press's anonymous readers were more than usually helpful. Specific chapters were improved by the criticism of Richard Kenneth Atkins, Jeff Kasser, Robert Lane, Martin Lefebvre, Catherine Legg, and Charles Rubin. The geologist, Victor Baker, deserves special mention, as it was his comment, that Peirce wrote philosophy like a scientist, that planted the seed.

A Note on Citation of Sources

I employ the usual abbreviations in citing Peirce's writings: those of the form n.m are to paragraph m of volume n of the *Collected Papers*, while those of the forms Wn:m are to page m of volume n of the *Writings*, EPn:m to page m of volume n of *The Essential Peirce*, RLT:n to page n of *Reasoning and the Logic of Things*, PM:n to page n of *Philosophy of Mathematics: Selected Writings*, and Rn to unpublished manuscript n, as numbered in Richard Robin's catalogue (Robin 1967). The Bibliography contains more information about these editions. Whenever possible, I will cite EP instead of other editions, as that is the source most readily available to most readers. Other references, as that to Robin just made, are by author and date, as listed in the Bibliography. An exception is made for citations of classical works, for example, those by Aristotle, Descartes, Hume, and Kant. In their case, I use standard forms of citation that will enable the reader to locate the passage cited in any good edition or translation. That is more useful than citing a page number to a particular edition, and therefore I have listed no such editions in the Bibliography. I cite particular editions of these classic works only when quoting a translation, and those translations are listed in the Bibliography.

CHAPTER I

Peirce's Life in Science: 1859–1891

... the writer ... may almost be said to have inhabited a laboratory from age six until long past maturity; and having all his life associated mostly with experimentalists, it has always been with a confident sense of understanding them and of being understood by them. – *Peirce in 1905, EP2:332*

Biography is irrelevant to philosophy, normally. For the purpose of understanding Peirce's thought, however, it is helpful to know the extent to which he had been immersed in mathematics and scientific research from childhood onward. This history is well known to students of Peirce's philosophy, yet his philosophical writings are seldom interpreted in light of the scientific milieu in which they were written. Hence the present chapter. By describing his scientific work and enumerating his accomplishments in diverse fields, I hope to render plausible this book's unusual orientation.

Of the history here recounted, I say nothing original.[1] As it would be misleading to omit Peirce's philosophical essays and lectures within the same period, I mention them also; however, philosophical or scientific matters discussed in later chapters are treated briefly. My explications of technical subjects may be too concise to help some readers, but one who reads through the chapter will get the gist, which is all for the present purpose that matters.

---

[1] In what follows, every undocumented biographical claim is derived from one or more of these sources: what has been published of Peirce's scientific work in the chronological edition of his Writings and in Volume 7 of the Collected Papers; the introductions, by Max Fisch and others, but especially the quite detailed ones by Nathan Houser, to various volumes of the Writings; Joseph Brent's biography of Peirce (Brent 1993; there is a later edition, but I prefer the first); Victor Lenzen's 'Charles S. Peirce as Astronomer' (in Moore and Robin, eds., 1964); and Ian Hacking's survey of Peirce's many-sided encounters with probability (1990, Ch. 23).

I

A

Charles Sanders Peirce, rhymes with 'curse', was born on September 10, 1839, the second of Benjamin and Sarah Mills Peirce's five children. Benjamin Peirce (1809–1880) was a Harvard professor of mathematics and astronomy, the only creative mathematician in the United States of his day and the second American mathematician, after his teacher Nathaniel Bowditch, to be internationally recognized. He was a friend of Emerson and Longfellow but was especially close to Louis Agassiz, the Swiss expatriate and naturalist who founded the Harvard Museum of Comparative Zoology and the last major biologist never to be converted to Darwinism. Benjamin was close also to Henry James, Sr., a Swedenborgian mystic who is remembered today primarily for his sons, the philosopher, William, and the novelist, Henry, Jr. Charles was thus raised in a scientific milieu, but not one narrowly scientific.

Together with Agassiz and other leading scientists, Benjamin in 1863 founded the National Academy of Sciences. For seven years, while retaining his Harvard professorship, he served as a superintendent of the US Coast Survey (later, the Coast and Geodetic Survey; today, the National Oceanic and Atmospheric Administration). He was elected president of the American Association for the Advancement of Science, convinced Abbot Lawrence to endow the Lawrence Scientific School at Harvard, and founded the Harvard Observatory under Coast Survey auspices. It was within these institutions, which owed so much to his father, that Charles studied and worked.

Benjamin's oldest son, James Mills, became like his father a professor of mathematics at Harvard. Yet, as the boys were growing up, it was with Charles that Benjamin would discuss his own researches. For, early on, he discovered in Charles the marks of genius. He raised him accordingly, instilling in the boy a habit of intense and prolonged concentration. Benjamin and his mathematical colleagues believed that Charles had a stronger mind for mathematics than did his father.

After desultory study at Harvard, graduating near the bottom of his class in 1859, Peirce earned a Bachelor of Science degree in chemistry *summa cum laude*, from the Lawrence Scientific School, in 1863. Between Harvard and the Lawrence School, he worked as a temporary aide to the Coast Survey, then spent half a year studying taxonomy with Agassiz. After the Lawrence School, he attained a regular position in the Coast Survey. His work at the Survey, being in the national interest, excused him from service in the Civil War. He would have made a terrible soldier.

From July 1861 to June 1867, Peirce worked for the Coast Survey as a 'computer'. At first, much of this was at the Harvard Observatory, reducing observations of occultations of the Pleiades by the moon, thereby correcting earlier determinations of longitudes (by triangulation from time differences in such observations taken at different locations). This was a full-time job, but during that period, he had also completed his degree at the Lawrence Scientific School, married, and published a brief paper on 'The Chemical Theory of Interpenetration' (W1:95–100). In 1865, he gave a series of twelve lectures at Harvard on 'The Logic of Science' (W1:162–302), and a different series of twelve under almost the same title at the Lowell Institute the next year (W1:358–504). These lectures intermix comment on the views of Kant and mainly English philosophers with various forays into syllogistic logic, Boole's new calculus of logic, and probability theory.

Perhaps of most interest, the 1865 lectures announced a third mode of inference, in addition to deduction and induction, named 'hypothesis' (comparable to Karl Popper's idea of 'conjecture' propounded nearly a century later). William Whewell had emphasized the importance of hypothesis; Peirce turned it into a form of inference. This tripartite division of inference is frequently repeated throughout the rest of his career, during which hypothesis became renamed 'retroduction' (less often, 'presumption') and, finally, 'abduction'. Abduction is variously defined as well as variously named, but, roughly, it either introduces an explanatory hypothesis or provides a reason either for tentatively accepting it or for examining and testing it. Confirmation of a hypothesis is inductive. At this time, it was in terms of syllogistic logic that Peirce distinguished the three forms of inference: induction is one and abduction is another of well-known deductive fallacies.[2] What counts as a fallacy or, conversely, what counts as validity, is relative to the aim of inference: in deduction, the aim is to conserve truth; in induction and abduction, it is to extend knowledge. To extend knowledge, error must be risked; the hope is that in the long run errors will be eliminated, growth of knowledge being the residue of the process. The analogies, to diversifying risks in investment and to selection among chance mutations in biological evolution, have often been made – but only many years after Peirce wrote.

---

[2] 'All A is B. All B is C. Therefore, all A is C' is deductively valid; while 'All A is B. All A is C. Therefore, all B is C' is deductively invalid but is the pattern of induction, and 'All A is C. All B is C. Therefore, all A is B', also deductively invalid, is the pattern of abduction (for, if all B is C, then A's being B's would explain why A's are C's).

4 Charles Peirce and Modern Science

At the beginning of 1867, upon being elected to the American Academy of Arts and Sciences, Peirce read or otherwise presented five remarkably concise papers (W2:12–97), published in its *Proceedings* of 1868. In these, some of the topics discussed in his lectures were separately treated and further developed. 'On an Improvement in Boole's Calculus of Logic' makes important amendments to Boole's new notation (adapting the signs and rules of arithmetic to logic), increasing its expressiveness and facilitating its application to probabilities. 'On the Natural Classification of Arguments' is a study of syllogistic logic that includes induction and abduction (named 'hypothesis'). 'Upon the Logic of Mathematics' sketches a formal deduction of mathematics from 'propositions ... taken as definitions of [mathematical] objects' (W2:59). It is not logicism, as in the attempt by Frege and Whitehead/Russell to deduce mathematics from logical axioms; instead, it is closer to what the logicist program ended up being, where one or another axiom is nonlogical. I think the most interesting paper is the last, 'Upon Logical Comprehension and Extension'. It has received little comment but represents a deep strand of Peirce's thought that was further developed in later years, in his doctrine that symbols grow in meaning ('comprehension') while not losing, or even while also growing in, their range of reference ('extension'), thus embodying growth of knowledge (in this essay named 'information'). The third of the American Academy papers, 'On a New List of Categories' (EP1:Ch.1), is the one most celebrated by his philosophical readers, as, in it, he seems to have anticipated so much of his later thought: it is examined in Chapter 5.

Beginning in 1867, Peirce published a number of book reviews on mathematical, scientific, and philosophical works in the *North American Review* and then, after 1868, a great many in the *Nation*. An 1867 review (W2:98–102) was among the first to recognize the importance of the frequency theory of probability, proposed by John Venn in 1866. That theory is an alternative to the classical conception of probability (Pascal, Bernoulli, Laplace, et al.). Classically, a probability is a rational number determined a priori on the basis of ignorance; for example, we have no reason to expect heads more or less than tails, so the probability of a flipped coin's landing heads-up is 1/2. On Venn's account, a probability is a real number, viz., the limit toward which an actual ratio – say, of heads to flips – tends over the long run. It is approximated empirically by examining as much of the run as we can. The frequency theory is one that Peirce thereafter maintained consistently but often revised: it is of enormous importance to many departments of his thought.

Two further items, out of a great many that might be mentioned, indicate Peirce's range. In a letter of 1869 to the *Chemical News*, he proposed a table of chemical elements (W2:282–84). Much attention was then being given to the question of how to classify the elements. Peirce's scheme might have been of some importance had it not been eclipsed, almost immediately, by the Periodic Table that Mendeleev presented to the Russian Chemical Society in the same year. And in 1870, he reviewed, sympathetically, *The Secret of Swedenborg*, by his father's friend, Henry James, Sr., a book notoriously more obscure than the mystical doctrine it was meant to elucidate (W2:433–38).

B

In June 1867, Peirce's astronomical work changed, from computation exclusively, to include observation as well. From that time until 1875, he participated in a variety of astronomical observations and measurements at the Harvard Observatory and from other vantage points under the auspices of the Coast Survey. The results to which he contributed, including micrometric measurements of celestial positions, were published in Observatory reports and other journals. 'The investigations included double stars, nebulae, satellites, asteroids, comets, and occultations of stars and planets by the moon' (Lenzen 1964, p.36). The Observatory acquired a spectroscope in 1867, of which Peirce made much use, including making, in April 1869, the first spectroscopic analysis of an aurora borealis. In August 1869, he was part of a Coast Survey expedition to Kentucky to observe a solar eclipse. In June 1870, Peirce traveled to the Mediterranean to find suitable sites for observing the solar eclipse predicted for December, and he was part of the party, under the direction of his father, that made the observations from Sicily (another party did the same from Spain). These included determining the polarization of the solar corona.

It should be understood that the use of instruments in scientific measurement involves painstaking work, many calculations, and fresh thought. This work is not mechanical and requires theoretical reasoning. For example, photographs were taken and micrometric measurements made of the 1869 eclipse to determine the radii of sun and moon, but Peirce found that the results were uncertain, due to unsystematic variations in the tilt of the photographic plates relative to the optical axis of the telescope. In connection with this work of 1869, he also devised a graphical method by which to map the moon's shadow, minute by minute, as it crossed the United States.

Let me pause here to emphasize a point. This work done in 1869 illustrates two quite different but complementary aspects of Peirce's overriding interest in logic: problems in making accurate observations and techniques of representation. For, while we can look at what we cannot comprehend, we can observe (make an observation of) only what we can represent (e.g. name, describe, or conceive of), and knowledge is therefore advanced by these two means. Both to observation and to representation, Peirce in all of his remaining years gave persistent, penetrating, and highly original attention. We will pay special attention in Chapter 7 to his studies of observation; his general study of representation in all its forms is to be found in his theory of signs or 'semeiotic'.

Also in 1869, Peirce delivered fifteen lectures at Harvard, on 'British Logicians', in which William of Ockham, Duns Scotus, and other medieval logicians were prominently featured (only some fragments survive: W2:310–47, 533–38). His historical studies of logic were being taken deeper in time; eventually, they would reach beyond the medieval period through the Hellenistic age to classical Athens; but at this point, the thirteenth century predominated. That was not without an influence on his philosophy. Already in 1868–1869, he had published a series of three papers in the *Journal of Speculative Philosophy*,[3] in which he launched an attack on Descartes and, through Descartes, on all of modern philosophy (EP1:Chs.2–4). Although not endorsing the views of medieval logicians, he compared favorably their style of thought to that of Descartes and his successors and, in stunning paradox, associated the pattern of their inquiry with that of modern science (*vide infra*, Ch.5, A). This critique of modern philosophy was explicitly logical and implicitly moral. It issued in a novel theory of cognition and reality, and also in a novel theory of the self, in which the individualism and egoism of the modern age were challenged. But these are themes I develop in later chapters.

C

Now, we must begin to describe Peirce's contributions to formal deductive logic. In order to appreciate their importance, the reader should know that there had been no major addition to formal deductive logic for over two millennia, from the founding of that subject by Aristotle in the fourth-century BC to the year 1847. To be sure, well before 1847, there had

---

[3] This quarterly journal, published in St. Louis, was the first philosophical journal in the English-speaking world (W2:xxv). Peirce's 1868 papers appeared in its second year of publication.

been additions to Aristotle's theory of the syllogism; most importantly, his brief remarks on propositional logic were developed by his student, Theophrastus, and then by others. During the course of the Hellenistic period and the Middle Ages, there had been a profusion of subtle studies of logic; a far greater share of intellectual energy was devoted to logic in those centuries than has been devoted to it since. And yet, there was no advance either in the techniques of formalization or in the range of deductive logic. Then, from 1847 to 1935, there occurred a revolution in logic resulting in a stream of stunning discoveries: that mathematics cannot be reduced to logic; that mathematical truth, even with respect to arithmetic alone, cannot be defined as what may be deduced from axioms, logical or nonlogical; and that reasoning cannot be wholly reduced to routine, that is, to rules mechanically applied.

As to techniques of formalization: in 1847 and in 1854, George Boole, a self-taught English mathematician of humble origin, published two books that formalized logic in the style of arithmetical algebra. However, Boole's algebra of logic was limited to the range of Aristotle's syllogistic and propositional logic, though he also applied these techniques to probabilities; it did not cover inferences concerning relations. Boole's class logic and Aristotle's syllogistic embrace the logic of predicates taking subjects one at a time, such as 'x is red' and 'x explodes'. But there is a need for a logic of predicates taking subjects two or three or more at a time, such as 'x is larger than y', 'x is y's father', and 'x gives y to z'. We may thus speak of predicates, and of the properties or relations they represent, as being of different 'orders' or 'adicities': monadic (Rx, where R is something predicated of a single subject, x), dyadic (Rxy, where R is predicated of an ordered pair of subjects, x and y), triadic (Rxyz), etc. Without extending logic to dyadic relations, we cannot show that even so simple an inference as 'All men are animals, therefore the head of a man is the head of an animal' is valid. The example is due to the English mathematician, Augustus De Morgan, who used it in 1860 to show the inadequacy of syllogistic logic.

Earlier, De Morgan, Peirce, and others had attempted to extend the principles of syllogistic to inferences concerning relations. De Morgan published his 1860 memoir in 1864, which Peirce read in 1868 (W2:xliv). He began working on a non-syllogistic logic of relations in the late 1860s and in 1870 published a long paper (W2:359–432) with a long title – 'Description of a Notation for the Logic of Relatives, Resulting from an Amplification of the Conceptions of Boole's Calculus of Logic' (in the *Memoirs of the American Academy of Arts and Sciences*) – in which he developed a logic of relations in Boole's style.[4] He was the first to have done so. Subsequent papers, published in the *American Journal of Mathematics*, in 1880 (W4:163–209) and 1885 (W5:162–90), refined and extended that system. Thereby, he established the subject. The importance of this to the development of modern mathematical logic cannot be overstated; there could not have been a logical analysis of mathematics without it. Peirce's only equal in developing a logic of relations was the German, Ernst Schröder, whose later work made use of Peirce's. Schröder's writings, in turn, were fundamental to Russell and Whitehead's *Principia Mathematica* (1910–1913) and hence to the revolution in modern logic.

D

In the year 1870, as well as traveling twice to Europe in connection with observing the solar eclipse and in addition to publishing his first major paper on the logic of relations, Peirce wrote and saw published a long review of a new edition of the works of Bishop Berkeley (W2:462–87). This review is of generally acknowledged importance. It marks a further depth taken in his studies of medieval logic and a correspondingly stronger criticism of modern individualism. In these pages (anticipated in his 1868 article, at EP1:52–53), he derived from medieval discussions a definition of 'real' – as that which is independent of what anyone thinks about it – by which to make sense of the medieval controversy between realism and nominalism, as to whether individual things alone are real. He took the side of the realists, that is, of those who affirmed the reality of that which cannot be reduced to any finite collection of individuals, such as types of quality and types of individual. His realism continued to grow in later years, in both depth and breadth. But we will discuss realism at length later (Chapters 4 and 8).

In 1872, Peirce began two new assignments at the Coast Survey. One, continuing through 1875, was to determine the 'magnitudes', that is, relative brightness, of stars instrumentally. Always previously, differences in magnitude were judged by eye, unaided. The ultimate purpose of this study was to determine the shape of our galaxy, the pattern of distribution of stars of various magnitudes in it, and our own location within

---

[4] For detailed comparison of this paper to De Morgan's work, in which the logic of relations had begun to be formalized albeit in a different and less satisfactory way, and also to the elder Peirce's *Linear Associative Algebra*, which appeared with Charles' help in the same year, see Daniel D. Merrill's introduction to W2, W2:xlii–xlviii.

it. It resulted in the only book Peirce ever published of his own work, *Photometric Researches* (1878). As Lenzen reports, 'In his pioneer contribution, based upon scant data, Peirce deduces general forms of the surfaces of equal star-density throughout the [galactic] cluster' (Lenzen 1964, p.48 – but all of pages 48 and 49 should be consulted for the technical details and also regarding recognition by later astronomers of the importance of this work). In this book, Peirce described his experiments correlating judgments of brightness to differences in light energy, confirming Fechner's psychophysical hypothesis that the strength of sensation varies as a logarithm of the strength of the physical stimulus. He also summarized the results of his research in 1875–1876 in European libraries, examining ancient and medieval star catalogues, and included translations of the major catalogues, the translation of Ptolemy's being his own. These psychophysical experiments and historical comparisons attested to the objectivity of judgments seemingly subjective: see Chapter 7.

The other assignment was to measure the Earth's force of gravity at various points on its surface, by which to determine the distribution of mass in the Earth. This was done by timing the period of a swung pendulum. As with the preceding example, these measurements were extremely exacting, requiring much adjustment of the apparatus and training of the observer, as well as complex calculations by which raw data were reduced to scientifically meaningful data. After 1875, Peirce's work at the Survey was wholly devoted to gravity measurements, partly including the training and supervision of assistants. The pendulum apparatus was a major concern, and several variants of it were tried. Extensive trips were made to Europe in 1875–1876, 1877, 1880, and 1883, to measure gravity from different locations, to pick up an improved apparatus from a firm in Hamburg and later to bring a design of Peirce's own to that firm, and to communicate, to a geodesy conference in Paris,[5] his finding that a flexure in the support of the pendulum affected the period. That source of error was corrected in the apparatus Peirce designed, on which two pendulums are swung simultaneously in opposite direction.

During these and his earlier trips to Europe – two-and-a-half years *in toto* – Peirce took advantage of the opportunity to meet with various mathematicians and logicians such as De Morgan, to consult with Clerk Maxwell and other scientists on geodesy, and to visit the great libraries to read rare

---

[5] 'The first international scientific association was geodetic' – it was founded in 1864 – and Peirce was 'the first invited American participant in the committee meetings of an international scientific association' (Fisch, W3:xxiv–xxv).

manuscripts in logic and in the early history of science, particularly but not only the early star catalogues. This included early studies of magnetism; he made a translation, now lost, of Petrus Peregrinus' thirteenth-century treatise on the loadstone. The fine arts were not neglected; indeed, his puritanical first wife, who disapproved of his attending the opera, returned, for that or for other reasons, in haste to the United States. In addition, he began learning Arabic and was tutored in Médoc by a French sommelier.

E

The eclipses observed in 1869 and 1870 posed a problem for use of the method of least squares. All measurements, to the extent that they purport to be exact, are liable to be wrong. Exactness is improved by making many measurements of the same quantity and then taking the true measure to be the value from which the actual measurements (discarding those far from the mean) vary least (i.e., the number which is such that the sum of the squares of its differences from each actual measurement is least). But this method presupposes that errors will tend to occur more or less symmetrically on either side of the true value. And that is not the case when observing the time at which a star or other body emerges from occultation. Peirce's paper addressing this problem, 'On the Theory of Errors of Observation', appeared in 1873 (W3:114–60). It is remarkable for applying the logic of relations to probability and probability to the analysis of inductive inference. That treatment of induction was further developed in later papers, discussed below.

The 1873 paper is remarkable, also, for reporting an experimental study, carried out by Peirce himself, of the effect of training on improving an observer's accuracy in observing a phenomenon 'not seen coming on', like the emergence of a star from behind the moon. This and a later study, in connection with his photometric researches, of the effect of training on judgments of brightness, were Peirce's first forays into experimental psychology. Both are discussed in some detail in Chapter 7.

The science of experimental psychology had only recently been initiated in Germany – in fact, from the beginning of the century, but Fechner's important book did not appear until 1860 and Wundt did not formally establish what is often said to be the first laboratory in experimental psychology until 1879. William James, who had studied with Wundt in Germany, began his experimental studies in psychology in about 1874; there is no exact date at which his laboratory in experimental psychology can be said to have been established, but its beginnings were no earlier than 1875 (Perry 1935, Vol. II, pp.12–15). Peirce's 1873 paper thus preceded

James in this type of inquiry. It might, however, have been James who, returning from Germany in the late 1860s, alerted his friend to the new developments taking place there. One generalization we might make from this and preceding examples (Boole, Venn, DeMorgan, and Whewell) is that Peirce was always quick to pick up on a new idea and to extend it further; another example of this was provided by Darwin's theory, of which we shall later make much (Chapters 2, 6, and 9).

F

The years 1872–1878 were occupied in large part by scientific work, often making geodetic observations with aides under adverse conditions in a variety of locations, including a failed attempt in a deep vertical mine shaft. In 1877, Peirce was elected to the National Academy of Sciences. In 1877–1878, he published a series of six articles in the *Popular Science Monthly*, under the general title, 'Illustrations of the Logic of Science'. The first two of these are his best-known philosophical essays, 'The Fixation of Belief' and 'How to Make Our Ideas Clear'. 'How to' is supposed to contain the first published statement of pragmatism, though that term was not used. The remaining four essays develop themes begun earlier. The third is on the frequency theory of probability, and the last reformulates the three classes of argument, still syllogistically. The fourth essay, to which the fifth is a religio-cosmological codicil, deserves separate mention, as follows.

'The Probability of Induction' applies the frequency theory of probability to an analysis of inductive inference, developing a line of thought already evident in the paper on errors of observation. An induction can result in a false conclusion from true premises. Why, then, should anyone make inductions? Peirce said that if there is a reality, then repeated inductions will tend over the long run to correct short-run errors and thus approximate to the truth – a truth not already contained in the premises. But his argument is not so facile as such a summary statement may seem to suggest. It applies the mathematics of probability to the case where induction consists in taking the proportion of a pre-designated (this qualification is essential) characteristic in a randomly selected sample of pre-designated size to be the proportion of that characteristic in the entire, perhaps indefinitely large population. Refined in 1883, in 'A Theory of Probable Inference' (W4:408–49), in 1902 (2.102, 2.773–791), and in 1905 (2.755–772), this account anticipated the idea of 'confidence interval estimation' advanced in the 1930s by Jerzy Neyman and E. S. Pearson (see Hacking 1980 and Levi 2004).

Although not the first to claim that induction is self-corrective (Laudan 1973), Peirce was the first to make the statistical argument, and in such a way as distinguishes his view from, for example, the later view of Reichenbach (Levi 1980). In this way, he supported a theme that he had stated much earlier, especially at the conclusion of his three 1868–1869 essays, and continued to maintain the rest of his life, that types of argument essential to the growth of knowledge, namely, induction and abduction, are not valid in the short run. The implication, which he drew in dramatic form, is that logic itself requires us to transcend egoism, by taking an interest in the long run, which is a run one does not live to see completed. Except as contributing to what others will eventually believe, our inductive and abductive inferences are illogical. This extreme conclusion was implicitly modified in his later work, but its anti-egoistic spirit was retained.

G

In 1877–1878, Peirce developed what he named a 'quincuncial projection' of the Earth: a two-dimensional map in which the angles found on a globe between any two points are preserved, as they are not in other two-dimensional projections (see W4:69, where the map, a thing of beauty, is reproduced).

In 1879, continuing to 1884, Peirce was appointed a part-time Lecturer in Logic at the newly formed Johns Hopkins University, in Baltimore, still continuing his full-time work for the Survey. The lectureship appears to have stimulated his work in formal logic. In addition to the aforementioned long papers of this period on the logic of relations (1880 and 1885), he published two shorter papers in *The American Journal of Mathematics*, 'On the Logic of Number' and 'Associative Algebras', as well as a number of short pieces privately or locally published.

Johns Hopkins was the first university formed in the United States on the model of the German research universities, something that Benjamin Peirce many years previously had urged should be done. It attracted an especially able and eager group of students, including John Dewey and Thorstein Veblen, neither of whom seems at that time to have been greatly influenced by Peirce. Those he did influence include Allan Marquand, Christine Ladd, B. I. Gilman, Joseph Jastrow, and O. H. Mitchell. About Jastrow, more in a moment. The other four are represented in a book Peirce edited while at Johns Hopkins, *Studies in Logic* (Boston, 1883), consisting of essays by his students and one of his own ('A Theory of Probable Inference', mentioned earlier, to which he added two appendices; the second appendix, 'The Logic of Relatives' is long and also important). The students' papers are impressively sophisticated. One of Marquand's two was on logic machines; the other students produced original investigations in the algebra of relations. Marquand later founded Princeton University's art museum and Gilman became director of the Museum of Fine Arts in Boston. Christine Ladd, due to her sex, was permitted at Johns Hopkins only by special arrangement; she later, as Christine Ladd-Franklin (having married another of Peirce's students), achieved some renown as a logician, mathematician, and psychologist. She remained in touch with Peirce on matters of logic. Her papers in psychology pertain to color vision, one of Peirce's special interests.

The most important paper in the collection is that by O. H. Mitchell, which introduced a system of quantification into the logic of relations (incorporated with modifications in Peirce's 1885 paper). A formal theory of quantification – universal quantification expressed in ordinary English by the words 'any', 'every', or 'all' and existential quantification expressed by the words 'some' or 'there exists a' – was essential to the development of modern logic. Thereby, for example, it can be shown why the inference, from 'There is a woman whom all men love' to 'Every man loves some woman', is valid, while the converse inference, from 'Every man loves some woman' to 'There is a woman whom all men love', is invalid. The example is Peirce's.

It is impossible to tell how much Mitchell, who died not long after, owed to his teacher, but the debt must have been great. Quantification was first developed by Gottlob Frege in 1879, but his work was little noted – Peirce was certainly unaware of it – until the twentieth century, and the Mitchell-Peirce system was the first to have had an influence on other logicians, for example, Leopold Löwenheim and Thoralf Skolem in their important work (done independently of Russell and Whitehead's *Principia*, though published in 1915 and later). Frege's system was, however, the one cited by Russell and Whitehead, and for that reason and because of his priority he has usually been given sole credit for the invention of quantification. Peirce's contributions to the development of modern formal logic were for a time mostly forgotten but have recently been recovered (see Putnam 1990, Ch.18, Hintikka 1997, and Sowa 2007).

H

Peirce also guided a single student, Joseph Jastrow, in setting up and carrying out an experiment that holds a place of importance in the history of psychology (7.21n1). The resulting paper, 'On Small Differences of Sensation', published in 1884, presents their experimental findings and argues against the assumption (by Fechner and others) of a 'least perceptible difference' or *Unterschiedsschwelle* of nerve excitations (*vide infra*, Ch.7). As well as its conclusion, the design of the experiment was important. It 'was the first experiment in which the sequence of trials was chosen by an artificial randomizer … built into the analysis of the data' (Hacking 1990, p.205). Jastrow, who cited this experiment as his introduction to the possibility of making an experimental study of a psychological problem, went on to become a leading American psychologist. Philosophers remember him as the source of the 'duck-rabbit' of which Wittgenstein made so much.

In 1880, Peirce was elected to the London Mathematical Society, and in 1881 to the American Association for the Advancement of Science. In 1883, he was made a contributing editor to the newly conceived and very ambitious *Century Dictionary* (twenty-four large volumes, 1889–1891), responsible for all definitions in logic, metaphysics, mathematics, mechanics, astronomy, and weights and measures. In addition, he contributed to definitions in several other areas of philosophy, science, and education, especially words pertaining to universities. Eventually, he wrote, contributed to, or edited over 15,000 entries, many of them quite long (the *Century Dictionary*'s 'definitions' are akin to encyclopedia articles, technical and condensed). From October 1884 to February 1885, Peirce was in charge of the United States Office of Weights and Measures.

It should be noted that this outline omits the many short papers Peirce published, especially in the years 1879–1884, on logical, mathematical, and scientific topics. He was the first to propose using a wavelength of light as a unit of measure – a unit that, unlike the standard meter, would not be subject to change by physical causes (W4:269–98). In addition, he knew many languages, had an interest in Shakespearean pronunciation, wrote on recent developments in economics (Hoover and Wible 2020), and perhaps had an influence on geology (Baker 2009).

Toward the end of this period, Peirce's thought took a dramatic turn, toward an evolutionary cosmology. This began in about 1883 and was first expressed in a lecture, 'Design and Chance' delivered at Johns Hopkins in 1884 (EP1:Ch.15). It culminated in a series of five articles published in the *Monist* in 1891–1893 (EP1:Chs.21–25).[6] The idea, briefly, is that the fact that

---

[6] *The Monist* was the second philosophical journal in the United States. Both it and *The Journal of Speculative Philosophy* were founded in the Midwest; neither had academic affiliation; both had Germanic roots, the first in the philosophy of Hegel, the second in the theological interests of a German immigrant industrialist named Hegeler.

there are laws of nature – and these particular laws rather than others – requires to be explained, and that the only way to explain laws without presupposing other laws is to suppose that they evolved from out of chaos. As Chapter 6 examines this hypothesis and its devolution, I will say no more about it here, except to note, as it is germane to our present theme, that the attempt grew out of concern with the baffled state of physics in the 1880s and was based on earlier advances in nineteenth-century science, in physics and biology. That is to say, it was not a 'philosophical' speculation formed independently of the then current state of scientific knowledge.

I

This chapter is about Peirce's life in science and not his life generally, but the reader, I fear, will demand to know why his scientific career ended so abruptly when he was only fifty-two. He lost his position at Johns Hopkins in 1884 and his position in the Coast and Geodetic Survey in 1891. He never again held a post in any institution, academic or scientific. He earned a living, meagrely, by writing articles, book reviews, and dictionary definitions. For a time, he and his wife, Juliette, lived in New York City, fugitives from Pennsylvania justice, where they were sued for non-payment of debts for work done on a house purchased there in the small town of Milford. At one point, Peirce threatened suicide. Eventually those debts were paid by his brother, enabling Charles and Juliette to return to their house, retiring in rural seclusion. They lived in deepening poverty, hungry and cold, dependent on charity organized by and sustained largely, if not wholly, by William James, by that time a celebrated Harvard professor of psychology and then of philosophy.

James, sometimes privately expressing exasperation with Peirce's improvidence, recognized his friend's genius and, in the late 1890s, did what he could to revive his career. In a lecture of 1898, in California, James announced a new doctrine, named 'pragmatism', which he attributed to Peirce. It was instantly popular. In the same year, he arranged a series of lectures for Peirce to deliver at a private house in Cambridge, Massachusetts. Peirce was not, at that time, permitted on the campus of Harvard College. Then, in 1903, James finally prevailed on President Eliot to allow Peirce on campus and he arranged another series of lectures by Peirce, this time on pragmatism. Each series of lectures was moderately remunerated.

The causes of Peirce's downfall have not been exactly determined, but there are many possibilities. He was arrogant, contemptuous of mediocrity, ill-tempered, and inclined to offend his superiors and colleagues. As long as his father lived, he had protection, but his father died in 1880. Perhaps more importantly, he was impractical in managing the financial and other details of life, careless with Survey apparatus and of his obligations to others, increasingly tardy in completing his assigned tasks, and had an irregular marital history. This last – it was discovered that he had lived with his second wife before they were married – was almost certainly why Johns Hopkins found it necessary to reorganize its program, finding slots in the new arrangement for every existing faculty member except Peirce. In the case of the Survey, his reports were long overdue. One, when finally completed, received a damning review by Simon Newcomb, a celebrated astronomer and mathematician who had been a prize student of Benjamin's and with whom Charles' relations always were rocky. And at the Survey there were a couple of public relations disasters partly Peirce's fault (see Houser, W5:xxviii–xxx, W6:xxx–xxxii). It is clear that Peirce was tired of the Survey work and desired an academic position in logic, but after Johns Hopkins terminated his employment, he was not employable in any college or university.

We are the beneficiaries. Freed from other duties, Peirce, after some years fruitlessly seeking ways of using his scientific expertise to make a fortune, worked full time, unremunerated, in logic and philosophy. In logic, he developed his system of 'existential graphs' – a complete system of truth-functional logic and first-order polyadic predicate logic with identity, with some suggestions for extensions into second-order predicate logic and modal logic.[7] This system is, as advertised, graphical, as Venn diagrams are; but it bears the same relation to the latter as the palace at Versailles bears to a grass hut. In philosophy, he developed the new sciences of phaneroscopy (see Chapter 8) and semeiotic, and framed a conception of three 'normative' sciences (Chapter 9). Under the rubrics 'pragmatism', 'pragmaticism', and 'critical common-sensism', he produced his most deeply considered accounts of scientific inquiry.

---

[7] An excellent introduction to the existential graphs is Roberts (1973), in which, additionally, metatheorems of consistency and deductive completeness are proven for some parts of the system. See also Shin (2002) and Bellucci and Pietarinen (2016).

CHAPTER 2

Peirce's Concept of Science

Until the mid-nineteenth century, the word 'science' retained the meaning Cicero had given it in the first-century BC, when he used *scientia* to translate the Greek philosophers' *epistēmē*. A science was a body of knowledge, a more or less finished system, such as Euclid's science of geometry. It was not a form of inquiry. Well into the nineteenth century, inquiry into nature was named 'natural philosophy'. The people whom we think of as being early scientists, such as Galileo, Newton, and Harvey, did not so designate themselves; they were natural philosophers or mathematicians or otherwise named. And their manner of inquiry, which was not wholly new but was newly regarded as of more than practical utility, was called experimental philosophy or mathematical philosophy. The explanations they sought and sometimes found were mechanistic, and therefore an idea of the world either as a vast machine or as consisting of mechanisms – 'the mechanical philosophy' – became associated with natural philosophy. The word 'scientist' did not exist until 1840, when William Whewell coined it to designate those – by that time numerous and organized – who experiment, measure, and calculate.

Today, by 'science' we mean that form of inquiry which has been growing in scope and power ever since the sixteenth century. Sometimes, in order to distinguish it from earlier speculations about nature, we speak of 'modern science'. Knowledge supposedly established is of course part of science; but even when we refer to *a* science, such as the science of physics, we mean a branch of ongoing inquiry, not a system of knowledge. This lexical change represents an intellectual revolution deeper than is generally recognized. Whereas inquiry had earlier been engaged in for the sake of coming to rest in a system of knowledge, now knowledge is sought for the sake of advancing inquiry, in order to make further discoveries. The new intellectual ideal is that of a restless and endless quest.

Peirce's thought about science was formed in the period when the contemporary meaning of 'science' had just become established. More than anyone else, then or since, he grasped its revolutionary character. But he took the identification of science with inquiry to an extreme, holding that the methods of inquiry and the metaphysics which they assume are themselves products on inquiry; for they are revised as inquiry continues, in light of the results obtained. If that is correct, modern science does not have a philosophy, for example, mechanist. How, then, is it to be defined?

A

In 1893, Peirce wrote:

> What is science? The dictionary will say that it is systematized knowledge. Dictionary definitions, however, are too apt to repose upon derivations; which is as much as to say that they neglect too much the later steps in the evolution of meanings. Mere knowledge, though it be systematized, may be a dead memory; while by science we all habitually mean a living and growing body of truth. We might even say that knowledge is not necessary to science. The astronomical researches of Ptolemy, though they are in great measure false, must be acknowledged by every modern mathematician who reads them to be truly and genuinely scientific. That which constitutes science, then, is not so much correct conclusions, as it is correct method. But the method of science is itself a scientific result. It did not spring out of the brain of a beginner: it was an historic attainment and a scientific achievement. So that not even this method ought to be regarded as essential to the beginnings of science. That which is essential, however, is the scientific spirit, which is determined not to rest satisfied with existing opinions, but to press on to the real truth of nature. (6.428)

There is much to be said about this passage. The remainder of this chapter is an explication of it. For the most part, that explication relies on what Peirce said in other writings.

Peirce here referred to meanings evolving, that is, as changing nonarbitrarily. This forces one to distinguish reference from meaning and to see, as in contemporary 'causal theories' of reference, that neither is wholly a function of the other. For only then does it become possible to suppose that, as more is found out about the referent, our idea of the referent and, hence, the meaning we give to our words for it, can change nonarbitrarily. The name 'Sun' refers to the same entity now as previously, but previously by that term was meant a body that orbits the Earth, which is not what we now think the Sun does.[1]

---

[1] The referent, or at least its recognized scope, may also change in light of discoveries made. For example, words deriving from the Greek word for amber were used at first to refer to static electricity

Now, if science is inquiry, not knowledge, then what sort of inquiry is it? In twentieth-century philosophy of science, science was typically identified by its supposed method (e.g., the hypothetico-deductive method). But it cannot be defined by its method if its method, as Peirce said, is itself a product of scientific inquiry. For in that case, inquiry was scientific before it found its method. But perhaps we can say that, after an inchoate struggle, the right method was found, and that the struggle itself may therefore be identified, retrospectively, as science or early science or proto-science, where 'science' is defined by this method, the method of science.

That, however, will not do. It is not the case that, after some centuries of bumbling, we suddenly struck upon the right method and that all was clear sailing from then on. After the advent of modern science, methods continued to evolve: new types of explanation emerged, generally attended by controversy, and with those changes came unanticipated refinements in the aim of science and in the subordinate values, for example, of simplicity and accuracy, that inform theory-choice (Toulmin 1961, Kuhn (1962/1970) and 1977). Techniques of observation, modes of representation, rules of calculation – all of these vary from one science to another, novel forms emerging with new lines of inquiry. Contrary to a popular dogma, not all theories yield predictions by which they may be tested: consider geology and evolutionary biology. Any idea of 'the' method of science must be either false or so vacuous as to leave the methods actually employed unspecified.

More to the present point, that is what Peirce thought. Often, he spoke of 'the' scientific method, but at least as often, even in the same works, he spoke of scientific methods in the plural, of their being discovered seriatim, and of their being still in process of being discovered. In his 1877 essay, 'The Fixation of Belief', he wrote in both ways but in more persuasive detail about methods in the plural. I am not referring to his famous four methods of 'fixing belief', only one of which is distinguished as 'the' method of science, but rather to an earlier section of the same essay in which he mentioned four historical examples of methods – all of them scientific. I take what Peirce said in those few pages to be of such importance,

only, but with Franklin's discovery 'electric' was applied also to moving charges. One might therefore argue that the reference of 'electric' was extended; or one might argue, instead, that, as electric charge is the same whether static or moving, this term always included lightning and other such phenomena in its extension – only, at first, we didn't know it. Another complication is presented when the referent has itself a history, as in the case of science, so that as it changes, the meaning of the term referring to it also changes. But these complications should not be allowed to obscure the truth, that meaning evolves and often does so as a function of discoveries made about the referent, which is relatively stable.

both for the theme of this chapter and for later chapters, as to warrant its detailed discussion, in the following four sections. Then we will return to the question of how, if not by its method, science can be defined.

B

Early in 'The Fixation of Belief', Peirce wrote that 'each chief step in science has been a lesson in logic' (EP1:111). By 'logic', Peirce here meant, as he usually meant, not formal deductive logic alone, but study of the methods of inquiry. That each chief step in science has been a lesson in logic, so understood, is the thesis for which Thomas Kuhn became famous (Kuhn 1962/1970). Kuhn called a chief step in science a change of 'paradigm', by which he meant that in a manner at once striking and successful there was a new theoretical idea combined with a novel technique of investigation, sometimes a new mode of explanation, and that this combination served as a model for inquirers in that field of investigation or in other fields where the same method might prove fruitful.[2] But let us turn to the historical examples of 'chief steps' that Peirce cited.

'Kepler undertook to draw a curve through the places of Mars' (EP1:110). The places of Mars are its observed positions at successive times, as, in Kepler's case, had been recorded by Tycho Brahe. Drawing a curve through those points could be classified as a method of description or of observation or of prediction or of explanation. It is how one observes an orbit, and the orbit thus described explains, or at least it enables us to predict, the observed positions of the planet. This method was not entirely novel: applications of geometry to astronomical observation, yielding predictions of apparent positions of celestial bodies, go back to ancient times. But Kepler's painstaking plotting showed Mars' orbit to be elliptical with the Sun at one of the ellipsis' two foci. This allowed Kepler to derive his three laws of planetary motion, which, in turn, Newton could show to be deductive consequences, given some simplifying assumptions, from his law of universal gravitation. Kepler's laws were therefore part of the

---

[2] Kuhn particularly emphasized that what is learned through studying a paradigm cannot be reduced to rules that can be learned from a textbook alone. A young scientist is educated by working with older scientists, by pursuing lines of inquiry under their guidance or by imitating their example. Peirce did not say this, so far as I know, but I think he would have agreed. Certainly, that is how he learned science. For example, he did not learn biological taxonomy by studying a textbook. He learned it by being handed a fish by Agassiz who told him to describe it and who then criticized every attempted description. Taxonomy is not independent of a mode of observing and that mode can be learned only from practice. Similar remarks apply to every science.

empirical confirmation of Newton's theory. Peirce, in citing this example, seems to have been suggesting that a method is established by success in its use (he did not cite Newton's use of Kepler's laws, but could assume knowledge of that fact on the part of his readers). Novelty alone does not make something a 'chief step'.

The next example was Lavoisier, whose method 'was to carry his mind into his laboratory, and to make of his alembics and cucurbits instruments of thought, giving a new conception of reasoning, as something to be done with one's eyes open, by manipulating real things instead of words and fancies' (EP1:111). The role of experimentation in modern science, as opposed to Aristotle's form of empiricism, could not have been more dramatically expressed. Peirce's point, however, seems to have been that experimentation needed to be established separately for each department of inquiry. The kinds of experiment carried out by Galileo, Torricelli, Newton, Harvey, and others were not the same as the kinds of experiment by which chemical interactions could be studied.

The specific contrast Peirce invoked was not to Aristotle but to the alchemists, whose method was to read and pray (in a famous maxim that he quoted), before trying out a recipe for transmuting lead into gold. Their methods did not include measuring interactants and their products. But why should they have measured? What would they have supposed they were measuring? Making measurements presupposed a new idea – of course vague – of what is going on in a chemical change: viz., that there are parts that remain constant in quantity. The parts are assumed to be physical; it is the type of interaction, producing changes in secondary qualities, that distinguishes chemistry from physics. Peirce did not say why he chose Lavoisier over Boyle and Priestly, who were earlier in chemical experimentation; perhaps it was because it was with Lavoisier that their methods proved, or proved most dramatically, to be successful. How silly thinking with cucurbits would have seemed had nothing come of it!

The last innovation, presented by a pair of nineteenth-century examples, was the introduction of statistical methods into natural science. Statistics had previously been employed, by the English and the Dutch in the seventeenth century, in drawing up actuarial tables (Hacking 1975, pp.102–21), and, in the eighteenth century, with respect to social phenomena for administrative purposes, a practice that grew with political centralization in France and Prussia (Hacking 1990, pp.16–34). Those uses were descriptive, not explanatory. Still earlier uses of probability, to calculate betting odds, were neither descriptive nor explanatory. The use of statistical methods in physics and in biology, by contrast, was explanatory.

It was a new form of explanation, not anticipated by Galileo or Newton. This is a complicated topic, and one important to us for later purposes. It therefore deserves extended discussion, to which the next three sections are devoted.

C

Peirce's discussion of the two examples he cited, the theory of gases and Darwin's theory of natural selection, poses several problems. To make proper use of the passage, quoted below, we shall have to take the time to resolve those problems.

Firstly, Peirce did not say or imply that statistical explanation was by probabilistic *laws*; he therefore did not anticipate quantum physics or its form of explanation, contrary to what has often been claimed. Rather, his thesis was that probability played a role in the *reasoning* by which some phenomena were explained. That reasoning pertained to ensembles of particles or populations of organisms, where each individual particle is presumed to be governed by the deterministic laws of Newtonian mechanics and where each organism may be assumed to consist of a complex of mechanisms operating in deterministic fashion. That he himself later questioned Newtonian determinism is irrelevant; it neither adds to nor detracts from the present point (and it, too, does not anticipate quantum physics).

Secondly, he wrote this before the advent of statistical mechanics: his reference to the theory of gases and to 'heat relations' is to the beginnings of the development of that science. It does no harm – it only strengthens his point – to recognize that what he meant by 'heat relations' includes the Second Law of thermodynamics, which was later explained in full generality, and not with respect to gases alone, by statistical reasoning of the kind first employed in the theory of gases.

Finally, his assertion of an influence of the theory of gases on Darwin is almost certainly incorrect. He himself later realized this. He expressed the idea far more cautiously in 1893 (EP1:358); and in a manuscript (MS334) of 1909–10, in which 'Fixation' was edited for publication in a new volume of essays (never published), he tacitly corrected himself by inserting, 'but he had been more particularly impressed by Malthus' book on population' (EP1:377n9; cf. EP1:377n10). Despite the admixture of error, Peirce was probably the first to recognize the analogy between Darwin's thinking and statistical reasoning in physics – a recognition usually attributed to R. A. Fisher (1930), who wrote fifty-three years later.

The passage in question, in full, is this:

> The Darwinian controversy is, in large part, a question of logic. Mr. Darwin proposed to apply the statistical method to biology. The same thing had been done in a widely different branch of science, the theory of gases. Though unable to say what the movements of any particular molecule of a gas would be on a certain hypothesis regarding the constitution of this class of bodies, Clausius and Maxwell were yet able, by the application of the doctrine of probabilities, to predict that in the long run such and such a proportion of the molecules would, under given circumstances, acquire such and such velocities; that there would take place, every second, such and such a number of collisions, etc.; and from these propositions were able to deduce certain properties of gases, especially in regard to their heat-relations. In like manner, Darwin, while unable to say what the operation of variation and natural selection in any individual case will be, demonstrates that in the long run they will adapt animals to their circumstances. Whether or not existing animal forms are due to such action, or what position the theory ought to take, forms the subject of a discussion in which questions of fact and questions of logic are curiously interlaced. (EP1:111)

One might suppose that statistical methods are merely another mode of calculation – one we fall back upon when ignorant of the details or when the details are too numerous to compute. But that is not what Peirce was saying. He was suggesting, instead, that statistical reasoning provides a new form of explanation. Thus it is a 'lesson in logic'.

As it has often been denied that a statistical explanation of the Second Law or of the ideal gas laws is different in kind from Newton's explanation of Kepler's laws, Peirce's view requires some explication and defense, as follows. Only after that, will we turn to what he said about Darwin's theory.

D

Philosophers' logical analyses of statistical explanation have usually been restricted to applications of probabilistic laws, such as those of quantum mechanics or the less precisely formulated generalizations assumed in the social sciences. Such explanations conform to the 'covering-law' model of explanation exemplified by the deduction of Kepler's laws from Newton's law of universal gravitation (together with his laws of motion and some assumptions about the particularities of the solar system). The only difference is that, in them, the 'covering' law is probabilistic and the deduction is therefore of a probability. We shall refer to such explanations as 'nomological', whether the laws assumed are deterministic or probabilistic.

If, in nomological explanation, it is a law that is deduced, it is of the same form as the law or laws from which it is deduced; it is a special case of them. It has become standard to refer to this as a 'reduction' of the law explained to the more general law that explains it. And it is usually claimed that statistical mechanics in similar fashion 'reduces' the laws it explains to the laws of mechanics that it assumes (the *locus classicus* is Nagel 1961, Ch.II). The passage quoted above implies a contrary view (Peirce did not say it does, as he wrote before anyone had urged this form of reductionism). I shall explicate that view in my own way as follows.

The phenomena explained are of a kind different from the laws assumed. The laws assumed are laws of molecular motion, but the phenomena explained are not laws of motion: they are laws of distribution, for example, of gas molecules (or their momenta) within a closed container; or of changes in distribution, for example, of heat (more precisely: of random translational kinetic energies of molecules) in a system that is closed thermodynamically; or of consequences of distribution, for example, the functional relations of the temperature, pressure, and volume of an enclosed gas. In short, the laws or phenomena explained are inherently statistical, involving averages and changes of averages within large populations; whereas, the laws assumed are not statistical in that sense, as they, whether deterministic or probabilistic, pertain to individual particles. This fact is inconsistent with the idea that statistical mechanics reduces the phenomena it explains to the laws of mechanics it assumes.

What, then, is the character of such explanation? Initially, the laws assumed were deterministic, not probabilistic; reformulation on the basis of the probabilistic laws of quantum mechanics made important differences to statistical mechanics, solving previously unsolved problems, but its reasoning – or characteristic parts of it – remains in form what it earlier was. That reasoning is not a deduction from laws directly; rather, it is a deduction from the fact that the motions so governed have no privileged direction. In an observable quantity of gas or liquid or solid, there are trillions of molecules moving about or jiggling in place in directions not perfectly coordinated. This condition, which we may name 'chaos', obtains even if each individual in the population behaves in a perfectly lawful and predictable way. It is the reasoning from the fact of chaos that is statistical or probabilistic; the laws assumed may be probabilistic or not.

We shall henceforth use the term 'statistical explanation' to refer to such explanation only, that is, to explanations that employ statistical reasoning and that are not nomological in the sense of subsuming phenomena under laws. I have no quarrel with the use of 'statistical explanation' to refer to nomological explanation from probabilistic laws; only, that is not how I shall use the term.

The term 'nomological explanation' has often been used to distinguish explanations such as that of the tides by Newton from explanations that specify mechanisms by which effects are produced. The latter sort of explanation was the initial ideal of early modern science and Newton himself was dissatisfied with his failure to specify a mechanism by which gravity works. But it should be noted that a nomological explanation can also be mechanistic in this earlier sense, if it adds a mechanical model to the laws assumed; and a mechanical model implies nomological explanation so far as the mechanism is understood to be acting according to general laws. We shall use 'mechanistic explanation' more broadly, as including nomological explanations *sans* mechanical models, if all the laws assumed are laws of mechanics, either Newtonian or quantum mechanical.

By a 'law of mechanics', I mean a general law, deterministic or probabilistic, that relates particular outcomes of a specified general type to particular conditions of a specified general type. Via such laws, particulars are explained by particulars; more precisely, particulars are explained as related by law to other particulars that occur or obtain either earlier or simultaneously. As with the example already cited, of Newton's explanation of Kepler's laws, mechanistic laws can also be used to explain other mechanistic laws.

By these definitions, statistical explanation, as in statistical mechanics, is not mechanistic, even though it assumes none but laws of mechanics and even though it yields new laws that are mechanistic. For it does not trace the trajectories and interactions of particular particles, thereby accounting for the particular effects of those causes; instead, without determining what those effects are, it calculates what must be their statistical pattern. Statistical explanation is a novel kind of explanation, neither mechanistic in the billiard ball and cogwheel sense nor mechanistic in the sense of subsuming phenomena under the laws of mechanics.

The nature of explanation in statistical mechanics is a large and difficult topic – one that has received and continues to receive a great deal of highly technical debate. I do not pretend to have provided its definitive account in a few paragraphs. I hope only to have said enough to make Peirce's view plausible, even though it runs counter to prevailing attitudes.[3] A few more words in that same vein may help.

[3] I say more in Short (2007), pp. 117–28, but that, too, is not enough.

A notorious problem is that the Second Law defines a direction in time, whereas the laws adduced in its explanation do not. How is that possible? The Second Law is the law that, in a thermodynamically closed system, heat flows only from a less equal to a more equal distribution. More generally, it is that entropy in a closed system can only increase toward a maximum, never decrease. More accurately, it is that the probability of a decrease being sustained for any appreciable length of time in any closed system large enough to be easily observed is vanishingly small. But the laws of mechanics – whether Newtonian or quantum – apply reversibly. A ball bouncing one way obeys the same laws when it is bounced back the other way. How can the reversible laws of mechanics explain an irreversible process?

This is much less puzzling if we drop the idea that explanation always subsumes the explained under the laws that explain it. The fact that the Second Law can be explained assuming no laws but those that apply reversibly suggests that Peirce was right, that what we have here is a new form of explanation, distinct from nomological forms of explanation. Because the *reasoning* is statistical, the phenomena explained are statistical forms of order, and these forms of order are not reducible to the laws assumed in their explanation. A major lesson of statistical mechanics is that some of the most important phenomena are, at bottom, statistical. Another major lesson is that forms of order that prevail at the macro- or observable level are not deductive consequences of, and cannot be reduced to, forms of order that prevail at the microlevel, even though the former would not exist did the latter not exist.

E

So much for physics, now biology. There has been a lot of discussion, continuing into the present, of the logic of the theory of natural selection. This includes recent arguments by a few philosophers that explanation by natural selection is essentially teleological in a nontheistic sense (Wright 1976, Brandon 1996); in Chapter 6, we will see that this view, with an important difference, was anticipated by Peirce in 1902. In any case, the difference between Darwinian explanation and explanation in statistical mechanics is more obvious than is the similarity that Peirce noted. We must take both similarity and difference into account.

Like the growth of entropy, the evolution of species cannot be reversed, giving us, for example, reptiles from birds. Life in all its aspects exhibits irreversibility; there are no Fountains of Youth. But these cases of irreversible process depend on taking place in a thermodynamically open system – all of life depends on inflowing and outflowing matter and energy – whereas the Second Law applies only to closed systems, including that of the universe as a whole. Living things resist the growth of entropy, but only in the biosphere: life does not violate the Second Law. Thus, the theory of natural selection applies within conditions far more complicated than clouds of gas molecules or iron bars heated at one end, and thus it differs in the specific form of its statistical explanations. Whereas statistical mechanics relies on principles drawn from the mathematical theory of probability, the theory of natural selection invokes a nonmathematical tautology, that when one of two already existing but rival inheritable features (alleles) favors the chances of reproductive success more than does the other, then it is likely to recur in subsequent generations with a frequency greater than does the other. In the phrase 'natural selection', Darwin captured the analogy of this to deliberate choosing, while denying deliberation. In statistical mechanics, there is nothing analogous to making a selection.

From these differences, other differences follow. The organic features selected do not constitute a more uniform distribution of matter and energy but, rather, the exact opposite. They eventuate in forms of organization by which one space is differentiated from another – a mouse here, a cat there. And that is why we are interested not only in the general course of evolution but also in its particular products. For this reason, Darwinian explanation bifurcates. At one level, it entails prediction, while at the other level it does not. That under certain conditions species evolve can be predicted as well as explained. That is what Peirce referred to when he spoke of adaptations occurring over the long run. But the evolution of a particular species cannot be predicted. It can only be explained post hoc, by inferring, or simply guessing, at the sequence of mutations that must have occurred in the parent stock to bring this result about, given an idea of why those mutations favored the chances of reproductive success more than did their rivals.[4] Explanations of this kind are like historical explanations, which also do not entail a power to predict. In fact, they *are* historical explanations, albeit of natural, not human history.

---

[4] There are other processes involved, in addition to mutation and selection, that drive evolution. Darwin and Peirce both mentioned some of them; other such processes are receiving growing attention today. But no new feature is likely to long survive if it reduces the chances of reproductive success.

F

In none of these cases – Kepler, Lavoisier, Maxwell, Darwin – is it at all plausible that a philosopher, just by thinking hard, could have discovered such a way of explaining phenomena. Certainly, a philosopher could not do this by explicating an already-formed concept of explanation. The methods reviewed here, and many more, could only have emerged in the course of an inquiry already underway, *a fortiori* employing less apt tools. And their value could not have been known before some stunning successes were attained by their means. With such successes, the concept of explanation changed. Method is inquiry's most important product.

What is it, then, that all methods of science must have in common? Geometrical astronomy, as by Ptolemy and Copernicus, predicted what it could not explain, whereas Darwinian natural selection explains what it cannot predict. But both methods are scientific. Therefore, neither explanation nor prediction is essential to science. And what do the several kinds of explanation that we have examined have in common? Historical explanations are post hoc, devoid of predictive power. Statistical explanations do not subsume phenomena under the laws assumed. Nomological explanations do not always specify mechanisms by which effects are brought about. What could be the idea of scientific explanation generally? Is there such an idea? To be sure, we explain in order to understand, and particular cases are understood when they are made to stand under general ideas. But that applies as well to Aristotle's taxonomic model of explanation and it applies to various explanations formed in the ordinary course of life, as when we attribute Jones' misbehavior to his jealousy. It does not distinguish scientific explanation; it does not delimit what may be accepted as a scientific explanation.

If science cannot be defined by its method, then we are left with the vague idea of the restless spirit of inquiry, a desire to find things out – in whatever form that may take. It is important to see just how vague this idea is. Peirce described the scientific spirit as one that will 'press on to the real truth of nature'. That seems fairly definite – if we know what truth, reality, and nature are. But it is to science itself that we turn to tell us what nature is and what is real; as science has developed, our concept of nature has changed. And tests of truth have changed with that change. Many philosophers hold that truth of theory is verifiability of a theory's predictive implications. But that is not what truth had always been thought to be. It is an idea that emerged with the advent of modern science. It cannot be found in classical philosophy or medieval philosophy. To say that science is the study of nature or of reality or that it aims at the truth, is therefore to utter an empty formula, an uninformative tautology. Or almost empty: it does suggest that science presupposes that there is something about which we want to find out more.

Science, it seems, can be identified only by 'the pure scientific Eros', as Peirce expressed it in 1898 (EP2:29): viz., the desire to learn, to find out about things, to discover what is there. This is intolerable. Nothing can be built on so vague a notion. Not unless it is just definite enough to enable us to employ the retrospective strategy that we earlier tried, with respect to method, unsuccessfully. Perhaps we can look at the current state of all that is called 'science' and take its form to be the best expression to date of the scientific spirit.[5] From that concrete vantage point, perhaps we can then discern the same spirit at work in the developments that led up to it. At first, that spirit will not have been recognized; it will have been weak and tangled up with other motivations; it may have been misconceived; but now it can be known from its effects, its current concrete embodiments.

That appears to have been Peirce's approach to the matter, at least c.1902, as we can see from the following seven passages:

> Given the oxygen, hydrogen, carbon, nitrogen, sulphur, phosphorus, etc., in sufficient quantities and under proper radiations, and living protoplasm will be produced, will develop, will gain power of self-control, and the scientific passion is sure to be generated. Such is my guess. Science was preordained, perhaps, on the Sunday of the *Fiat lux*. (7.50, c.1902)
>
> The greatest difference between the scientific state of the modern scientific era from Copernicus and the middle ages, is that now the whole concern of students is to find out the truth; while then it was to put in a rational light the faith of which they were already possessed. (7.87, 1902)

Here, the idea of truth takes on some slight measure of definiteness, by the contrast drawn to methods of inquiry circumscribed by dogmas that cannot be questioned; it is also, in the first passage, associated with self-control, hence, the process of correcting opinion, hence, the process of subjecting opinion to tests grounded in something independent of opinion.

---

[5] We need only exclude such self-proclaimed sciences as astrology, so-called Creation Science, Marxism, and Freudianism; we can do so on the ground that they are not part of the network of inquiries that depend on one another and contribute in their diverse ways to further discovery. This exclusion is not dogmatic: Creation Science, for example, could justify its title if it led to concrete discoveries. There are disputes among scientists about which methods or theories are legitimate, ergo, 'scientific', for example, the old dispute about ideas of 'vitalism' in biology: These are eventually resolved by progress in scientific inquiry itself.

Let us continue with passages of 1902. The following five were written as part of an introduction to a classification of the sciences as 'living' branches of inquiry, that is, as 'a pursuit of living men' (EP2:129–32):

> Let us look upon science, – the science of today, – as a living thing. What characterizes it generally … is that the thoroughly established truths are labeled and put upon the shelves of each scientist's mind, where they can be at hand when there is occasion to use them … while science itself, – the living process, – is busied mainly with conjectures, which are either getting framed or getting tested.

That seems to anticipate the view of Karl Popper, but Peirce did not, as Popper is often wrongly supposed to have done, identify testing with a simplistic comparison of predicted effects to observed effects. A theory is tested most notably in being developed and refined. It either succeeds by being made more concrete or fails by resisting improvement. Testing is therefore one with discovery.

But that requires specialized techniques and training. Specialization is essential to modern science:

> The man working in the right way to learn something not already known is recognized by all men of science as one of themselves, no matter how little he is informed.
>
> The life of science is in the desire to learn …. Such being the essence of science, it is obvious that its first offspring will be men, – men whose whole lives are devoted to it. By such devotion each of them acquires a training in making some particular kind of observations and experiments. He will thus live in quite a different world, – quite a different aggregate of experience, – from unscientific men, and even from scientists pursuing other lines of work than his …. Bring together two men of widely different departments, – say a bacteriologist and an astronomer, – and they will hardly know what to say to one another …
>
> … one will meet with men of the most deserved renown in science who will tell you that, beyond their own little nooks, they know hardly anything of what others have done.

We will make much of this emphasis on specialization, especially what it reveals about the purpose of modern science.

Peirce's approach to the problem of defining 'science' led him to anticipate one of the chief methods of contemporary sociology of science:

> Here, then, are natural classes of sciences all sorted out for us in nature itself, so long as we limit our classification to actually recognized sciences. We have only to look over the list of scientific periodicals and the list of scientific societies to find the Families of science ready named.

This method, of review of periodicals and societies, presupposes, and its success confirms, that science has become a network of specialized inquiries. The channels of communication form the network, which consists, not in a unified world-view, but in specific dependencies, varying in kind and changing over time, of work in one department on work in another.[6]

The scientific spirit, over a long period of development, created for itself the institutions – the periodicals and societies, laboratories and university departments – through which and in which it now lives. It created for itself a mode of life and a type of person – the scientist – who lives it. As that is the contemporary expression of the scientific spirit, it is our best evidence as to what that spirit is and, hence, as to what science is. We identify pre-modern thinkers as 'scientists' or as 'scientific' when they exhibit this spirit, at least partially, *avant la lettre*, for example, Archimedes or Ptolemy or, in his biological works, Aristotle.

G

Peirce did not often mention the famous advertisements of science, as by Francis Bacon, or the articulations of a scientific world-view, as by Hobbes in his *De Corpore*. These did not for him define science. A dozen years before *De Corpore* appeared, Galileo's pupil, Torricelli verified the conjecture that air has weight; he (and others following him: Pascal, Boyle) did so by measuring its weight. Torricelli is remembered as a scientist, Hobbes as a philosopher. I am not urging a simplistic distinction. Descartes was both philosopher and scientist, and Torricelli also wrote a general work on mechanics. The point, rather, is that it is by finding things out, and not in having a general idea of the world, that the scientist is distinguished. Ideas are recognized as scientific only when they lead to, and can be further developed or tested in, the sort of discoveries that specialized research, like Torricelli with his glass tube sealed at one end and dish of mercury, can make. The theoretician is a scientist rather than a philosopher, in the

---

[6] Sociologists of science tend to be 'social constructionists', holding the view that scientific theory is a tissue of arbitrary convention, political ideology, professional turf-wars, and so on. Peirce, to the contrary, held that professional divisions in science reflect divisions in nature. Research is organized by the techniques employed; but those are the ones that have been found to produce new and verifiable results. A classification of the sciences is therefore 'natural', albeit subject to revision. It is based on the ways scientists have come – without forethought, without benefit of philosophy – to organize their inquiries. Of course there will always be some distortion due to bias, to sources of funding, to personal ambitions, and so on, not to mention ignorance and error; but, as inquiry continues, nature itself determines how nature is to be studied.

current sense of the latter term, when his aim is to so frame ideas that they can be thus developed.

What, then, is science? What does the evidence show it to be? How does 'the scientific passion' – its 'desire to learn' – differ from other passions, for example, someone's desire to learn where his other sock has gotten to or Socrates' desire to learn how best to live? There are many passions and all sorts of desire to learn. In a perhaps presumptuous effort to clarify Peirce's idea, I should like to introduce a pair of terms – concreteness and fruitfulness – by which to identify the spirit of modern science. It should be noted, however, that these terms do not entail a specific aim *qua* kind of fact or type of explanation or theory that is to be sought.

By 'concreteness', which I shall not attempt to define except by incomplete enumeration, I mean a multitude of detail, delineation of parts or of steps, what can be calculated or proven, and especially a degree of quantitative exactness. Concreteness consists, for example, in knowing not just that an arrow soars and falls but that its path is parabolic; and that theory is made still more concrete by recognizing that air resistance prevents the trajectory from being perfectly parabolic. Concreteness is illustrated by quantitative prediction, but is not limited to predictive theories; much of biology, geology, archeology, etc., boast concrete detail *sans* predictive power. Concreteness is not limited to the physical; what can be calculated or proven in pure mathematics also satisfies that desire to learn which characterizes modern science. Even within physics, concreteness is not limited to the visualizable or to mechanical models: quantum mechanics exhibits the power of higher mathematics, and of ideas divorced from image, to yield a multitude of exact results.

By 'fruitfulness' I mean the use of concrete knowledge to produce more concrete knowledge: additional discoveries, each leading to further discoveries and, indeed, to an unending growth of knowledge. Fruitfulness is concreteness in prospect.[7] This, again, applies to mathematics as well as to empirical science. The English mathematician, G. H. Hardy wrote that 'a serious mathematical theorem ... is likely to lead to important advances in mathematics itself and even in other sciences' (Hardy 1940/1967, p.89). It was only by seriousness so defined – that is, fruitfulness – that Hardy found himself able to distinguish mathematics from chess problems.

[7] Peirce did not often use the term 'fruitful', though near the end of his life, in 1913, he did speak of fruitfulness – preferring the unusual term 'uberty' – as an aim of reasoning in tension with that of 'security' (EP2:Ch.3). In a letter, also of 1913, he added an adjective, apparently (and typically) of his own coinage: 'esperable uberty' (8.384).

These two virtues, of concreteness and fruitfulness, come at a price. Their price is incompleteness and specialization. A fruitful theory is by definition incomplete. Concreteness requires many more techniques than any one person can master; hence, it requires specialization. The adoption of concreteness and fruitfulness as values therefore transformed intellectual life. It caused new institutions to be formed, and it changed the shape of intellectual ambition.

The ancient sage imparted wisdom to his students; the medieval scholar professed, explained, and defended a body of truth already known. In both cases, there was in fact disagreement, debate, and an evolution of thought, a growing body of ideas and methods. But the assumption was that inquiry would come to a conclusion; that its conclusion could be comprehended in an individual mind (not perhaps any individual's mind, but those only of the fortunate few who possess intelligence, leisure, and discipline); that it would be a coherent vision of self, world, and God; and that, as such, it would guide the individual to living well and perhaps to governing the state well.

Socrates was not in all respects an exception. Life, in his view, may be examined endlessly, but not, as in modern science, progressively, that is, by accretion of factual discoveries. Knowledge was still that which can be comprehended in a single mind, and if what we know is only our own ignorance, there is, ironically, wisdom in that knowledge. Socrates, too, taught wisdom, albeit by the Socratic method. In different ways, Plato, Aristotle, and the scholastic doctors of the medieval universities taught methods of thinking to be employed endlessly; but these methods were never meant to form an inquiry that would endlessly progress. For Aristotle, *epistēmē* is knowledge of a systematic body of truth, possessed after inquiry is completed, which the philosopher may endlessly enjoy by running through it, over and over again, in his own mind, syllogism by syllogism.

Such being the aim of thinking, the test of a philosophy was its being comprehensive (as to all the important questions) and internally coherent, perhaps coherent also with quotidian experience and human sentiment. In the Middle Ages, Jewish, Christian, or Islamic, coherence with divine revelation became an additional desideratum. To demonstrate either a theory's irremediable incompleteness or its incoherence was to refute it. A system was defended dialectically, by revealing the incompleteness or incoherence of every alternative that had been offered.

The contrast to modern science could not be more striking. Neither incompleteness nor incoherence is fatal to a living theory; for such a theory exists to be worked on, that is, to guide research toward its correction and completion. A theory that is capable of being applied, or appears capable of being developed until it is applicable, does not consist merely in its verbal or mathematical formulation.[8] Knowing the theory includes knowing how to adapt it to different kinds of case; the theory has a living edge still growing. Thus, its incoherencies are not always obvious and are not always fatal. At one or another point in its career, a theory will be found to contradict the facts or itself, and may be adjusted accordingly. In its early stages, a theory may be sparse of concrete applications. What matters is the promise of concreteness. In modern science, there are no flaws fatal to a theory. It can even contain known errors – if they are ones we do not yet know how to correct. But a theory will die eventually if it fails to bear fruit or is contradicted by a theory that is more fruitful (Lakatos 1978).

That is why critiques of Darwinism, exhibiting its lacunae and unsolved problems, fail. They show only that the theory is part of living science, still under development. It has been and continues to be enormously fruitful. No scientist is going to reject the theory of natural selection in favor of some alternative, even if more coherent and complete, if that alternative does not guide research. Nothing could be more coherent and complete than the claim that God explains everything; but, as God works in mysterious ways, that hypothesis is neither concrete nor fruitful. To the scientific spirit, theology is a Barmecide feast.

Specialists rely on one another's results and borrow one another's techniques and tools, but the emphasis is on continued discovery in each department of inquiry, and not on cobbling all these results together into one grand system. Indeed, specialists in distinct areas employ distinct vocabularies, methods, and explanatory ideals. Even were a unified theory in physics found (Weinberg 1992), it would be limited to physics and probably not of much help to embryology or geology, albeit scientists in those departments use ideas and tools physicists have devised. A specialist, finally, does not address all those who are educated or intelligent, but only other specialists, perhaps a few dozen persons.

---

[8] This truth is obscured in popularizations of scientific theories and in the tendency of grade-school instruction in science to be degraded in that direction. Learning physics essentially involves laboratory experience applying the theories – of learning what it takes to apply them – and in reproducing significant experiments – learning what ingenuity is required to obtain significant results – and in solving textbook problems – learning that calculation is not always routine but importantly depends on discerning what is relevant. Similar remarks apply to other sciences; sometimes field work or observation of natural phenomena takes the place of experimentation. It is not at all like humanistic learning, of studying texts merely or ideas merely. An idea that can be mastered just by reading is not a scientific idea.

Thus, scientific inquiry does not have the unity of an individual consciousness. Instead, its unity is institutional: it is that of an indefinitely extended community, a loosely organized federation of specialists. The Royal Society was founded in London in 1660, preceded by shorter-lived societies such as the Academia dei Lincei at Rome, 1610–1630. Such organizations are fundamentally different from the older academies, beginning with Plato's in the grove sacred to Academus. They exist to promote discovery, not to impart wisdom. In their published transactions, the results of discovery are stored. Modern science is not a world-view that can be comprehended by one person; knowledge is no longer the possession of an educated person. It is, instead, the possession of a community of inquirers.

And thus one's aim is no longer to possess the truth oneself but is to contribute to a multifaceted pursuit of truth carried on by innumerable others, with no completion in sight. This makes for a new type of personality, one seeking satisfactions different from those of the classical sage. Ambition takes on a new form, hostage to future progress, including that made after one's own demise. It is not hostage to the future in the old way, where one hoped to be remembered, hoped for enduring fame. It goes deeper than that. The point is that one's ideas and discoveries have no value, no claim to truth, no significance, independently of what others can do with them. The proof is always in the further progress of inquiry. And therefore the scientist is a kind of person not previously possible, moved by a purpose not previously known.

Instead of the classical philosophical goal of a comprehensive system in which the human spirit can come to rest and in which we can find guidance for living, modern science offers a new, restless ideal of endless discovery with no promise of moral guidance. Knowledge is still an end in itself (a thesis defended in the next chapter), but it is now to be found in the process of inquiring rather than at inquiry's conclusion, and it is distributed over the community of inquirers, as it cannot be possessed except in small and uncertain pieces by any one individual. I think that the importance of this revolution in intellectual life has not been sufficiently appreciated, except by Peirce.

H

In 1896 – after a period in which he spent much time in the studio of the painter, Albert Bierstadt, and in which, desperate for a new source of income, he attempted to interest investors in one or another application of his scientific expertise, and in which, finally, he developed an astounding cosmological hypothesis (Chapter 6) – Peirce distinguished 'three classes of men', artistic, practical, and scientific:

> For men of the first class, nature is a picture; for men of the second class, it is an opportunity; for men of the third class, it is a cosmos, so admirable, that to penetrate its ways seems to them the only thing that makes life worth living. (1.43)

He continued,

> If we are to define science ... as a living historical reality, we must conceive it as that about which such men as I have described busy themselves. As such, it does not consist so much in *knowing*, nor even in 'organized knowledge', as it does in diligent inquiry into truth for truth's sake ... (1.44)

Six years later, in 1902, he wrote,

> The next most vital factor of the method of modern science [after 'love of truth'] is that it has been made social ....The scientific world is like a colony of insects, in that the individual strives to produce that which he himself cannot hope to enjoy. (7.87)

But already in his papers of 1868–1869, and repeatedly in later papers, Peirce had argued that the inferences scientists make – inductive and abductive inferences specifically or the whole rope of inquiry consisting of abductions, deductions, and inductions – are invalid in the short run of an individual's life. They lead to error in the short run and reliably to truth only in a run indefinitely long. Therefore, the inferences essential to science are invalid if not made as part of an inquiry that will be continued by others over an indeterminate future. Subordination of ego to the indefinitely extended community of scientists is therefore required by logic itself.

Peirce expressed that logical point in terms specifically Christian. Such an expression may seem to our secular age objectionably hyperbolic. His age, however, was secular also, though more newly and reluctantly so. So the hyperbole, if that is what it is, was intended. It was intended, anyway, to shock his audience:

> He who would not sacrifice his own soul to save the whole world, is illogical in all his inferences, collectively. So the social principle is rooted intrinsically in logic. (EP1:81)

This is repeated almost verbatim in 1878 (EP1:149), except that there the relation is reversed: it is said that 'Logic is rooted in the social principle'. And it is further recommended in 1910, with preference expressed for the initial formulation (2.661). The initial formulation, in the passage quoted, is preceded (without express attribution, none being needed) by Jesus' question, 'What shall it profit a man if he gain the whole world and lose his own soul?' (as Peirce wrote it, evidently quoting from Mark 8:36 in the King James version, omitting the first word, 'For'). Superficially, his words seem the opposite of Jesus', though saving the world is not gaining it for oneself. But Peirce could rely on his contemporaries knowing that Jesus' question was preceded by the statement, 'For whosoever will save his life shall lose it; but whosoever shall lose his life for my sake and the gospel's, the same shall save it'. Thus he was drawing an analogy between a person's acquiring the spirit of science and the Christian conversion experience. In place of the self-sufficient satisfaction of the sage, who understands the world and knows the Good, the modern scientist forgoes satisfaction in order to make a contribution. He overcomes the despair of finitude by giving himself up to an infinite enterprise.

Modern science, like Christianity, entails a morality. The scientist exists as such only as a member of the community of scientists, and thus has obligations – carefulness in observation, accuracy in measurement, honesty in reporting, logicality in inference, respect for criticism, and so on. To act otherwise, although there are temptations to do so, would be to negate the very reason one has for being a scientist. The temptations arise from extra-scientific motivations. Peirce therefore made some large claims for the moral character of scientists (e.g., 1.49, c.1896). Those claims are less plausible today, when the institutional growth and material rewards of science have strengthened extra-scientific motivations. But the essential point remains, that science *per se* imposes a morality.

It imposes *a* morality but not morality in its fullness. In some of the same passages where he praised the morality of science, and also in other passages, Peirce distinguished science from morality and insisted on their mutual independence. Science depends on speculative boldness and on questioning received doctrine, whereas 'morals is the traditional wisdom of ages of experience'; 'If a man cuts loose from it, he will become the victim of his passions. It is not safe for him even to reason about it ...' (1.50). Therefore, were science to be made a guide to conduct, its real character would be destroyed (1.55). Similarly, the religious cast of science is consistent with its being in tension with traditional forms of religion, which are conservative where science is progressive (6.429–33, this in 1893).

It is typical of Peirce – of his ability to weld seeming contradictions into a union playfully expressed or only implied – that he argued that science is at once amoral and morally justified. In a passage of 1898:

... the true scientific investigator completely loses sight of the utility of what he is about. It never enters his mind. Do you think that the physiologist who cuts up a dog reflects, while doing so, that he may be saving a human life? Nonsense. If he did, it would spoil him for a scientific man; and *then* the vivisection would become a crime ... (EP2:29)

But that's not all. Science, in that sense amoral, is at the same time a model of morality. The social character of science presented, for Peirce, a moral contrast to the materialism (in the moral sense) and individualism of the modern age, with its 'Gospel of Greed' (EP1:357). The sacrifices science demands of scientists could not be supported by such psychological and ethical doctrines as egoism and hedonism (both descended from Ockham's nominalism: EP1:359, EP2:70, 156). Those were doctrines that Peirce summed up as being the 'metaphysics of wickedness' (7.571).[9]

Peirce's emphasis on community is subject to misunderstanding. The subordination of self-interest to community-interest does not entail social control of the individual, as in the discipline of a Jesuit or a Communist Party functionary or, today, the limits imposed on speech, hence thought, by 'political correctness' and an exaggerated 'sensitivity'. Quite the opposite. If truth, as Peirce said (*vide infra*, Ch.4, E), is what the community of scientists would ultimately come to believe, that is because each inquirer thinks independently, however dependently on results established by other specialists. Consensus is a mark of truth's having been attained, but only if that consensus is neither coerced nor formed for the sake of agreement. It has to be the unintended, albeit desired, outcome of many lines of inquiry pursued independently. The scientist's education is not an indoctrination. Instruction in current theory and current methods makes freedom of thought possible, including the freedom to correct received ideas and to emend received methods. As a model for society, the moral that science teaches is individual freedom. The example of science – of what the education of a scientist enables the scientist to do – shows that freedom is a product of society and that a society is strong in proportion as it produces free individuals.

[9] Peirce included Mill's utilitarianism among the wicked errors descended from Ockham. That may surprise those who are impressed by the altruism that utilitarianism demands. But its ultimate end is hedonistic, the 'happiness' of each individual.

CHAPTER 3

Modern Science Contra Classical Philosophy

In the preceding chapter, we saw that Peirce conceived of science as a form of inquiry defined not by a method, a metaphysic, or an idea of what counts as a good theory or good explanation, since all of these are revised as this inquiry continues, but by its 'spirit', a restless desire for discovery fruitful of further discovery. Like any definition of science, this one is normative. But it is based on historical fact, that is, on what has come to be called 'science', in contradistinction to classical and medieval philosophy. Before the advent of modern science, endless growth was not a cognitive ideal: Restlessness was seen to be a moral defect; the aim was for inquiry to come to rest in a comprehensive and coherent system of general truths.

It is a commonplace that modern science broke decisively with the past, but is Peirce's implied view of that break correct? It is in several respects opposed to the commonplace view, that modern science is in metaphysic materialist, in explanatory ideal mechanist, and in purpose utilitarian. But while he held that modern science retains the classical aim of knowledge as an end in itself, he also held that it redefines that aim, because it reconceives knowledge. If that is correct, what, if anything, gives his definition of science its normative force, if, indeed, it has normative force? If a revolution in ideals is fundamental, there can be no principles cited in its defense. Any principles cited will be ones adopted in consequence of that revolution.

The first of these two questions, whether Peirce's concept of science correctly identifies the genius of modern science, is one of history: it can be persuasively but not conclusively answered. I shall argue that the question regarding normative force also is one of history. The history of the growth of modern science shows (a) that the spirit of discovery did not result from utilitarian motives but was a change in intellectual ideal and (b) that this change did not occur arbitrarily.

But how could a new cognitive ideal be other than arbitrary, if there is no principle that justifies it? The answer is that justification is not the only alternative to arbitrariness. Is learning from experience always, or ever, principled? That experience precedes principle, that it is from experience that we first learn the difference between better and worse, is fundamental to Peirce's idea of normative science (Chapter 9).

Some readers may be inclined to find an argument in this chapter where none is intended. They might suppose that the facts of history that I cite (Sections D–G) are premises, which yield Peirce's conclusion only given an assumed principle, which may be identified by logical analysis of the argument. What could that principle be? Only a very dubious one, such as that anything found satisfying is good, or such as that irreversible historical developments are invariably right – a version of might makes right. But what I am arguing is that there is no argument. There is no argument that takes us from a recital of historical facts to a normative conclusion. The facts recited show only that those who experience modern science in comparison to its predecessors *find* it to be good. It is our perception of value that is normative; normative principles can be established only by induction. It follows that history is germane to philosophical inquiry.

In support of Peirce's normative view of science, this chapter reviews established facts of the history of science. Novelty is risked only in the use I make of those facts, but even that use is in line with, though it goes beyond, the philosophically pregnant historiography initiated by Karl Popper, Stephen Toulmin, and Thomas Kuhn. As use cannot be made of facts not mentioned, I beg the knowledgeable to bear with me. The history of science here recounted becomes in Chapter 9 evidence for the Peircean idea of normative inquiry there defended.

But first, I attempt in the next three sections to make the significance of Peirce's view of science clearer, by contrasting it to two other views, both of them familiar to us, of the contrast of modern science to classical and medieval thought. These two alternatives, each of which exists in many variants, are merely sketched, but I believe my caricatures of them are accurate enough for the present purpose.

A

What used to be known as the 'scientific revolution' of the sixteenth and seventeenth centuries is now seen as part of an evolution – of idea, method, and aim – over a longer period. For example, the modern idea of quantitative laws of motion grew out of attempts in medieval universities to solve a problem in Aristotle's physics. Although it evolved, modern science may nonetheless be viewed as revolutionary in its effects.

In classical Greece and also in the Middle Ages, speculation about nature had not been wholly separated from other departments of thought, moral, political, and theological. Nor had that speculation uniformly contradicted common sense, by denying human experience and ideals a place in reality.

To be sure, some of the ideas discussed did anticipate modern science and its cultural consequences. Before Socrates, the atomists had portrayed reality in material and mechanical terms; and during Socrates' own time, the sophists had freed their moral and political teaching from speculation about nature, by cynically denying that there is any truth about right and wrong or perhaps about anything. But those were only some ideas among others, parts of a larger discussion. With modern science, that changed. The experimental and mathematical methods of Galileo and others – not new but newly harnessed to theory – yielded results so impressive that it became difficult to reject the materialist metaphysics with which they were initially associated; it became difficult to affirm the objective reality of purposes, ideals, and values. At the same time, the methods of modern science spawned specialist researches that proceeded independently of the dialectical debates that still occupied philosophers in the universities: The sciences developed their own institutional structures. Thus, what we today call 'philosophy' became institutionally separated from science – though philosophers have made science and its alleged materialism a major topic of debate.

A few terms drawn from that debate will be useful in the following discussion. As successive revolutions in physics redefined 'matter' out of all recognition, 'materialism' is no longer a term favored among philosophers. It has been replaced by 'physicalism', the doctrine, roughly, that reality is whatever physics will eventually conclude that it is, if its inquiries are pursued long enough. It is granted that present theories are tentative and, at best, no better than approximations to better theories that, we confidently expect, will replace them; this modesty distinguishes physicalism from materialism. But physicalism is still dogmatic on four points: that physics is the basic science and, hence, that reality is, at bottom, physical; that physics will always portray reality abstractly in mathematical language; that the test of a physical theory is that it yields accurate prediction (always conditional, that is, of the form, 'If A occurs at time and place X, then B will occur at time and place Y'); and that what can be tested in this way is fact not value, so that values have no place in reality. Physicalism thus embraces and affirms the revolutionary division conventionally attributed to science, between knowledge and valuation.

Physicalism entails the still more modest doctrine of 'scientific realism', the view that scientific theory is to be understood as representing reality, albeit imperfectly, as otherwise its practical success cannot be accounted for, and that, for all its momentary defects, science is our best guide to reality. Scientific realism is not committed to the view that all scientific truths are reducible to truths of physics. At its most modest, it might even permit one to think that reality is not exhausted by what all the sciences together can represent.

In contemporary philosophy of science, views opposed to scientific realism, and therefore to physicalism, may be, for our purpose, roughly collected under the label, 'instrumentalism'. Instrumentalism is, again roughly, the view that, as prediction is the test of theory, so also it is the whole meaning and aim of theory. In other words, scientific theory represents nothing but the evidence for it. Its seeming representations of a distinct reality, for example, of light as a wave or as corpuscular, should be interpreted as mere devices for making accurate predictions (it is no problem, then, that light in one context is seen as a wave, in another as corpuscular). The term 'instrumentalism' derives from the fact that prediction, because it is conditional, often, not always, facilitates control. It does so when we can either bring about or prevent the conditions specified. Thus, scientific theory is about the instrumental; or it is itself an instrument for controlling events.

Now, instrumentalism informs two, diametrically opposed, valuations of science. On the one hand, most instrumentalists, at least most academic philosophers who might be so labeled, maintain that scientific theory is our best example of knowledge, or even that it is the only genuine knowledge, in comparison to which all other purported modes of knowledge, for example, metaphysical, theological, or moral, are poor creatures indeed. In this, these instrumentalists agree with physicalists, even though physicalists and instrumentalists disagree about what scientific knowledge *is*. Both regard the classical and medieval union of physics and ethics to be an error happily outgrown. We might collect physicalists together with instrumentalists of this type under the label, 'scientistic'. It must be emphasized that scientific realists are not necessarily scientistic; nor are most scientists scientistic.

On the other hand, there are instrumentalists who, in contrast to the scientistic, deny that science is the only or the best form of knowledge. Precisely because it is instrumental only, it fails to count for much as knowledge. This view, found more often outside of philosophy departments than within them, regrets the demise of the classical or medieval unities of fact and value, physics and ethics, and would restore them by reducing science's role. Shared by persons of opposing political tendency, it has no convenient name. But as it has an ancestor in Gulliver's observations of Laputa and the Academy of Lagado, I shall call it Swiftian.

Unable to deny the practical success of modern science, Swiftians hold the value of science to be practical merely. 'Practical' is here to be understood as referring to means to ends, whatever those ends may be, and not to knowledge of what our ends ought to be; it is instrumental practicality. Knowledge of what our ends ought to be is practical in a deeper sense. Swiftians argue that if the test of truth in science is accurate prediction, which facilitates control, then, as far as science is concerned, truth equals utility. That alone, they add, shows that science does not comprehend all of truth; it omits what it is most important to know.

Without, for the moment, citing any particular Swiftian, but continuing our rough sketch, let us explore the issue as Swiftians tend to see it and also consider what might be said in response. The latter is my own invention, as there has been little dialogue between the opposing parties.[1] Science, Swiftians sometimes say, tells us how things work but not what they are. Classical and medieval philosophies, by contrast, told us what things are; most importantly, they told us what *we* are, not only in fact but also normatively. We are rational animals even though we often act irrationally, or we are made in God's image though often acting as the Devil tempts us to act. Clinical psychology, in contrast, has usually identified mental health with not acting in ways that thwart one's own desires, whatever those desires may happen to be. What one *should* desire is not a legitimate topic of research; 'being judgmental', that is, morally, is *verboten*. Political science similarly describes the structures and strategies of power, whereas classical and medieval political philosophies sought to establish what power should be used for, hence, what sort of regime is best. As modern science leaves out all that is most important, there is an urgent need to recover the lost unity of classical or medieval speculation.

Now, it is easy to refute the suggestion that modern science is merely instrumental and of no intellectual value. Even though its theories are tentative and incomplete, they are relatively well confirmed; being well confirmed, any better theories are likely to agree with them in certain respects; and in those respects they contradict the cosmologies of Aristotle and the Book of Genesis, etc. But, as its theories contradict what is not merely technical, modern science is not merely technical. It may fail to answer

---

[1] But see Haack (2007); opposed equally to scientism and to cynicism, Haack's sturdy commonsense is in tenor consistent with what I say here.

our moral questions, but it has moral significance by virtue of sapping the grounds of traditional answers to those questions. We cannot embrace the ethics and politics and theology of earlier thinkers unless we can free those views from the physics and cosmology and natural history with which they were entwined. That which made classical and medieval philosophies so satisfying – that they unite ethics with physics – is precisely that which today prevents our accepting them, because now we know that the physics with which they united ethics is mistaken.

Also, the distinction drawn between what things are and how they work is indefensible. It makes no more sense in Aristotle's philosophy, which is the alternative that seems to be alluded to, than it does in modern physics. Yes, in modern physics, mass, for example, whether Newtonian or relativistic, is defined by (even if it is not identified with) how it is measured, which is to say, by its effects. But so, too, Aristotle made the actuality of an individual its form, and form is not shape only but more importantly it is function (but even shape is known by its effects). This can be seen most obviously in his account, in *De Anima*, of *psychē* as the form of the living body: it is metabolism and growth and reproduction; in animals it is in addition sensation and locomotion; in humans it is in addition thinking and community. The real difference is that Aristotle defined function in terms of purpose, whereas purpose has no place in the dynamic relations that define the entities postulated by modern physics.

But this last brings us back to the strength of the Swiftian view, which depends dialectically on the premises that the scientistic also accept. They point out that, if modern science denies the reality of any purpose (beyond what is in fact desired), then it leaves us morally adrift, which is intolerable. Modern science cannot even account for itself. For, it subscribes to an ideal, namely, truth, at which it aims; and it imposes values on its practitioners, such as honesty in reporting facts and carefulness in measurement; and yet, by making accurate prediction the measure of truth, it implies that there is no truth about ideals and values. Ideals and values pertain to what should be done, not to what is done, and therefore they ground no predictions. They are not reducible to how things work, that is, to actual behavior. In scientism as a matter of doctrine, and in modern science as a matter of practice, Swiftians note, values are relegated to subjective desire and then subjectivity itself is given no place in objective reality. If we look for joy and sorrow in the brain, all we find are chemicals.

Scientists are not perturbed by the failure of science to explain itself, much less to justify itself, much less to provide a unified vision of the world. For they *are* specialists. Swiftians triumphantly conclude that scientists are not philosophers. That they find intellectual satisfaction in their work is irrelevant. They may enjoy solving puzzles; so do people who work the daily crossword; but what matters is whether science has intellectual value to the society that supports it. And the obvious truth is that society supports science for its practical benefits alone – more food, cures for diseases, deadlier weapons, more leisure. These benefits have seduced us away from the important questions. Society in general has followed the lead of its scientists in spurning theology and in relegating philosophy to the pursuit of a few harmless professors. Thus modern science has corrupted our society and trivialized our culture, which has been reduced to entertainment. Philosophy itself, and liberal education more generally, are no more than leisure time activities, supported by society perhaps for the sake of keeping malcontents off the streets.

From this point of view, Peirce was headed in exactly the wrong direction. He wrongly elevated specialist inquiry to the status that rightly should be reserved for comprehensive theory and then, topping that error by a worse one, he proposed that philosophy itself should become scientific in this degraded sense. Instead of offering the guiding vision we need, he urged endless, amoral inquiry.

B

I have cited no authors to whom these various doctrines may be attributed, lest we be distracted by their nuanced variations from the starker contrasts that define the issues. It needs to be said, however, that physicalism is widely assumed in contemporary philosophy – most of all when, as in ethical theory, it is not expressly affirmed.[2] However, the most interesting philosophies of science, for example, Kant's, Pierre Duhem's, and Thomas Kuhn's, do not fall neatly into one or another of the categories that I have distinguished.[3] But now I will name a couple of Swiftians, as their

---

[2] For physicalism, see Jaegwon Kim's *Physicalism, or Something Near Enough* (Kim 2005). In Bernard Williams' well-known work in ethics, something near enough to physicalism is expressly affirmed though renamed 'the absolute conception' (e.g., Williams 1985).

[3] Duhem's view c.1914 is that a theory can be successful only if it is a 'natural classification' of phenomena, achieving an 'economy of thought' 'anticipating experiment', which is useful but also satisfies aesthetically, yet lacks the metaphysical depth of theology (Duhem 1954). Kant in his first Critique and Kuhn toward the end of his life (Kuhn 2000) attributed genuine knowledge, good for itself and not just for its utility, to science, while being skeptical, for very different reasons, of the power of science to represent reality. Each of these three is therefore neither purely a scientific realist nor purely an instrumentalist, and the first two clearly (Kuhn much less clearly if at all) shared Swiftian concern with what modern science omits.

argument from history, by its defect, will help us to appreciate the depth of the revolution modern science has made.

Straussian political theorists (Kennington 2004) and radical feminists (Merchant 1980) – strange bedfellows! – claim that the motivating idea of modern science is that we should conquer nature, turning its mechanisms to our purposes, making our lives easier, more secure, and longer. We know this, they say, because that is what Francis Bacon and René Descartes, writing in the seventeenth century, said is the aim of the new science. Both cite passages from Bacon and Descartes that announced a new way of knowing, one that will serve practical purposes by mastering nature; feminists turn that into a rape metaphor (Merchant, p.171). That there are other passages in the same works, expressing interest in knowledge for its own sake, does not deter these scholars.

But, as Bacon and Descartes disagreed about method (one being inductivist and the other rationalist) and as scientists have followed neither prescription (Newton and Boyle professed but did not perfectly practice Bacon's methods), why suppose that their statements of the aim of science are authoritative? Today, the most popular account of scientific method, due to Karl Popper, is that it consists of 'conjecture and refutation' (Popper 1934/59, 1963, 1972). This omits most of what scientists actually do, but it is generally accepted, even by scientists, as an account of scientific inquiry more accurate than is either Bacon's inductivism or Descartes' rationalism. Popper, however, did not suppose that the aim of science is utility. It would seem, then, that there is no reason to accept as authoritative what Bacon and Descartes said about science. That *they* thought its *raison d'être* is utility – *if* that is what they thought – is no proof that it *is* utility.

In fact, argument from the texts of Bacon and Descartes, as if these were canonical, begs the question. It assumes that modern science is a system of ideas that can be explicated by the textual methods of humanistic scholarship. But there are no canonical texts in modern science. There are historically important texts, but none that are canonical. One does not today learn science from Newton's *Principia*, much less from Descartes or Bacon. One learns science by applying theories currently used, and as currently formulated, to concrete examples (textbook problems, laboratory work, field work), thus learning the associated techniques of observation, representation, and calculation. Whatever the limitations of such an education, does it deprive scientists of an understanding of their own discipline? If for three centuries few scientists have studied Bacon, does that mean that for three centuries they have not understood what science is, that only humanistic scholars, including some who have never been inside a laboratory, understand what science is?

Such absurdities force one to admit that science is not a system of ideas (complete with a set of 'founders'). It is, instead, what Peirce said that it is: a form of inquiry woven of specialist investigations that spawn a variety of techniques of discovery. To be sure, ideas guide these inquiries; but those ideas are revised in light of the results of inquiry – its failures as well as its successes. As this form of inquiry has no irrevocable presuppositions, it neither is nor has a philosophy in the usual sense.

That conclusion cuts against physicalism as much as it does against Swiftianism. But if modern science is without a philosophy, does that mean that it is without intellectual value, that it is merely instrumental, its only value being utility? Peirce, for one, did not think that modern science abandoned classical philosophy's aim of knowledge for its own sake. He was not an instrumentalist, despite what many have thought his 'pragmatism' entails (see Chapter 4); he was, as I have defined the term, a scientific realist. Much less did he suppose that the purpose of inquiry is to make our lives easier and longer. Instead, he grasped the fact that modern science sustains the classical ideal of knowledge in the only way that it can be sustained, by revising it. The revision is radical, but it is a revision, not a rejection.

The success of specialist inquiries in refuting Aristotle's physics and cosmology (see vide infra in Sections F–G) shows that what must be abandoned is the ideal of an established body of truths invulnerable to correction. The knowledge to which we can reasonably aspire has to be identified, rather, with the process of discovery: to understand a theory is to know how to use it to find out more. In being used, it is tested and refined. Such knowledge as we can be said to possess must always be mixed with errors from which it is not yet distinguished. This is neither relativism nor historicism – it does not imply that truth itself changes – but is what Peirce named 'fallibilism', the doctrine that we know much but can be certain of nothing (1.8–14, 141–75).

As often said, modern science shifted attention from static kinds of thing to dynamic relations and processes. That is true not only of physics, with its laws of kinematics and dynamics: it is even more obvious in biology. From Aristotle to Agassiz, biological taxonomy was of forms of life assumed to be unchanging; once granted that species evolve, taxonomy had to be reformulated so as to represent lines of descent, subordinating taxonomy to changes and their explanation. But the same transition from static to dynamic was made also in method and aim, when the epistemic ideal of final system gave way to the ideal of unending inquiry.

C

Swiftians will object that, nevertheless, Bacon and Descartes articulated a 'technological project' that supports and is supported by modern science. This project, they say, and I agree, has changed the way we see ourselves in relation to nature: it defines the modern ethos, and, even as it exalts us over nature, degrades us. It degrades us by denying that we have any but the lowest and most subjective ends, viz., whatever it is that we happen to desire. For it admits no other ends. It degrades us, furthermore, by implying that human nature, like the rest of nature, is nothing but machinery to be manipulated: by advertisers for profit, by propagandists for power, and by the well-meaning 'for your own good'. That, however, is a different argument, not pertaining to the nature of science itself. This project does not define scientific inquiry. It is inconceivable apart from modern science, but modern science is not inconceivable apart from it.

Indeed, Peirce shared these Swiftian concerns without sharing Swiftians' view of science. We have seen (Ch.2, H) that he deplored modern materialism and individualism – a 'metaphysics of wickedness' supporting a 'Gospel of Greed'. But we also saw that, far from attributing these evils to science, he made the life of inquiry a model of morality, a form of selfless devotion nearly or quite religious. In his opinion, the fault lay not with science but with nominalism, the fourteenth-century philosophy of William of Ockham, through the influence of which science has been misunderstood, even by scientists (EP2:67–74, a statement of 1901 improving on that of 1871 at EP1:104; cf. 1.20).

Nominalism and the issues it raises will be discussed in Chapters 4 and 8. In Chapter 5, we shall see that Peirce, with evident delight in paradox, associated modern science with the 'scholasticism' that nominalism defined itself against and that modern science is usually supposed to have refuted. He called himself a 'scholastic realist', extending that doctrine to the laws of physics and also to possibility and community (Chapters 8 and 10). In Chapter 6, we shall see that he argued that nineteenth-century science reintroduced the idea that nature contains processes exhibiting purposefulness, and Chapter 9 cites that development as explaining how a normative science is possible. Thus, Peirce addressed Swiftian objections to modern society but he did so on the basis of modern science. For none of his assertions were doctrines a priori. They grew out of empirical inquiry (Chapter 7) and remain subject to empirical tests.

This humble recognition, that our most vital interests depend on empirical discoveries and on progress in science yet to be made, distinguishes

Peirce's thought from that of the Swiftians. They, or some of them, want us to recover certitudes that they suppose were once known and are now occluded by modern error, intellectual, and moral. Thus they deny the lesson of modern science, that knowledge cannot be separated from inquiry, that it is a growing body of concrete but fallible results. But, if that is correct, then what are we to do for moral guidance in the meantime? And have we the option, and would it be a good thing, to leave moral knowledge to specialists, scientific experts in right and wrong? Finally, can morality survive uncertainty? Does not it, as it is always assailed by temptation, require confidence in moral truths? These three questions seem a devastating rebuke to Peirce's idea of normative science specifically and to his celebration of modern science generally.

However, that is to overlook the distinction he drew between theory and practice. By 'normative science' he meant a study that is indeed normative but is nonetheless theoretical, where theory is understood to be a long-run pursuit of truth for its own sake. It is not practical in the sense of being of immediate use, a guide to us in present action. In this distinction, between the long-run pursuit of truth and the beliefs we live by in the present, all three of the preceding questions are answered, as follows.

At about the time when he was beginning to think of philosophy as a science, Peirce argued that this would require our not relying on philosophy in any matter of 'vital importance'. That was in the first of a series of lectures delivered in 1898 (RLT, 105–22). He there asserted that science progresses by trying out conjectures that depart as far as possible from common sense. Such conjectures will be illuminating if true but are likely to be false. They are tested by experiments in which refutation will be instructive, not catastrophic. In matters of vital importance, Peirce said, we are better off relying on custom, sentiment, and instinct. For these have been shaped by eons of experience, and, although they likely are admixed with error – error which is sometimes productive of evil – it is unlikely – since we have survived so far – that they will lead us into total disaster. Reasoning arrives at the truth in the long run, wherein one's own reason and experience is woven with that of innumerable others. An individual's own reasoning, about any but technical matters, is unreliable in the short run. Nothing is more dangerous than the radical who by his own reasoning thinks he knows what is good for us all.

Peirce described this view of practice and of morality as a 'conservatism' that complements the 'radicalism' of purely theoretical inquiry. But this sort of conservatism is not a dogmatic confidence in the truth of traditional views; instead, it entails skepticism – skepticism *sans* cynicism. For, what has been shaped by experience is subject to amendment in light of further experience – including advances in normative science if such a science comes to be. Only, those amendments ought themselves to be made with conservative caution, Peirce said.

Custom, sentiment, and instinct are unreasoned sources of guidance; we are so guided without conscious justification, indeed, without much consciousness of being guided. But over time, reason, that is to say, the conclusions of scientific inquiry, can supply the missing explanations. Peirce suggested that Darwin's reasoning shows why instinct is more reliable in matters of vital importance than is reason. Fortunately, instinct being what it is, we did not have to wait for Darwin to tell us to rely on it.

Curiously, Descartes had made a similar move. Having resolved to dismantle all that he had learned and to begin afresh, he for practical purposes had to erect a temporary dwelling, as he expressed it, the first principle of which was to obey the laws and customs of his country and observe its religion (*Discourse on Method*, Part Three). Peirce did not agree that it was either possible or necessary to begin afresh; inquiry, he repeatedly asserted, begins and can only begin with what is presently believed, which may later be amended. Nor did he suppose that final answers could with certainty be attained. But, as scientific inquiry begins with what is already believed and corrects it only as compelling grounds for correction emerge, it presumes that there must be some truth in opinions formed in the long course of pre-scientific experience (a presumption that could only be identified and defended in light of conclusions attained by its means). Descartes could not have given that reason for his temporarily reposing confidence in custom and religion. He gave none.

D

Now let us turn to the history of science.[4] Does it bear out Peirce's view, or not? We shall first, in this and the next section, see that the historical facts are inconsistent with any idea that modern science was founded on a turn to empiricism or to mechanistic explanation or to a practical goal; it was not 'founded' at all.

---

[4] Historical claims for which I cite no authority are among those generally accepted; see such well-regarded histories as Dijksterhuis (1950/1986), Crombie (1952/1969), Butterfield (1957), Koyré (1957), Clagett (1961), Hall (1981), and Cohen (1985). These histories draw upon a much larger literature, for example, studies of the ancient and medieval roots of modern physics that go back to Pierre Duhem's many publications beginning in 1905. Duhem's overstatements were corrected in the 1940s and 50s by Anneliese Maier and others (see Maier 1982 and, e.g., Wilson 1956); similarly, Koyré's overstatements were corrected by Stillman Drake in publications over many years (see Drake 1990).

It is not the case that modern science began one day when Galileo and some others had the bright idea that one should observe nature to see how it works, that is, mechanically. Neither empirical methods nor mechanistic explanation was new, though they were not always combined with one another and with prediction. Astronomy always had been an observational science: Paths of the planets were described, permitting prediction of their future positions. So far as there were mechanistic theories in ancient astronomy, for example, that heavenly bodies are carried about in crystalline spheres, those theories were not regarded as predictive – except of what was already known. Observation and prediction in astronomy were thus at least partly independent of mechanistic theory.

Conversely, mechanistic theories do not need to have predictive power. There were before Aristotle many mechanistic theories. One was that everything is composed of a continuous matter, water or air, existing in various stages of compression or dilation. Atomism was an opposite but equally mechanistic view, that matter comes in discrete pieces some of which hook together, forming visible bodies. Each of these conjectures was suggested by one or another experiential analogy but none yielded the sort of empirical tests now expected of theories. Nor was that seen as a defect.

Aristotle, by contrast, was much less conjectural, much more rigorously empirical. But his idea of explanation was not mechanistic; it was taxonomic and teleological. Understanding is seeing what more general taxon each more specific taxon stands under, in a system of taxa arranged from the most specific to the most general. Such a taxonomy is formed by abstracting from observations made of particulars: observations made and sorted until, from out of them, a stable system of classes emerges (*Post. An.*, II, 19). Living nature and society are further understood teleologically, in terms of ends served. That, too, is empirical, as it is based on observed patterns of self-sustaining development (growth and reproduction): As the process is sustained by its products, the latter were concluded to exist for the sake of the whole (*Phys.* II, *Pol.*, I, 1–2). Mechanistic explanation was not denied; it was presupposed (the 'co-operative causes' (Jowett trans.) Plato cited in the *Timaeus*); but neither taxonomy nor teleology is concerned with the mechanics of how things come about. They are not for that reason any the less modes of understanding or any the less based on observation.

Archimedes' famous solutions to mechanical problems are seen retrospectively as having been in the spirit of modern science. But that claim should be qualified, as they were not at that time regarded as being of any theoretical interest; they were thought, probably by Archimedes himself

(Dijksterhuis 1938/1987, pp.13–14), to be of merely instrumental value. Theory was seen by the Greeks, the sophists excepted, to be noble precisely because its interest does not depend on utility. It is good in itself, and also as instructing us about ultimate ends, fitting the educated for political rule. In consequence, the technical advances made throughout the Hellenistic and medieval periods – windmills, pumps, etc. – though we today can see that they bear suggestions for mechanistic theory were made by those innocent of any pretension to theory.

The same division, between noble-because-useless theory and ignoble practicality, may be seen in the history of mathematics, where arithmetic developed largely in response to the needs of commerce but the study of conic sections was pursued, as Whitehead somewhere said, for 800 years without any idea of application. It was not until Galileo noted that projectile motion is parabolic and Kepler demonstrated that planetary orbits are elliptical that the theory of conic sections gained interesting application. That application, however, was not at first of any practical use. Archers already knew to aim high; they did not need to be told about parabolas.

Applying conic sections to the analysis of physical motion violated another dichotomy that was sometimes asserted in the classical period. Aristotle, in anti-Platonic mood, argued that, as geometrical figures are ideal, their study does not illuminate the actual (*Phys.*, II, 2): a tangent touches a circle at but one dimensionless point, whereas a wheel touches a road along a line of some length. Thus we have a trichotomy: on the ignoble side, machines, bookkeeping, etc., and, on the noble side, two distinct kinds of science, one of the ideal, the other of the actual. Astronomy was an exception, in its use of geometry, but the exception is a limited one; furthermore, it carries the implication that the celestial is more ideal than is the terrestrial, making the former a model for our emulation ('Bright star! would I were steadfast as thou art'). We shall later note the importance of this to Aristotle's philosophy.

The idea of a mathematically formulated law of motion developed slowly in the medieval universities as scholars struggled with an unsolved problem in Aristotle's physics, that of projectile motion: what keeps an arrow moving after it leaves the bow? Aristotle tried two answers (in different books of the *Physics*), each mechanistic, neither convincing. In the sixth century, John Philoponus, a Christian Neo-Platonist of Alexandria, proposed as an alternative that the bow imparts to the arrow a motive force – a ghostly push *sans* pusher – that accompanies it in its flight, keeping it going but gradually wearing out. The idea of an 'impressed force' emerged again in the universities at Oxford and Paris after Aristotle's physical works became known there, in the thirteenth century. As this force cannot be seen, what keeps the idea of it from being empty words masking the truism that projectiles fly because they do? At the university in Paris in the fourteenth century, Jean Buridan proposed a quantitative theory of 'impetus', defined as the force required to move a body at a given speed; impetus, thus, is measured by speed times the 'quantity of matter' (weight) in the body moved. In that way, the impetus theory was made more than tautological. But this innovation presupposed the development of means of representing functional relations. Nicolas Oresme developed a system of geometrical representation on two axes, with time marked off on the horizontal axis and velocity on the vertical axis: constant velocity appears as a horizontal line while uniformly accelerated or decelerated velocity appears as a diagonal, and the distance covered is equal to the area under the line. Theorems could thus be proven, such as the mean speed rule.[5] All of this took place wholly within theory and out of an interest wholly theoretical.

Of course, opinion is never uniform. Already in the thirteenth century, Roger Bacon wrote, in his vehement fashion, abominating the pursuit of knowledge of nature for its own sake, rather than for its usefulness. But the primary use he found for it was in the interpretation of Scripture; only secondarily was its use material improvement, and for that use, he specially praised alchemy. Alchemy, metallurgy, and medicine were at that time studies practical without being, to any great degree, theoretical; they are the roots of chemistry, which became a theoretical science only very gradually (Partington 1957). In the fifteenth century, however, practice and theory were approaching one another, as each became more mathematical: Engineering, civil or military, became a profession (Leonardo da Vinci's). Thus the question was in the air, whether theory should be practically beneficial and whether that should be its purpose. But it was only a question. It does not follow that utility was the aim of Galileo or of those whom he influenced.

It has often been remarked that a major part of the achievement of Galileo and some others was to have brought the mechanical knowledge of craftsmen into relation to theoretical inquiry, which Archimedes had not done. But this does not have to be seen as a subordination of theory to practice. It is more naturally viewed as the reverse: practical application serving the ends of theory. Theory, though it is then no longer useless and

---

[5] In modern terms, the rule that, where acceleration is constant, distance equals mean velocity times time. This was discovered at Merton College, Oxford in the early fourteenth century and later proven graphically by Oresme.

can be praised for its usefulness, may continue to be nobly pursued for its own sake.[6] Galileo also opposed the other classical dichotomy, the one between mathematics and physics: '... it was no small part of Galileo's purpose to overcome a certain traditional resistance to the use of mathematics in the solution of physical problems' (Drake 1974, p.xxi). That issue would seem to be about values exclusively cognitive.

Had Galileo's aim been merely practical, he would not have run afoul of the Church when he defended Copernican heliocentrism. Copernicus' system could have been defended consistently with Church doctrine the way that his posthumous editor, Osiander, did in fact defend it, as an elegant device for conveniently calculating where in relation to the fixed stars a given planet can be observed at given times. But Galileo defended the system as representing the way things really are. Interest in the way things really are is theoretical, and theory can contradict Church doctrine.

There is, then, little evidence for the view that modern science was 'founded' on a practical turn away from theoretical understanding. It is not clear even what 'founding' might mean in the case of modern science, as it evolved over a long period, from a variety of sources.

E

That modern science began by a turn away from airy speculation to observation is even less plausible; we noted above that observations had been made from the beginning of thought about nature, including the nature of man and society, and that Aristotle's philosophy in particular was based on observation, as by his own account. The difference, rather, was in what was observed and in the logical relation of these observations to theory. But those innovations were themselves discoveries made, viz., that observation is a more effective test of theory when it is quantitative than when qualitative and that observation of any sort is more telling as a test of theory than it is as a source of theory (a point Karl Popper emphasized). The historical sequence bears this out, as follows.

It is obvious that the Sun orbits the Earth: We see it every day rise in the east and set in the west. Copernicus did not have a separate stock of observations from which to draw the opposite conclusion. Rather, he entertained a hypothesis (not original with him but by him elaborated) that revealed an ambiguity in what is seen: The same phenomenon could

---

[6] In his early treatise on machines, Galileo proclaimed the usefulness of that study, but he did not claim utility as its sole value (1590–1600/1960, pp.147–50).

be explained differently on a different, less obvious assumption. This alternative explanation was a product of mathematical imagination. How might observation decide between these rival hypotheses? In the next section, we will examine Galileo's defense of the Copernican system, which was in large part by deducing implications of Aristotle's physics (but of terrestrial, not celestial phenomena) that could be tested against observation. Of course, theories had earlier been sometimes examined in light of their implications; and in the modern period observation continued to be a source of ideas. But after Galileo, the emphasis shifted from careful generalization of experience to bold conjectures that can be tested against experience.

Testable implications are predictions of what has not yet been observed (or, anyway, noted), and which, often, it takes special effort to observe. Thus their test leads to making observations that otherwise would not be made. Such observations are typically of phenomena inherently trivial and ordinarily ignored. Often, these phenomena cannot be observed at all without the use of special instruments and techniques devised for that purpose (to take a later example, by microscope and cell-staining). Often, they do not occur naturally but must be created artificially via experimental contrivance. This expands the empirical base of science. Trivial, remote, or artificial, the phenomena observed are real, and therefore they serve their epistemic purpose. A theory made to yield a prediction of what is otherwise unexpected is likely to be refuted; conversely, when the unexpected surprisingly *is* observed, that is strong evidence for the theory tested – stronger evidence than that the theory agrees with the observations that suggested it in the first place and which it was designed to explain.[7] The upshot is fourfold: Rigor is enhanced as more theories are eliminated; the realm of permissible ideas is expanded to include conjectures that contradict common sense; the range of observation is vastly extended; and that range includes novel discoveries, creating a taste for discovery.

As to what is observed: the application of mathematics to the study of nature, suggested by the medieval development of laws of motion and retrospectively appreciated in Archimedes' famous achievements, augmented these four features. Postulated quantities add to the stock of conceptions subject to empirical test. When their reality is confirmed, by the success of attempts to measure them, the detail and precision of empirical

---

[7] Attempts to use probability theory to explain our intuitive sense of this difference in epistemic force of the two relations of observation to theory go back at least to Peirce (*vide supra*, Ch.1, F); it does not follow that the difference can be quantified.

knowledge is increased. Conversely, measurement and other forms of quantitative observation eliminate a greater variety of hypotheses than does qualitative observation. By rolling balls on an inclined plane, Galileo was able to observe that their path is parabolic; air resistance means that projectile paths will not be perfectly parabolic, but even so this experiment raised a question about Aristotle's physics which that physics itself never raised. Measurement is never perfectly exact; there are degrees of exactness; yet, even a very inexact measure is inconsistent with a greater variety of quantitative predictions than is qualitative observation with qualitative predictions.

In brief: conjecture, especially when quantitative, and the deduction of consequences, especially by calculation, expanded empiricism and made it epistemically more powerful. This has been generally admitted once Karl Popper's writings became well known, but it needs to be restated here. The difference between ancient science and modern science is not that of speculation versus observation but almost the reverse: modern science introduced a form of speculation that deepened empiricism.

Much the same applies to the idea that modern science began with the introduction of mechanistic explanation. Mechanistic theory, we have noted, was nothing new. Rather, modern science transformed what counts as mechanistic explanation. The original idea of such explanation derives from how machines (levers, pulleys, gear wheels, the Archimedean screw for raising water) operate, by one part moving another part, via direct contact. The 'mechanics' that grew out of Galileo's and Newton's work – laws of statics, kinematics, and dynamics – was not mechanics in that original sense; indeed, Newton denied that the idea of gravity explained anything, as he knew no mechanism by which it worked. As to wave mechanics, statistical mechanics, and quantum mechanics, each is a unique way of looking at a distinct set of phenomena, requiring respective techniques, mathematical and experimental, that are novel; each form of mechanics has been a product, not a presupposition, of inquiry.

F

As modern science cannot be identified by any supposed founding principles, it must be identified as the upshot of debates, lines of thought, and investigations that gained momentum in the sixteenth and seventeenth centuries: it is what was established in the process by which Aristotle's physics lost its credibility. But what was thus established? Let us examine this history, so as to test Peirce's concept of science.

One might suppose that it began with the famous observations. In 1572, a new star appeared to amazed observers and in sixteen months it faded. In 1577, Tycho Brahe showed that a comet's path that he had plotted cut through the crystalline spheres supposed to hold planets in place. In 1604, another new star appeared. In 1609, Galileo learned of the invention of the telescope, in Belgium, constructed one many times stronger, and, by its means, observed such celestial imperfections as spots on the Sun and craters on the Moon; he also noted four moons orbiting Jupiter, which was inconsistent with the Ptolemaic principle of there being but one center of motion in the cosmos. He observed phases of Venus, verifying what had been regarded as a counterfactual implication of the Copernican system. He detected a multitude of stars additional to those seen by the naked eye. These telescopic discoveries, published in 1610 (those of sunspots in 1613), are what first brought Galileo fame and gained for his later works a broad audience.

It is not quite so simple, however. Stars had been observed to be born and to die before 1572, and some other puzzling phenomena, such as meteorites ('falling stars'), were common. They were puzzling because they did not fit into the accepted Aristotelian system, about which more in a moment. But what is merely puzzling is not a refutation of an important world-view; life is replete with unsolved puzzles. The difference was made by the growth of new ideas, alternative to Aristotle's, into which those strange phenomena did fit: the idea of a mechanistic terrestrial physics and the idea that that physics might be extended to the heavens. It was the latter which suggested turning a telescope to the heavens. Most importantly, these new ideas were presupposed, as framing possibilities, in what Galileo saw through the telescope. The moon's craters appear also to the naked eye, though only as dark areas; but even with a telescope, craters are seen as such only by inference – from the analogy of their changing patterns of light and dark to those of the Earth's mountains and valleys in changing relation to the Sun. The inference is of the type Peirce named 'abductive', but the abduction introduces or presupposes the possibility of a likeness between terrestrial and celestial phenomena. Similarly, one does not see four bodies orbiting Jupiter without assuming that the spots seen are bodies and that they are the same bodies in successively different positions; then one can infer that they orbit Jupiter because that would explain their changing arrangement (varying numbers on one side of Jupiter or the other but always in a line and within a maximum distance of the planet).

Galileo's observations had tremendous impact. In 1611 – twenty-one years before he published his defense of the Copernican system (though at the conclusion of his 1610 *Starry Messenger*, he indicated that he would publish such a defense) – John Donne wrote that 'the new philosophy calls all in doubt .... all coherence gone'. What was the coherence that was gone? These observations broke down the Aristotelian distinction between the terrestrial and the celestial. To appreciate what was at issue, we must take a moment with Aristotle's system, based on commonplace observations. These attest to the imperturbable perfection of the Heavens in contrast to what we know of life on Earth. Chunks of earth lofted fall back to Earth, whereas the stars seem eternal and keep to their courses, the aforementioned anomalous phenomena aside. Thus it appears there are two kinds of matter: terrestrial matter can be moved only by the imposition of force – except in falling, wherein it seeks of itself to return to its proper place at the center of the cosmos – whereas celestial matter glows and orbits eternally, without any imposition of force, in *its* natural place.

Aristotle's physics and astronomy supported his ethics, politics, and theology and were reflected in his poetics. Man can observe the perfection of the Heavens, which teach him of God, defined as the self-sufficient being; for the stars in their way emulate God; and this gives man an ideal to emulate, viz., self-sufficiency. Alas, we are terrestrial and imperfect and cannot escape dependency on one another, which is the origin of the *polis*. Tragedy evokes our fear and pity, as we contemplate one who, nobler than most, forgets his natural place in the cosmos and, striving too high, falls. Comedy evokes laughter at one who acts beneath his natural place. Man, by observing the stars and emulating God, is more than earthly yet Earth-bound. The prescriptions made in Aristotle's ethics and politics presuppose that fact; they are based on observations of human nature and what it takes to attain the deficient kinds of self-sufficiency possible for us. Judeo-Christian-Islamic theology modifies without destroying this system, by adding revelation to observation: God is no longer to be thought an unmoved mover but a loving and often angry creator; our dependency is not only on one another but is more decisively on Him; and eschatology replaces the ideal of self-sufficiency. But the celestial still differs radically from the terrestrial – and we remain at the center of the cosmos.

Galileo's defense of the Copernican system, published in 1632, in the *Dialogue on the Great World Systems*, united what Aristotle had divided. His key move (Butterfield 1957) may briefly be stated. Whereas Aristotle supposed that all terrestrial motion but falling requires a force, leaving projectile motion a problem, Galileo proposed that force is required only to account for change in motion; matter is conceived of as having the intrinsic property of inertia, that is, of continuing in whatever motion it is in. Impetus disappears; it is not needed to explain projectile motion.[8] And the changeless motion of heavenly bodies does not require its own physics – assuming, as Galileo did, that inertial motion over long distances is revealed to be circular and that planetary orbits are circular. Terrestrial gravity replaces projectile motion as an unsolved problem but its effect, as force, on falling bodies and projectiles can be computed. There is, then, a united physics of Earth and Heaven, one set of laws describing both. That there is one physics, not two, is sometimes said to be the Galilean revolution.

But if we suppose that theoretical unification is what matters, as it did in the classical ideal of theory, then Galileo's unified physics is less impressive than has been suggested. For its effect was to disunite physics and ethics. The 'great world systems' referred to in the title of Galileo's book were of astronomy (Ptolemaic and Copernican) only; Aristotle's system, by contrast, combined everything from astronomy and theology to politics and poetry. Thus it and its Christian amendment in the system of St. Thomas Aquinas were more comprehensive, more satisfying than anything Galileo offered. We must therefore look elsewhere than to theoretical unification for the reason Galileo's alternative was perceived by the Church as a threat.

One might suggest that, obviously, it is the observations that matter – not only the ones listed above, but more importantly those that Galileo showed in his *Dialogue* to contradict the implications which he drew from Aristotle's physics. He deduced from Aristotle's physics, for famous example, that a stone, if it is dropped from the mast of a ship moving forward, will strike the deck behind the mast and not, as is the fact and as inertial physics predicts, at its foot. It does not matter that such phenomena were of little interest to Aristotelians or Thomists; it does not matter that laws of motion and prediction of effects had no place in their conception of physics. For, what a theory implies, it implies; and if what it implies is false, then the theory is false.

We have already noted that things are not so simple. One does not reject a theory, much less a satisfying world-view, because some minor problems have been found with it – not, that is, unless a potentially better alternative beckons. And, while Aristotle's system faced many difficulties, so did, and does, the new physics. Not only was Aristotle's unsolved problem of projectile motion replaced by the unsolved problem of gravity, but the latter is a far more important problem in the perspective of the new physics than is

---

[8] The measure of impetus remained, reconceived as the measure of a different quantity, momentum. Momentum, unlike impetus, does not explain continued motion; instead, it explains the measurable effect, in collision, of moving bodies on each other's velocity.

the former in the perspective of Aristotelianism. And I mentioned, in passing, two erroneous propositions upon which Galileo relied, that inertia is circular and that the planetary orbits are circular. Kepler had already shown that Mars' orbit is an ellipse, which Galileo knew of but was unconvinced by. And not long after Galileo wrote, Descartes (allegedly on the basis of pure reason, not observation) claimed that inertia is rectilinear – which then raises all over again the question, why planets orbit the Sun. What bends their path out of the straight line? When, over half a century later, Newton framed a law of gravity from which Kepler's laws and a law of falling bodies were alike deduced, as well as the tides, etc., that still left the force of gravity a mystery. Like Galileo, Newton left most of the questions that his own theory raised unanswered; he did not calculate what he did not know how to calculate, for example, the gravitational effects of the planets on one another.

At first glance, this history makes the triumph of the new physics harder to understand; I think, however, that the difficulty itself points to the true explanation. The alternative that beckoned was not another system; it was, instead, an alternative to all systems. The ideal of a system is to be comprehensive and coherent, in a word, complete: unsolved problems are therefore defects, even if minor. By contrast, an inquiry that is concrete, that measures quantities and tests hypotheses about how, exactly, things happen and what, exactly, things are made of, cannot be expected to be completed any time soon, if ever. And that makes a difference to how problems are viewed. In this sort of inquiry, unsolved problems, even ones deemed major, are not so much defects as they are opportunities: They define work that remains to be done. In place of completeness, progress is the ideal. And, as long as progress is being made, it is reasonable to hope that an unanswered question or unsolved problem will yield to investigation, eventually. Even some degree of incoherence, for example, regarding the geometry of inertia, is tolerable, as long progress is being made.

The issue, then, was not a simple one of comparing theories to facts. Because progress was being made, facts of the sort that matter in this new type of inquiry acquired a weight they had not formerly had. A system in which mechanical details are trivial was being challenged by a form of inquiry in which those same details are crucial. To suppose that Galileo's university opponents were willfully blind dogmatists and that his Church opponents were self-serving careerists, does less than justice to Galileo himself, as it implies that his claims were obvious, which they were not. Was a scholar who would not look through a telescope (to take a notorious example) refusing to acknowledge relevant facts? More likely, he was denying that such facts as lunar craters *are* relevant to the great questions of philosophy. He was denying that gadgets like telescopes and childish activities like Galileo's, of rolling balls on an inclined plane – activities of the kind lampooned by Swift – are proper means of deciding important questions. These were intelligent and serious men, who, whatever their personal motivations, could see what was at risk: religion, morality, and political order. How could where a stone falls be allowed to tell against a world-view that for ages had defined the worth of man?

To understand how Galileo's arguments were effective, we have to see that his achievement went beyond the observations and calculations that refuted Aristotle's physics. Galileo's genius was to have grasped the potentiality of this new form of inquiry and, by a stream of concrete discoveries, to have exhibited its power to advance theoretical knowledge. His achievement was to have overturned the classical ideal of knowing. Knowledge as an end in itself was not rejected, but it was reconceived. Knowledge is still what inquiry results in, but now it is measured by its use in making further discoveries.

This revolution in the ideal of knowing, from completed system to ongoing inquiry, was clearly expressed by Galileo and Newton, in statements prefacing their greatest works. It is easy today to miss what was revolutionary in those statements: in reading them, we have to recall the classical ideal of knowledge which they by implication denied.

Galileo's last book, the *Two New Sciences*, based on work he had done some thirty years earlier, was written when he was under house arrest and was published in 1638, in the Protestant Netherlands, after he had become blind. One of the 'new sciences' is about the cohesion of bodies, specifically, about why the parts of larger machines and organisms had to be proportionally more massive to escape breaking, and the other is about terrestrial motions, for example, of projectiles. In naming them new sciences (*nuove scienze*), Galileo meant that they were systems of knowledge; for that is what 'science' meant in his day. Yet he presented them as unfinished inquiries:

> It has been observed that missiles or projectiles trace out a line somehow curved, but no one has brought out that this is a parabola. That it is, and other things neither few nor less worthy of being known, will be demonstrated by me, and (what is in my opinion more worthwhile) there will be opened a gateway and a road ... (Galileo 1638/1974, p.147)

He meant a gateway and a road to further such discoveries, *a fortiori* by others. It is astonishing that Galileo, instead of apologizing for it, praised this incompleteness, calling the road opened *more worthwhile* than the results already obtained. Therein, he rejected the classical ideal of knowing.

The same attitude was expressed forty-nine years later by Newton, in
the preface to the first edition of his *Principia* (his *Mathematical Principles
of Natural Philosophy*):

> I wish we could derive the rest of the phenomena of Nature by the same
> kind of reasoning from mechanical principles .... but I hope the principles
> here laid down will afford some light either to this or some truer method of
> philosophy. (Newton 1687/1962, p.xviii)

In this spirit, Newton in later editions made additions and corrections that
he in many cases cheerfully attributed to the work of others. That says a great
deal about the character of this new mode of intellectual life, as Newton
(unlike Galileo) was not a markedly generous or cheerful man. Note also
that Newton did not suppose that the question of method had been settled
once and for all: some method 'truer' may yet be discovered, he said.

It seems to me that this history confirms – at least, it makes plausible –
Peirce's concept of science as an inquiry of a type that of necessity must
be carried out by specialists in a community of investigators and that lacks
any definitive method or metaphysics but is defined, instead, by its ideal
of concreteness fruitful of further discoveries and by its hope of endless
progress, its 'esperable uberty', as Peirce wrote (*vide supra*, n.14).

G

What gives this conception of science its normative force, if it has one?
Swiftians object that the argument Galileo made against the Aristotelian
or Thomistic systems begged the question, as it substituted a new ideal of
knowing for the classical or medieval one. At least they recognize the complexity of the issue, missed by those who suppose that Aristotle's physics
was defeated simply by looking at the facts, as if its defeat did not require
learning a new way of looking. As Peirce said about the controversy over
Darwinism, 'questions of fact and questions of logic' – logic being for
Peirce a normative science, though it was only much later that he said
so – 'are curiously interlaced' (EP1:111). In other words, cognitive values or
intellectual aims and standards are part of what is at issue.

The obvious approach to the normative question is to look for some
principle – abstract enough to be shared by ancient and modern – by
which the new might be justified or might fail to be justified as against the
old. Are there intellectual aims and/or standards common to classical philosophy and modern science which the latter better satisfies than does the
former? One thinks of such standards as accuracy, scope, and simplicity.

As Thomas Kuhn pointed out, however, these standards seem constant only because they are ambiguous. 'Accuracy, as a value, has with time increasingly denoted quantitative or numerical agreement, sometimes at the expense of qualitative. Before modern times ... [quantitative] accuracy ... was a criterion only for astronomy ... Elsewhere it was neither expected nor sought' (1977, p.335). Similarly, what counts as simple depends on one's idea of simplicity: the Copernican system as amended by Kepler's laws is free of epicycles, but at the cost of replacing circles with ellipses having two foci. And there have been changes, too, in the relative weighting of these values. 'Or consider scope. It is still an important scientific value, but important advances have repeatedly been achieved at its expense, and the weight attributed to it at times of choice has diminished correspondingly' (1977, p.335). Kuhn appears to have had in mind specific instances of the diminished importance of scope, but that change was illustrated most dramatically by the advent of modern science itself, in which moral and other concerns were put aside in the interest of a more concrete grasp of a subset of phenomena, viz., those measurable.

In Section E, we noted that the new sorts of argument and observation eliminated a greater quantity of alternative theories – an increase in rigor, if rigor is so defined. But the very idea of entertaining alternative hypotheses and attempting to refute them is foreign to Aristotle's inductive method, wherein conjecture is to be avoided and the road to truth is careful generalization from experience. If we seek elsewhere in classical thought for an example of rigor it would be in the deduction of theorems in Euclidean geometry. To be impressed by the rigor of modern science, as measured by the elimination of error, is to adopt a new idea of rigor, a new standard by which to evaluate intellectual work. Therefore, rigor, too, cannot be cited as a universal principle by which the choice of modern science over classical systems can be justified.

If there are no universal and unchanging standards of theory-evaluation, might there nonetheless be intellectual aims that are universal and unchanging? Plausible candidates would be knowing the truth and understanding things. But those aims, too, are ambiguous. We noted above that understanding for Aristotle was not what it was for Galileo and Newton. Hence, the truths desired were not the same. It has never been the case that we want to know all truths: which truths matter is part of what is at issue. Therefore, modern science cannot be justified on the ground that it better realizes the same, univocal ultimate aim that classical philosophy realized less well. We can conjecture that there *is* an ultimate aim; but if there is, our idea of it has changed. Our idea of what counts as understanding the world changes as our idea of the world changes. What is understanding, truly? That remains to be discovered.

There appears to be no nonquestion-begging principle by which modern science can be justified. That does not mean that no account can be given as to why it is superior to its classical and medieval predecessors; only, that account is in terms of principles that are part of modern science, at least as it has so far developed, and not part of classical philosophy. As that is indeed circular, Swiftians conclude that the new ideal triumphed only in an unprincipled way, by promising material rewards in place of wisdom. We might remind Swiftians, however, that even they no longer think it true that the Sun orbits the Earth. This fact of changed belief cannot be ignored simply because it is humdrum. It shows that our idea of knowledge *has* changed. Swiftian protests to the contrary are like the 'paper doubts' that Peirce famously derided (EP2:349): They are merely verbal. Classical philosophy or medieval theology are what Swiftians want to believe that they believe; in practice, Swiftians accept modern science just as the rest of us do. What they really believe is shown by their practice.

If all justification is by deduction from principle, then fundamental principles cannot be justified. They can, however, be learned. One of the things we have learned from experience and from history is that we can learn from experience and from history. The preceding section detailed the course of experience by which a new ideal of knowing was learned. A new form of intellectual life developed in which new sources of intellectual satisfaction were found: The excitement of discovery was at the price of incomplete theories and continued uncertainty, but the conclusions drawn, albeit tentative and fragmentary, were by their concreteness of greater credibility than the grand syntheses they discredited. The obvious flaws of the new theories – fatal by the old standards of consistency and completeness – were seen as opportunities for further discovery. The promise of fruitfulness supplanted the dialectic of systems. History shows that this revolution in cognitive ideals was neither arbitrary nor anti-intellectual. Although it turns on a judgment of the type Peirce named 'aesthetic', it is irreversible. We will discuss his theory of normative inquiry in Chapter 9.

That the new cognitive ideal is not arbitrary is presupposed in what is felt by many to be the crisis of modernity, that scientific specialization forgoes any pretence to wisdom, to providing moral guidance. For, that can be a crisis only if there is no going back to earlier forms of knowing.

CHAPTER 4

The Meaning of Pragmatism

It is the reality of some possibilities that pragmaticism is most concerned to insist upon. – *Peirce in 1905, EP2:354*

Peirce did not use the word 'pragmatism' in print or in his public lectures until his sixties, after William James had made the doctrine famous and attributed it to his old friend, then living in obscurity. In a lecture of 1898, 'Philosophical Conceptions and Practical Results', subsequently published in several variously amended versions, James cited Peirce's 1878 article, 'How to Make Our Ideas Clear' as expressing the doctrine, unnamed, in the form of a rule for clarifying ideas by relating them to their practical consequences. This rule has come to be known as 'the pragmatic maxim'. In 1903, Peirce, through the kind offices of James, delivered a course of seven lectures at Harvard on pragmatism. Later, there were three articles on pragmatism in the *Monist*, 1905–1906, in a series not completed. The first of these, 'What Pragmatism Is', introduced a new term, 'pragmaticism', as being 'ugly enough to be safe from kidnappers' (EP2:335). The kidnapper was of course James. That may seem ingratitude, but James' version of pragmatism was not Peirce's.

In lectures and articles from 1902 on, and in unpublished manuscripts of the period, everything that Peirce had been thinking or was then working on was brought under the new label or its ugly sibling: some as parts of an alleged 'proof' of pragmatism, some as among its 'consequences'. Phaneroscopy, semeiotic, normative science – all were drafted into service as parts of the proof.[1] Even his new, graphical system of logic, the 'existential graphs', was made to serve. Following Peirce's lead, students

---

[1] Whether pragmatism admits of a proof, or what 'proof' in its case might mean, is a question: see Houser at EP2:xxxiii–xxxviii; also Roberts (1978), Fisch (1986), Ch.19, Robin (1997), and Colapietro (2012a).

of his thought have tended to label the whole of it 'pragmatism' or, sometimes, 'pragmaticism', though other labels, equally awkward, that he had invented, such 'synechism' and 'critical common-sensism', would serve as well or better. Of neologisms he was prolific. In addition, he called himself an 'idealist' and a 'realist'. These terms (antonyms only in the lexicon of the vulgar) have had varied meanings in the history of philosophy, of which meanings Peirce freely availed himself. At different times, he espoused mutually incompatible versions of idealism, while his realism became ever more encompassing. For his varied idealisms, see the next two chapters; for his realism, the next section.

Now, idealism and realism are metaphysical doctrines, whereas pragmatism, as it is usually understood and as it was most often described by Peirce himself, pertains to meaning alone or, more broadly, to logic as theory of inquiry. However, Peirce's later reflections on his pragmatic maxim affirmed its need of support by a realist metaphysics. In express contradiction of what he said about the maxim in its first publication, Peirce later argued that what would be and what may be are realities; that is, he argued for modal realism. Thus the epigram of this chapter (EP2:354). Pragmatism, in Peirce's later understanding of it, is a doctrine not only of logic, though he continued to name it so, but also of metaphysics.

Despite the evolution of his pragmatism and realism, certain features of each were constants of Peirce's thought. It will smooth the road taken in later chapters if this one is devoted to an examination of those doctrines and the successive changes made in them. Section A of this chapter defines 'idealism' and, in more detail, 'realism' as these terms will be used in this book. Section B outlines the series of Peirce's philosophical publications and lectures, locates pragmatism within them, and traces in them the stages of his realism. Then, in Section C, the pragmatic maxim is read in light of his concept of science as it was described in Chapter 2. On that basis and on other bases, I reject the prevailing reading of the maxim, that it anticipates the verification theory of meaning; it is not a theory of meaning at all. In subsequent sections, problems in applying the maxim are exposed, which lead to and account for its later, modally realist interpretation. Among the applications considered is that to the concept of a 'final opinion': the set of conclusions to which inquiry leads – or, under the later assumption of modal realism, to which it *would* lead, *were* certain conditions fulfilled. Peirce identified truth with the final opinion and reality with what that opinion represents or would represent. Reality, represented to be independent of its representations, explains inquiry's progress toward its representation.

The chapter ends by noticing the version of the pragmatic maxim with which Peirce concluded his 1903 Harvard lectures. It is not, as it has usually been taken to be, a figurative restatement of the 1878 maxim. It differs from it essentially, so as to account for the meaning of the modal realism it presupposes.

A

I shall now say the least that can be said about idealism and realism to establish what in this book is meant by those terms.[2]

Idealism is one of three alternatives, the other two being materialism and dualism. 'Materialism' is the term current in Peirce's day; were we to replace it by 'physicalism' (*vide supra*, Ch.3, A), that would complicate our formulation of the issue but not change it essentially. The issue is whether mind is reducible to matter or matter to mind or neither to the other. X is *reducible* to Y if our concept of X can be defined in terms of our concept of Y, or, in other words, if in reality X is no more than Y, or some parts of Y in some sort of combination.

Materialism is the doctrine that blind, thoughtless, unfeeling matter is the whole of reality, that everything consists of matter and its motions, and that mind, if it exists at all, is no more than some sort of matter in some sort of motion or, perhaps, that it is the motion itself or its functional organization (assuming that function is reducible to mechanics; otherwise, functionalism is a nonmaterialist theory of mind).

Dualists hold that mind and matter both exist, neither being reducible to the other; in the case of Descartes, matter is one sort of substance, extended in space, while mind is thinking substance and has no spatial extension. The problem for dualism is to account for the interactions of mind and body in perception and in action: how can matter's motions produce thoughts and how can thoughts move bodies?

Idealism, in starkest form, asserts that matter is reducible to mind, that is, to thought and/or to feeling. These are not necessarily any particular person' s thoughts or feelings. Idealisms divide (a) on whether it is thought or feeling that is made basic to mind and (b) on whether mind consists of individual minds or is impersonal. That individual minds and their

---

[2] Lane (2018) is a careful and comprehensive, thoroughly documented, account of Peirce's idealism and realism; it quotes variant formulations that I here ignore and cites sources that I here omit. Lane defines 'idealism' more broadly than I do (and, in my opinion, more broadly than the history of the term warrants); he also finds Peirce's early statements of idealism to be less problematic than I do (*vide infra*, Ch.5); but otherwise I think his readings support mine.

contents exhaust reality, as in Berkeley's philosophy, has often been named 'subjective idealism'; subjective idealism is one form of idealism, perhaps the only one, that Peirce clearly never adopted. However, the alternatives need not be so stark as here presented: Peirce introduced unexpected nuances by which his idealism, in any of its versions, retained aspects of materialism and dualism.

Realism varies with what is claimed to be real. Peirce at first (1868) affirmed what he named 'scholastic realism', referring to a debate in the medieval schools, between 'realists' and 'nominalists', over whether 'universals' are real. In the technical argot of the schools, 'universal' is made a noun, so that 'a universal', 'some universal', 'all universals', etc., are not solecisms. A universal is a quality, for example, white, or a type, for example, horse, that may be predicated of any of many individuals; it is, then, what is represented by a monadic predicate, that is, a predicate true of individuals taken singly. Nominalists, such as William of Ockham, maintained that individual things and events alone are real, and that to take universals as real is to mistake representation for reality: Universals exist in name only. The realists did not deny individual existence but maintained that universals, or some of them, are real also: that is, they maintained that at least some universals are irreducible to their instances. Whether they exist separately from those instances is another question.

In lieu of using 'universal' as a noun, Peirce later introduced the word 'general' as a noun (shorn of its military sense). That is probably because he extended scholastic realism to include relations that are not represented by monadic predicates and also to include laws. Relations, as distinct from universals, are represented by dyadic and triadic predicates, that is, predicates that apply to pairs or to triplets of subjects. A relation such as 'larger than' may be predicated of any of many different ordered pairs (X is larger than Y), and, so, it is a general. Similarly, relations such as 'gives' embrace many ordered triplets (X gives Y to Z). The word 'relation' is then extended to include universals, thus, what any predicate represents.

Laws of physics are differently represented – not in predicates but in equations – but they are generals because they apply to any number of instances. If I let go of this stone, it falls and if you let go of that stone, it falls: two instances of one law. As his conception of law deepened, Peirce saw that scholastic realism entails the modal realism aforementioned. A law determines not only what is or will be under given conditions but also what would be under conditions that might not or do not obtain: even if I never let go of this stone, it remains true that were I to release it, it would fall and that had I released it, it would have fallen. It follows that, if law is real, possibility, too, must be more than a *façon de parler*.

In addition to scholastic and modal realism, Peirce began in the 1870s to develop a physical realism. 'Physical realism' is not a term he used; by it, I mean a doctrine that there is a spatiotemporal world of causally efficacious individuals existing independently of their being known. A physical realist may be either a materialist or a dualist or even, to a degree, an idealist: Peirce came eventually to hold that *what* an individual thing *is*, is what it would be *thought* to be, were it known and, hence, that material things, while existing independently of being thought of, are not independent of the nature of thought in general.

For the same reason, his physical realism entailed scholastic realism and modal realism. For, what a material individual is, consists of general properties, including causal dispositions – laws of the individual's behavior, which, like any laws, exceed their actual instances. This lump of sugar is soluble even if never put to the test; and if it is put to the test, that can only be once, whereas it would have dissolved had it been put into unsaturated water at other times. Of course, many physical realists, under the influence of nominalism, would deny that physical realism entails scholastic realism and modal realism. But, if Peirce was right, their view is incoherent.

Now, all of this presupposes a definition of 'real' that does not beg questions, as would defining reality as matter, or as what actually exists, or as individual things and events, or as truth, or as thought, etc. What would a nonquestion-begging definition of 'real' be? Peirce in 1871 pointed out that in ordinary parlance we distinguish reality from dream, wish, delusion, and fiction, on the basis that the latter are exactly as they are felt, thought, or said to be, while 'The real is that which is not whatever we happen to think it, but is unaffected by what we may think of it' (EP1:88). We may generalize this by substituting 'represent' for 'think', where representation is understood to include words, images, and feelings as well as thoughts: the real is that which is what it is independently of its being so represented. Notice that, while the fictional or the dreamt, etc., is unreal, the fiction or dream is real; for, a representation is what it is independently of what it is represented to be.[3] This definition of 'real', Peirce suggested, was

---

[3] In this connection, it is useful to notice that there can be no ignorance or error if there is no reality, but nonetheless that one can be ignorant of or mistaken about what is not real. Twain's novels are real; thus, one can fail to know who Huck Finn is or one can mistakenly believe that he has an Aunt Polly.

presupposed in the medieval controversy, as it leaves open the question whether reality may include universals as well as individuals.

Does something real, say, a thought, consist of facts about something else, say, brain events? Does something's being really possible consist of facts about what is (or was or will be) actual? We shall use the terms 'realism' and 'realist' to refer to doctrines that combine claims of reality with claims of irreducibility. Realism about some class of entity (say, possibilities) maintains not only that those entities are real but also that they are not reducible to entities, or to facts about entities, of some other class (say, actualities). Thus, there are two ways to dispute a given sort of realism.

Peirce's definition of 'real' presents a difficulty. It derives from something he asserted three years earlier, in 1868, and never rescinded: that 'the absolutely incognizable is absolutely inconceivable' (EP1:51). In other words, it is nonsense to talk of that which is not capable of being known. He made some argument for this (EP1:24–25), but we will take it to be axiomatic. It follows that the errors we make are subject to correction and that what we are ignorant of is subject to being discovered. In other words, (a) what is independent of being represented must be representable and (b) those representations must be capable of being found to be correct. The difficulty is indicated by the qualification 'absolutely', which presumably is motivated by a reluctance to limit reality to what can in fact be known, granted the limitations of existing inquirers. By the 'absolutely incognizable' Peirce would seem to have meant that which could not be known even were all of our limitations to be removed. But what counts as such a limitation? Put it the other way around: to say that something is knowable is to say that it could be known under certain conditions. But how broadly may those conditions be construed? For example, do they include conditions conceivable but not physically possible?

In Section E, we will review Peirce's 1878 discussion of one such question. For the present, I should like to make this observation: the problem we have delimiting the knowable means that 'real', as Peirce defined it, will not always have an easy, uncontroversial application. But that does not preclude its being a useful term. It will often be the case that its application is straightforward, and, when it is not, it is useful to have the difficulty of a difficult case revealed.

B

While it is not my purpose to present an overview of Peirce's philosophical writings, brief attention must now be given to that topic, lest confusion ensue. I shall here assign various doctrines to their major sources in

Peirce's literary remains. Some of my formulations are controversial, but in ways that will be defended later. Those of his writings and lectures that usually are deemed 'philosophical' appeared in four discrete clumps, but I will more politely say 'sets'. Each has a thematic unity and is separated from the preceding or succeeding set by a lapse of eight or more years. This neat scheme is marred by a couple of intermediate items that must be mentioned.

The first set, or rather the part of it most celebrated, consists of an 1867 paper 'On a New List of Categories' and a series of three articles of 1868–1869 in the *Journal of Speculative Philosophy*. The latter three papers frame an idealism I shall name 'conceptual': one that identifies reality with conceptual thinking, actual or potential. These papers also contain prominent assertions implying physical realism and attempts (in my opinion unsuccessful) to reconcile the two doctrines. Scholastic realism also is asserted. I discuss the 1867 paper and the 1868–1869 idealism, and their continuities and discontinuities with Peirce's later thought, in the next chapter. The 1868–1869 papers contain much, formulated in the context of conceptual idealism, that was later reformulated in other contexts; these persistent themes are important, and thus those papers are cited also in other chapters, for example, in Chapter 2. An intermediate item: a long 1871 review of Berkeley's works reaffirms scholastic realism but was a step away from the conceptual idealism of the 1868–1869 papers and toward the physical realism expressed (more convincingly than in 1868–1869) in the next set.

The second set is a series of six articles published in the *Popular Science Monthly* in 1877–1878, under the rubric, 'Illustrations of the Logic of Science'. In it, scholastic realism is barely present, is even rendered problematic, but physical realism is affirmed albeit not so named. In the first of the papers, 'The Fixation of Belief', it is asserted that the method(s) of science rest on a 'fundamental hypothesis', that there exist 'real things' 'upon which our thinking has no effect' but which 'affect our senses' (EP1:120). The series' second essay, 'How to Make Our Ideas Clear', provides the text – the famous maxim – for this chapter's sermon.

The third set consists of a series of five articles in *The Monist*, 1891–1893, in which Peirce developed a bold cosmogonic hypothesis, first announced in a lecture of 1884, that is intended to account for the existence of laws as having evolved from chaos. That hypothesis took several forms, of which one is the doctrine that everything is feeling. That is another form of idealism, inconsistent with conceptual idealism; it could be mistaken for Berkeley's subjective idealism, except for the fact that Peirce supposed that these feelings occur unfelt by any individual; he named it 'objective idealism'. I describe the strange career of this cosmogony in Chapter 6. A lecture series of 1898, though of great interest, is like the Berkeley review in not marking an epoch but being intermediary; it represents yet another stab at the cosmogony while also evincing a growing interest in the relation of philosophy to science, which led to the last set.

The fourth and final set consists, in part, of the aforementioned lectures and essays on pragmatism from 1903 to 1906. At least as important as these, however, are a large mass of other writings from 1902 continuing until near the end of Peirce's life: book reviews, dictionary definitions, private letters, some later articles, a long grant application that was rejected, and a trove of unpublished manuscripts. In the published and unpublished writings together, Peirce developed two new sciences, phaneroscopy and semeiotic; outlined a conception of three normative sciences; proposed that philosophy should consist of a set of sciences, including those aforementioned; implied a phaneroscopic defense of realism, scholastic, modal, and physical; framed an idea of final causation paradoxically made consistent with modern science; refined his ideas about perception and, under the rubric of 'critical common-sensism', refined his account of scientific inquiry; and, as if all of that were not already beyond what we would expect is possible even for a genius, invented the system of existential graphs. A few strands only of this extraordinary production will be mentioned in Chapters 8 and 9.

C

Now let us turn specifically to pragmatism. In 'How to Make Our Ideas Clear' (EP1:124–41), Peirce wrote:

> ... our action has exclusive reference to what affects the senses, our habit has the same bearing as our action, our belief the same as our habit, our conception the same as our belief; and we can consequently mean nothing by wine but what has certain effects, direct or indirect, upon our senses; and to talk of something as having all the sensible characters of wine, yet being in reality blood, is senseless jargon. (131)
>
> ... how impossible it is that we should have an idea in our minds which relates to anything but conceived sensible effects of things. (132)
>
> It appears, then, that the rule for attaining the third grade of clearness of apprehension is as follows: Consider what effects, which might conceivably have practical bearings, we conceive the object of our conception to have. Then, our conception of these effects is the whole of our conception of the object. (132)

The rule for attaining 'the third grade of clearness of apprehension' is the so-called pragmatic maxim. The first two grades were earlier identified as familiarity, that is, feeling able to recognize typical examples, and verbal definition. Those two grades, Peirce argued, are what Descartes called clearness and distinctness, respectively (124–25).

The contrast drawn between 'senseless jargon' and what we can 'mean' by wine, presumably by the word 'wine', suggests two things often claimed about this maxim: First, that it expresses a general theory of meaning, that is, of the meanings of words; second, that it is motivated at least in part by a desire to get rid of meaningless words. If we repeat meaningless words without realizing that they are meaningless, we might suppose that we have ideas when we do not have ideas. How impossible it is, Peirce said, that we should have 'an idea in our minds' that relates to aught but the sensible. Put as crudely as possible, this gives us an equation: idea = meaning = sensible effects. That equation connects thought, words, and sensation. As words are a social product and sensation and thought are functions of body and mind, respectively, the equation also connects body, mind, and society. An entire philosophy appears to be entailed by this simple maxim.

That sounds, in content and in motivation, like the 1920s doctrine of logical positivism. The logical positivists wished to eliminate theology and metaphysics as so much meaningless verbiage; they espoused a verification theory of meaning, variously formulated. Roughly speaking, the verification theory holds that the meaning of a statement is the sensible conditions that can verify it and that the meaning of a word is the difference it makes to the verification conditions of the statements in which it occurs. Somewhat less roughly, meaning is *a rule* that specifies verification conditions. As Peirce wrote that 'our conception' of sensible effects is 'our conception' of the object conceived of, it is clear that he would have identified meaning with the general rule, and not with any number of particular conditions – *if* he were to identify it with either. In a manuscript of 1906, he said that his repetition of 'derivatives of *concipere*' was intended 'to avoid all danger of being understood as attempting to explain a concept by percepts, images, schemata, or by anything but concepts' (5.402n3; see also 5.3).

Thus it has been held that Peirce anticipated the verification theory of meaning (Misak 1995, Ch.3), as if that were to his credit, from which it follows that the pragmatic maxim is subject to all the same objections, and perhaps to some others as well, that the verification theory is subject to. One of those objections is that this theory of meaning is too narrow, as it eliminates not only theology but also moral judgment, mathematics, and much else.

A second objection is that we can sometimes understand what is being said without knowing how to test it. For example, that light has a velocity is understood by those who have no idea how its velocity might be measured. Indeed, the idea must have occurred before anyone knew how to make the measurement; why, otherwise, would they have tried?

A third objection is that, if to understand a term is to know its meaning, and its meaning is the verification conditions of predications of the term, then no one can understand what he himself says.[4] For, no one who uses a term can have all of its verification conditions in mind or even be able to list them on demand. The list would be long, perhaps endless. Take a trivial example: In how many ways can we verify that this table is round? We could try rolling it. We could look at its shadow. We could take an opinion poll. And so on, not to mention various mathematical techniques. Nor are all the ways of verifying something as yet known: Discoveries of additional physical properties suggest new tests for already known substances. That chemical elements when heated produce light of characteristic wavelengths was not known before 1859. Novel tests will not always change our conception nor its range of reference but normally they will enable us to discover additional instances of that to which they already refer. Spectroscopy reveals the presence of distinct elements in distant stars.

The first objection, that the theory is too narrow, fails in the case of Peirce, since he never claimed that the 1878 maxim was a universal criterion of meaningfulness, much less a complete theory of meaning. The maxim occurs in the second of the series of articles, 'Illustrations of the Logic of Science', and is not asserted to have broader application than within science. To be sure, the introductory statement, quoted above, is uncompromisingly general: '... how impossible it is that we should have an idea in our minds which relates to anything but conceived sensible effects of things'. But in a 1907 comment on the 1878 maxim, Peirce wrote that pragmatism is limited to the meaning of 'intellectual concepts', those on which 'arguments concerning objective fact may hinge' (EP2:401). And in 1903, in explicating the maxim, he said that 'meaning' is a technical term referring to 'the intended interpretant of a symbol' (EP2:218); now, symbols are but one kind of sign and in his semeiotic writings, Peirce used the word 'meaning' more generally but also loosely and with many subdivisions, usually identifying it with one or another type of 'interpretant'

---

[4] A. J. Ayer, though sympathetic to verificationism, made this objection specifically to Peirce's maxim (1968, p. 58).

of a sign – not only signs testable but also commands, metaphors, stories, natural signs, and even music (Short 2007, Chs.6–9).

The second objection, that one can understand a term without knowing how to verify its predications, can be answered by taking the first two grades of clarity seriously: deficient as those grades are, they are not vacuous and, as they lead us to seek clarity at the third grade, they serve a purpose. This can be supplemented by Peirce's later semeiotic, as some of the other dimensions of meaning it distinguishes apply within science, accounting for our ability to entertain a hypothesis before we know how to test it. In the development of a theory, there is analogy, metaphor, modeling, picturing, diagramming, and representing by equations. All these bear in various ways on the possibility of working out verification conditions, but they cannot be reduced to those conditions. A differential equation, for example, represents quantities, rational and irrational, smaller than anything observable. Dimensions of meaning such as the pictorial do not fall under any of the three grades of clarity. As a hypothesis is refined, some earlier dimensions of its meaning may be replaced by rules of verification, but others will not be thus eliminated.

This answer to the second objection shifts our attention from meanings as already formed to the growth of meaning. The third grade of clearness is an ideal to be worked toward. But then it is not a theory of what meaning is in its entirety; it is not even a necessary condition of meaningfulness. It is, I suggest, not a theory at all but, rather, a prescription, one that reflects a cognitive value. And that gives us an answer to the third objection, that a totality of verification conditions will often exceed what one who understands a term can comprehend. Let us take a moment with this.

Look again at the maxim: it refers to 'our conception' and to 'the object of our conception', not to words or their meanings. An object, presumably, may be an individual thing, such as the Sun, or a kind of thing, such as electrons or genes, or a substance, such as water, or a process, such as osmosis or convection, or a property, such as solidity or negative charge. An individual theorist's conception of one of these objects is not necessarily what a word designating it means within a community that shares that word and uses it successfully to communicate. Therefore, a maxim for clarifying concepts is not the same as a theory of meaning. Let me show this by an example.

Suppose that, after flying a kite in a lightning storm or, rather, prudently employing a boy to fly it for me, I tell you that lightning is electricity. You know what I refer to by 'lightning' and I know what that word means to you. But, though its referent remains the same, 'lightning' now means more to me, because I now conceive of lightning as electricity; for,

I was able to make it produce effects (in a Leyden jar) that are already identified as electrical. My concept of lightning has been deepened. (My concept of electricity has been changed, too, with some consequences for its range of reference or, perhaps more precisely, its recognized range of reference: I now have to distinguish between the static and the dynamic forms of electricity.) It will take some time for the *meaning* of 'lightning', that is, the understanding of that word shared by those in a community (e.g., of scientists or of the educated) who use it, to incorporate my (if you insist, Franklin's) new *conception* of it.

Although there are connections between word-meaning and conception, which Peirce indicated, his maxim refers to conception only and, furthermore, only to what is *ours*. *Our* conception of something is subject to change: to growth and to correction. Now, is not a concept clarified a concept *changed*? An idea that has been clarified is not the same as it was. You can make clearer to me what 'justice' means without changing that meaning, but you cannot succeed in this attempt without changing my idea. An idea may be clarified by sorting out what we think its object's sensible effects are (e.g., distinguishing the effects of temperature from those of heat), by defining those effects more precisely (not just refraction but its angle), and by adding to their number (as when we discover that an electric current deflects a compass needle). Clarification, then, can be growth in knowledge. When Peirce wrote of clarifying our ideas, did he mean explicating the meanings of words, leaving those meanings unchanged? There is little reason to suppose so.

On this reading of it, the maxim does not specify what must be understood by a person who uses a term, and therefore the third objection is evaded. The maxim is to an entirely different effect. It is not put forth as a tautology; it is not a theory of meaning; it is not a theory of any sort; rather, it is a prescription – 'a rule', as Peirce said. It urges that we make our concepts *clearer* by identifying verification conditions: The more we can add, the greater will be our understanding of the object of the concept and the more fruitful will we have made that concept. In an 1897 comment on the three grades of clearness, Peirce wrote, 'The third grade of clearness consists in such a representation of the idea that fruitful reasoning can be made to turn upon it ...' (3.457).[5] Note the words 'can be made':

---

[5] This 1897 understanding of the 1878 maxim is contradicted by a comment of 1913 in which the maxim (dated 1871, the time of its presumed oral expression) is associated with 'security' as opposed to 'uberty', that is, fruitfulness (EP2:465); this inconsistency shows that we must take Peirce's later accounts of his earlier thought *cum grano salis*.

The maxim is not about understanding what a word already means but is about how to improve an idea in such a way as to make its use in inquiry more fruitful.

A verificationist reading of the pragmatic maxim, if limited to scientific or factual contexts and not construed as a general theory of meaning, is not easily dismissed. There are many passages, especially in Peirce's 1903 lectures on pragmatism, that strongly suggest it. But there are other passages in those same lectures that convey other suggestions; indeed, a major theme of these and other late writings is that the maxim is a rule for the 'admissibility of hypotheses' (EP2:234). At the end of this chapter, we will notice a passage in those same lectures that appears to gloss the 1878 maxim but which in fact adds to it, presenting an account of meaning clearly opposed to verificationism. Was Peirce inconsistent? I think, rather, that the root idea is protean and has many potentialities, some of which might be realized in mutually incompatible ways, but each of which may be illuminating and none of which should be prematurely ruled out.[6]

That the maxim is a rule for growing knowledge would be consistent with its pertaining primarily to science, given Peirce's idea of science as dynamic, that is, as inquiry, not doctrine. Read as prescriptive, the pragmatic maxim is part of the logic of scientific inquiry; for, logic is in fact normative, as Peirce in 1902 asserted (Ch.9, A). Perhaps the best proof that this was his intention is to be found in the remaining essays of the series, 'Illustrations of the Logic of Science', wherein he applied the maxim to what was then an idea newly found to be of use in science, viz., probability. In philosophical debates about probability theory, the question is not what 'probability' already means but is about what, for scientific purposes, we should make the word mean, that is, what idea of probability we should adopt; and, in historical fact, new applications of the vague idea of probability have resulted in new definitions of 'probability' together with new ways of calculating probabilities. Peirce's argument (beginning in 'The Doctrine of Chances', the sequel to 'How to') is based on determining 'what real and sensible effect there is between one degree of probability and another' (EP1:145).[7] On that 'pragmatic' ground, Peirce argued for the frequency theory, as opposed to earlier ideas of probability; in that process, he refined the theory.

[6] See Skagestad (1981), Misak (1995), and Hookway (2012) for alternative views of pragmatism's relation to verificationism.
[7] Jeff Kasser persuasively argues that probability is the central focus of the 'Illustrations of the Logic of Science' series (Kasser 2016, Section 1).

As prescriptive, the maxim might also have been intended as a recommendation to philosophers about how they should proceed, which is the way James took it. Its implication, then, would be that philosophy should be made scientific: It should aim at discovery, if not of surprising facts, at least of the true nature of the familiar. The verification theory belongs to the project, as it was originally conceived, of analytic philosophy, which was to explicate concepts *qua* meanings of words. Peirce's maxim belongs to his idea of philosophy, in which the aim is not to explicate concepts but is to improve them by increasing their empirical content, making them more informative hence more useful.

D

Peirce's idea of science was broad, including, among much else, mathematics and historiography. He therefore extended the pragmatic maxim to those studies, raising some problems which it will advance our discussion to examine. First, mathematics.

Over many years, Peirce consistently maintained that all mathematical reasoning consists in making 'experiments' on diagrams (one-dimensional as in algebra, two-dimensional as in geometry, possibly of more dimensions), and 'observing' the results (EP1:227–28, in 1885, and many later passages, e.g., EP2:206–7 and PM: *passim*). Conventions are essential to every diagram (PM:81). In the case of geometrical diagrams, one convention is to idealize, by ignoring the thickness of the lines and any errant wiggles. Most importantly, there are the conventions that govern permissible manipulations of the diagram: In Venn diagrams, an 'x' may not be inscribed in a shaded lune; in ordinary algebra, the laws of addition, multiplication, and their inverses must be conformed to. Given these conventions, a diagram, and any results obtained by manipulating it, may be interpreted as representing this or that: Such assignments of meaning to the diagram are additional to albeit limited by the conventions.

Given the rules governing shading and inscribing 'x's, Venn diagrams can be interpreted as representing relations among classes, wherein shading represents emptiness and an 'x' in a lune represents possessing a member. Dropping the 'x' notation, Venn diagrams can equally be interpreted as representing truth-functions of propositions, wherein shading in the lune where circles p and q overlap means 'not both', that is, that propositions p and q are not both true. So also, small changes in ordinary algebra give us importantly different alternative algebras that may be put to a variety of uses. That was how Boole produced his algebra of propositional logic, which turns out to be interpretable also as representing electrical switching circuits.

Insofar as experiments on diagrams reveal something about what the diagrams represent, that is because certain relations in the represented are identical with relations in the diagram. We may say, then, that what the diagram most directly diagrams are those relations. These relations are *in* the diagram but they are also *in* other things, such as electrical circuits. Taken in themselves, the relations diagrammed are pure possibilities; they need not be instantiated anywhere. They might not obtain even in the diagram itself *qua* physical object. Relations among dimensionless points and lines without width, for example, are present in geometrical diagrams only as they are 'read' in conformity to the idealizing conventions, and not as observed chalk dust or ink. It follows that mathematical reasoning pertains most directly to the purely hypothetical, that is, to the relations diagrammed – mere possibilities.

One mark of this feature of mathematical reasoning is that it does not require observation of a physical diagram; a merely imagined diagram will do; one can reason with eyes closed and hands at rest. Moreover, imagination, whether or not abetted by pencil and paper, is essential to the observations made. One 'sees' that an alternative result *cannot* be obtained; for, one cannot imagine a way, in conformity to the conventions, of getting an alternative result. To take a simple example: if, of three overlapping circles, A, B, C, you shade in the lune of the A outside B and the lune of B outside C, then all of A outside C is shaded in; no contrary result is possible. And this proves the transitivity both of class-inclusion and of truth-functional conditionals. So also, no matter how you set about adding up the figures in your checkbook, you cannot get a different result without violating the rules of arithmetic, proving, alas, that you have over-drawn your account. Mathematics establishes necessary truths, that is, truths about every possibility of a specified kind, and these truths apply to actual instances of those possibilities.

An experiment on a diagram is a manipulation of it (perhaps an addition to it) that the conventions allow. As it is permitted, not required, the experiment is in that sense arbitrary, hence, voluntary. Genius consists in hitting upon arbitrary moves that prove revelatory. For example, dropping a perpendicular from the apex of a triangle to the line of its base enables one to see something about triangularity (its area) that cannot be deduced from triangularity's definition. That is how Peirce accounted for the distinction between what he called corollarial and theorematic reasoning. The latter discovers necessary truths that, far from being tautological, are surprising; and not only surprising, but also significant, as opening a door to further discoveries (PM:27–29,63–64; cf. Hintikka 1983).

That diagrams are observed and that this involves acts of imagination seems to me clearly correct and yet very far from being clear; more work is needed on this (Legg 2014 is an initial effort), but it falls outside of our present topic. Without attempting such explication, we can nevertheless recognize that this sort of observation deserves to be distinguished from empirical observation, which is always of the actual and always depends on sensation, or something like sensation (see Chapters 7 and 9 for Peirce's extension of observation to include feelings), never imagination. Empirical observation informs us about the actual and not about the necessary consequences of the merely possible. Peirce, c.1902, noted that the fact that no fraction = $\sqrt{2}$, 'means nothing at all in regard to what can be expected in physical measurements' (5.541). He added, however, that it 'relates to what is expectable for a person dealing with fractions'. This last evidently refers to the consequences of making calculations, that is, experimenting on diagrams. The passage occurs in a discussion meant to show that 'all belief' involves 'expectation as its essence' (5.542). But if thus the pragmatic maxim applies to mathematics, it applies beyond the empirical.[8]

E

History poses a problem that Peirce discussed in the final pages of 'How to': What of 'all the minute facts of history, forgotten never to be recovered … the buried secrets? … Do these things not really exist because they are hopelessly beyond the reach of our knowledge?' (EP1:139). If factual claims are ones that can be verified if true, then it would seem to follow that a statement about a buried secret is not factual. Peirce replied, '… it is unphilosophical to suppose that, with regard to any given question (which has any clear meaning), investigation would not bring forth a solution of it, if it were carried far enough' (139–40). But this desperate gambit fails. To be sure, it is imprudent to suppose that *a given* question can no longer be answered. It does not follow that there may not be questions that can no longer be answered. Surely, there are many such; it is 'unphilosophical' only to suppose that we can know which ones they are.

Take, for example, the vexed question whether Peirce's mysterious French second wife was of the aristocratic origin she claimed to be, and

---

[8] Misak (1995, p. 111) and Hookway (2012, p. 2) deny this; I dispute their view in Ch.7, A.

not of the *demi monde* she was suspected to be. We know how that claim could have been tested at the time, by a sufficiently energetic investigator, but the evidence is very likely no longer available. We cannot know for sure that nothing will be found to settle the issue, but let us suppose that there is no longer any decisive evidence. The law of excluded middle arguably does not apply where there is no conceivable way to prove or to disprove a claim – as is the case with some mathematical propositions. But where, as in this case, we can conceive of how the proposition could have been tested, the law cannot be denied. Either her claim is true or it is false, and if it is either, it is meaningful. It is meaningful even if neither it nor its negation can be verified – now.

Indeed, in the case of many now unanswerable historical questions, there was a time when persons existed who *did* know the answer. We do not know, but Richard III knew whether or not he had ordered his nephews to be murdered. Mrs. Peirce, who presumably knew the truth about her origins, is another example. Thus the issue of 'buried secrets' raises a further issue: whose knowledge is relevant? Peirce's discussion implies that the only knowledge that matters is ours, where 'ours' denotes that of an indefinitely extended community of investigators to which we belong. What Richard III and Mrs. Peirce knew is not a component of 'our' knowledge. As we shall see in Section F, Peirce's famous definitions of truth and reality in terms of a 'final opinion' are similarly restricted to a community.

There is a reason why Peirce could not have embraced the obvious alternative, that a hypothesis about a past event is meaningful if a *possible* investigator, *had he been* properly positioned, *could have* verified or disverified it. For, earlier in 'How to', he denied that subjunctive conditionals have any meaning distinct from that of finite sets of indicative statements. After stating the rule for clarifying ideas, he, by way of illustration, applied it to 'what we mean by calling a thing *hard*', which is that 'it will not be scratched by many other substances'. So far, so good, but then he added: 'There is absolutely no difference between a hard thing and a soft thing so long as they are not brought to the test'; '… the question of what would occur under circumstances which do not actually arise is not a question of fact, but only of the most perspicuous arrangement of them' (132). This contradicts our commonsense conviction that an untested diamond is hard, an untested marshmallow soft. It makes everything to depend on what *has been* or *will be* discovered, rather than on what *would be* discovered under conditions that might never occur or *would have been* discovered under conditions that, in fact, did not occur. In other words, Peirce in 1878 denied modal realism, and that is why at that time buried secrets presented so intractable a problem to him.⁹

One might argue that in this instance common sense is supported by physical theory, and in such a way as to avoid implying modal realism. For, as molecular structure, binding forces, and so on explain hardness, and an untested diamond has a certain molecular structure, then it is indeed hard despite not being tested. Its hardness consists of actual structure, not of what would-be. But that only takes the problem down a level, as structures and forces must be explicated in terms of what would happen under such-and-so conditions. To say that there is X binding force between molecules A and B means that X amount of force *would be* required to separate them. Peirce surely knew this; he wrote to such effect in 1905 (EP2:357), after the passage next to be examined.

In 1905, Peirce expressly reversed himself on this matter, referring to the 1878 denial as a mistake. He tried to excuse it – 'The article of January 1878 endeavored to glose [sic] over this point as unsuited to the exoteric public addressed; or perhaps the writer wavered in his own mind' (EP2:354) – but the mistake seems to have been made by his failing at that time to realize that scholastic realism entails modal realism. The passage quoted continues:

> Another doctrine which is involved in Pragmaticism as an essential conse-quence of it, but which the writer had defended … before he had formu-lated, even in his own mind, the principle of pragmaticism, is the scholastic doctrine of realism … that there are real objects that are general … But the belief in this can hardly escape being accompanied by the acknowledgment that there are, besides, real *vagues*, and especially, real *possibilities* … Indeed, it is the reality of some possibilities that pragmaticism is most concerned to insist upon. (EP2:354, Peirce's emphases, also his inconsistent capitalization and his making 'vague' a noun)

That is to say, the unactualized possibility (what would have been) and the possibility that might never be actualized (what would be) are as real as what actually happens; reality is wider than actuality. This is entailed by scholastic realism; for, if the general is not reducible to its actual instances and unactualized possibilities are what the general is over and above its actual instances, then, if the general is real, unactualized possibilities must

---

⁹ His expressions were not always consistent with this denial; notice, for example, the subjunctive for-mulation in the passage from EP1:139–40 quoted above, the 'would … if it were'. If modal realism is implicit in common sense and cannot be escaped, then this inconsistency is no surprise and testifies to the fact that Peirce had not yet thought the matter through.

be real. Conversely, possibilities are always general; for, lacking the full specificity of the actual, they remain actualizable in infinitely diverse ways. Modal realism and scholastic realism, properly understood, entail each the other.

If pragmatism or pragmaticism is 'most concerned to insist upon' modal realism, that must be because modal realism is implicated in any talk of the practical bearings of ideas. What would have happened had you disregarded my warning, is every bit as much a part of my warning's practical bearing as is your happy actual condition after having nimbly side-stepped the falling anvil. You rightly thank me for having saved your life: 'Had that anvil hit my head, I'd be dead now'. What would have been matters.

Nominalists will of course claim, correctly, that the only way we can know about possibilities is by observing actualities; from which they infer, incorrectly, that talk of possibilities has no meaning apart from a perspicuous arrangement of facts about the actual – just as Peirce in 1878 said. Nominalism finds an ally in verificationism. As verification is by what actually happens, and as the actual consists entirely of individual things and individual events, verificationist theories of meaning entail that it is nonsense to speak of anything but actual individuals. But that line of thought runs into a problem: sets of verification conditions and rules for verifying a statement include possible as well as actual instances. A verifiable statement might be verified this way or that, by you or by me, now or later or never. Rules are general; the conditions specified in explicating meaning are general, not particular. Verificationism presupposes what nominalists correctly claim that it banishes, which makes the doctrine self-contradictory. (Later, in Chapter 8, Section H, the same conclusion is drawn in another way, on the ground that generality and unactualized possibility are implicated also in what individuals actually are and are perceived to be.)

Be that as it may, verificationism, in its heyday, was understood nominalistically, by logical positivists and logical empiricists, and thus it generated problems akin to that of buried secrets; these were much discussed. One concerned properties, as in Goodman's famous 'grue' paradox (Goodman 1965, pp.74–75). Another problem was to distinguish a law of nature from a regularity, that is, a possibly accidental pattern among actual events. If a law cannot meaningfully be said to be anything but its actual instances, then what distinguishes it from an accidental regularity? One suggestion made was that a regularity is a law if and only if it can be deduced from a network of general statements, or theory, and/or is confidently projected into the future (so also Goodman's resolution of his 'grue' paradox: Goodman 1965, pp.84ff). But that distinctly Humean strategy makes law to depend on its representation, making it unreal. If, to the contrary, we adopt modal realism, then we can say that law is distinguished from accidental regularity by its determining what would be and would have been (albeit this cannot be known directly nor with certainty but only by inference from what actually happens). That is what Peirce later maintained (*vide infra*, Sections F–H and Ch.8, Sections F–G).

To be sure, our only evidence for law consists of observed regularities, but on the modal interpretation of law, what observed regularities are evidence for is more than regularity. The doctrine that meaning consists of nothing more than verification conditions limits what verifications can be evidence of, viz., only more of the same. But what, beyond its verification conditions, is meant by a statement about what would be? That topic is deferred to Chapter 8, but we can see already that modal realism entails rejecting the verification theory of meaning. Hence, the pragmatic maxim not only is not that theory but, modally interpreted, it contradicts verificationism. I shall henceforth assume a modal interpretation of the pragmatic maxim.

F

The concept of 'the final opinion' was always central to Peirce's thinking (see Lane 2018, Chs.1–2, *passim*). Foreshadowed in the 1868–1869 papers (see EP1:52, quoted below in Ch.5, B), and in earlier lectures, it was first introduced by name in the Berkeley review of 1871, then restated in 1878 in 'How to'. The final opinion is the unique set of conclusions (not uniquely formulated) toward which inquiry through many misadventures proceeds as long as it is continued. That there is such an opinion – that there is an irreversible direction of inquiry – is not a tautology: It is a logically contingent proposition – a hypothesis. Yet, because it refers to an indefinitely long run and because the progress it postulates is not asserted to be monotonic, it is not such a hypothesis as could be refuted in any finite time: Any failure of inquiry might be a temporary reverse. And therefore there is no test which this hypothesis can be said to have survived. The most that can be said in its support is that, since the advent of modern science, there *appears* to have been progress, indeed, very impressive progress. Theories rise and fall but their instrumental power has kept growing and the body of particular facts seemingly known has kept growing (sometimes they have had to be reformulated in light of changes in broader theories).

Now, Peirce identified truth with the final opinion and reality with what that opinion represents. Those identifications cannot be taken as conceptual analyses of what the words 'truth' and 'reality' mean. To do so would result in absurdity, that if inquiry does not in fact progress irreversibly, then the truth is that there is no truth and, in reality, there is no reality. If we call Peirce's identification of truth with the final opinion a *definition* of 'truth', then it is such a definition as is common in the sciences: It is theory-laden. The definition of 'color' as wavelengths of light is not a tautology but depends on the truth of a theory; no more is it a tautology that truth is the final opinion. Peirce did offer, as tautologies, other definitions of 'truth' and 'reality'. We saw above that he defined 'real' as something's being independent of what it is represented to be. And in 'Fixation', he said in passing that '… we think each one of our beliefs to be true, and, indeed, it is mere tautology to say so' (EP1:115). The latter anticipated the currently popular redundancy 'theory' of truth, which, as a conceptual analysis of what 'truth' means, is a tautology, not a theory.

As originally stated, the idea of a final opinion was infected by the same nominalism that initially troubled the pragmatic maxim, producing related problems. In the Berkeley review, in connection with his adoption of scholastic realism, and therefore presumably in opposition to nominalism, Peirce wrote:

> … there is a definite opinion to which the mind of man is, on the whole and in the long run, tending. On many questions the final agreement is already reached, on all it will be reached if time enough is given …. This final opinion, then, is independent, not indeed of thought in general, but of all that is arbitrary and individual in thought; is quite independent of how you, or I, or any number of men think. Everything, therefore, which will be thought to exist in the final opinion is real, and nothing else. (EP1:89)

Why 'will be thought' and not 'would be thought'? By making reality to be what *will be* thought to exist *if* inquiry continues long enough, Peirce made reality itself to depend on a contingent fact about actual thought. Which is to say, he made the real unreal, by his own (tautologous) definition of 'real'. In 1871 as in 1878, he was fighting shy of modal realism – with absurd consequences. But let us put that problem aside for a moment, and glean what else we can from this passage.

We see in it that the final opinion was never intended to be a single answer to every question, the universe rolled up into a ball. It is a consistent set of answers to be achieved piecemeal. Reference to 'the' final opinion at which inquiry 'in general' aims emphasizes the relatedness of diverse questions. From that relatedness, it follows that we can never be sure of what is the final answer to a given question before all questions have been answered, since the answer to one may undermine the answer to another. If there is no Santa Claus, then who gave me that teddy bear? More precisely, it is not required that all questions are answered, but those only that in the end are recognized as meaningful. For, as we continue to inquire, we discover that some questions are based on false assumptions. 'How much does Santa Claus weigh?' has no true answer. Therefore, although we already possess the final opinion in some parts, we cannot be sure which parts of what we think we know really are parts of the final opinion. Peirce said that on many questions the final opinion is already reached, but he did not say that we could know for sure which questions these are. That is so, even if in many cases a large measure of confidence is justified.

There is, in this passage, an emphasis not only on the relatedness of questions but also on the relatedness of inquirers. As long as there is disagreement, none of us can be sure of his own answer to a question. The final opinion is 'the final agreement'. But this is not agreement simpliciter, no matter how arrived at. Earlier in the same paragraph, an example was given of a deaf man and a blind man, proceeding from entirely different sensory data, arriving at the same conclusion, that a murder had been committed; let us add that these two men are somehow able to communicate, comparing their conclusions. In many places, Peirce emphasized the importance in science of diverse lines of inquiry, employing distinct methods and different data, converging on a single answer. Convergence produces greater confidence in the answer than would any one line of inquiry, no matter how carefully conducted. We assume that such confidence is justified; showing that it is, is another matter, one of inductive logic and statistical theory. Notice, however, that it is not a question of logic merely, for it depends also on the truth of a physical hypothesis: The deaf man and the blind man each assume that what they see or hear proceeds from a single reality (a quarrel that one sees and that the other hears) affecting them both. Only by being about the same supposed reality, could their respective conclusions either agree or disagree. It follows that the Hegelian tone of the passage quoted – 'a definite opinion to which the mind of man is, on the whole and in the long run, tending' – is misleading: the mind of man has not that tendency of itself, but only because it discovers and applies methods that make opinion to be determined by something 'upon which our thinking has no effect' – as Peirce later put it in 'Fixation' (EP1:120). The relatedness of inquirers is through a world that exists independently of them but affects them all, even if in different ways.

This emphasis on convergence misled Quine (1960, p.23), who wrongly supposed that Peirce was assuming that scientific inquiry as a whole is like a series of measurements made of the same quantity, the mean values of the successive totals of which vary by decreasing amounts, monotonically approaching a limit. But Peirce was not so naïve. There are two points that must be noticed: fluctuation of opinion and divergence of lines of inquiry. As to the latter: while inquiry eliminates some questions, it also produces new questions. The discovery of subatomic particles raises questions that formerly would have been meaningless, about their mass, charge, and spin. As inquiry converges on answers to some questions, the number of questions to be addressed grows and, hence, lines of inquiry diverge. Far from his having denied this, Peirce emphasized that progress in science entails a proliferation of specialized inquiries (*vide supra*, Ch.2). And as to fluctuation of opinion: progress is rarely monotonic. Light was once supposed to be undulatory, then corpuscular, then undulatory again but not in the same way as before, then corpuscular again, though not corpuscular in the way formerly supposed but somehow undulatory also. The history of science is replete with such examples, and Peirce had studied that history.

If opinion can fluctuate, how shall progress be defined? Progress, let us stipulate, entails irreversibility. But irreversibility over the long run is consistent with reverses in the short run, and no upper limit can be assigned to short runs; in science, a short run may last centuries, or longer. Think of all the excellent work, the accumulation of precise observation in astronomy for over two thousand years – all under the mistaken assumption that the Earth is at the center of the cosmos; those observations remain valuable, though many of them have to be restated in ways inconsistent with their original statement. With respect to inquiry, irreversibility might be defined in this way: if inquiry continues forever, then, for any given question (of a large number, perhaps infinite, of questions, but not necessarily all questions), there is a finite time (but we cannot say what that time is) after which the last answer that had been given to that question (which in some cases will be that the question is ill-founded) will never thereafter be rejected (though it may be improved – made more complete and/or precise). This definition of irreversibility somewhat resembles the mathematical definition of a limit; however, it is not the same, as nothing follows about answers growing 'closer' to the final answer.[10] And therefore it is an

[10] Following Popper, much was written about the concept of 'verisimilitude', that is, of degrees of closeness of a theory to the truth, the upshot of which was that verisimilitude resists definition. The present gloss on Peirce's idea of a final opinion avoids that conundrum.

error, one that has often been committed, to think that the idea of a final opinion is an idea of a limit which inquiry approaches. Quine's criticism of Peirce was based on that mistaken reading.

But what if inquiry does not continue forever? That is the problem noted above, to which we shall return in a moment.

The 1871 treatment of the idea of reality was elaborated in 'How to', where the definition of 'X is real', as Xs being independent of every actual opinion about it, is relegated to the second grade of clearness (EP1:136–37). A clarification at the third grade is then demanded:

> But, however satisfactory such a definition [the one at the second grade] may be found, it would be a great mistake to suppose that it makes the idea of reality perfectly clear. Here, then, let us apply our rules. According to them, reality, like every other quality, consists in the peculiar sensible effects which things partaking of it produce. The only effect which real things have is to cause belief ... (137)

The language employed here is not to be taken literally: Reality is of course not a quality like a color and belief is not a sensible effect like seeing a color. Nonetheless, the real is to be known by its effect on our thought. Reality understood at the second grade of clarity is like a pot without a handle. It gives us no mark by which to identify real things; for how is independence from opinion to be determined? Reality understood at the third grade, in terms of the final opinion, provides the missing handle. If inquiry progresses irreversibly, then some of what we now agree about will be sustained as inquiry continues. Therefore, what we find we agree about after having inquired diligently is what we may take, not with certainty but justifiably, to be real.

Later, in 'How to', the doctrine is summed up in this way:

> The opinion which is fated to be ultimately agreed to by all who investigate, is what we mean by the truth, and the object represented in this opinion is the real. That is how I would explain reality. (139)

Notice the wording: 'what we mean'. Who are 'we'? Not, I suggest, all speakers of English but only the author and his readers: those who may be presumed to have adopted the ideal of scientific inquiry. The identification, then, is prescriptive, not analytic. It is not an explication of what 'true' means in ordinary usage; instead, it recommends a concept of truth suitable to the project of modern science.

The word 'fated' in this passage is crucial. Contrary to what is sometimes said, Peirce did not identify truth with consensus, since consensus could be achieved arbitrarily, for example, through intimidation or through one's desire to conform. Consensus is only a mark of truth – and only insofar as it is achieved by persons forming opinions on grounds other than their desire to reach agreement:

> So with all scientific research. Different minds may set out with the most antagonistic views, but the progress of investigation carries them *by a force outside of themselves* to one and the same conclusion. (138, my emphasis)

'Fated', then, refers to the power of something on which our thinking has no effect – and which is in that sense 'outside' of us – to influence our thinking, *if* we earnestly inquire. (As thoughts and thinking also are real, we have to understand 'outside of themselves' as referring to what is independent of a specific inquiry.) Peirce did sometimes refer to the final opinion as a 'consensus'; but that consensus has to be understood as one that is fated if we continue to inquire earnestly.

At the third grade of clearness, reality is identified as the object represented in the final opinion. But reality is also what is assumed in the hypothesis that there is a final opinion. It is a power to constrain thought: a force 'outside' of inquirers. Thus a threefold doctrine: reality is independent of what we think about it; it is what it is thought to be in the final opinion; and it is what explains there being a final opinion, that is, an irreversible direction in inquiry. If reality explains the final opinion in which it is represented, then the final opinion represents its own cause.[11]

But, how can reality be defined both as independent of what we think about it and as what it is thought to be in the final opinion? Only by the latter thought being potential, the former actual. But, then, it is not necessary that the final opinion ever be attained; it is not even necessary that each part of it be attained in some finite time. That is not necessary, because potentiality does not depend on future actualization. So the modal realist claims. As long as Peirce rejected modal realism, he could not consistently assert that there *is* a final opinion, except on the assumption

---

[11] May we conclude that Peirce held a correspondence theory of truth? There are several versions of such a theory, some of which he, at least in later years, rejected, for example, in 1903, the absurdity that we can directly compare our beliefs to reality (7.628). In 1906 he declared that the simple statement, that truth is correspondence to reality, is not incorrect but merely 'nominal', that is, tautological, not illuminating (EP2:379). Lane (2018), pp. 45–51, maintains that Peirce held a correspondence theory, since 'a pragmatic clarification' can be given of 'what it means to say that something *accurately represents reality*' (p. 50). If that clarification is the general one stated in 'How to', it verges on vacuity; however, theories represent their purported objects in a variety of ways, and some of these theories, physical, physiological, and semiotic, describe those ways, accounting, nonvacuously, for the success of those representations. Such explanations give concrete meaning to the idea of correspondence. Donald Davidson concluded similarly (1984, Ch.3).

that it *will* be attained – which is inconsistent with his definition of the real, as being independent of any actual opinion about it.

In light of Peirce's later adoption of modal realism, we can say, consistently, that the final opinion *is* what *would be* thought – that is, under conditions possibly counterfactual or that cannot be known to be factual or as to which there is as yet no fact, such as that inquiry continues without end. That there is such an opinion – hence, that there is something real – is a hypothesis – a hypothesis about what is possible. Here, however, we must proceed cautiously. For there are several kinds of possibility. The reference is not to logical possibility but to physical possibility, as determined by physical law. And there is much about those laws that remains to be discovered. We learn from quantum mechanics, for example, that some measurements which we had formerly supposed possible are not possible. The kinds of thing that we suppose the final opinion covers is amended as we advance toward that opinion.

The identification of truth with the final opinion and of reality as the object which that opinion represents is therefore to be taken less simplistically than it often has been taken. For example, there can be buried secrets, because reality is not dependent on what will actually be discovered or even on what can still be discovered. For another example, the idea of a final opinion extends beyond science, many of Peirce's remarks to the contrary notwithstanding. The reason is that science is not interested in every fact. Most of reality it would be a great bore to record. Reality contains not only a multitude of buried secrets but also an enormous pile of matters of no interest. Most are of no interest at all; some are of intense interest to you or to me (which of us does Sally love?) but not to the community of inquirers. They are matters nonetheless about which the truth *would be* known *were* conditions favorable and *were* sufficient inquiry made.

G

There are ambiguities and puzzles in Peirce's 1878 discussion of what was later named the pragmatic maxim that I have not yet mentioned. They are to be expected, given his practice of sketching ideas in ways suggestive, not final. Some might have been introduced intentionally, either to provoke questions he chose not to frame, as he did not yet have answers to them, or to warn the reader that his essay represents only a fragment of a complex topic.

Sometimes, 'How to' cites the practical effects of belief: 'different beliefs are distinguished by the different modes of action to which they give rise'

(129–30), and, 'To develop its [thought's] meaning, we have, therefore, simply to determine what habits it produces' (131). But other times, it cites the sensible effects of the things our beliefs, concepts, thoughts are about: 'our conception of these effects' – referring to the 'conceived sensible effects of things' – 'is the whole of our conception of the object' (132). Are beliefs distinguished by *their* effects, or by the effects they represent their *objects* to have? The two may have been intended to be equivalent, on the ground that 'our action has exclusive reference to what affects the senses' (131); but such equivalence is not an identity. Furthermore, the emphasis on practicality is practically deleted by the qualification that the sensible effects an object is believed to have need only 'conceivably have practical bearings' (132). Any sensible effect is *conceivably* practical.

Another problem: 'How to' does not discuss what counts as a sensible effect. From the examples given, for example, of hardness tested by a knife-edge, we can deduce that Peirce's idea of sensible effects was physicalist, not phenomenalist: that is, sensible effects are not sensations but are what is sensed. But if sensible effects are physical, then they, in turn, are to be understood in terms of their effects, and so on, *ad infinitum*. That is a problem if the maxim is a theory of meaning: as we cannot define a term by terms we do not understand, we are launched on an infinite regress. But if the maxim is a prescription for clarifying our ideas, then the regress is avoided. It is avoided, because (a) it is granted that an idea may be to a degree unclear yet applicable, and (b) the aim is only to make an idea more clear, not perfectly clear. In other words, the infinite regress of definitions is replaced by an infinite progress of discovery. The first is an absurdity, the second, an adventure.

Then there is the problem posed by religious belief, which Peirce might well have ignored; instead, he acknowledged that in ordinary usage 'belief' refers primarily to 'religious or other grave discussions' (127–28). The problem is that the actions religious belief produces are not always performed with an intent to produce a sensible effect – in this world. To square this with the pragmatic maxim, Peirce spoke of the possibility of there being sensible effects 'hereafter', and thus he undercut his own example of 'senseless jargon', viz., 'talk of something as having all the sensible characters of wine, yet being in reality blood'. He wrote: 'It is foolish for Catholics and Protestants to fancy themselves in disagreement about the elements of the sacrament, if they agree in regard to all their sensible effects, *here or hereafter*' (132, my emphasis). This curious remark cannot be dismissed as an error or a joke merely. The same point was made several times in various essays, for example, in 'Fixation' regarding the Assassins who 'used to rush into death' in the belief they would thereby 'insure everlasting felicity' (114; cf. 5.541, c.1902). If the pragmatic maxim was intended to apply to science only, then this remark raises a question about just how far the community of inquirers may extend.

Finally, the pragmatic maxim's reference to practical effects raises questions that Peirce in 1878 could not answer. That a proposition is testable might suffice for the purposes of theoretical inquiry, but where success matters practically, some degree of confidence is required that the prediction *will* come true. It is not enough that we can test claims that bread nourishes, arsenic kills; we need to suppose that those claims' repeated confirmation warrants confidence in them. Furthermore, as we saw in Section D, practical action takes place with respect to what would be as well as with respect to what was, is, and will be: Its practical significance depends on what, but for it, would have been. Without pausing here to argue the point, these two desiderata, of knowing what would be and having confidence in what will be, are connected. And thus Peirce's nominalistic gloss on the pragmatic maxim, regarding untested diamonds, makes nonsense, in both respects, of his own talk of practical consequences. Now, it is improbable that he had no awareness of this difficulty. Perhaps, then, it was to it – to the fact that he was leaving fundamental questions unanswered – that his unsettling allusions to religious belief pointed. Perhaps he had meant to create in the reader a sense of skating over thin ice, of there being more work to do.

In any case, a quarter century later, in 1903, Peirce added a new clause to the maxim – one which permitted an account of the meaning of modal locutions, irreducible to non-modal meaning. We shall notice this addition briefly now but in more detail later, in Chapter 8.

H

At the very end of the 1903 Harvard 'Lectures on Pragmatism' we find a 'maxim', as it was there named:

> The elements of every concept enter into logical thought at the gate of perception and make their exit at the gate of purposive action; and whatever cannot show its passports at both these two gates is to be arrested as unauthorized by reason. (EP2:241)

This has usually been taken to be a figurative restatement of the 1878 maxim (e.g., Skagestad 1981, p.89). And, indeed, both maxims connect concepts, perception, and action. However, beyond that important similarity, they are fundamentally different. The new maxim is not about what concepts are or how they might be made clearer; instead, it refers to 'elements' of concepts and stipulates two conditions which these elements must fulfill. Stipulating conditions that must be fulfilled is not a matter of degree, as clarification is. So that is one difference. Another is that there is no reference to elements of concepts in the 1878 maxim or anywhere else in 'How to'. To be sure, the pragmatic maxim makes a concept a conditional relation of two other concepts ('X is *hard*' means 'X will not be *scratched* if X is *pressed by a knife-edge*'). But, as we shall see in a moment, by 'element', Peirce did not in the 1903 maxim mean the protasis or apodosis of a conditional; he meant, instead, something more subtle.

As to the second gate: we must suppose that the action may be potential merely; the 'element' is then identified as potentially making some difference to action, presumably to one's choice of which action to perform for a given purpose or to how to perform it. That a concept must bear on actions is assumed in the 1878 maxim; so, the second gate reflects that maxim. It is, we might say, the pragmatic gate.

The first gate is another matter. Peirce did not say in 1878 that a concept (much less its elements) must originate in perception. This gate, most surprisingly, is Lockean. It is a reversion, though only in part, to Locke's 'historical, plain' method, of establishing an idea as genuine – that is, as not a word empty of meaning – by tracing it back to its original in sense perception (*Essay*, Bk.I, Ch.I). Peirce's version is that each element of a genuine idea – that is, one capable of being employed in logical thought – must have first occurred in perception. There is no hint of this in 'How to'. Pragmatic clarification refers forward only, to uses that may be made of an idea, and not backward to its origin. So, the first gate is an addition to the original, or pragmatic, maxim.

The first gate, however, is not quite Lockean, since Peirce's idea of perception is very different from Locke's. That is a complex and difficult topic which must be deferred to Chapter 8, after we have in that chapter gained some acquaintance with the three phaneroscopic categories. For, as we will then see, it is those categories that Peirce had in mind when he spoke of the 'elements' of concepts: each conceptual element represents something in experience belonging to the class of phenomena that a phaneroscopic category represents. Anticipating much of Chapter 8: the phaneroscopic categories may be interpreted modally, accounting for the empirical meaning of modal locutions. In particular, the third category, which Peirce unhelpfully named 'Thirdness', is of what would be, would have been, and so on. Hence, it accounts for the empirical meaning of our idea of lawfulness as more than a possibly coincidental regularity. Rather than either protasis or apodosis of the conditionals into which the 1878 maxim analyzed concepts, Thirdness is conditionality itself.

The section of Lecture VII that concluded with this new maxim began by declaring that pragmatism has 'two functions': to rid us of 'ideas essentially unclear' and to 'help to render distinct, ideas essentially clear but more or less difficult of apprehension'. Peirce added, '... in particular, it ought to take a satisfactory attitude toward the element of Thirdness' (239). Thirdness – law, lawfulness, etc. – is thus implied to be an idea essentially clear (it is part of almost any concept applying to existing things), yet difficult of apprehension (witness the appeal of nominalism). It is clear to common sense, difficult for philosophers. Pragmatism is addressed to the latter.

CHAPTER 5

Misleading Appearances of System

I consider Schelling as enormous; and one thing I admire about him
is his freedom from the trammels of system, and his holding himself
uncommitted to any previous utterance. In that he is like a scientific
man. (letter from Peirce to William James, 1894)[1]

In an unfinished manuscript of 1887–1888, Peirce expressed an ambition 'To erect a philosophical edifice that shall outlast the vicissitudes
of time …' (EP1:246). These words have often been quoted as showing
that he was a philosopher with 'a system', or at least wanted one. What
is a system? In philosophy, it is perhaps an overview of how everything
fits together, a structure within which scientific discoveries (thus, vicissitudes) will find their assigned places – without requiring any amendment of the whole.

However, the words so often quoted are unusual in Peirce's literary remains (8.254–7, of 1902, is another example, albeit the system
claimed is not the same). They were accompanied by a reference to the
Naturphilosophie of Schelling (EP1:247). A related series of five essays,
published in 1891–1893 (EP1:Chs. 21–25), also begin with an allusion,
but this time not unambiguously positive, to system (EP1:286) and later
refer favorably but not uncritically to Schelling (EP1:312–13). In unpublished manuscripts of the period there occur stronger statements of debt
to Schelling (eds. note, W8:391–2), though Schelling is not mentioned
similarly, or hardly at all, in later writings. It is therefore significant that
toward the end of this period, in 1894, in the letter to James quoted in the
epigraph of this chapter, Peirce praised Schelling not as a system-builder
but as free 'from the trammels of system' and willing to change his mind,
being in that respect 'like a scientific man'.

---

[1] Quoted in Perry (1935), vol.2, pp.415–16.

To be sure, the scientist inquires systematically, and with the purpose of discovering systematic aspects of nature. But that is not the same as having or building a system. The great achievements of system – Newtonian mechanics, the Periodic Table, the theory of evolution, quantum theory and relativity – were or are works in progress, more important for facilitating discoveries, by which they are supplemented, extended, and/ or amended, than for unifying past discoveries in one coherent and final scheme. And a philosopher can be intensely aware, as Peirce was, that answers to questions in different departments, say, of logic, metaphysics, and ethics, bear systematically on one another, without claiming to have a system in which all answers have a place, or even thinking that such a system is possible – or desirable.

The statement of 1887–1888 may be dismissed, I suggest, as the expression of a momentary enthusiasm. It occurred amid pages in which Peirce began to work out a cosmogony, first intimated in a lecture of 1883. Perhaps, like all newborns, it evoked admiring wonder in its parent. But the cosmogony proved problematic during its adolescent years, in papers of 1891–1893, and then was discretely hidden away, but for two failed attempts at reform (in 1898 and 1904); we shall examine it in the next chapter.

The statement of 1887–1888 aside, there are striking – beguiling – appearances of system in Peirce's writings. They are misleading. There were indeed important continuities in his thought, as one would expect there to be; but also there were fundamental revolutions. The latter have been missed because Peirce continued to employ much the same terminology with reference to much the same formal structure, even while interpreting those words and that structure in radically different ways. And then, too, some features of Peirce's genius were constants: he always saw the individual, whether a person or an object or a thought, as a part, whether of a society or a physical system or an inquiry; and he always understood the whole as consisting in the relations of its parts, or, rather, their evolving relations, hence, as a process. But as to what those wholes and relations and processes are, he did not always think the same. His philosophy itself – if we are to speak of his having one – was a process. The path he cleared is more significant than are the camps he set up *en route*. In that respect, his philosophical writings bear the character of modern science.

Section B of the preceding chapter divided Peirce's philosophical writings into four sets, distinguished chronologically and thematically. This chapter is about the first set: the 1867 essay 'On a New List of Categories' and the three essays published in *Journal of Speculative Philosophy* in 1868– 1869. The 'New List' (hereafter NL) sketched a system of metaphysical categories similar in some ways to a later list developed in the 1900s, and the other three essays (hereafter JSP) sketched a theory of signs that reappears, transformed, in a later, more elaborate theory, again of the 1900s. NL and JSP are independent of one another (citations of NL in JSP are inessential to the latter's argument). Though developed together (W1:161–528 *passim*), each follows a distinct line of thought in its own way. However, both express an idealism that is conceptual: an identification of reality with concept. And that idealism distinguishes them from the doctrines they respectively anticipate. Peirce's methods in the 1900s were opposed to the methods of 1867–1869, and, far from expressing a conceptual idealism, his later conclusions contradict that doctrine.

A

I will begin with JSP, as it is far more accessible than is NL. This section briefly states basic themes of JSP (EP1:Chs. 2–4)[2] on which commentators are generally agreed and about which Peirce himself had no later doubts. Those themes are essentially negative. In the two sections following, we shall examine the positive doctrine of JSP. That doctrine has had a more confused reception, reflecting its confused expression; it was not repeated in later writings.

JSP is most notable for its, at that time, highly original attack on Descartes' quest for certainty, a quest not limited to Descartes but shared in one way by his rationalist heirs and their empiricist opponents and in another way by Hegel and the 'absolute idealists' (Bradley et al.). Whereas the former sought certainty at the beginning of inquiry, rationalist or empiricist, the latter sought it at the end of a dialectical exercise. In effect, modern philosophers prior to Peirce made theory of knowledge primary: all other inquiries require justification by it. Peirce called Descartes 'the father of modern philosophy' (28), implying that he meant, in refuting Descartes, to refute all of modern philosophy.

In the case of Descartes, the rationalists, and the empiricists, the quest for certainty depended on these assumptions: (a) that what is known non-inferentially is known intuitively, that is, without mediation[3]; (b) that what is known intuitively is without possibility of error; and (c) that we

---

[2] Comprising pages EP1:11–82; hereafter, in this and the next three sections, unadorned numerals in parentheses denote pages among those pages.

[3] In philosophical usage from the eleventh-century, an intuition is unmediated cognition: see the note at EP1:11 citing St. Anselm. It will become important later, in Chapter 8, that one can deny intuition without maintaining that every judgment is inferred. Of course, 'intuition' can also be used in other senses, as Peirce sometimes did.

can be certain that our beliefs are true if and only if they are founded, by inferences intuitively valid, on cognitions (either rational or empirical) intuitively true. Peirce named (c) the 'chain model' of reasoning. It assumes that once error is allowed to creep in, all of our inferences become uncertain and soon we have no idea whether any belief is so much as probable. But that, it is alleged, is our present situation. We must therefore make a clean sweep of existing opinion, so that we may begin over again, building securely on firm foundations, namely, intuitive cognitions. Thus 'foundationalism', a term coined in the 1950s when its denial, anticipated by the absolute idealists, began to become popular.

One prong of Peirce's attack on foundationalism was to reject the chain model of reasoning, espousing in preference to it the cable model exemplified by the scholastic philosophy of the thirteenth century, which wove its conclusions from diverse authorities (28–29). In his view of it, modern science also exemplifies the cable model: It is woven of specialized inquiries employing diverse methods, beginning from different bodies of data. It is the unplanned (albeit desired) agreement of conclusions arrived at differently that attests to their truth. The data themselves are not secure independently of that agreement: for mistakes in observation can be made; especially, theories assumed in making observations may turn out to be mistaken. Truth, then, resides not in secure beginnings but in final destination, later named 'the final opinion' (*vide supra* Ch.4, F).

Hegel and the absolute idealists had already identified truth with the conclusion of inquiry; but they supposed that finality resides in conceptual coherence, achieved dialectically. Peirce's originality was to substitute empirical inquiry for conceptual dialectic. But then the cable model applies to theory of knowledge itself: we cannot know what knowledge is and how it is possible prior to progress being made in the various sciences.[4] Indeed, 'Philosophy ought to imitate the successful sciences in its methods ... and to trust rather to the multitude and variety of its arguments than to the conclusiveness of any one' (29). Like the idealists, Peirce supposed that every belief formed along the way is fallible; unlike the idealists, he supposed that we must always be on the way. Inquiry's endlessness is entailed by the ideals of concreteness and fruitfulness which science, by Peirce's day, had come to embrace.

This contrast of modern philosophy to scholasticism, and the surprising association of modern science with the latter, occupies the beginning

---

[4] Some might object that Peirce in the 1860s, as in his 1902 classification of the sciences, made metaphysics to rest on logic. Yes, but in what respect and at what point in the progress of inquiry? That foundationalist reading of Peirce is refuted below, in Ch.8, A.

of the second article of JSP, 'Some Consequences of Four Incapacities', but it was anticipated in two ways, superficially at odds with one another, by the argument of the preceding article, 'Questions Concerning Certain Faculties Claimed for Man'. On the one hand, that argument employs empirical evidence to refute a rationalist doctrine, viz., that knowledge must be based on intuition – a doctrine supposed by rationalists to be established independently of empirical evidence and, indeed, before any argument from evidence can be made. On the other hand, there is the scholastic form in which Peirce cast his argument.

Let us begin with the latter. Peirce's argument in 'Questions' is modeled on the formal debates in medieval universities known as *quaestiones disputatae*, which were structured by a series of questions that a master set to his students.[5] In this case, there are seven questions, the answer to each building on the answer to the preceding. It begins with the seemingly fussy question, whether we can intuit whether a cognition is intuitive, and concludes with the major question, whether there are intuitive cognitions. But that nod to scholasticism was only a rhetorical flourish, one that throws into relief the contrasting, far-from-scholastic strategy of the way in which Peirce answered these questions.

For, the answer to the first question depends completely on a recitation of seventeen empirical facts (12-18), proceeding from ones less telling (third: 'the very complicated trick of the Chinese rings') to the somewhat more compelling evidence of physiological psychology (e.g., 'A single sensation does not inform us how many nerves or nerve-points are excited'); and therefore the answers to all seven questions depend on those same, not entirely secure, empirical facts. Now, if these facts *tout ensemble* convince the reader, that both illustrates and is evidence for the thesis, that multiform argument from uncertain premisses outweighs a single strand of argument from an axiom deemed indisputable. Only, these uncertain premisses, unlike those of scholasticism, derive not from various canonical texts but from varied observations and investigations.

In short, though Peirce did not make a point of it – he left it for the reader to discern – the nature of his argument, cable-like and empirical, was a second argument. The official argument refuted the hypothesis that there is intuitive cognition, ergo, firm foundations. The character of

---

[5] Murray Murphey said that this paper is 'modeled on that of a Scholastic commentary' (1961, p.107); it isn't. However, Thomas Aquinas wrote some of his noncommentary treatises, such as his *de Veritate*, on the model of the *quaestiones disputatae*, and one of these treatises might well have been Peirce's more immediate model.

that argument was an argument *qua* convincing example – hence, it was implicitly an argument from experience – for what is to replace foundationalism and also idealist dialectic, namely, argument from experience. But how can an argument from experience refute an argument purely rational? The point is that this example shows, from experience, that it can. That stratagem had a precedent: rationalism had already been discredited when Newton used empirical facts to refute Descartes' theory of vortices; it is not unlikely that Peirce had this in mind. The artistry, the rhetorical cleverness of JSP has not been sufficiently appreciated.[6]

JSP also disputed some of Descartes' further theses, that we know our own states of mind intuitively and that we know the physical world only by inference from our states of mind. Peirce argued, to the contrary (and empirically), that the infant begins by being aware of the world around it, without distinguishing that world from itself. When it begins to think about that world and itself, it is in a language taught it by others. As its expectations are disappointed by experience and as its statements are corrected by others, the infant comes to a consciousness of itself as distinct from the world and from other persons. One's self is thus first apprehended as a locus of ignorance and error (18–21). Positive attributes may be assigned to that negatively defined being, but only as inferred from its publicly observable behavior: 'We can admit no statement concerning what passes within us except as a hypothesis necessary to explain what takes place in what we commonly call the external world' (30). Later, Peirce admitted introspection and affirmed an inward life (e.g., in 1907 at EP2:412; see Colapietro 1989); but he never supposed that introspection is an intuitive cognition of one's own mind. And the essentially negative definition of one's self, underlying all positive description, was not erased.[7]

---

[6] Cornelius Delaney, in the most detailed and best discussion of JSP, writes that this argument is impotent against Cartesians: 'For a philosopher like Peirce who does not invoke a sharp dichotomy between science and philosophy, such empirical considerations are obviously very weighty. Most foundationalists, however, are among those who think that philosophical considerations are in principle different from empirical or scientific considerations, and since their foundationalism is a philosophical position, they are not disposed to feel threatened by these kinds of empirical arguments' (1993, p.94). Thus Delaney misses the deliberate cleverness of Peirce's mode of argument. Worse, he supposes that foundationalism can be refuted only by reasoning a priori, ergo, only by a foundationalist argument, which is to say that foundationalism is inviolable. But, though this may come as a surprise, philosophers are people; thus, they can be reached by an argument addressed to them from outside of the prison walls of their own ideas (when the walls are thick, shouting is necessary).

[7] How can something defined negatively become a subject of positive attributes? In later years, Peirce spoke of 'hypostatic abstraction' as postulating an entity defined indirectly (through such locutions as 'that which') by relation to another; it may then be made subject of further predications (Short 2007, Ch.10). Relations to others can be negative.

We have seen (Ch.2, H) that Peirce in later years drew out an implication of this doctrine, by arguing that philosophical egoism, the 'metaphysics of wickedness', derives from the falsehood that selves are substantial entities out of which societies are built, rather than the other way about.

A last thesis of Cartesianism that we shall note is that mind and body differ in substance, the one extended in space and thoughtless, the other pure thought without spatial extension. Peirce was not the first to object that an ontological dualism of mind and body makes their interaction inexplicable. However, he took the objection a step further: '... that anything *is* thus inexplicable can only be known by reasoning from signs. But the only justification of an inference from signs is that the conclusion explains the fact' (29). Thirty years later, that became a principle of logic: 'Do not block the way of inquiry' (EP2:48–49). Now, the interaction of mind and body requires some continuity between them. In general, then, logic requires that we must seek out continuities in place of dichotomies – a corollary that in 1892 he named 'synechism' (EP1:313).

The rejection of Cartesianism frames all of Peirce's subsequent thought. It also frames much of contemporary philosophy. Denial of an ontological dualism of mind and body was alone common before Peirce wrote. And it took the form of reducing either mind to matter or matter to mind: hence, not, as with Peirce, by affirming their continuity whilst maintaining their distinction.

B

What is to be offered in place of intuition? Peirce's answer in 1868–1869 was his theory of 'thought-signs': not merely that thoughts are signs, a doctrine he never abandoned, but that every thought-sign interprets a preceding thought-sign and is interpreted in a subsequent thought-sign. This fascinating theory is absurd but instructive. Threads of it appear rewoven in Peirce's later thought. Not subsequently developed, it was later implicitly denied.

Peirce never rejected the Cartesian assumptions that intuition, were it possible, would be certain and that certainty is impossible without intuition. Instead, he embraced uncertainty, a position he never relinquished, eventually naming it 'fallibilism'. But what of the assumption that non-inferential knowledge must be intuitive? In JSP, Peirce did not deny that, either (later he did: *vide infra*, Ch.8, G). Instead, he argued in the first essay that every cognition is inferential, concluding on that basis that there is no intuition (25–7). As he put it in the next essay: 'We have no power of intuition, but every cognition is determined logically by previous cognitions' (30).

There is, then, no first cognition. How is that possible, if thought began at some time or if an individual's thinking begins at some time or if one's thinking about a certain topic begins at some time? The answer Peirce gave is that thinking is a continuum and therefore contains an infinity of thoughts in a finite span. Take a finite line segment from 0 to 1 inch. That line is infinitely divisible. Consider only its fractional divisions, or only some of them. Proceeding backwards from 1 by halves, we obtain 1/2, then 1/4, then 1/8, and so on, drawing ever nearer to but never reaching 0. So also if we trace our thoughts back through the brief span of time they fill: '… there is no absolutely first cognition of any object, but cognition arises by a continuous process' (30). Continuity remained a key concept in Peirce's thinking; to its mathematical analysis he returned repeatedly. It is not adequately defined in terms of the rational numbers; ultimately, he denied that even Cantor's analysis of it into real numbers suffices, a point that for the present we may ignore. What we must keep in mind, however, is that divisibility is not division: it consists not in actual but in possible divisions. Anything continuous is divisible but undivided.

That thinking is a continuum of thoughts yet inferential stretches what we ordinarily suppose is inference, in which premises and conclusions are discrete. We are nonetheless invited to suppose that logical analysis applies to a continuous process. Peirce did not explain how that is to be done, though the system of 'existential graphs' that he developed in the 1900's was perhaps an attempt in that direction, as its rules of inscription and erasure were described as putting 'before us moving pictures of thought' (4.8; see also the very important 4.572, both of 1906).

Another difficulty, or two, is that, in addition to portraying thought as a continuum, Peirce hinted that it is continuous with pre-conscious processes. That is a quite different way of denying that there is a first thought. Can these two alternatives be combined? Furthermore, this second view requires a second extension of the idea of inference: 'Something, therefore, takes place within the organism which is *equivalent to* the syllogistic process' (31, my emphasis). What the equivalence is, is not said, though the implication is that it suffices to make logical analysis applicable.

That all thought may be analyzed as valid inference (38) is next restated as a doctrine of signs, on the ground that '… whenever we think, we have present to the consciousness some feeling, image, conception, or other representation, which serves as a sign' (38). The idea seems to be that thought must consist of something, and that what makes that something (whether feeling or image or words or numerals, etc.) a thought is that it is a sign. Peirce was here drawing on a long tradition of logical theory, from Aristotle through the Hellenistic and medieval periods to Locke and Berkeley, in which 'sign' (also *signum*, etc.) has not the restricted application that it has in ordinary usage. A sign is *of* something, its object; being-of is the essence of thought; so, thoughts are signs.

But what makes one thing to be 'of' another? What *is* being-of? One possibility is that X is of Y when X elicits a thought of Y. Crusoe saw a footprint and thought of a man, so the footprint was to him the sign of a man. But if to signify is to be interpreted by thought and if thoughts are themselves signs, then it follows that every thought must elicit another thought which interprets it. It is only by interpreting it in a second thought, that we know what a given thought signifies, i.e., what it is a thought of. But then that second thought must be interpreted in a third, and so on, *ad infinitum*. That 'all thought is in signs' had already been asserted in the preceding essay, in which it was concluded, 'From the proposition that every thought is a sign, it follows that every thought must address itself to some other, must determine some other, since that is the essence of a sign' (24). Peirce named the interpreting thought a sign's 'interpretant'.

There is an obvious problem here: significance is assumed in and therefore cannot be explained by one thought's interpreting another. Peirce was aware of the problem but his attempt to wave it away does not succeed: 'It may be objected, that if no thought has any meaning, all thought is without meaning. But this is a fallacy similar to saying, that, if in no one of the successive spaces which a body fills there is room for motion, there is no room for motion throughout the whole' (42). Nothing is said to show that the similarity is such as to render the objection fallacious. Significance is in later years linked to interpretation in another way.[8]

Granted that each thought must be interpreted in another, the series of thought-signs is infinite in either direction. A present thought interprets a prior thought which determined it, and so on, infinitely; and it determines a subsequent thought in which it is interpreted, and so on, infinitely. The infinite *regressus* leads back to the object thought-of. The infinite *progressus* leads forward to what is thought about that object. I think I see a rhinoceros in your garden. What made me think that? I saw something large and gray and ugly which snorted. What made me think I saw something large and gray which snorted? Betwixt green leaves I saw patches of gray

---

[8] See Short (2007, Ch.2), §§5&10, for more detailed refutation of Peirce's argument.

extending from here to there which I assumed were of some continuous object lurking behind the leaves, and at the same time I heard sounds like snorting. And so on, back and back. Now, in the other direction. What does it mean to think of a rhinoceros? I think a rhinoceros is an ill-tempered quadruped from Africa, that a quadruped is a four-legged animal, and that an animal is … etc. Also, what can we expect if this ill-tempered beast is in your garden? And what should we do about it? The meaning of my thought is to be found in the further thoughts which it elicits. Between the real object and my present thought, there is an infinity of thoughts; between my present thought and any action I may take, such as running fast, there is also an infinity of thoughts. Fortunately, as thinking is a continuum, it does not require an infinite amount of time either to draw a conclusion or to take an action.

The forward-directed series of thoughts interpreting thoughts is not to be confused with that other forward-directed series of thoughts named 'inquiry'. Inquiry, which might continue forever and takes place in discrete steps, leads toward a final opinion. Inquiries being instituted and additional data sought, it turns out that the rhinoceros I thought I saw was your grumpy gardener, large, gray-clothed, and ugly, snorting as he digs. Inquiry, unrestricted in time, determines truth. The other forward-directed series of thoughts, compressed in a finite time, constitutes meaning. I knew what I meant by there being a rhinoceros in your garden; I knew it before I discovered my error; I could not have discovered the error had I not known what I meant. There is no truth or error without meaning. In JSP, Peirce did not distinguish these two forward-directed processes, and even left an impression of having identified them: 'The real, then, is that which, sooner or later, information and reasoning would finally result in, and which is therefore independent of the vagaries of me and you' (52).

That easily corrected conflation of two processes aside, this doctrine of thought-signs is astounding. It denies its own terms – ones that it draws from common ways of talking. For, it makes individual thoughts to be fictions. They are arbitrary divisions, artificial albeit useful for certain purposes, of what is in reality a continuous process. And that process has no first thought, though there was a time before thought began. This doctrine has no anticipation in common sense. As such, it is pleasing in the way that modern science is pleasing. Reading JSP is like first learning that the Earth moves, that sound is a wave, that air has weight, that light takes time to travel (hence, that seeing is not simultaneous with the seen), or that heat is motion. It is not an explication of what we already think – it is not philosophy as conceptual analysis – it is something new and surprising and throws common sense into question.

To be sure, there are many problems with this new, radically original idea, some of which we noted above. But let us put those problems aside. Every new theory engenders problems not immediately solved: work that remains to be done. What seems absurd, such as that the Earth moves, and poses new problems ('Why don't we feel it move?', 'What keeps it in orbit?'), later is made commonplace; many, not all, of the problems are solved. It would be unfair to expect Peirce to have worked out this new idea in all of its aspects. Precisely because his mode of thought, even from the start, was not that of conceptual analysis nor that of system-building, but was that of conjecture, of trying ideas out, what he wrote is surprising, fruitful, and unfinished, replete with ambiguities and problems.

C

However, there is one difficulty which we will discuss, as the JSP papers struggle with it unsuccessfully and as it explains why Peirce later abandoned the doctrine of thought-signs. The real, he said, is that which 'information and reasoning would finally result in'. But what reasoning results in is judgment and what it would result in finally is the so-called final opinion. We might suppose that this does not mean that the real *is* the final opinion but, rather, that it is what that opinion *represents* (its 'object', we shall say). We might suppose that the final opinion represents its object to be distinct from itself, and to be, in part (the physical part), distinct from all judgment. But what distinguishes a true judgment from its object? The claim, that the real is what reasoning results in, is ambiguous. And there is much in JSP which implies that there is no distinction of judgment from object, as well as much that implies that there is.

The doctrine of thought-signs allows for two ways of making the distinction; neither succeeds. One possibility derives from the fact that inquiry can never be finished. About the object of a true judgment there are additional truths (other features, features more exactly specified, relations to other things) which may be represented in subsequent true judgments. Thus the object of any actual judgment is distinguished from that judgment. But it is not thereby distinguished from the final opinion or from judgment in general: 'Over against any cognition, there is an unknown but knowable reality; but over against all possible cognition, there is only the self-contradictory' (25).

The other possibility is that the object is distinguished as the cause that initiated thought (and perhaps that explains thought's progress) – a cause that is not itself a thought, hence, not in the series of thought-signs. Much in JSP suggests exactly that idea; e.g., a reference to '... a real effective force behind consciousness' (42). And in the fourth question of 'Questions', Peirce argued, against the supposition that self-knowledge is introspective, that '... our whole knowledge of the internal world is derived from the observation of external facts' (22, repeated at 30). Nowhere in JSP is this use of 'external' versus 'internal' defined, but it would seem to refer to the publicly observable physical world versus the private world of one's thought.[9] (Would it not follow that the evidence for the theory of thought-signs consists of facts about the physical, including the physiological? Indeed, we have seen that it is precisely on such basis that the first question in 'Questions' was answered.)

However, this commonsense assumption of a physical world that affects us, that explains much of our thinking, and that comprises an important part of what we think about, is undermined by a defining principle of the doctrine of thought-signs, that '... every cognition is determined logically by previous cognitions' (30). For then no room is left for physical explanation:

> ... to adduce the cognition by which a given cognition has been determined is to explain the determinations of that cognition. *And it is the only way of explaining them.* For something entirely out of consciousness which may be supposed to determine it, can, as such, only be known and only adduced in the determinate cognition in question. (25, my emphasis)

Peirce made it a principle, in JSP, to use the rules of logic alone to explain thought: '... we must, as far as we can, without any other supposition than that the mind reasons, reduce all mental action to the formula of valid reasoning' (30).

Notice, however, the caveat: 'as far as we can, without any other supposition'. We are being told that an attempt is being made, and not that it will certainly succeed. An alternative is intimated, that from a given cognition we may 'adduce' something 'entirely out of consciousness' that explains it. But most that we think we know is already what we think is 'out of consciousness': the 'adduction' is already made! That, however,

---

[9] Much in JSP suggests that 'the external' would best be defined as the limit of the series of thought-signs traced backwards, just as 0 is the 'external limit' of the series $1/2, 1/4, 1/8 \ldots$, because it is not a member of the series it limits. In neither use of 'external' is the spatial metaphor taken literally: while the physical is spatial, it is not outside of thought, as if thought itself occupied a space.

is not the line of thought to which JSP is dedicated. We are to read that essay as the working out, up to a point, of an idea that is no more than a conjecture, viz., that thought is to be explained only by thought. As well as its partial success, the failure of this conjecture is instructive.

Just as physical explanation is proscribed, so also is reference to anything, such as the physical, that lies outside the series of thought-signs:

> For what does the thought-sign stand …? The outward thing, undoubtedly, when a real outward thing is thought of. But still, as the thought is determined by a previous thought of the same object, it only refers to the thing through denoting this previous thought. (39)

As with 'external', 'outward' is nowhere defined in JSP; we must suppose that these terms are used synonymously. But if reference is always through previous thoughts, then, tracing the series of thought-signs backwards, we never get to the 'real, physical connection of a sign with its object' which, only two paragraphs later, Peirce named 'the *pure demonstrative application* of the sign' (40). As in that statement, so throughout JSP, there are references to the physical. But those references are undermined, as I've said, by the doctrine adumbrated. Perhaps that is why, only a little later in the same essay, pure demonstrative application, again with those words italicized, is identified not with a physical connection but with a 'force of attention' (46). Now, a physical connection would presumably be causation proceeding from object to thought-sign; whereas, attention would presumably proceed in the other direction from thought to its object. But if reference is attention, then what is it that is being referred to? Is it not determined by thought?

Consequently, we find Peirce struggling to maintain that thought has an object distinct from itself, even while denying the same:

> At any moment we are in possession of certain information, that is, of cognitions which have been logically derived by induction and hypothesis from previous cognitions which are less general, less distinct, and of which we have a less lively consciousness. These in their turn have been derived from others still less general, less distinct, and less vivid; and so back to the ideal* first, which is quite singular, and quite out of consciousness. This ideal first is the particular thing-in-itself. It does not exist *as such*. (52, Peirce's emphasis)

It does not exist 'as such': but if not as such, then *as what*? The note Peirce appended (where the asterisk occurs) is: 'By an ideal, I mean the limit which the possible cannot attain' (52n). Here, 'the possible' must refer to what is possible as we trace the continuum of thinking backwards.

The preceding passage continues its agonized struggle in this fashion: 'That is, there is no thing which is in-itself in the sense of not being relative to the mind, though things which are relative to the mind doubtless are, apart from that relation' (52). This, it would seem, means that the object of thought is as it is thought to be (in a true thought of it), but exists independently of its being thought of. Unfortunately, that commonsense sentiment depends exactly on what we want from the doctrine of thought-signs and that it does not give to us: viz., a way of distinguishing the object thought-of from the thought of it. To repeat: '... over against all possible cognition, there is only the self-contradictory'.

The same problem appears in JSP in another guise. Thought is concep-tual, concepts are general, and thought, we think, is in great part about individuals. Indeed, the definition of generality, as applicability to many individuals, requires there to be individuals – ones that we conceive of in general terms. But in JSP, thought-signs are assumed to be wholly con-ceptual, and that makes reference to individuals problematic. In the words quoted above, cognitions are derived from previous cognitions, and 'These in their turn have been derived from others still less general, less distinct, and less vivid; and so back to the ideal first, which is quite singular, and quite out of consciousness'. The implication is that thought is always gen-eral, albeit in varying degree, and that the individual (or singular) is there-fore 'out of consciousness' and 'does not exist as such'.

This problem is addressed in JSP identically with the first of the two ways, discussed above, of distinguishing the object of thought from the thought of it. The singular is defined as the infinitely specifiable: 'When an image is said to be singular, it is meant that it is absolutely determinate in all respects. Every possible character, or the negative thereof, must be true of such an image' (47). While here images only are referred to, in 1870 Peirce wrote that the individual exists, but only as that about which more always remains to be determined (W2:390n8). While 'horse' in general has a finite definition, one can never finish describing a particular horse. The particular is distinguished from the general, then, as infinite specification differs from finite specification. The trouble with this solution is that an infinity of concepts still is no more than conceptual; were, *per impossibile*, the infinite series of specifications to be completed, the result would still be general. It would be so, because it could be supposed that there is more than one individual of that same description.

Peirce himself, earlier in the same paragraph, mentioned the missing sense of individuality: 'A singular may mean that which can be but in one place at one time'. Amazingly, he dismissed that sense on the ground that, '... it is *not* opposed to the general' (47, my emphasis). The reason for the latter assertion is that an individual (rather: any physical individual) is of some size and some duration. Therefore, it occupies infinitely many subspaces of the space it occupies, has different properties at these different subspaces, and will be the same individual at other times, whether in the same place or in other places, even with changed properties. To which we may answer: yes, individuals in those ways implicate generality; but that does not make them 'generals' in Peirce's sense.[10] Location in space and time makes the individual, despite its size and variable characteristics, unique, hence, not general. And no amount of description in general terms can specify a location. For each location is itself individual. If description is purely conceptual, then the infinite series of specifications mentioned above cannot include location. And therefore they do not individuate.

As Murray Murphey was the first to declare (1961, pp.298–300), a major revision of Peirce's thought began by 1885 when he recognized that, in addition to general terms predicable of individuals, there are (and must be) terms that pick out individuals through some connection that is not conceptual but is itself individual, for example, pointing. As Peirce wrote in 1885, '... the subject of discourse ... can, in fact, not be described in general terms; it can only be indicated. The actual world cannot be distinguished from a world of imagination by any description. Hence the need of pronouns and indices ...' (EP1:227). While Peirce earlier (in NL) used the term 'index' in somewhat this manner, indices, as Murphey noted and as we shall see (Section D), were not then conceived of as signifying nonconceptually. Once logical analysis revealed the need for nonconceptual signification, then other developments ensued (the phaneroscopic analysis of 2ndness discussed, in Chapter 8).

As nonconceptual signification was not acknowledged in JSP, Peirce's argument in those essays, perhaps contrary to his intention, entailed a conceptual idealism: that is, a view in which nothing but the conceptual, the irreducibly and exclusively general, could consistently be admitted.

This has not been a complete account of the three JSP papers; they contain a richness barely touched on here. I have focused on just one strand of thought in them, for the sake of making perspicuous their conjectural, exploratory, and transitory character. My thesis is that Peirce should be

---

[10] We do not predicate Fido of each part of Fido; rather, of each part we predicate 'part of Fido' (or 'this is Fido's paw', 'this is Fido's tail'). Again, as to space occupied, when we say that Fido is lying partly on the pillow and partly on the formerly clean sheet, it is 'Fido lying on' that is predicated of pillow and sheet. The individual dog is never predicated of anything and, therefore, it is not general. But this interesting technical issue is not one we need for the present purpose to examine.

read, especially in these early papers, as trying out ideas, and not as building a system. We have more to learn from these papers by taking their ideas neat, and tracing their implications to their logical conclusions, however absurd, than by diluting those ideas with the sobering soda water of common sense.[11]

D

'On a New List of Categories' (EP1:1–10), written with baffling concision when Peirce was twenty-seven, is remarkable for having anticipated much of his later thought, when he was in his sixties. In what manner anticipated is the issue. NL has been called 'the keystone' of Peirce's 'system of philosophy' (EP1:1, Editors' introduction). And yet, major problems in understanding this 'keystone' have been little discussed, in some cases never even acknowledged. In Sections E–G, I refute the reasons given for calling it the keystone of a system.[12]

We shall begin, in a moment, with a thumbnail sketch of NL's argument. But first, problems of interpretation are posed already by NL's opening words, the one-sentence §1[13], which, in its entirety, reads as follows:

> This paper is based upon the theory already established, that the function of conceptions is to reduce the manifold of sensuous impressions to unity, and that the validity of a conception consists in the impossibility of reducing the content of consciousness to unity without the introduction of it.

There is no indication of where, when, or by whom this theory was 'established'. As the words translate those Kant used in the *Critique of Pure Reason*, it might seem that the allusion was to that work. Indeed, the editors of EP1 append a note citing it, as if Kant's was the theory which Peirce held to have been established. That, however, is surely mistaken.[14]

---

[11] For a more sober reading, thoroughly documented, consult Lane (2018, Ch.4). Lane and I differ in what we read for: it is clear that Lane wishes to determine what Peirce really thought, assuming that Peirce said what he thought, whereas I wish to learn from what Peirce said, without assuming that the ideas he was trying out invariably reflect his real convictions. Lane labors to interpret Peirce's words in ways that make his claims maximally consistent, whereas I am happy to maximize the contradictions. As Marx claimed in the economic sphere, contradictions explain progress – in this case, Peirce's – and maximizing them produces progress – in this case, ours. Besides, clear contrasts and sharp corners seem to me more fun.

[12] Short (2014) contains additional argument and textual evidence.

[13] As all of NL's fifteen sections but the last are brief, some only a sentence or two, it will be convenient to cite passages by their section numbers. In *Collected Papers* 1.545–59, the nth section of NL is numbered n+544.

[14] It is a mistake I also made in Short (2007), p.31, which I now contritely correct.

In Peirce's audience at the American Academy of Arts and Sciences, the few who could have caught that allusion would have known that Kant's theory was *not* established, as it was rejected by prominent contemporaries, such as Mill, Whewell, and Comte, whose views had been discussed at length by Peirce himself in public lectures in the preceding two years.

Unless he was ironically alerting his audience not to take his premises too seriously, he was probably not referring to Kant at all but to what he himself had argued (and thus claimed to have established) in Lecture VIII of his 1866 Lowell lectures. That lecture we do not possess, but the opening words of Lecture IX refer to what 'we found' in 'the last lecture', including that 'the first impressions on our senses … are grasped into the unity which the mind requires, the unity of the *I think* …' by 'predicates which the mind affixes by virtue of a hypothetical inference' (W1:471). This is Kantian only in part. The reference to 'hypothetical inference' entails that the 'validity of a conception' depends on its empirical success, that is, on its being sustained in subsequent inquiry, which contradicts Kant's view that certain conceptions – his list of categories of the understanding – can be established a priori.

That the premises of NL are not to be taken too seriously anyway is suggested by a second problem posed by this opening statement, namely, that it is contradicted by the argument of JSP. I am not aware that this contradiction has been noted by Peirce's commentators. If there is no first cognition and if aught that precedes cognition is an ideal limit that does not exist 'as such', then the 'manifold of sensuous impressions' or 'first impressions on our senses' does not or do not really exist. In JSP, sensation itself is absorbed into the inferential continuum: '… a sensation is a simple predicate taken in place of a complex predicate; in other words, it fulfills the function of an hypothesis' (42). It might be supposed that between 1867 and 1868 Peirce had changed his mind on this fundamental point, except for the fact, noted above, that the themes of JSP and NL were developed together in earlier lectures and writings. It therefore seems to me that Peirce knew that the view he had been developing faced problems not yet resolved and that in his published articles he was trying out first one hypothesis and then another, seeing how far each would take him.

Let us begin with a thumbnail sketch of NL's argument (quotations not otherwise identified are from §§1–9, italics deleted). It will convey an impression that Peirce *did*, after all, argue a priori – and very much in the manner of Kant. Only, whereas Kant based his categories on the logical types of judgment (affirmative or negative, categorical or conditional, etc.), Peirce based his on an analysis of judgment-*formation* – a typically

Peircean shift of attention from product to process. He took affirmative
categorical judgments as the only case; but that would seem to be on the
assumption, unstated, that what applies to their formation applies like-
wise to the formation of judgments of other types. After having asserted,
very much as did Kant, that 'the function of conceptions is to reduce the
manifold of sensuous impressions to unity', he defined categories as 'universal conceptions' implicated in *any* reduction of sensuous impressions to
unity; whereas, for Kant, categories represent the different kinds of unity
to which sensuous impressions may be reduced. 'The unity to which the
understanding reduces impressions is the unity of a proposition', Peirce
said, connecting 'the predicate with the subject'. The concept of this unity
is therefore a category, that of *being*. At the opposite extreme is the category of *substance*, the 'universal conception which is nearest to sense': it
is 'of the present, in general'. Between substance and being there are other
categories, rather mysteriously explained in this way: 'one such conception
may unite the manifold of sense and yet another may be required to unite
the conception and the manifold to which it is applied; and so on'.

Working down, from being to substance, the next category after being
is that of *quality*, comprising whatever is predicated of any (one) subject.
But any quality must be understood independently of the subject of which
it is predicated and must therefore be abstract. Hence, quality is defined
as 'reference to a ground' or 'pure abstraction'. But such abstraction can
be attained only by comparison of subjects alike in quality and contrast of
subjects unlike in quality, and thus the concept of reference to a ground
leads to a concept of 'reference to a correlate'; this is the category of *relation*. But any comparison requires 'a mediating representation' in which
the items compared are both represented, and that representation is named
'an interpretant' because 'it fulfills the office of an interpreter', saying that
one of the represented represents what the other represents (in this case,
that each represents the same quality). Thus, the last category proceeding
from being to substance is *representation* or 'reference to an interpretant'.
This gives us five categories: two framing categories, being and substance,
and three intermediate categories, quality, relation, and representation.

Many questions are raised by this brief sketch, few of which can be
answered by citing other passages in NL. For example, is substance the
idea of the sensuous manifold or is it the idea of any subject a proposition
might have? The two are distinct in Kant's thought, where a subject of
predication is an object introduced by conception, the contents of sense
experience being understood as qualities (or as exemplifying qualities or
as signs of qualities) of those objects. In NL§3, Peirce said only that the

category of substance is 'nothing but the general recognition of what is contained in attention'. Is what is contained in attention the manifold or is it a subject introduced by conception? In §4, he said that 'If we say "The stove is black," the stove is the substance ....' Here, substance is indicated by a proposition's subject-term. Is the stove *qua* subject the sensuous manifold so far as already unified under the concept of stove, or is it an object distinct from the manifold, in relation to which the manifold, conceived of as so many qualities of the stove, is unified? In §6, we find the phrase, 'reduction of the manifold of substance to unity', which suggests the non-Kantian doctrine, that substance *is* the manifold. But this evidence of what Peirce meant is inconclusive.

Consider another problem. Being, or an instance of it, is expressed by a proposition; quality, or an instance of it, is expressed by the proposition's predicate; and substance, or an instance of it, is expressed by the proposition's subject-term. Relation and representation, however, are not expressed in the propositions they are adduced to explain. We seem, then, to have two kinds of category. Three, being expressed in propositions, are discerned by logical analysis; and two, not so expressed, are introduced in order to explain what is expressed. This division does not coincide with the division into two framing and three intermediate categories. Do explanatory concepts belong in the same list with analytic concepts? Are they all categories in the same sense of that word?

NL contains comments on its method, but these only deepen our perplexity. In §8, Peirce said, 'Empirical psychology has established the fact that we can know a quality only by means of its contrast with or similarity to another'. But in §6, he wrote that all five categories are derived by the same method of abstraction, named 'prescision' (notice the spelling), that was introduced in the preceding section; and he added that empirical psychology only 'discovers the occasion of the introduction of a conception'. But the claim in §8 is not about an occasion merely. Our confidence in Peirce's claim in §6, that the categories are derived by abstraction, is further undermined by a note he made in the next year, 1868, where he implied that his method was empirical: 'It may be doubted whether it was philosophical to rest this matter on empirical psychology. The question is extremely difficult' (W2:94).

Prescision is described in §5 as a 'mental separation' that 'arises from attention to one element and neglect of the other', and attention is said to consist in 'a definite conception or supposition of one part of an object, without any supposition of the other'. 'Prescision', Peirce adds, 'is not a reciprocal process'; for example, 'I can prescind ... space from color ...; but

I cannot prescind color from space …'. Certainly, this is not empirical psychology. Is it, then, introspective? Not according to §6: '… introspection is not resorted to', and 'Nothing is assumed respecting the subjective elements of consciousness which cannot be securely inferred from the objective elements'. But what are these 'objective elements'? Are they concepts? Are they words? And what makes such entities objective? How do we apprehend them? Peirce did not say. In any case, both in his reference to empirical psychology and in his account of prescinding, he seems to be suggesting that the categories are not wholly founded on logical analysis *à la* Kant.

I am not attempting to explicate NL; I am only noting the problems that an explication must either solve or turn into criticism. It is alarming that the accounts that have been given of NL fail even to raise these questions, much less answer them.[15] Whether NL commits the fallacy that Peirce in other places named 'psychologism', of substituting psychology for logic, has been discussed, so far as I know, by two authors only.[16] Some difficult questions, which our sketch allows us to ignore, have however been raised by other commentators (especially Murphey 1961, pp.55–94); the preceding are those that even a summary statement of NL's argument forces on us.

E

The continuity of NL with Peirce's later thought has been asserted by many. These assertions have been of varying strength, from NL's being the keystone of his supposed later system to NL's three intermediate categories being an early version of his later, more famous list of three categories. I will refer to any and all such assertions as 'the continuity hypothesis'. It is supported on four grounds.

The first ground is that there is a formal analogy between NL's three intermediate categories and the later lists of three relationally defined categories. To understand this, we must briefly outline these later developments. Predicates are assumed in NL to be monadic, that is, to apply to but one subject at a time. Shortly after NL's publication, Peirce began developing an algebra of relations, in which predicates, and the relations

---

[15] Including Savan 1952, Thompson (1953), pp.19–36, Murphey (1961), pp.55–94, Buzzelli (1972), Rosensohn (1974), pp.19–51, Esposito (1980), pp.82–121, Apel (1981), pp.19–25, 37–42, Hookway (1985), pp.90–97, De Tienne (1989), and Parker (1998), pp.9–10. De Tienne does make a strong argument that NL's method anticipates Peirce's later phenomenology; see also his 1996 *passim*.
[16] See De Tienne (1996, pp.233–37), and his citations of Joseph Ransdell's 1966 PhD dissertation.

they represent, are distinguished as monadic, dyadic, triadic, or of higher orders.[17] On the assumption that relations of higher than triadic order can be represented as logical compounds of those of lower order, whereas not all triadic or dyadic relations are similarly 'reducible', Peirce began, in 1885, to speak of three categories defined relationally, sometimes calling them 'One, Two, Three' (W5:235ff), later as 'firstness', 'secondness', and 'thirdness' (often capitalized). I prefer and will use their numeral variants, '1stness', '2ndness', '3rdness', though Peirce rarely used them. From 1885 through the 1890s, he applied the list of three categories in diverse ways – physical, psychological, cosmological, etc. – describing them as 'vast, though vague ideas' (EP1:251) and admitting, 'Perhaps it is not right to call these categories conceptions; they are so intangible that they are rather tones or tints upon conceptions' (W5:237).

Later, c.1902 and after, the three categories were defined unambiguously as conceptions that apply universally: that is, each to a distinct aspect universally present in experience and in what is experienced. These categories still are applied in a variety of ways, but those ways are now systematically arranged, beginning with their phenomenological or phaneroscopic identification and proceeding to their modal and metaphysical generalization. As that is the topic of Chapter 8, I will now say only as much as is needed for the present purpose. As to phaneroscopy, 1stness is the qualitative content of experience, 2ndness is the sense of action/reaction or force/resistance, and 3rdness is the element of generality or continuity in experience. 3rdness, combining many, is irreducibly triadic; 2ndness is irreducibly dyadic, as there can be no force felt without feeling a resistance to it, and vice versa. Notice that named qualities, for example, blue, are 3rds, not 1sts. For, the exact shade of blue in a given instance is unique, nameless, and a 1st, whereas blue is a continuous spectrum of such shades, hence, a 3rd. Blue as a physical property is another sort of a 3rd, not phaneroscopic but involving causal laws.

Now, in NL§12, Peirce had already remarked on the 'numerical' character of the intermediate three categories. This has been taken to mean that the three are respectively monadic, dyadic, and triadic, though those terms do not occur in NL. The category of quality is monadic (despite its

---

[17] Not that Peirce earlier ignored relations, but those discussions (e.g., in 1866 at W1:382–7) did not have the clarity achieved by distinguishing predicates in this way. Hence, they vainly attempted to work out the logic of inferences concerning relations within the framework of syllogistic principles. His first contributions to the logic of relations distinct from syllogistic was in 1870: see above, Ch.1, B.

'reference' to a ground) in the sense that NL conceives of qualities as predicable of but one subject at a time. The category of relation, as concerning two items, a relate and a correlate, is dyadic. And the category of representation is triadic in combining relate and correlate, the combination, or 'reference to an interpretant', being a third item. It is therefore alleged that there is a formal identity of these categories with the phaneroscopic categories.

But is it not surprising that orders of relational complexity should have emerged within an essay based on the assumption that all predicates are monadic? Does not this feature of the intermediate categories undercut the assumption of the essay? And, if so, did Peirce intend that from the beginning? Was NL written ironically? Or is NL, instead, where Peirce first discovered the inadequacy of syllogistic logic? Or was he unaware of the problem? These questions have not been discussed in the vast literature on Peirce, as they have not been raised.

Another surprise should be noted: Peirce never announced the deletion of the two framing categories, being and substance, much less explained why they were deleted. On the continuity hypothesis, that silence is a mystery. Why, if NL is the keystone of his system, did he never again mention five categories or say anything to explain why he dropped two of them? Another mystery is why this mystery has been so little discussed. Max Fisch, who may have been responsible for the idea that NL is a keystone,[18] said only that 'Peirce soon reduced the five to three by sloughing off Being and Substance'; he offered no explanation (W1:xxvi). 'Sloughing off' is a remarkably casual description of what happened to parts of a keystone, especially as they are seemingly essential parts of a seemingly rigorous argument. But put the keystone metaphor aside. Even if the later and earlier lists are no more than variants of the same idea, why did the later not need the framing categories the earlier needed?

A third and final surprise: during the eighteen years that elapsed between NL and 1885 – the year when Peirce began to write of three categories – he did not discuss categories at all and rarely even referred to categories.[19] This makes Fisch's remark that the categories were 'soon' reduced from five to three even more mysterious. When in those silent eighteen years did

---

[18] The idea first appears in an editorial note (W2:502) in a volume of which Fisch is listed as 'Consulting Editor' but of which he was actually the guiding spirit.

[19] The *Collected Papers* contains two passages on the categories seemingly written between 1867 and 1885; but they – 1.353, dated c.1880 and 1.337, dated c.1875 – are now dated 1885 and 1886, respectively (W5:497,499).

the sloughing-off occur? And when categories were again mentioned, the admitted vagueness of their conception (*vide supra*) contrasts dramatically with the rigor or seeming rigor of NL's list. More than being and substance was 'sloughed off'. These surprises and mysteries and discontinuities aside, we will take this first ground for the continuity hypothesis seriously and examine it in the next section.

The second ground of the continuity hypothesis is that Peirce never made an argument for the necessity of any of the later lists of categories and, hence, that he must have been relying on the argument made in NL. Murray Murphey, who held that NL and phaneroscopy are mutually incompatible systems, claimed that the doctrine of NL follows 'from a rigorous analysis of the concept of representation' and that the 'presupposition underlying the categories' is that there are truths a priori about 'laws governing symbols' (1961, p.91); by contrast, 'the phenomenology does not show why it [the relational analysis of experience] should be made' or why those 'categories are either necessary or particularly important' (1961, p.368). Notice Murphey's assumptions, that a philosopher must propound a philosophical system and that a philosophical system must consist of necessary truths demonstrated a priori. Other scholars, also making those assumptions and agreeing, implicitly, with the contrast Murphey draws between the rigor of NL's argument and the absence of argument in phaneroscopy, suppose, for those very reasons, that the argument for the phaneroscopic categories *is* the argument of NL (e.g., Apel 1980, pp. 84–85). To draw that conclusion, they do not need to assert that NL and phaneroscopy are identical systems or even that NL's three intermediate categories and the phaneroscopic categories are exactly the same. But they do have to assume that there is sufficient commonality between the two lists of categories that NL's argument is adaptable to the phaneroscopic categories. And that would make NL, as it provides a key argument otherwise missing, the keystone of Peirce's system.

The third ground is that there is much else in NL, in addition to the three intermediate categories, which anticipates features of Peirce's later thought. First of all, the category of representation is described – as in JSP's doctrine of thought-signs – as involving three items: the representation itself, its object, and the 'interpretant'. And this, it is said, anticipates his later theory of signs, famously triadic. Secondly, in NL§14, representations are subdivided into 'Likenesses', 'Indices or Signs', and 'Symbols', according as to whether their 'relation to their objects' consists in or is grounded on, respectively, a 'community in some quality', a 'correspondence in fact', or 'an imputed character', and this, with important amendments, is the later division of signs (NL's 'representations', not its 'signs') into icons, indices, and symbols. Finally, the Hellenistic and medieval 'trivium' – grammar, logic, and rhetoric – is reinterpreted, in NL§15, as studies of 'the reference of symbols in general' to, respectively, their 'grounds or imputed characters', their objects ('the formal conditions of the truth of symbols'), and their interpretants ('their power of appealing to a mind'), and in succeeding years that revision was repeatedly revised and renamed, eventually dividing the theory of signs into three compartments. It is as if Peirce had an entire system of philosophy in mind from the very first.

The fourth and last ground for the continuity hypothesis is that Peirce himself in his later years many times praised NL in the highest terms. Examples will be cited in Section G, where those passages will be shown not to mean what they have so often been taken to mean. In the next section, the first three grounds are examined and rejected.

F

Let us begin with the second ground, that phaneroscopy needs an argument of a kind that is wanting, unless it is supplied by NL. It rests on a mistaken assumption. Murphey remarks, as if it were a devastating fault, that Peirce's 1902–1903 classification of sciences '… made it impossible for him to prove that his categories are either necessary or particularly important' (1961, p.368). Exactly. If philosophy is to become a set of empirical inquiries, of which phaneroscopy is one, then, like the other empirical sciences, it must proceed by way of conjecture, followed by hard work, without the comfort of guarantees a priori. There can be no proof, before making the attempt, that a relational analysis of experience will result in anything interesting, or even that it is possible. Certainly, it is not necessary to parse experience in that way, or in any way. What reason Peirce may have had to suppose that a relational analysis of experience *might* prove fruitful is a different question, one we shall address in the next section.

The second ground, in other words, fails to take Peirce's extension of empiricism to philosophy seriously. It assumes, mistakenly, that *more geometrico* remains philosophy's ideal. If NL's argument could be adapted to the phaneroscopic categories, and if Murphey is correct that that argument is a priori, then the phaneroscopic categories would not be empirical; they would not be phaneroscopic.

Even were an argument wanted, one for the five categories of NL could not be an argument for the three phaneroscopic categories, as the differences between the two lists are too great. To show this, let us examine the continuity hypothesis' first ground, that the two lists are the same, or are so essentially.

All categories are concepts; what is conceived of may be conceptual or not. The first two phaneroscopic categories are of nonconceptual aspects of experience. Are NL's supposedly corresponding categories, of quality and relation, also concepts of the nonconceptual? No, they are not. NL defines quality as 'reference to a ground' and describes a ground as 'abstract'; but abstraction is general and conceptual. NL's category of quality comprises monadic qualities only, but those qualities are not phaneroscopic 1sts; rather, they are *types* of monadic quality; they are 3rds. The relation of a relate to a correlate, as it pertains to their likeness or difference *in quality*, is conceptual, too, if quality is conceptual. It is not a category of the dyadic element in experience.

The same conclusion may be established in a second way, on Peirce's own authority. NL derives its list of categories by an analysis of what is implied in any propositional unification of the manifold; but a proposition and all the terms it contains are said in NL§15 to be symbols, and symbols in NL§14 were distinguished from other representations by their being general; from which it follows that NL's categories not only are general but are *of* the general, that is, the conceptual, only. Twenty-nine years later, in 1896, Peirce, referring to NL, rejected its implication that propositions can be wholly analyzed as in all respects general. A proposition, to be assertible or deniable, true or false, requires, he argued, in addition to symbols, signs that are not general in meaning (2.332–43). In having assumed in NL the opposite, '… there I was wrong' (2.340).

The only item in NL that is portrayed as nonconceptual is the manifold of sense impressions. It is nonconceptual because it is waiting, as it were, to be unified under concepts. The contents of this manifold, as being impressions, that is, compelling attention, would seem to be 2nds, and the contents of these 2nds would seem to be 1sts. But no such account of the manifold is provided in NL, which provides no account of it at all. We can think about the manifold in terms of the phaneroscopic categories, but that does not prove that Peirce in 1867 was thinking about it in those terms.

No statement in NL suggests an idea of phaneroscopic 1stness, despite there being some places where it would have been natural to introduce 1stness, however named, had Peirce then had an idea of it. There are two seeming suggestions in NL of phaneroscopic 2ndness, one in §2, the other in §3. In the first, 'attention' is described, as also in JSP, as being 'the pure denotative power of the mind' bereft of 'connotation' – bereft, therefore, of conception. But this gives the game away. Peirce's phaneroscopy does not teach us that 2ndness is a power of mind to 'denote' an object; instead, phaneroscopic 2ndness consists in a consciousness of a force exerted against our resistance or of something resisting a force we exert. It implies activity on our part, but it also implies an opposing force. It is an awareness of that opposition. It is not a power of attention. However, in §14, opposition is cited, indeed emphasized; this is the second suggestion of phaneroscopic 2ndness. There, the category of relation is divided in twain, according as relate and correlate either are compared in quality alone or 'the correlate is set over against the relate, and there is some sense of *opposition*' (Peirce's emphasis). In the former, the quality is prescindable from the relation, while in the latter the relate and correlate share a feature not prescindable from their opposition – a feature, then, though Peirce did not say this in so many words, that consists in their mutual opposition.[20] This definitely suggests the phaneroscopic idea of 2ndness, or would have done so had Peirce said anything to imply that the 'sense of opposition' is not conceptual. He appears to have glimpsed a prospect that NL could not accommodate.

The third ground, that NL anticipates much of Peirce's later thought, does not pertain directly to the list of categories and therefore it cannot make up for the failure of the first two grounds. It does, however, embrace some intriguing and problematic passages, such as the one last noticed, in which the framework of NL is transcended, not to say burst asunder, and other passages in which similarity of structure masks difference in content. The division of representations, into likenesses, indices, and symbols, illustrates the point. Likeness is defined as 'community in some quality' (NL§14), where a quality, remember, is an abstraction, a concept.[21] Indexicality is defined as 'correspondence in fact', without any explanation of what this correspondence might be. We noted in connection with JSP that it was not until 1885 that Peirce discovered the need for signs, namely, indices, that relate nonconceptually to their objects. The fact that he saw this as being a discovery proves that he had not earlier conceived of indices as signifying nonconceptually.

[20] Where I have used the word 'feature', Peirce wrote 'quality', which suggests that the category of quality should be subdivided into the monadic and the dyadic, that is, into qualities prescindable from relation and those not prescindable from relation. But that would be inconsistent with the way in which NL defines the category of quality – and also inconsistent with this quality being phaneroscopic 1stness.

[21] In the same passage, NL§14, symbols are distinguished from likenesses and indices in being general, implying that the latter are not general. But this contradicts the assertion that likeness consists in 'community in some quality'.

G

Statements that Peirce himself made, from 1896 to 1909, praising NL and asserting its importance, constitute the fourth and final ground for the continuity hypothesis. The four chief of these are: 'On May 14, 1867, after three years of almost insanely concentrated thought, hardly interrupted even by sleep, I produced my one contribution to philosophy in the "New List of Categories"'; 'after the hardest two years' mental work that I have ever done in my life, I found myself with but a single assured result of any positive importance'; NL is the work 'perhaps the least unsatisfactory, from a logical point of view, that I ever succeeded in producing'; and NL was one of his 'two strongest philosophical works'. These are usually quoted (e.g., in editorial comments at W2:502 and EP1:1) exactly as here, out of context. We shall now examine them in context.

We must separate what is demonstrably unreliable in Peirce's recollections from what may be taken more seriously. The most famous claim, that NL is 'my one contribution to philosophy', is from the draft c.1905 of a letter possibly never sent (8.213). The claim in it, of 'three years of almost insanely concentrated thought, hardly interrupted even by sleep', is patently false, as during those years he was employed full time at the Coast and Geodetic Survey and delivered two sets of public lectures, a dozen each, all highly original and on wide-ranging erudite topics, only some of which bear on the topic of NL. In the next remark quoted above, from a never completed manuscript of 1907, the three years have been reduced to two (EP2:424). In addition to these claims, there are a number of similar claims made with reference to the same years concerning the time spent studying Kant's first Critique. As NL is obviously a product of that study, these claims should be compared to the two foregoing, as supporting or contradicting them. In 1898, Peirce wrote, 'In the early sixties I was a passionate devotee of Kant, at least as regarded the Transcendental Analytic in the *Critic of the Pure Reason*'; he then described difficulties in Kant's list of categories, concluding, 'Here there was a problem to which I devoted three hours a day for two years …' (4.2). But in a passage c.1897, the hours per day were remembered as two rather than three, the years as three rather than two, and the whole Critique, not the Transcendental Deduction alone, was studied, '… until I almost knew the whole book by heart …' (1.4). The amount of time spent and the period within which it was spent are not important. Despite their exaggerations and inconsistencies, these claims are evidence that Peirce genuinely felt that he had worked hard at the Kantian problem that issued in NL and that it resulted in a 'single assured result' of 'positive importance'.

But what was that result? What was the 'one contribution to philosophy'? In the letter draft c.1905, the contribution is not specified, unless it is by words occurring in the next two sentences: '... this is, if possible, even less original than my maxim of pragmatism;... My three categories are nothing but Hegel's three grades of thinking'. Elsewhere, he distinguished his categories from Hegel's (EP2:164,177). The reference to Hegel is especially problematic, as his references to that philosopher are among his most inconsistent. This passage does not state that it was by reading Hegel that he came to these categories; in 4.2, quoted above, Peirce said that in 'the early sixties' he knew Hegel only through a book about his philosophy and that he was 'repelled' by him. The main point to be gleaned from all this is that it is not NL as a whole that Peirce said was his one contribution. That contribution, he said, was 'in' NL. Might it be nothing but the three intermediate categories?

The reference to a 'single assured result' occurs in a context at once more helpful and more problematic. That result is specified in the next sentence:

> This was that there are but three elementary forms of predication or signification, which as I originally named them (but with bracketed additions now made to render the terms more intelligible) were *Qualities* (of feeling), (dyadic) *Relations*, and (predications of) *Representations*. It must have been in 1866 that Professor De Morgan ... [sent] me a copy of his memoir ... I at once fell to upon it ... (EP2:424–25)

Here we have by Peirce himself an unambiguous identification of NL's intermediate three categories with the three phaneroscopic categories. It might seem that this answers all our questions and that much wasted effort could have been avoided had I quoted it earlier. However, it cannot be trusted. The reference to De Morgan was by way of explaining how Peirce discovered at so early a date three categories distinguished by orders of relational complexity. For, it was De Morgan who, in 1860, in a memoir not published until 1864, demonstrated the inadequacy of syllogistic logic to account for reasoning about relations. But if Peirce had read that memoir before or while composing NL, why is that essay based on an assumption of the adequacy of syllogistic logic? Daniel Merrill notes that 'Peirce's later recollections', about when he read De Morgan's memoir, 'are contradictory and even inconsistent with known facts', and he gives reason to conclude that Peirce did not receive the memoir until after April 1868 (W2:xliv).

It would seem, then, that in this comment Peirce was reading his later thought into NL, composed forty years earlier. Certainly, he did not in NL describe the intermediate three categories as 'forms of predication or signification'! Far from it; they are introduced as implicated in monadic predication. And, far from making those categories 'more intelligible', their phaneroscopic glosses are inconsistent with the definitions of them given in NL, at least those of 'quality' and 'relation'. 'Quality of feeling' was Peirce's term for phaneroscopic 1stness, which, as we have seen, NL's 'quality' is not.

We have arrived at this point: Peirce's one contribution, on his own express telling of it, is not NL. Instead, it is his three phaneroscopic categories. They are somehow 'in' NL but made 'more intelligible' in his own later, phaneroscopic writings. This, however, is not the whole story.

Peirce's praise of NL 'from a logical point of view' might readily be dismissed, but that would be a mistake. It could be dismissed for this reason: a work can be 'strong' or well-argued even while being wrong. Furthermore, Peirce's reference to NL as 'the least unsatisfactory ... that I ever succeeded in producing', so often quoted, occurs in a context, not quoted, which makes it ironic. We looked at that context, 2.332–43, earlier: it is an extended criticism of an error NL committed ('... there I was wrong'). Peirce's 'least unsatisfactory' is, in his own estimation, unsatisfactory. I think, nevertheless, that his praise of NL, albeit ironic, is to be taken seriously. It was important to him that NL was argued rigorously; for, it is the very rigor of its argument that makes NL's failure – the emergence within it of three 'numerical' categories that explode its assumptions – significant. A *reductio ad absurdum* succeeds only if it is rigorous.

And that rigor remained important, even crucial, to the later development of Peirce's thought, his phaneroscopy especially. This, for the reason already cited: there is no a priori demonstration that a relational analysis of experience will result in anything interesting. There is no accounting at all for Peirce's developing this new science, nor for the specific way in which he developed it, turning to the algebra of relations for a descriptive vocabulary, except on the ground that he already had a good idea of what such an analysis would show. He had that idea, because orders of relation emerged within a study based on the contrary assumption, that a logic of monadic predicates suffices. Their emerging despite that assumption, showed that orders of relation have a power not to be denied. Many years had elapsed before that discovery was fully appreciated and thirty-five elapsed before it began to be mastered.

In the manuscript of 1885 in which he returned after a nineteen-year hiatus to thinking about categories, Peirce said this of Kant:

> It is remarkable that although the system of formal logic upon which Kant founded his list of categories was extremely imperfect, yet his categories themselves are at least highly important conceptions. (W5:236)

Something similar applies to the 'New List'. Peirce, in commenting on Kant, may well have been thinking of his own case.

H

Peirce's style of thinking was conjectural, to state a bold hypothesis starkly. Making an idea definite enough to imply much, without being committed to every detail, is characteristic of theoretical work in modern science. Inquiry is advanced by exploring those implications and seeing whether the idea, with this or that modification, can successfully be applied and prove fruitful. Softening the contours of Peirce's theory of thought-signs in JSP, so as to make it consistent with common sense, with his own later views, and with itself, is like smoothing out the facets of a cut diamond, so as to restore it to the dullness of a pebble. It forecloses learning from the conjecture. Reading Peirce's later views into NL similarly deprives us of a theory illuminating to explore. And it makes a mystery of his intellectual development.

CHAPTER 6

Devolution of the Cosmogonic Program

We expect that a flipped coin will turn up heads sometimes and sometimes tails, in no particular pattern, with the two outcomes over the long run being about equal. If the coin keeps landing heads-up, much to the benefit of our opponent, we demand an explanation. So also if no money is at stake but the coin persistently turns up one way five times in a row and then the other way five times in a row over a long series of flips. Disorganization requires no explanation; organization does. In 1884, Peirce delivered a lecture at Johns Hopkins, 'Design and Chance' (EP1:215–24), in which he declared that laws of nature are in need of explanation as much as anything is:

> Among the things that demand explanation, then, are the laws of physics; and not this law or that law only but every single law .... What is the cause of the restriction of extended bodies to three dimensions?
>
> And then the general fact that there are laws, how is that to be explained? (218)

One law might be explained by being shown to be a special case of a broader law, but that strategy must leave at least one law unexplained. It could not explain why there are any laws at all; it could not explain the fact of lawfulness. Now, how could the general fact of law be explained, unless by laws having evolved out of lawlessness?

> We want a theory of the evolution of physical law. We ought to suppose that as we go back into the indefinite past not merely special laws but *law* itself is found to be less and less determinate. (218–19)

In his fragmentary, unfinished treatise of 1887–1888, 'A Guess at the Riddle', Peirce wrote to the same effect:

> ... conformity with law is a fact requiring to be explained; and since Law in general cannot be explained by any law in particular, the explanation must consist in showing how law is developed out of pure chance, irregularity, indeterminacy. (EP1:276)

That, at its most general, is Peirce's cosmogony. As so far stated, it does not differ from the ancient Greek idea that the ordered Cosmos emerged from an initial Chaos, except that the reference to law is to the laws of modern physics. The details concern how those laws might have evolved, and that, too, distinguishes this cosmogony from its classical forebears. Peirce extrapolated from types of statistical explanation that had newly appeared in the nineteenth-century science, and the statistical ideas employed therein did not exist before the modern period (Hacking 1975 traces our idea(s) of probability to 1660).

There are two criteria which this theory, in one or another of its detailed formulations, must satisfy. The first, taken for granted, Peirce did not state. It is that the explanation of how laws might have evolved must make sense. In coin-tossing, chance is variability of cause and absence of pattern among outcomes, but each toss presumably conforms to the laws of mechanics. So also in physics and biology, it is assumed that individual events are lawful, and thus it is not obvious that one can extrapolate from statistical explanations in those sciences to an explanation of lawfulness in general. The interest of Peirce's cosmology or cosmogony – he used both terms, the latter narrower – centers on the ways in which he attempted to make his hypothesis work. He tried in several ways, producing a sequence of mutually inconsistent variant cosmologies.

The second criterion is one that Peirce stated several times, as it was central to the motivation of his theory. It was that the cosmogony should prove fruitful in guiding empirical research in the special sciences. By the 1880s, physics had seemed to come to a standstill. Peirce's idea was that an account of how laws evolved will entail something about their form, or the kinds of law they are, and that this, by narrowing the range of possibilities, should aid in the discovery of laws additional to those already known. However, he never developed the hypothesis to a point where it could prove fruitful, and therefore it was not fruitful, and therefore it did not satisfy this second criterion.

Some months after the 1884 lecture, Peirce lost his position at Johns Hopkins. In the ensuing years, he worked with enthusiasm on his cosmogony. In 1891–1893, he published a series of five cosmological articles in the *Monist*. Between the appearance of the first and second of these articles, he lost his position at the Coast and Geodetic Survey and never after acquired a reliable source of income. After 1893, there are diminishing references to the theory. We will note interesting variants proposed in 1898 and 1904. Peirce never admitted defeat, but the cosmogony was allowed to fade away. Only the general idea of it – that laws must have evolved and that chance ('absolute chance', that is, utter lawlessness) is a positive factor in the universe – remained.

Gestated in a period of personal turmoil, Peirce's cosmology has had an equally troubled reception. Andrew Reynolds, in his useful book, begins by dividing comment on it in twain: critical by scientifically minded philosophers and sympathetic by those less scientifically minded (2002, p.1). And this, as Reynolds implies, is odd. For, the cosmology was intended to be scientific. The critics, then, would seem to have the better part of the argument. Those who celebrate the theory ignore Peirce's own view of what it should be; they write as if its abstract statement suffices and as if that statement is an argument a priori establishing the cosmology as a fundamental part of a grand system.[1] Nor do they attempt to answer the trenchant criticisms made by W. B. Gallie (1952, pp.215–42) and by Rulon Wells (1964). Most remarkably, they have provided no detailed explication of the several difficult texts in which Peirce tried hardest to explain how laws might evolve. The closest to such an attempt was by Murray Murphey (1961, Ch.XVI), who did not conclude that Peirce succeeded. Christopher Hookway, in a note to his own critical but sympathetic yet inconclusive discussion (1985, Ch.IX), remarked that 'Peirce's cosmology has not received any fully adequate treatment in the secondary literature' (p.291n2); Reynolds, quoting this statement, writes, 'Today, seventeen years later, the situation remains arguably unchanged' (2002, p.1). Reynolds himself provides much-needed background about the nineteenth-century science that Peirce presupposed (see also Hilary Putnam's commentary on the final three of the 1898 lectures, RLT:78–102), but expressly omits a 'deeper analysis' of the cosmology.

The aim of this chapter is twofold. Successful or not, Peirce's variant attempts at a cosmogony are fascinating, especially when they are not conflated with one another but each is examined in its own terms. I sketch each of these.[2] Secondly, my purpose is to refute the view that Peirce was engaged in building a system of which the cosmogony is a part. His cosmogony was not a brick in a philosophical edifice but a rough sketch of a hypothesis to be developed and tested. Hence, it defined a program of scientific research. The devolution of that program was part of Peirce's progress.

---

[1] For example, Turley (1977), Esposito (1980), Raposa (1989), Hausman (1993), pp.168–93, Sheriff (1994), Anderson (1995), pp.63–67, and Parker (1998, Ch.8).

[2] This chapter is based on two articles, Short (2010a, 2010b), which provide more detail.

It is not my purpose to discuss the relation of Peirce's cosmogony to contemporary cosmological speculation, which is at least as bold as his and sometimes similar. Peirce's cosmogonic writings preceded relativity theory, quantum mechanics, and the discovery of subatomic particles[3], on all of which contemporary cosmology builds. Though he cannot be said to have anticipated theories that are grounded differently than his, what he did anticipate – because his reason for it was sound – is that any progress in physics, after the 1880s, would have to depart so far from common sense as to challenge our assumptions about what makes a theory intelligible. That argument is found in the reflections, described in the next section, that led Peirce into cosmological conjecture.

A

Even in his twenties, when he was supposed to have been immersed in Kant's first Critique, Peirce's concern was with the growth of empirical knowledge. In his 1865 Harvard lectures, he substituted for Kant's question, how synthetic judgments a priori are possible, a broader question: 'The question of this whole course of lectures is how are synthetic judgments in general possible' (W1:248). By broadening Kant's question, he abandoned Kant's project (the point was repeated in 1878, EP1:167–9). The question about judgment turned out to be one about how 'material', that is, nondeductive, inference is valid: '… the fundamental inquiry of the whole course, [is] that of the grounds of inference' (W1:286). In these lectures (*vide supra* Ch.1, A), Peirce discussed induction and introduced a second form of material (later, he would say 'ampliative') inference, viz., abduction (then named 'hypothesis'). Induction generalizes from a sample. Abduction introduces an explanatory hypothesis; its premises include a description of a phenomenon to be explained. Now, the premises of an ampliative inference may be true while its conclusion is false. What, then, makes such an inference valid? This is the question that led, in a series of steps, to the cosmogony.

In 1865, but more dramatically in the 1868–1869 papers in the *Journal of Speculative Philosophy*, the validity of ampliative inference is defined with reference to the long run of scientific inquiry, which combines all three forms of inference; such validity consists, not, as in deduction, in

---

[3] The first subatomic particle discovered was the electron, by J. J. Thompson in 1897. The last of Peirce's cosmological trial-balloons, in 1898 and 1904, show no effect of that discovery.

never going wrong, but in progressing through error toward the truth. Without abduction, there would be no theories to test, so inquiry begins with abduction. From theories, predictions of regularities may be deduced, so that observation yields either refutation or partial inductive confirmation. And induction, as additional samples are taken, is self-corrective. However, there is a problem with this account. As there are an infinite number of possible explanations of any given phenomenon, if our abductions are random guesses, then it is infinitely improbable that we should, in any finite time, hit on the correct explanation. How is it that our abductions have been close enough to the truth often enough for progress to have been made? We know that Peirce recognized this problem at least by 1878, because that is when he provided a solution to it, in the fifth of his six articles on the logic of science in the *Popular Science Monthly*, 'The Order of Nature' (EP1:170–85). An improved statement of that solution was made in 1883, in 'A Theory of Probable Inference' (W4:408–50).

As Peirce put it in 1883, progress in inquiry depends on our having 'special aptitudes for guessing right' (W4:447). In 1878, he had explained those aptitudes by natural selection: 'Without something like geometrical, kinetical, and mechanical conceptions, no animal could seize his food …' (EP1:181). Thus we have an 'instinct for truth', for apprehending the world under concepts suited to that world, so far as concerns practical purposes. However, this explanation of past progress in science had an unsettling corollary: as inquiry extends beyond the mid-range and near-by phenomena with respect to which we conduct our daily struggle for survival and our vertebrate ancestors conducted theirs, our instinct for truth will likely falter. And that prospect was already beginning to appear in nineteenth-century science, with respect both to the large or distant (the geometry of the universe) and to the small (the constitution of matter) or fast (light). Non-Euclidean geometries were developed early in the nineteenth century, based on alternatives to Euclid's parallel postulate; in his 1884 lecture, Peirce described the difficulty of determining empirically which postulate holds for the universe as a whole. And in the first of his 1891–1893 *Monist* series, 'The Architecture of Theories' (EP1:285–97), he mentioned a few examples of the increasing strangeness of science concerning light and matter, concluding, 'Thus the further progress of molecular speculation appears quite uncertain'. Indeed, 'There is room for serious doubt whether the fundamental laws of mechanics hold good for single atoms. And it seems quite likely that they are capable of motion in more than three dimensions' (288). The reference is to molecules and atoms, because this was written before the discovery of subatomic particles.[4] But if we are to examine hypotheses invoking varied numbers of dimensions, the possibilities, for that reason alone, are myriad.

What is one to do? How are we to sift the plausible from the possible, so as to have some chance of finding the truth? Galileo, whose 'principle appeal is to common sense and *il lume naturale*', '... always assumes that the true theory will be found to be a simple and natural one', but 'The further physical studies depart from phenomena which have directly influenced the growth of the mind, the less we can expect to find the laws which govern them "simple," that is, composed of a few conceptions natural to our minds' (287). If simplicity can no longer be a guide, then

> To find out much more about molecules and atoms, we must search out a natural history of laws of nature, which may fulfill that function which the presumption in favor of simple laws fulfilled in the early days of dynamics, by showing us what kind of laws we have to expect ... (288)

By a 'kind of laws' Peirce meant such forms of law as being inverse square. We have found inverse square laws to be simple and they have proven reasonably accurate; perhaps other forms can be predicted to characterize laws yet to be discovered. In October 1885, he wrote to William James,

> I have something very vast now .... It is ... an attempt to explain the laws of nature, to show their general characteristics and to trace their origin & predict new laws by the laws of the laws of nature. (Quoted in an editorial note, EP1:242)

By a new law, Peirce meant one newly known, not one newly evolved, contrary to what some commentators have assumed.[5] In a letter of about the same time to his older brother, Peirce wrote of his 'duty' to 'set forth the true nature of logic', without which 'molecular science must remain

---

[4] N-dimensional geometries had already been formulated (by Arthur Cayley in 1843; Peirce often cited Cayley); but atoms were still the smallest known particles, the electron not being discovered until 1897. It is not clear why Peirce thought that the smallest particles might move in more than three dimensions. In previous sentences, he mentioned perplexing phenomena concerning heat and light, but the sentence quoted is preceded by one that begins, 'When we come to atoms ...', suggesting a change in topic. Crookes' cathode ray experiments of 1878, published in 1879, were surely known to Peirce (he referred in the same paragraph to Crookes' radiometer experiments). Crookes concluded his 1879 paper by speculating that 'matter may exist in a fourth state', that is, neither solid, liquid, nor gas (Boorse and Motz, 1966, vol.1, p.362); but that does not entail a fourth dimension. Murphey (1961, p.327) suggests that Peirce may have had the Michelson–Morley experiment of 1887 in mind; however, his similar remark of 1885 to his brother (quoted below) suggests inspiration of an earlier date.

[5] For example, Murphey (1961, p.326). That laws may still be evolving is a possibility Peirce cautiously stated and made to be minute and slow, not something to be observed in any reasonable period.

at a stand-still. It must continue what it is, idle guess-work' (quoted in
W5:xxxvii).

The problem is more complicated than merely judging plausibility,
difficult as that itself would be. Tests vary in expense and time required,
and an implausible hypothesis might be easily disconfirmed if false but
extremely fruitful if confirmed. In such cases, the implausible should
be tested first. Peirce discussed this under the rubric, 'the economics of
research'.[6] However, judgments about ease of testing and significance
are like judgments of plausibility in depending on general ideas about
how the world works, hence, on speculative generalization from theories presently accepted. Thus Peirce in 1902 wrote, 'In light of one's
metaphysics and general conception of the department of truth dealt
with, one considers what different hypotheses have any claims to investigation.' (7.83).

That, then, is the purpose of the cosmogonic program. It was to take
the place of *il lume naturale* in guiding research. The aim was not to frame
a cosmology for its own sake, or not for its own sake only. Though Peirce
was surely interested in cosmology for its own sake, he still regarded the
test of his cosmogonic hypothesis to be its success in leading to the discovery of laws additional to those already known. This, notice, does not mark
a radical distinction between cosmology and other scientific inquiries,
but at most one of degree. Any novel hypothesis, if partially confirmed,
will suggest new lines of inquiry the success of which will provide further
confirmation.

Peirce repeatedly emphasized the scientific intent of his cosmological
thought. Thus, in 'A Guess', he wrote:

> Such is our guess of the secret of the sphynx [sic]. To raise it from the rank
> of philosophical speculation to that of a scientific hypothesis, we must show
> that consequences can be deduced from it with more or less probability
> which can be compared to observation. We must show that there is some
> method of deducing the characters of the laws which could result in this
> way ... (EP1:277)

Again, three years later, in the first article of the *Monist* series:

> ... before this can be accepted it must show itself capable of explaining the
> tridimensionality of space, the laws of motion, and the general character-
> istics of the universe, with mathematical clearness and precision ... (293)

---

[6] From 1876 on: 1.122–25, 5.600–4, 7.139–61, 220–23, 226, 230; see Rescher (1978, Ch.4) for insightful
comment; thus he anticipated Karl Popper's similar reflections (1963, pp.217–20).

He never developed his hypothesis to the point where it could be shown to have testable implications. There were only some brief and murky attempts – far from mathematical precision – to account for time and space (EP1:278, 323–24). Later, in 1898, there are some mathematical arguments (RLT:264–67), but they depend on topological assumptions additional to the cosmological hypotheses and lead to 'predictions' of doubtful testability that, in any case, are not of the forms of laws.

Its failure to satisfy the purpose Peirce gave to it aside, does his cosmogony make sense? Any cosmological hypothesis, as it seeks to account for the world within which our ideas have developed, necessarily teeters on the edge of nonsense. Take, for example, time. The word 'time' is understood in relation to irreversible processes – of memory, experience, and expectation, of birth, growth, decay, and death – and it is measured by the periodicity of processes like pendulums swinging, the rising and setting of the Sun, the sequence of the seasons. If all of these regularities are to be explained as having evolved out of some earlier, less regular state of the universe, then are we not talking about what was before time? And by what ingenuity can we rescue the phrase 'before time' from being oxymoronic? In 1887–1888, Peirce wrote, 'Our conceptions of the first stages of development, before time yet existed, must be as vague and figurative as the expressions of the first chapter of Genesis' (EP1:278). Does its being figurative make cosmology unscientific? What scientific ideas, for example, Boyle's speculation that the air has a 'spring' or Bohr's planetary model of the atom, were not initially figurative? We noted earlier that part of the work of scientists is to find ways of making an idea testable. Whether an idea is testable, or is nonsense, is not always obvious *ab initio*. Cosmology is merely an extreme case of what scientists do, which is to create intelligibility where none was.

B

How might order evolve from out of chaos? There are several well-attested examples of exactly such a process (in which, however, the chaos is not perfect), and from these Peirce extrapolated the first formulation of his cosmogony, in the aforementioned lecture of 1884.

The nebular hypothesis of Kant and Laplace, explaining the formation of the solar system, assumes deterministic laws but also an initial cloud of particles in uncoördinated motion. The number of planets and their exact orbits could not have been predicted (*sans* impossibly precise knowledge of the position and momentum of each particle), but it was nonetheless claimed that gravitational attraction and Newton's laws of motion explain how from that cloud an orderly solar system evolved. Similarly, Peirce described a game of chance of repeated plays and wagers with a large number of participants, each of whom has initially an equal sum to wager: after a long sequence of plays, a certain distribution of winnings is predictable even though, if the game is fair and skill is not a factor, it cannot be predicted where any individual player will fall into that distribution; it is as if they at first formed a homogenous cloud which later was differentiated into an order of distinct parts, winners and losers. Similarly, under conditions prevailing in the biosphere, it can be predicted that types of organism and an ecological order will evolve, though the specific forms and specific order cannot be predicted. The disorganized cloud of mechanical events and chemical reactions eventuates in interdependent forms of life, reproducing their respective kinds and occupying their respective ecological niches, generation after generation. Matter is made less homogenous by being differentiated into organic cells and into organisms, each having an inside and an outside, and each sustaining itself by imposing its organization on less organized material that it draws into itself from outside itself.

In addition to those examples, Peirce also mentioned the explanation that had then been recently developed by Maxwell and others of ideal gas law, that the volume of an enclosed gas varies with temperature and inversely with pressure: it was shown to be a statistical consequence of the uncoördinated motions of trillions of molecules, assuming that each conforms to Newton's mechanics. The Second Law of thermodynamics, that in a thermodynamically closed system, heat, if unevenly distributed, will flow toward even distribution, was also explained statistically from the same assumptions. As with games of chance and the nebular hypothesis, it is not by tracing the steps of mechanical processes that order is shown to be a consequence of disorder.

There is, however, a fundamental difference between the statistical reasoning involved in the theory of natural selection, in explaining the formation of the galaxies, and in playing games of chance, on the one hand, and its use in deriving Maxwell's laws, on the other. Whereas the former (A) are examples of local order – a solar system here or there, these winners and those losers, life on the Earth's surface – the latter (B) are universal laws. And whereas A are the products of a temporal evolution, B are the immediate consequences of the uncoördinated motions of molecules.

Within B there are other differences of interest. The gas law, like laws of mechanics, applies reversibly: changes in temperature can produce changes in volume, and changes in volume can produce changes in temperature.

But heat in a closed system will flow in but one direction, toward equal distribution. The evolutionary processes in A also have a unique temporal direction (organic decay is not the reverse of organic growth, as it does not result, alas, in youth). But they are toward differentiation and increased order, whereas the Second Law describes an evolution toward the boring uniformity of disorder. Evolutions from chaos to order do not violate the Second Law, because they occur only in systems that are open to exchanges of matter and energy with a larger world. For that reason, such evolutions must always be local.

Thus, when, in the 1884 lecture, Peirce said that 'A most important premise, playing a great part in the establishment of the Nebular Hypothesis or the Theory of Natural Selection, is that things must on the whole have proceeded from the Homogeneous to the Heterogeneous' (218), he was mistaken. On the whole, things must go the other way, toward what has famously been named 'the heat death of the universe'. Or, if not, it is for reasons not contained in the theories and explanations Peirce cited. Nor is it so much a premiss as it is a conclusion, that in A heterogeneity evolves from out of homogeneity. And only if 'proceeded' is taken in a nontemporal sense, can we speak of some laws of physics as having proceeded from the chaos of molecular motion. The use of these examples to suggest how the laws of nature may have evolved is therefore questionable. The first examples (A) are not of the evolution of universal laws and they are not examples of the evolution of order on the cosmic scale. The second set (B) are not examples of evolution.

In addition, there is this problem. Both sets are indeed examples of how 'chance begets order', to use a phrase of 1893 (EP1:358), where universal law as well as local organization is taken to be a form of order. But 'chance' cannot refer in these cases to lawless occurrence. For, in each case, it is assumed or, at least, not denied, that individual events (molecular motions, coin flips, genetic mutations, the adventures and misadventures of organic life) conform to laws, for example, of mechanics. Chance, in these cases, consists in causes varying unsystematically in ways not known, so that, from the types of past outcomes, the type of the next particular outcome cannot be predicted. In that sense, the particular outcomes are mutually independent. For example, a coin landing heads-up this time has no effect on the probability that it will land heads-up next time. In a gas, molecules whiz around with no effect on one another (gravitational attraction being negligible) except in the relatively rare cases of collision, so that the location at a given time of one molecule is independent (largely, not entirely: for example, no two can be at the same point at the same time) of the locations of all the others. But, for his purpose, Peirce had to suppose that, in the beginning, individual events conformed to no law at all and that, in later stages of the evolution of law, not all events conform perfectly to such laws as have begun to form.

Peirce was aware of this difference. It is why he introduced the term 'absolute chance' and distinguished it from 'ordinary chance' (219). Absolute chance is lawless occurrence (either where there are no laws at all or as departing from existing laws).[7] Chance in the ordinary sense, he said, is 'merely relative to the causes that are taken into account'; that is, it depends on not all causes being taken into account. Ordinary chance thus suggests the classical idea of probability, that it is a measure of our ignorance. Peirce, as we saw (Ch.1, A) adopted Venn's alternative, which makes ordinary chance to be a relative frequency, empirically measurable.

Whether chance is absolute or is ordinary, and whether the calculus of probability be interpreted classically or in terms of the frequency theory, the applicability of that calculus depends on the events in question occurring independently of one another. Let us be precise: events of type X are mutually independent with respect to a second type, Y, when the probability that a given event of type X is also of type Y is not conditional on other events of type X being, or not being, of type Y. It makes no difference whether independence is a factor of the causal situation or is due to there being no causality at all. That must be the reason why Peirce asserted that 'The laws of the two kinds of chance are in the main the same' (219).

So far, so good. But in order to apply the laws of probability, there must be events of some sort. There must be discrete events and they must be of definite kinds. There must be events of type X which vary in being either of type Y also or not being of type Y. Now, in a condition of complete lawlessness, can there be any events at all? Any event must be of a type and being of a type is conforming to a law. Peirce himself admitted the problem three years later in 'A Guess at the Riddle' (hereafter, 'A Guess', EP1:245–279):

> The existence of things consists in their regular behavior .... Not only substances, but events, too, are constituted by regularities .... The original chaos, therefore, where there was no regularity, was in effect a state of mere indeterminacy, in which nothing existed or really happened. (278)

---

[7] Contrary to what is so often asserted, Peirce did not anticipate quantum physics, and not only because he could not have anticipated the reasoning that led to the quantum revolution. His idea of absolute chance was of lawlessness, not probabilistic law. At most, one can say that Peirce and quantum physics both make chance to be a positive factor in the universe. So did Lucretius, in the first-century BC.

If nothing existed or really happened, if there were no events of identifiable types, then there was nothing that the laws of probability may be applied to. There were no heads, no tails, no coins to flip, and no flips. The statistical reasoning of a Maxwell or a Darwin presupposes that there are things of determinate character; and therefore Peirce's extrapolation from the examples he cited does not work. Gallie noted that fact already in 1957 (pp.127–28), only to be ignored, not answered, by Peirce enthusiasts.

C

'A Guess', having recognized the problem, then struggles with it. After the words last quoted, Peirce continued:

> Out of the womb of indeterminacy we must say that there would have come something by the principle of firstness, which we may call a flash. Then by the principle of habit there would have been a second flash. (278)

Suddenly, as it were by a flash, we are offered two 'principles', not mentioned in 1884. Where do they come from? What do they mean? Are they consistent with the original idea of the cosmogony?

As noted above (Ch.5, E), Peirce in the 1880s and 90s applied his vaguely conceived and numerically designated categories in a variety of ways. Here, in 1887–1888, 'the principle of firstness' is, apparently, the principle that something may occur without cause, ergo, second to nothing and in that sense 'first'. But after 1902, occurrence *per se* falls under 2ndness; it would never be named a 1st. In 'A Guess', a few paragraphs earlier, he wrote that '... three elements are active in the world: first, chance; second, law; third, habit-taking' (277). But law, in the phaneroscopy, is quintessentially a 3rd (as there is no 4thness, habit-taking would be ranged, with the habits taken, under 3rdness). These discrepancies between Peirce's earlier and later usage need cause us no worry. The only error would be ours, if we supposed that his uses of the same terms always denote the same categories.

'The principle of firstness', then, would seem to be that something – a determinate flash – can come from sheer indeterminacy, that is, nothing. But what was this first flash or, for that matter, the second? What was its content or character? How can flashes be distinguished as two? And what makes one first, the other second? Indeed, what makes them flashes?

The second principle, 'the principle of habit', evidently refers not to the operation of a habit but to the formation of a habit. As Peirce said in a fragment of 1886, 'If the universe is thus progressing from a state of all but pure chance to a state of all but complete determination by law, we must suppose that there is an original, elemental, tendency of things to acquire determinate properties, to take habits' (EP1:243). If laws are products of evolution, then, like the habits organisms acquire, they at first were not but later were: hence this broad use of the word 'habit' to encompass laws of nature. However, to assert habit-taking as a 'principle' is to add to the cosmogonic hypothesis as originally formulated. In order to explain known laws of physics, Peirce postulated a principle unknown in physics. Nor is it, like the laws of probability theory, a truth of mathematics; if it is a law at all, it is a positive truth about the actual world, a logically contingent fact. Now, habit-formation is exemplified, so far as has ever been observed, nowhere but among ourselves and other animals (Peirce tried in 1892 to extend it to vegetable life also: *vide infra*, Section E). The fact that animals, through experience, acquire habits, might be explained in one way or another. Projected onto the universe, a principle of habit-taking looks a good deal like a law, albeit one of tendency only: that what has been done will tend to be repeated and, more often repeated, more likely to be repeated. But why is there this law? There can be no explanation. For, as this law is 'original, elemental', it is inexplicable.

Thus the aim, to explain all positive law, was abandoned. Or so it would seem. But in these same pages, Peirce reiterated that aim (as quoted above, in the first paragraph of this chapter). What are we to make of this? Despite the claim, made by the editors of *The Essential Peirce*, that 'A Guess' is 'perhaps Peirce's greatest and most original contribution to speculative philosophy' (EP1:245), we should not ask too much of a work that was not made ready for publication – that was, in fact, only the sketch of a few chapters of a book never brought closer than that to completion. The importance of 'A Guess' is, rather, that in it we can hear, as it were, Peirce thinking aloud, struggling to work out some new ideas and to solve the problems they raise. It is not surprising that in it we should witness him trying to combine the two halves of a contradiction. It is unfair to Peirce to label such writing his 'greatest' contribution. To be sure, he himself, in these pages, grandly declared: 'Such is our guess of the secret of the Sphynx [sic]' (277). But that is only the rhetorical trope under which he hoped to organize the book which he at that point thought he could write; we are not justified in accepting it as a considered judgment about what he actually achieved. Respect for an author requires that we do not ignore his own judgment about what was fit to be published. Let us turn, then, to what he did publish on this theme, the series of five cosmological articles in the *Monist*, 1891–1893.

D

The first article, 'The Architecture of Theories', outlines the doctrine of the whole and names it 'objective idealism' (a term Peirce used only in this period):

> The one intelligible theory of the universe is objective idealism, that matter is effete mind, inveterate habits becoming physical laws. (293)

Matter, hence, material objects, hence, organisms and, presumably, persons have evolved out of mind, which comes first. 'Mind' is here to be understood as denoting feeling, primarily, where feeling is defined as 'all that is immediately present, such as pain, blue, cheerfulness ...' (290). Present to what? Peirce did not say, but presumably he meant present to consciousness. Before there was a physical world, however, there could have been no one and nothing that is conscious. It follows that feelings must initially have been unfelt, that is, not located in anyone's consciousness. Thus, '... in the beginning, – infinitely remote, – there was a chaos of *unpersonalized* feeling ...' (my emphasis): feeling 'sporting here and there in pure arbitrariness' (297). We shall see (Section E) that Peirce's doctrine in this period was that consciousness is substantival, consisting not in the possession of feelings but in the feelings themselves. Hence, if there were feelings sporting unfelt, there *was* consciousness – before there were any beings capable of being conscious. What we call *a* consciousness – a person or organism that is conscious – must therefore be something more than consciousness *per se*, that is, feelings. Perhaps such a consciousness is an organization of feelings in which some feelings are central and heightened, others peripheral and dim; and perhaps such organization occurs only through – or is – an organism.

That the world is essentially mind is idealism. That this mind is not yours or mine or anyone's but is independent of persons makes it objective. Thus the label, 'objective idealism'. Normally, an idealism that is objective, such as Hegel's, identifies mind with conceptual thinking or reason, not with feeling, and an idealism, such as Berkeley's, that identifies mind with the nonconceptual, is subjective. Peirce did it differently, though only in the 1890s; his earlier idealism, in the 1868–1869 essays, was conceptual. In the 1890s, he objectified what most philosophers suppose is subjective, viz., the contents of sensation and emotion. One extraordinary implication of this extraordinary doctrine is that we are acquainted with the nature of primordial existence by reflecting on our own minds, since the original chaos was composed of the sort of stuff that forms the immediate contents of our consciousnesses. Cosmology by introspection!

Matter is comprised of substances, such as earth, air, and water, of particles, such as electrons, and larger entities, such as stones and stars; and each of these is what it is because of how it behaves. An electron that does not repel other electrons is not an electron; a stone that floats and vanishes and has a sense of humor is not a stone. The laws of the behavior of physical things are here said to have been originally habits of mind, that is, habits that evolved from feelings sporting – we shall postpone to the next section considering what that might mean – and that have become exceptionless or nearly so. Matter, being law-governed, is 'effete mind' because it has lost the spontaneity of feelings sporting arbitrarily. This suggests that our minds – indeed, that we – fall between the arbitrariness of the initial chaos and the dead regularity of matter. All living things are where, in the present stage of the universe, spontaneity is still possible, by which novel organizations may be created and new laws formed. '… no exact conformity is required by the mental law. Nay, exact conformity would be in downright conflict with the law; since it would instantly crystallise [sic] thought and prevent all further formation of habit' (292).

Why is this the 'one intelligible theory of the universe'? A dualism of mind and matter, Peirce suggested, is unintelligible, because it makes of the relation of mind to matter a mystery. That leaves two possibilities, that matter explains mind or that mind explains matter. On the assumption that the first fails, that leaves idealism as the only intelligible option. In 'Architecture', however, this is hardly more than asserted: 'The materialistic doctrine … requires us to suppose that a certain kind of mechanism can feel …', which is 'repugnant' to common sense and 'irreducible to reason' (292). In addition, freedom or creativity cannot be explained mechanistically: '… exact law obviously never can produce heterogeneity out of homogeneity; and arbitrary heterogeneity is the feature of the universe the most manifest and characteristic' (289).[8]

In addition to these supposed advantages, an objective idealism of feeling-qualities had another attraction for Peirce. He consistently, from at least 1871 (EP1:91), maintained the doctrine of immediate perception or naïve realism, namely, that the world is generally as it appears to us to be. Not everything that looks blue is blue, but blue, as it is experienced, is a genuine feature of the world; so also for all the other so-called secondary qualities. And not those only, but also such emotional qualities

---

[8] But is not that exactly what the Kant-Laplace hypothesis asserts – that out of the undifferentiated cloud of cosmic matter, the deterministic laws of Newtonian physics produced the solar systems, with its central sun and orbiting planets?

as cheerfulness. If we find a spring day, with its fresh breeze and blue sky and buds bursting and birds chirping, cheerful, that is because it is. Now, how can this doctrine be defended against the clear teaching of modern science that, in reality, colors, etc. are purely physical and fully described mathematically (by shape, size, energy, wavelength, etc.) alone? Well, that objection to the doctrine of immediate perception would be blocked were feelings the stuff of the universe.[9]

We now know what the 'flashes' spoken of in 'A Guess' are: they are feelings. These flashes come from nothing, but the physical universe has a source, as it comes from them. However, its evolution is no longer to be explained by the laws of probability alone. Instead, a positive law of habit-taking is assumed, now referred to as the 'law of mental action' or 'law of growth of mind' and described as 'generalization' (291). Later, as in the title of the third essay of the series, it is named 'the law of mind'. Thus, it is only physical law, and not all positive law, that is to be explained. Peirce still struggled against that conclusion, but with only partial success, as follows.

'Architecture' reasserts the original aim of the cosmogony: 'Law is *par excellence* the thing that wants a reason' (288) – no restriction here to physical law! And therefore habit-taking is itself said to be something that evolved: the chaos of feeling sporting arbitrarily '… would have started the germ of a generalizing tendency. Its other sportings would be evanescent, but this would have a growing virtue. Thus, the tendency to habit would be started …' (297). In later essays in the series, habit-taking is twice referred to as 'primordial' (EP1:331, 347), but the second reference is followed by a statement that the 'principle of habit' is '… itself due to the growth by habit of an infinitesimal chance tendency toward habit-taking …'. Habit is adduced to explain the growth of habit, and therefore habit remains primordial. The *reign* of the law of mind – its *being a law*, one might say – is thus explained as an evolutionary product – but only because that law was present from the beginning albeit in germinal form. Habit-taking, then, is not explained but is assumed. By virtue of itself, it grows in strength over time, becoming a law. But for that to happen, it had to have been there already.

It follows that the 1891–1893 cosmogony differs fundamentally from the cosmogony of 1884. Use of the mathematical theory of probability is supplanted by a nonmathematical 'law', or at least by a primordial tendency.

---

[9] Peirce's experimental studies of observation, discussed in the next chapter, work toward a defense of immediate perception in another way, without assuming that feelings sport primordially.

References to statistical explanation are barely present in the *Monist* essays. Its demoted status is made clear in the last essay, 'Evolutionary Love' (EP1:352–71). Three theories of evolution – generalizations of three explanations of biological evolution – are presented, only one of which, the Darwinian theory of natural selection, is couched in statistical terms. It should be noted, contrary to what has sometimes been supposed, that Peirce did not reject Darwin's theory, but only added two others to it; Darwin himself said that evolution can have other causes in addition to natural selection and gave examples. However, Peirce argued that 'agapastic' evolution – presented as Lamarckian but defined as habit-taking and otherwise described as 'love' (in New Testament Greek, *agapē*: I Cor. 13) – is the most basic (360–63). Nothing remotely like that was suggested in 1884 or even in 1887–1888.

E

It would be unfair to Peirce to omit from this summary of the second version of his cosmogony – less ambitious yet even more extraordinary than the first one – the clarifying and explanatory statements he made in the three intermediate essays of the *Monist* series, though these raise further questions and present further difficulties.

The second article, 'The Doctrine of Necessity Examined' (EP1:298–311), was more important in its day, 1892, than it is in ours. Least in need of comment, it is the essay of this series that has been most commented on. In light of the quantum revolution, we need no convincing that physical events are not always determined by prior conditions. Before that revolution, however, determinism (the doctrine of necessity) was generally accepted as axiomatic, as if it were inconceivable that something can happen unless it is made to happen. And it was supposed that the deterministic laws of Newtonian physics had been established beyond any doubt. Science was assumed to be deterministic. To make room for his principle that 'absolute chance' plays a positive role in the universe – a principle that in the next essay was named 'tychism'[10] – Peirce had to argue that

---

[10] From the Greek word for chance, *tychē* (EP1:312). It would be a mistake to suppose that Peirce had Aristotle's use of *tychē* (*Phys.* II, 4, *Meta.*K,8) in mind. Aristotelian *tychē* is illustrated by two persons, each going his own way for his own purpose and neither with the purpose of meeting the other, who encounter one another, fulfilling a purpose one or both had but was not at that time acting for. 'Oh! I didn't expect to see you here, but – how lucky! – I've been wanting to ask you ....' It is what could have been done purposefully that was not done purposefully. Chance in this sense, or luck, has nothing to do either with variable causes or with Peirce's absolute chance.

determinism is not in fact established by empirical science. This he was well qualified to do, having spent so much of his scientific career making measurements and estimating their margins of error. Since no measure is exact, there can be no empirical proof of any law's applying exactly. The doctrine of necessity can therefore be defended only on other grounds, and here Peirce claimed to have the advantage. Absolute chance, he argued, is as intelligible as is determinism and it permits the explanation of law and of the growth of heterogeneity, whereas determinism must assume law as inexplicable and is inconsistent, he said, with the growth of heterogeneity.

The third article, 'The Law of Mind' (EP1:312–33), hereafter, 'Law', begins by introducing a second principle, after tychism, named 'synechism' and defined as 'The tendency to regard continuity ... as an idea of prime importance in philosophy ...' (313). Synechism seeks to replace ontological dualisms by continuities – e.g., making mind and matter to differ by degree – on the ground that only so may their relationships be explicable. The argument of these essays presupposes that principle.

Take the question we earlier postponed: what could it possibly mean to speak of disembodied feelings forming habits or, as Peirce otherwise described the law of mind, as becoming more general? In 'Architecture', we are told that 'The one primary and fundamental law of mental action consists in a tendency to generalization. Feeling tends to spread; connections between feelings awaken feelings; neighboring feelings become assimilated' (291). We could understand these claims were they about persons and the universe as presently constituted. Feelings spread from person to person through sympathy; qualities felt may spread spatially and temporally, as the rosy sunset spreads across the sky or a musical note is prolonged. Songs, poetry, opera, ballet unite image, music, and story, connecting feelings, awakening or intensifying one by its association with another, and forming more complex feelings. Perhaps some associations of emotional with sensational feeling become habitual, forming new values, communicated by one person to another. But persons, music, and stories, even the sky, space, and time, are what this cosmogony is supposed to explain; and therefore the spreading, neighboring, generalizing, and becoming habitual that we experience cannot be what these same words denote, if they denote anything, in the primordial chaos. Or so one might think.

But the principle of synechism entails continuities of meaning as well as of things, permitting us to model the explanation on the explained. We are to look for analogies to human experience among the lower animals, then in plant life or living tissues generally, and so on: animals learn from experience, plants are responsive to changes in their environment, crystals grow as their structure assimilates ambient molecules; and we may suppose analogies beyond those that we can identify. Recall that in 'A Guess', Peirce wrote, 'Our conceptions of the first stages of development, before time yet existed, must be as vague and figurative as the expressions of the first chapter of Genesis'. Thus, we may not know what, exactly, it means for feelings in the original chaos to spread and form habitual combinations, but we are to assume that in some manner they behave *like* the feelings we directly experience. Recourse to analogy was not new: in the Middle Ages, some theologians argued that we can speak intelligibly about what we cannot comprehend if we suppose that God's attributes are *like* human virtues except for being – *in some unspecifiable way* – infinitely superior.

Not only is synechism presupposed by Peirce's method in cosmology, it must also be kept in mind, as a hermeneutic principle, while reading 'Law'. In that essay words shift in meaning, without warning or explanation, as they refer first to one part and then to another part or to the whole of a single continuum. This continuity of usage reflects the continuum discussed. That is true especially of the word 'idea'. By attending to the shifts in meaning of this word, we will better understand how Peirce was thinking about the relation of human mentality to primordial feelings sporting.

In 'Law', 'idea' sometimes refers to concepts and sometimes to all modes of mentality, feelings especially. For, concepts are held to be evolutionary products of feeling. In a fragment of 1888, consciousness is divided into three modes, 'Single, Dual, and Plural', the last being described as 'synthetic consciousness', an awareness of a 'process of learning', in which 'I put things together'; yet, feeling is held to form 'the warp and woof of consciousness, or in Kant's phrase its matter' (EP1:282–83). In 'Architecture', this triad becomes 'feelings', 'sensations of reaction', and 'general conceptions', the last implied to consist of a rule of connection among feelings: 'When we think, we are conscious that a connection between feelings is determined by a general rule, we are aware of being governed by a habit' (291). 'Law' later asserts that 'Three elements go to make up an idea', which are its 'intrinsic quality as a feeling', 'the energy with which it affects other ideas', and 'the tendency of an idea to bring other ideas along with it' (325). Thus, when, many pages earlier, Peirce said '… there is but one law of mind, namely, that ideas tend to spread continuously and to affect certain others …' (313), that is a doctrine that applies to feelings primarily, and it is their spreading and affecting one another that accounts for the existence of ideas *qua* concepts, which continue the process of generalization and connection. Consciousness, then, is feeling; the more developed forms of consciousness are feelings organized; organization is a product of feelings initially unorganized; and this organization grows out of feelings' intrinsic nature.

The irreversibility of time is asserted to be a consequence of an alleged fact that one idea (feeling?) affects another without being affected by it (322–23). Feelings (that is now the word used) are next said to have 'intensive' continuity (pertaining to their 'intrinsic qualities' along several 'dimensions', of which 'we can now form but a feeble conception') and also to have 'spatial extension' (323–25). As time and space (especially the number of its dimensions) and physical causality are supposed to be what this cosmogony explains, we are forced to conclude that the flow of ideas, their asymmetric affectability, and their extension and other continuities are all to be conceived of as analogous to physical time, space, and causality, even though we are unable to say what the analogy is. Physical time and space would then be accounted for as the order that evolved, along with the laws of physical causation, from out of the disorderly sporting of feelings intrinsically possessed of extension (in various dimensions) and affectability. Far from being a consequence of the physics of the nervous system, our subjective sense of the irreversible flow of time reflects the primordial nature of feeling, from which the physical universe evolved. The dimensions of physical space are a paring down of the greater number of dimensions of feeling, as any one organization can be achieved only at the expense of other possible organizations (324).[11]

This cosmogony thus differs from that of 1884 by its not attempting to explain the evolution of lawfulness from unlawfulness. Instead, it supposes that lawfulness in all its aspects (spatial and temporal dimensions, causality, etc.) is present from the beginning in germinal form, albeit not as physical but as features of 'feeling'. This anticipates the later, phaneroscopic doctrine that none of the three categories is reducible to the other two: in particular, 3rdness or law is irreducible. The specific laws that have evolved were not determined by law, but by which feelings happened to 'sport' first and in which combinations – a matter of chance. (What 'combination' could mean without referring to space and time, I do not know.)

[11] All highly speculative, of course, but so is the current interest of many physicists in string theory, which also exists in several variations, differing by the number of dimensions, some very large, in which it is postulated that strings vibrate. It, too, supposes that vibration in these dimensions can account for the physical phenomena we observe in three spatial dimensions. And it, like Peirce's conjecture, has yet to be made to entail testable implications or to have led to new discoveries.

However, those chance combinations became habitual, not because of the mathematics of probability, but due to the law of mind, the effect of 'love'.

There is more in 'Law' than there is room here to discuss. For example, there is a tension between two assertions, that as 'an idea spreads' it loses its power of 'affecting other ideas' (325) and that, as feelings 'flow together' into 'general ideas', the latter attain a 'peculiar vivacity' and 'are just as much, or rather far more, living realities than the feelings themselves' (330). More positively, there is in 'Law' a long and important discussion of the mathematics of continuity (314–22) and an intriguing comment on personality as a 'coördination or connection of ideas' (330–31). But enough has been said about that essay for our purpose.

F

About the last of the three intermediate articles of the series, 'Man's Glassy Essence' (EP1:334–51), hereafter 'Essence', I shall also be brief. It is a puzzling essay, certainly the most puzzling of the cosmological five. One would therefore expect it to have received the most comment; in fact, it has received the least comment.[12]

The most obvious objection to the 1890s cosmogony is that it contradicts our commonsense idea that feelings do not occur except as felt – that is, felt by one person or organism or another. It also contradicts what many say is the metaphysics of modern science, that matter and its laws are primary. 'Essence' addresses these objections (without announcing that that is its purpose) by attempting to use what were then the most recent advances in physiology, biology, and chemistry to derive the ideas at issue. It seeks to turn the tables on the metaphysics of modern science by deploying against it the discoveries of modern science. In the process, common sense, too, is revised, though I suspect that the opinion I here attribute to common sense is one that Peirce would have argued is a corruption of common sense by the outmoded metaphysics of early modern science.

'Essence' begins with and is more than half occupied by a cogent and wonderfully concise account of then-current molecular science (334–41). It next discusses the complex molecules that make up what was at the time supposed to be the substance of a living cell, the 'life-slimes' named 'protoplasm'. Protoplasm is the substance of a cell outside the nucleus, now named 'cytoplasm'; the discovery that the nucleus contains an organism's

---

[12] More in Short (2010b), building on Reynolds (2002), than elsewhere, yet far from enough.

inheritable 'blueprint' makes this discussion sadly dated; but let us continue. Protoplasm is irritable: disturb it at one point and it begins to liquefy, which liquefaction spreads out from that center until, the disturbance being evaded or removed, the protoplasm regroups itself anew (342). In some cases, 'The course which the spread of liquefaction has taken in the past is rendered thereby more likely to be taken in the future ...' (343). This, Peirce said, is 'habit-taking' and, hence, '... there is a fair analogical inference that all protoplasm feels'. The analogical inference is from the fact that when one of our habits breaks down and a new habit is formed we become conscious of what we were not conscious of while acting habitually.

The premise of this inference, and the suggestion of an analogy, is drawn from William James and other psychologists of the time. James wrote that 'habit diminishes ... conscious attention' and, conversely, that when habits fail their purpose and break down, attention to stimuli is called for (1890, v.I, pp.114–15). While he held that it is by introspection that we understand what consciousness is, James emphasized that habit can be observed in the behavior of others: 'When we look at living creatures from an outward point of view, one of the first things that strike us is that they are bundles of habits' (v.I, p.104). So also, when habit breaks down, that may be observed. The publicly observable and privately introspectable thus are correlated. In 'Essence', Peirce mentioned James in a related connection, but for this purpose instead cited the 'principle of accommodation' of another psychologist, James Mark Baldwin, quoting from the latter's 1889 *Psychology*: 'Physiologically,... accommodation means the breaking up of a habit .... Psychologically, it means reviving consciousness' (348n).

Now, Peirce made a persuasive argument that protoplasm's habit-taking can be explained mechanically, given the instability and other characteristics of its molecules (343–46). But of the correlative, analogically supposed feeling, he said, 'Yet the attempt to deduce it from the three laws of mechanics ... would obviously be futile' (347). He did not explain why it must be futile. In addition, his assumption that mechanistic explanation must be Newtonian ('the three laws' obviously refers to Newton) is open to question (Hookway 1985, p.275, Murphey 1961, pp.345–46). Instead of providing needed argument, Peirce moved swiftly to an unexpected conclusion, much as if he were pulling a rabbit out of his hat. As habit-taking entails feeling and there is no mechanistic explanation of feeling, then habit-taking can be mechanical only if 'physical events are but degraded or undeveloped forms of psychical events' (348). That is to say, the feeling must be there already, in the materials that acquire habits, if habit-taking can be explained mechanically. His mechanistic account of protoplasm's habit-taking was thereby turned into an argument for objective idealism: 'Thus we see that the idealist has no need to dread a mechanical theory of life' – an example of Peirce's rhetorical inclination to startle, by standing a doctrine on its head.

As non-habitual action is associated with increased consciousness, and as feeling *is* consciousness, Peirce concluded that 'Wherever chance-spontaneity is found, there, in the same proportion, feeling exists. In fact, chance is but the outward aspect of that which within itself is feeling'. In the 'primeval chaos in which there was no regularity' there was no physical reality but there was 'an intensity of consciousness' dwarfing our own (348). In general, then, the physical and the psychical are dual aspects of things: 'Viewing a thing from the outside,… it appears as matter', while 'Viewing it from the inside,… it appears as consciousness' (349). Notice that Peirce here adopted James' inside/outside mode of expression but extended it beyond 'living creatures' to all material things, adding that 'These two views are combined when we remember that mechanical laws are nothing but acquired habits ….'

What could 'inside' and 'outside' mean in this case? One thinks of physical things, such as baseballs: an outside surface and an inside stuffing. But the inside is in this case consciousness, and I cannot find your consciousness by taking you apart. The distinction draws on a different sense of 'inside', one in which spatial meaning is attenuated. You hide your thoughts or feelings from me, as if within your body, which I observe from outside. So, we speak of your inner life and outer behavior. But, for the most part, you do not refer the data of introspection to locations inside your body: the pain in your toe, yes, but your thought of the morrow, no. It must be that Peirce meant by 'inside' the introspectable.[13] But, then, one can 'view' nothing but oneself 'from the inside'. What could he have meant by claiming that material things and chance sportings have an 'inside' which is consciousness? This idea depends on two assumptions: that consciousness is substantival, consisting of feelings; and that feelings can exist unfelt. A feeling unfelt is 'inside' nothing but it is 'inside' in this sense: it is the sort of thing that in certain conditions *is* introspectable;

---

[13] In his 1868–1869 papers, Peirce famously denied that there is such a thing as introspection, holding that what we know of the 'internal world' is 'derived from the observation of external facts' (EP1:22–23). That he now admitted introspection does not mean that he accepted the Cartesian doctrine that in 1868–1869 he was combating. For, to assert that there is introspection is not to assert that it comes first, the external world being inferred (see 2.62, 2.539, 1.310, dated 1901 to 1907). Indeed, observation of the world about one provides by analogy introspection's vocabulary.

'inside' has now lost its spatial reference altogether. This strange doctrine becomes somewhat more intelligible if we consider its source.

In the *Monist* series of cosmological essays, Peirce alluded to William James but twice (324, 346), both times to the latter's 1890 *Principles of Psychology*. That famous book's most famous chapter is 'The Stream of Thought', which appeared earlier under a different title in an 1884 issue of *Mind*. Peirce evidently read both (Girel 2003 and Houser's introduction, W8:xxxvi). In it, the word 'thought' is used as a generic term encompassing feelings. In James' 1892 abridgment of his *Psychology*, the *Briefer Course*, that chapter was renamed 'The Stream of Consciousness' and was rewritten, substituting 'consciousness' for 'thought'. In either version, James attempted merely to describe our 'mental life' (1890, v.I, p.1). Such description he characterized as 'introspective' and he regarded the thesis that there is something to introspect as 'the most fundamental of all the postulates of Psychology' (v.I, p.185). His descriptive method excluded anything explanatory, theoretical, or assumed (v.I, p.224). In particular, what is described is not ascribed to any underlying substance:

> The first fact for us, then, as psychologists, is that thinking of some sort goes on. I use the word thinking … for every form of consciousness indiscriminately. If we could say in English 'it thinks,' as we say 'it rains' or 'it blows,' we should be stating the fact most simply and with the minimum of assumption. As we cannot, we must simply say that *thought goes on.* (v.1, pp.224–25, James' emphases)

Thoughts (feelings, etc.), then, are reported *as if* free-floating, independently of their being functions or attributes of any organism. But that does not mean that James asserted that they *are* independent. While being careful (in this part of his book) not to say what does the thinking, he nonetheless did explicitly, indeed emphatically, suppose that thinking is 'personal' (v.I, pp.225–29). Only, he was careful to avoid any explanatory hypothesis in his descriptions of thoughts, hence, any claim either positive or negative about what they are in reality and whether they in reality depend on anything else.

I suggest that Peirce's 1891–1893 essays' fundamental assumptions are an ontologization of the descriptive method James introduced: they take what James described independently of explanatory hypotheses as being *in fact* independent of aught else. Feelings thus become independent existents, something that may sport unfelt. In standard metaphysical language, Peirce took feelings to be substances. Doubtless, this transposition of James' method into a metaphysical doctrine was done deliberately in

full consciousness of its boldness. Nearly two decades later, James followed
Peirce in taking this step.[14]

G

Many who have written on Peirce suppose that he had always been an
objective idealist. They are right to this extent: He always was an idealist of some sort and never a subjective idealist. But he himself used the
term 'objective idealism' only in the 1890s and only to denote the doctrine
he then held. The idealism of his 1868–1869 essays was one of concepts
and reasoning, not of feelings (*vide supra* Ch.5, B). At the conclusion of
'Essence', Peirce acknowledged the discrepancy while trying to minimize it: 'Long ago ... I pointed out that a person is nothing but a symbol
involving a general idea; but my views were, then, too nominalistic to
enable me to see that every general idea has the unified living feeling of
a person' (350). Nevertheless, the opposition is clear. Earlier, as we have
seen, he described general ideas as being of the nature of words and dismissed an idea's 'material quality', for example, a feeling, as unimportant.
It was deemed unimportant, because it is no more constitutive of an idea's
meaning than sound or ink is of a word's meaning.

As well as being at odds with his earlier idealism, the doctrine Peirce
named 'objective idealism' is at odds with his later idealism. This fact has
been missed by commentators who suppose that his c.1902 idea of final
causation, which he said distinguishes mind (7.366, quoted below), is
simply the 1890s 'law of mind' restated. But the two are fundamentally
opposed, and therefore final causation supplanted the supposed law. And
if it is by final causation that mind is distinguished, then that final causation is real is another form of idealism. To see the opposition of these two
forms of idealism, we must take a moment to examine the later doctrine.
I shall be brief, as I have elsewhere explicated and defended it at length
(Short 2007, Chs.4–5). The topic is important for many reasons, one of
which is that Peirce's c.1902 idea of final causation is essential to his c.1902

---

[14] In the last book published in his lifetime, *A Pluralistic Universe* (1909), James, in Lecture V, rejected
his argument in the *Psychology* (v.I, pp.158–62), that 'states of consciousness' cannot 'compound' –
as if he here adopted Peirce's theory that ideas, of themselves, do influence one another. More
astoundingly, in this and in his earlier-written but posthumously published *Essays in Radical
Empiricism* (1912), he appears to have followed Peirce in ontologizing the contents of introspective
psychology. It is difficult to trace the influence of either man on the other, so intimately connected
were they and, as inhabiting the same scientific milieu, subject to the same influences.

concept of normative science; the following paragraphs are to be recalled in Chapter 9.

Teleological explanation is usually identified as explanation by final causes, that is, by *types* of possible outcome, in contrast to mechanistic or, more generally, efficient causes, which are *particulars*, whether things, events, or forces. The latter are of course *of* types – thus they instantiate general laws – but, unlike final causes, they are not themselves types. The idea but not the terminology goes back to Aristotle and Plato. References to teleology or to final causes occur sparingly in Peirce's writings before 1902, always affirmatively but never with any account of what was meant. Then, in 1902, he produced a seminal account of final causation, reversing Aristotle's idea in one respect, in order otherwise to preserve it:

> … we must understand by final causation that mode of bringing facts about according to which a general description of result is made to come about, quite irrespective of any compulsion for it to come about in this or that particular way;… The general result may be brought about at one time in one way, at another time in another way …. Efficient causation, on the other hand, is a compulsion determined by the particular conditions of things, and is a compulsion acting to make the situation begin to change in a perfectly determinate way; and what the general character of the result may be in no way concerns efficient causation. (EP2:120)

In this passage, the two kinds of causation are distinguished by two patterns of phenomena. In one, there is uniformity in type of outcome and variation in steps toward that outcome (we use another method if the first doesn't work); in the other, there is uniformity in sequence of steps unaffected by outcome. In both, there is something general: in one, the general element is the law, say, a law of mechanics, by which particular conditions determine particular outcomes; in the other, the general element is the type of outcome toward which a tendency is. A type is general, because it can be realized in any number of different ways and need not be realized at all. Later in the same paragraph, Peirce said that the two 'modes of action' are 'polar contraries' (EP1:121). Making variation in steps the mark of final causation contradicts Aristotle's claim that final causation is shown when things come about always or for the most part in the same way, as teeth grow (Phys. II, 8). But thus, Peirce said, he was able to 'conserve the truth' of Aristotle's doctrine (EP2:120). That truth, I suggest, is that there is causation by type of outcome. It was conserved by being shown to be entailed by some developments in modern science.

How can a type of outcome explain a tendency toward its actualization? A type is nothing actual; it can exert no force. That is only more obvious when the type is of an outcome not yet achieved, perhaps never to be achieved. Early modern science supplanted teleological explanation by mechanistic explanation. We, in consequence, think of causes as always being particular things or events or conditions, producing their effects forcefully. Something is explained when we know what *made* it happen. This does not have to be perfectly deterministic. A probabilistic law, as in quantum mechanics, is also a law of efficient causation, as here defined, because it, too, is a general rule connecting particular conditions to particular outcomes; if the cause does not quite make the effect to happen, it at least makes it more probable or less improbable that it will happen. We therefore are disposed to reject out of hand the idea that a mere type can be a cause. The modern take on teleological explanation is that it is an erroneous extrapolation from human purposefulness: we desire a type of result and this guides our action, but our action's cause is not the type desired; it is the desire itself, which, as a particular neurological arrangement, mechanically causes our muscles to contract, relax, contract, producing motion.

However, the Latin root, *causa*, of our word 'cause', like the root of the corresponding Greek word, *aitia*, is juridical, concerned with assigning responsibility. A cause is something that is responsible for an effect, no matter in what way responsible. We shall say, then, that a cause is *that which must be cited in order to explain a phenomenon*. I adopt this as a fundamental principle. It opens the question up. It is, however, vague: it is a guide-post, not a definition. In mechanical causation, for example, not only the particular event but also the law that relates it to its effect must be cited; but we can take the law as understood in citing the event as the cause, and therefore the customary distinction between causes and causal laws is convenient.

What must be cited to explain such phenomena as that heat, in a closed system, becomes equally distributed or that, in a given population, longer-legged antelope evolved? Earlier (Ch.2, C–E), we saw that Peirce had already in 1877 recognized that a new form of explanation had emerged in the nineteenth-century science to account for such phenomena. He described that form as 'statistical', and we have adopted that label, distinguishing statistical explanation from mechanistic explanations even when the laws that the latter assume are probabilistic. But now we are to see that statistical explanations always invoke one or another type of outcome, in order to explain uniformity of result from variable mechanical causes.

The reason why heat, under the specified conditions, always becomes equally distributed is that equal distribution is a type that encompasses nearly all of the particular distributions of molecular kinetic energies that are possible in those conditions. The reason why one genetic variant supplanted a rival variant over many generations in a given population is that the one more than the other produced outcomes of a type (say, outrunning a predator) that favored reproductive success (a second type of outcome). In neither case can the type of outcome be omitted from the explanation and, therefore, that type is a cause of what is explained.

For each type of explanation, there is a corresponding type of phenomenon. Recognition of this principle answers the argument from 'causal closure', that the mechanistic explanation that is necessary to account for a particular outcome also is sufficient, and thus there is no room left for other types of explanation (Kim 2005). A simple counterexample: tracing mechanical causes and effects within a population of trillions of gas molecules, were that possible, would explain the exact redistribution of the molecules from moment to moment, but it would not explain the fact that a gas always expands to fill its container or the fact that the pressure it exerts on the walls of that container always varies with its temperature. Similarly, explaining Smith's death mechanically, in terms of the neurological events that caused Jones' muscles to so contract that he raised and pointed a pistol and squeezed its trigger, does not explain why he would have used arsenic instead, had he some on hand and no pistol. The argument from causal closure assumes that there is nothing to be explained but particular outcomes. But in the phenomena of life and even in steam engines, statistical uniformities matter: they are consequential. Paradoxically, they are consequential as accounting for particular events: A steam engine works because of the statistical fact that heat flows in but one direction, toward equilibrium.

Statistical explanation is a broader category than is teleological explanation. Four years before writing the above passage, but evidently already thinking along its line, Peirce said of such irreversible processes as the diffusion of a gas or of heat, 'If teleological is too strong a word to apply to them, we might invent the word *finious*, to express their tendency toward a final state' (RLT:220). What is the difference? Here, I must fill in a blank Peirce left. To call an explanatory type a final cause or purpose, there must be selection of means to that end. The selection *of* an allele, say, one coding for longer legs, is selection *for* some consequence it has, say, speed, which directly or indirectly favors reproductive success. The 'of' and 'for' marks a distinction between means and ends; it constitutes something's being a purpose. A purpose, or final cause, is a type for which selection (of something else, more specific) is made. Selection can be for a purpose consciously entertained, or one not conscious, as in ants' repeatedly traveling a path found to food, or for one that is no one's, as in agentless 'natural

selection'. Tendencies due to selection are more complex than is the diffusion of heat; among other things, in them, failure is possible, that is, when
the type selected-for is not attained.

Now, the 'law of mind', as defined in the essay of that title, is a law of
efficient causation. To be sure, it is not a law of mechanical action and it is
not deterministic; it specifies no more than a tendency. But the tendency
is asserted, not explained. And the tendency is for things to change in a
determinate way, regardless of what results. According to this law, a feeling
or idea, once occurring, will tend to spread or to generalize, losing vivacity;
feelings co-occurring will tend to combine, gaining vivacity; and so on.
The law of mind does not specify a type of outcome that is to be attained,
by hook or by crook, in one way or another. And therefore it is the opposite of final causation. The very idea of a law of mind distinguishes it from
final causation, because final causation has no law. The general element in
final causation is a type of outcome, not a law of sequence.

The passage of 1902 quoted above is from a long but incomplete draft of
a book known as the 'Minute Logic', so far published only in disconnected
pieces. In another of its pieces, Peirce wrote: '… the distinction between
psychical and physical phenomena is the distinction between final and efficient causation' (7.366). He still identified consciousness with feeling – '…
consciousness is nothing but Feeling, in general …' (7.365) – but denied that
consciousness is essential to mind, that is, intelligent action. Consciousness
is necessary only to the higher forms of intelligence (7.366, cf. 5.493). By
1902, then, he had rejected the 'law of mind' as an account of how the mind
works. If the mind works by final causation, it does not work according to
a law.[15]

---

[15] There is some excuse for confusing the 1890s idea of a law of mind with the view that the mind works
by final causation. In 1887–1888, Peirce wrote, in words much like those of 1902, '… it is precisely
action according to final causes that distinguishes mental from mechanical action' (EP1:266). But at
that time he still identified mind with consciousness, and the end sought was merely to remove 'a
source of irritation'. He did not yet have a clear conception of final causation. And in 1892, he implied
that the 'law of mind' is 'purposive', but did not explain how (EP1:369). Finally, in 1902, in Baldwin's
Dictionary of Philosophy and Psychology, he wrote that 'the tendency of things to take habits …
is the one sole fundamental law of mind' and, on that ground, that 'it would be perfectly true to say
that final causation is alone primary'. That seems definitively to identify the law of mind with final
causation! However, he continued, 'Yet, on the other hand, the law of habit is a simple formal law,
a law of efficient causation; so that either way of regarding the matter is equally true, although the
former is more intelligent' (6.101). Here we have an explicit declaration that the 'law of mind' is a law
of efficient causality – but also an attempt to identify it with final causation. And that is contrary to
the other statement of 1902, that the two modes of causation are polar opposites. This puzzle is easily
resolved. 1902 is the *Dictionary's* date of publication, whereas the 'Minute Logic' was *written* in 1902.
The dictionary entry, therefore, was written first, and its close relation to, yet inconsistency with, the
'Minute Logic' proves that Peirce was only then working out his idea of final causation.

Notice, also, that final causation, in Peirce's account of it, is something known by observation: it is revealed in phenomenal patterns of the afore-mentioned kind and in their statistical explanation. Therefore, unlike the supposed 'law of mind', our knowledge of final causation depends neither on introspection nor on analogical inference from the data of introspection.

Mechanical events and their laws are implicated in any instance of final causation. If there were no neurological events in the brain, there would be no thinking. If there were no mechanical events, such as being crunched in the jaws of a predator, there would be no natural selection. If nails were not driven in by hammering them, no one would hammer nails. Particular events must have particular causes, which are mechanical: these are what Plato in the *Timaeus* named the 'co-operative causes' (Jowett trans.). But they do not explain a patterned outcome, for example, why all of the carpenter's muscular contractions resulted in a house or all of the electrochemical exchanges across Newton's synapses resulted in a coherent theory. Those patterns – statistical, general – require a corresponding type of explanation. In the same long paragraph of 1902 quoted above, Peirce wrote that 'Final causality cannot be imagined without efficient causality...' (EP2:121). Certainly, in the accepted examples of finious process cited – the diffusion of heat, the evolution of species – mechanical events and their laws are assumed.

Peirce also asserted the converse, that efficient causation depends on final causation (EP2:124), perhaps because the relation of law to its particular instances is 'ideal', not itself mechanical (EP2:120–21); but that ideal relation does not satisfy Peirce's own definition of final causation as a process having a tendency. Be that as it may, replacing the 1890s law of mind by final causation cancelled the specific 1890s cosmogonic variants, though not the general idea of explaining laws as having evolved.

H

Peirce never did deduce testable consequences from his cosmogonic specu-lations. Perhaps that is why those speculations became less prominent in his thought after 1893. There are two subsequent variations of the cos-mogony that I know of. One, in 1898, is inconsistent with every preceding variant; the other, of 1904, is a variant of that variant.

In 1898, in the eighth and last of his 'Cambridge Conference' lectures, he turned the 'law of mind' (without so naming it) on its head, arguing that continuity precedes occurrences of feelings:

... we must not assume that the qualities arose separate and came into relation afterward. It is just the reverse. The general indefinite potentiality became limited and heterogeneous. (RLT:259)

Yet, vestiges of the earlier doctrine remained:

... the cosmos of sense qualities which I would have you to suppose in some early stage of being was real as your personal life is this minute, had in an antecedent stage of development a vaguer being, before its dimensions became definite and contracted. (RLT:259.)[16]

'The sense-quality', he proceeded to explain, 'is a feeling' that is 'intense' independently of any 'reaction' or 'feeling another' (RLT:259). Thus, by sense qualities being 'real as your personal life', he meant the intensity of consciousness, which he presumed to inhere in the qualities themselves rather than in any organism that senses them. He still attributed a kind of force, actuality, reality to feelings *per se*. And thus he was able to write that a particular sense quality 'can emerge from the indefinite potentiality only by its own vital Firstness, and spontaneity' (RLT:259). He had not yet clearly distinguished 1stness, as a mere may-be, from 2ndness, or actuality, and both from 3rdness, or lawfulness, as described, in Chapter 8.

Another strain of thought in this lecture raises a question about what Peirce meant by 'sense-quality':

... the existing universe with all its arbitrary secondness is an offshoot from, or an arbitrary determination of, a world of ideas, a Platonic world ...

The evolutionary process is, therefore, not a mere evolution of the *existing universe*, but rather a process by which the very Platonic forms themselves have become or are being developed. (RLT:258, Peirce's emphasis)

It is difficult to know what an evolution of Platonic forms might be, though Plato in *The Sophist* wrote similarly. 'And among the things so resulting are time and logic' (RLT:260). Even logic! Peirce ended this lecture by applying some theorems of topology to the hypothesis of an original undifferentiated continuum, so as to conclude that time must be circular.

An essay c.1904 (EP2:300–24), apparently intended to preface a book on mathematics, manages to restate, consistently with the phaneroscopic categories, the idea of an evolution from a primordial continuum, now conceived of not as undifferentiated sense-quality but as an indeterminate symbol, 'essentially a purpose'. This symbol means to grow in definiteness:

---

[16] The editors of RLT inserted a bracketed 'as' before the word 'real', which seems to me mistaken. Peirce was not making a comparison of degree. One's sense of personal existence *is* the vitality that feelings have in their original, spontaneous sporting.

a 'representation that seeks to make itself definite', by producing 'an end-less series of interpretants' (321–24). So, the universe begins not with 1stness but with 3rdness, and it proceeds, not by a law of spreading, or general-ization, but by a teleological process of fulfilling a purpose, of becoming more concrete, which means a selection from among possibilities. Logic (still supposed as having evolved?) requires this: '… the first of all logical principles is that the indeterminate should determine itself as best it may' (324).

Thus the cosmogonic program: a sequence of fascinating variants, increasingly bold, mutually inconsistent, and with diminishing prospect of being brought to the empirical test they were intended to be brought to. It is a disservice to Peirce to conflate all of these variants into one vague smear of an idea – and then to proclaim it a triumph of speculative meta-physics! It is, rather, the kind of hypothesis that drives scientific inquiry, not always successfully.

CHAPTER 7

Experiments Expanding Empiricism

Readers of Volume 5 of the *Writings of Charles S. Peirce: A Chronological Edition*, if they happen upon it unprepared, must wonder. They confront eighty-one pages (W5:26–106), plus another twenty-six or so pages of editorial notes (W5:426–33) and textual apparatus (W5:524–42), devoted almost entirely to nothing but lists of names of supposedly 'great men', including a few women. The names are repeated, it seems endlessly, in different combinations, sometimes under such labels as 'men of feeling' and 'men of action', sometimes ranked numerically, sometimes with biographical details appended. The biographical data, where they occur, are mostly quite trivial, and seem to be in answer to a uniform questionnaire, also included. All of this is without the least explanation. There is no explanation because none has survived from the years Volume 5 covers, 1884–1886. Such explanation as we can obtain from Peirce himself was written retrospectively in c.1900 (7.256–66), where he refers to a 'study of great men' he conducted with his students at Johns Hopkins in 1883 (the year, we gather, when the study was begun). But the principles of the Chronological Edition forbid including material from years later than the volume covers. Nathan Houser, in his introduction to the volume, draws from Peirce's later statement and other sources, but very briefly (W5:xxiii–xxiv). He mentions the interest that Peirce and others at the time had in great men and their 'comparative lives', but this cannot explain the most salient feature of what is printed, which is the paucity and triviality of the characterizations of the men and women listed, which suggests, rather, a lack of interest in them and their greatness. This study of great men must have had a purpose other than studying great men.[1]

---

[1] Nonetheless, Peirce was genuinely interested in a comparative study of great men, a theme to which he returned in later years: see Houser's introduction to W8:lxv–vii and his 2013, also Peirce's 1901 essay, 'The Century's Great Men in Science' (Peirce 1958, pp.265–74).

That study involved several students and much time. Houser (W5:xxiii–xxiv) reports that it began as a course and was continued, but not completed, in extracurricular fashion after the course concluded. It would seem (7.256–61, 265) that the study was conducted as follows. The students were asked to draw up preliminary lists of great men, construct a uniform questionnaire, and divide the labor among themselves of reading biographies whereby to answer the questionnaire. The questionnaire included such topics as 'sexuality, how shown' and 'shape of chin'. But some random facts also were allowed, such as that Rabelais wrote while eating in bed (W5:87). Then the whole class was exposed to these gleanings, and each member, independently, ranked the great in order of greatness. That was done, initially, in small batches, but ultimately 288 were ranked (7.265), though 574 names occur in W5's lists. Peirce himself then subjected these rankings to statistical analysis. The class never discussed the concept of greatness or agreed upon criteria of greatness. The rankings are specifically described as 'impressionistic'. Indeed, the rankings were done 'while carefully abstaining from any analysis of greatness or of the reason for the impression we felt' (7.257). The dubiousness of such a procedure is exacerbated by these rankings being sometimes made across disparate categories, including categories sparsely represented. The ancient and the modern, poets and tyrants, soldiers and scientists, just one chess master (Morphy), and just one actress (Mrs. Siddons) were compared. Who is greater, Socrates or Joan of Arc? Racine or Morphy? Cleopatra or Newton?

If not about greatness, what was the study about? Houser (W5:xxiii–iv) cites Peirce's later comments that its purpose was to train his students in 'inductive investigations' and that it illustrated 'statistical investigations' based on 'impressionistic data'. Contemporary interest in great men appears to have provided a topic for an exercise in induction. But why impressionistic data? How is working with such data training in induction? Would not definite facts serve better? What was the statistical investigation and what was it meant to prove?

In fact, this study was an experiment that fits in with, and can only be understood as fitting in with, the long train of experiments Peirce made, first to improve observation, then to push observation beyond its supposed limits. It was a capstone on those experiments. Together, they expanded what is commonly thought to be observable. And thus they prepared the ground for Peirce's later idea of philosophy as a set of empirical (he said, 'positive') sciences. The thesis of this chapter is twofold: that Peirce expanded what is to count as empirical inquiry, and that he did this not by redefining terms or by dialectical argument but on empirical grounds.

As to the latter: something is shown to be observable by observing it. We begin with a discussion of what that means.

A

As detailed in Chapter 1, Peirce spent a great part of his time, up to age 52, measuring minute quantities. In that line of work, one must identify possible causes of error in the instruments used, in the observer, and in the method, and estimate ranges of possible error. Improving accuracy is part of the work. Statistical analysis of measurements made reveals their pattern of inaccuracy – on the assumption that there really is a quantity that is being measured. It also verifies that assumption, by showing that the measurements agree more than can be explained by chance. But that works only if we can conceive of an alternative to chance, that is, some idea of causality by which the observed might conceivably be a cause that explains why observations of it agree to the extent that they do. The distribution of errors also matters: it should be of a pattern that can be explained causally. Recall (Ch.1, E) Peirce's 1873 paper on a problem in using the method of least squares. That method presupposes that errors will occur about equally on either side of the true value, but there is an obvious causal explanation of why errors timing the emergence of a celestial body from occultation will occur asymmetrically. That explanation, like any explanation, presupposes a metaphysics, in this case, mechanistic.

This interplay – of measurement (more generally, observation), mathematics (statistical analysis), and metaphysics (any idea of causality) – is essential to everything said in the remainder of this and in the next two chapters.

Observation is always of that which is presumed to be a cause of the observation. And that presumptive object is presumed to explain, as well, the statistical agreement of multiple observations of what is presumed to be that same object. There is no observation without at least a vague (often, very vague) idea of causal explanation. 'Vagueness' here means lacking specific detail, as in pre-scientific knowledge that low temperatures freeze water, which was without any idea of why or how low temperatures produce crystallization or, indeed, that freezing *is* crystallization.[2] Now, even

---

[2] One must emphasize this, because logicians have expended much energy analyzing the idea of vagueness *qua* 'fuzzy borders' of application, so that they tend to assume that fuzziness is the only meaning 'vague' has. Vagueness *qua* lacking specificity is, I think, more important than fuzziness is to the analysis of the growth of scientific and other ideas; I have analyzed 'inspecificity' (my coinage) in Short (1988) and Short (2007, Ch.10).

when vague, the causal explanation of observation should bear not only on the agreement of observations but also on how disagreements may occur. In addition, even a vague explanation must fit in with what else we know about the world (when explanations are made more specific, as in scientific inquiry, 'fitting in' becomes more detailed and rigorous).

To show, by observing it, that something can be observed, is therefore a complicated matter. Consider the following cases, each of which, in its own way, illustrates the triad of (putative) observation, agreement/ disagreement, and explanation. (a) Even when there is agreement, a claim to have observed may be disputed if that agreement is explained more persuasively on other grounds than that the object claimed to have been observed exists, for example, that it is wishful thinking, or an optical illusion, or due to the power of suggestion. That is how we counter claims to have seen a ghost, even when many people agree in having seen it. An explanation that omits reference to the item putatively observed is an argument that the alleged observation is bogus. Conversely, (b) even when putative observations are sparse, they are accepted as genuine if their causal explanation is convincing. The chemical composition of stars is observed not in a variety of ways but only by spectroscopic analysis; however, the underlying theory, that different chemical elements when heated emit characteristic spectra, is well attested in the laboratory and has been developed in detail on the basis of other well-attested theories in chemistry and physics. (c) But it is not always necessary that the explanation be detailed. Before the advent of modern science, our idea of color was not such as to provide a detailed explanation of how colors are perceived; the idea of ghosts was not any vaguer (*qua* lacking specific detail) than that of color – perhaps it was less vague. However, there was detailed knowledge about how lighting and perspective and contrast to adjacent colors correlate reliably with variations in color-judgments; and all of this analysis of agreement and disagreement, in which spatial relations figure prominently, cohere around the idea that colors (whatever they are) somehow produce sensations of color in one who is looking at the objects deemed colored. Whereas, no like patterns of agreement and disagreement, much less reliable ones, support the hypothesis that ghosts really do appear to those who claim to see them. In this case, the metaphysical assumption that there is a causal explanation, though it remains essential, retreats into the background and emphasis lies, instead, on analysis of the pattern of agreement/disagreement.

Suppose that a new field of observation is claimed: for example, that the chemical composition of stars can be observed; that telescopic evidence of irregularities in the moon's surface may be accepted as genuine (and not an artifact of the instrument); that the microscope reveals tiny 'animalcules' cavorting; that cathode ray experiments establish the particulate character of electricity and that other experiments actually measure the mass of those hypothetical entities; that psychologists trained in introspection can reliably identify aspects of consciousness (Titchener); that dreams reveal subconscious desires or fears (Freud); that one can by telepathy know what another is thinking. How are those claims established or contested? That is done, I suggest, by attempting the observations and finding a pattern of agreement (and disagreement) that can plausibly be explained on the assumption that the putatively observed is real. The explanation is plausible if its assumptions are otherwise supported; yet, it may be quite sketchy. In addition, this new field of observation must prove, eventually, to be fruitful of further discoveries. In short: *each empirical science establishes its own empirical base* – not by some sort of philosophical principle or argument a priori, but – *empirically.* Or it fails to do this and goes out of business.

This, we shall see, is the strategy Peirce followed in the long and varied course of experiments and related studies by which he attempted to push empirical inquiry into new and surprising territories.

Before examining those experiments and studies, there is an alternative way of understanding Peirce's expansion of the empirical that must be acknowledged – and then refuted. As we saw in Chapter 4, Section D, Peirce held that mathematics is an observational science: Its discoveries are made, he said, by observing the results of experiments on diagrams. On this basis, Cheryl Misak concludes that Peirce 'broadens the *notion* of the empirical' (1995, p.111, emphasis mine). I think this is doubly mistaken. It is not the *notion* (idea, concept, definition) either of 'observation' or of 'empirical' that is at issue; what is at issue is what is *in fact* observable. And Peirce did not claim that mathematical truths are empirical truths.

Take the latter point first, as it might seem trivial and is in any case simpler. In the passage Misak cites (5.541, quoted above in Ch.4, D), Peirce did not use the word 'empirical' or any of its cognates; in fact, he rarely used those terms, especially in application to his own thought.[3] And elsewhere he clearly distinguished mathematics from the 'positive'

---

[3] In his 1871 Berkeley review, he referred to 'English empiricism', not as a methodology but as a metaphysical doctrine (EP1:95, 104); otherwise, he used the term as physicists often do, to refer to a formula induced without being explained (see, e.g., EP1:195, where an 'empirical formula' is said to become a 'law of nature' once it is embedded in a theory).

sciences, that is, sciences about the actual world (*vide infra*, Ch.8, A). Mathematics is about possibilities that can be diagrammed, regardless of whether they are actual or can be made actual; and what is thereby discovered are necessary truths, that is, truths about any possible world. This leaves us free to define 'empirical' as broadly as Peirce used 'observation' or as narrowly as he used 'positive'. Misak is quite right to lay firm hold of Peirce's insight, that it is through the compulsive aspect of experience, signalized by the word 'observation', that truth is gradually sifted from error – as much so in mathematics as in physics. But it is important, too, to not lose sight of the difference between necessary truths and positive facts.

Like Misak, Christopher Hookway writes that Peirce '… rejected *a priori* sources of knowledge: mathematicians study abstract structures by (empirical) experiments upon diagrams' (2012, p.2, Hookway's parenthetical insertion). But what is discovered in mathematics about any possible world applies to the actual world without our having to observe it, and that is *precisely* what '*a priori* knowledge' has always meant. By restricting 'empirical' to knowledge based on observation of positive fact, we avoid the risk of seeming to deny the difference between mathematics and the positive sciences – as if we thought that Peirce agreed with J. S. Mill's theory of mathematics, often named 'empiricist'. In 1893, whilst disparaging Mill's view, that arithmetic is 'experiential', Peirce explained how loose use of the word 'experience' obscures the distinction between mathematics and knowledge of 'the existing world' (4.91).

As to the first point: in none of the examples cited above, from spectroscopy to telepathy, is the question one of changing the meaning of such terms as 'observe'; the question in each case is one of fact. Can chemical composition actually be observed by analysis of electromagnetic spectra? Can one really read another's mind? The studies and experiments that we shall examine in this chapter do not depend on any redefinitions of terms: they were not exercises in conceptual legerdemain. They may result in new definitions, but do not depend on them. Peirce, I shall argue, initiated an expansion of empiricism by showing that we can in fact make observations of kinds that in the modern period had been thought impossible. And he did this by attempting such observations. Whether sufficient agreement and explanation and fruitfulness was attained to warrant their being admitted as genuine observations is another question. But in any case, his attempt was empirical, as we shall use that term; that is, it was an attempt to observe the alleged positive facts.

B

I have referred to the series of Peirce's experiments and studies of observation as if they tended, altogether, in one direction; and I think that they do. But it is also true that there are several dimensions in which he explored the limits of observation. He was interested in (a) what is not deemed observable, (b) what is not deemed observation albeit of what is granted to be in other ways observable, and (c) whether powers of observation may be improved.

At first, (c) was the focus. The aforementioned 1873 paper, on the method of least squares, also described an experiment Peirce made in training an observer to greater accuracy in determining a signal's onset. An auditory signal was produced by a machine that recorded its time in thousandths of a second; the observer was to respond by tapping a key, 'nicely adjusted', which produced a record of equal minuteness. Although the stimulus was auditory rather than visual, errors were asymmetric in the same way as in the timing of astronomical bodies emerging from occultation: to varying degrees too late, but rarely too early. Peirce tested the apparatus' accuracy and adjusted it. He then employed a youth of eighteen with no previous experience in observation and had him tap the key each time he heard a sharp rap. This was done five hundred times a day, six days a week, for a month. Over the month, the unfortunate young man's accuracy improved dramatically. His probable error gradually decreased until it did not exceed 1/80th of a second. 'I think that this clearly demonstrates the value of such practice in training the nerves for observation' (W3:137). The training was of 'nerves' rather than of judgment, as the intervals in question hardly permit conscious thought.

Eleven years later, Peirce conducted a similar experiment, mentioned above (Ch.1, H), with his student Jastrow at Johns Hopkins. Here, too, an instrument was employed that produced effects differing minutely in degree – in this case, differences between two successive pressures on a fingertip – accurately recorded by the instrument itself. A number of subjects were asked to judge which pressure was the stronger. As the differences became smaller, the subjects denied that they could detect a difference and yet, told to guess, their guesses were correct more often than would be explained by chance. Without the subjects being conscious of the difference in pressure, that difference must somehow have been the cause of their guesses' accuracy. It was therefore concluded that perceptual discrimination occurs beneath the level of conscious discrimination. No lowest limit was found beneath which guessing had not some bias toward the truth. Thus the hypothesis of Weber and Fechner, that there is an *Unterschiedsschwelle*, or least perceptible difference of nerve excitation, was questioned.

In those two experiments, the observations made were of a physical fact independently determined, by which the accuracy of the observations could be measured. Peirce's comparisons of the brightness of stars (Ch.i, D) posed a different problem. The instrument he employed required the observer to compare the brightness of a star seen through a telescope to the brightness of an 'artificial star', a point of light projected into the same telescopic field. The light of the artificial star could be made brighter or dimmer by turning a knob until, in the judgment of the observer, it matched that of the real star (I am simplifying). Then the brightness of the latter could be assigned a number from the setting to which the knob had been turned. And in that way, the brightness of different stars, as determined by successive observations, could be compared. As there was no independent measure of brightness, the only test of accuracy was by the agreement of judgments of brightness with one another.

Causal considerations were nevertheless introduced in adjusting the instrument and in other ways; Chapter III of Peirce's 1878 book, *Photometric Researches*, contains a minutely detailed description of those adjustments and considerations, including extensive tables of numbers attesting, by their agreement, to the reliability of the results (W3:389–475). The instrument used was a Zöllner astrophotometer. The artificial star was generated by the light of a kerosene lamp passed through a Nicol prism; its brightness was controlled by rotating the prism through a graduated circle. The light, however, varied in strength depending on the trim of the wick in the kerosene lamp, which therefore had to be trimmed very precisely, and by drafts, changes in temperature and humidity, etc. To avoid problems with drafts, Peirce had to alter the instrument's construction. There also were problems with the shapes of the pinholes – six different ones were used – through which the light was passed. Not only the instrument but also its use by the observer was a source of problems. 'The most difficult part of the observations … consists in putting the eye straight to the telescope' (W3:405). Furthermore, 'It was also, of course, necessary that both real star and photometer star should constantly fall on fixed parts of the retina. Here came in another source of error, owing to these parts being unequally fatigued by the varying lights …' (W3:406). It was necessary to take the observer's fatigue into consideration – but first it was necessary for the observer to be aware of where, on his own retina, the light fell!

Let me interject here a general remark pertinent to later considerations. Instruments of observation serve to improve accuracy; sometimes they turn qualitative judgments into quantitative judgments, posing a question of accuracy that formerly did not arise. But every use of an instrument depends nonetheless on human sensitivity. For example, in using a mercury thermometer, tactile judgments of temperature are replaced by ocular judgments of the gradation at which a column of mercury ends: the latter more accurately distinguishes between higher and lower temperatures and yields a measurement of them, but still it is subject to error in proportion to the precision sought. Also, every use of an instrument assumes the truth of one or another causal theory, for example, that materials expand in constant proportion to increases in temperature (false, but true enough for some purposes). But causal assumptions are also implicit in relying on one's own senses. Peirce's attention to the human factor in using the astrophotometer was characteristic of his studies of mensuration. Sometimes, as we have seen, he proved that accuracy exceeds what the observer is conscious of and can control; other times, as in this case, he held that accuracy is increased by self-consciousness and self-control, as by becoming aware of how one's eye is positioned.

The most obvious source of error in these observations of stellar brightness was changes in atmospheric conditions from night to night or from one minute to another. Judgments had therefore to be made about whether conditions were favorable, and those judgments were fallible. This and the other sources of error could not be entirely eliminated but were mitigated by making repeated observations of the same stars. Each star was observed four times, not in succession but in regular rotation (thus correcting for fatigue), and observations were made again on different nights from different locations. From these data, more accurate values were obtained by the method of least squares.

There was yet another problem in judging brightness: The astrophotometer had another Nicol prism, with an interposed quartz plate, by which the color of the artificial star could be adjusted. The reason for this is that stars vary in color and color affects judgments of brightness, red appearing brighter than blue (how the latter fact was determined will be described in the next section). Peirce found, however, that, since the objective lens of the artificial star was not achromatic, it had to be refocused with each color adjustment. Difficulties in doing this introduced another source of error. Therefore, he fixed the color prism in one position and, in order to judge of brightness accurately, he trained himself to discriminate brightness independently of color. To verify that he had acquired that ability, he produced a table of his judgments which showed sufficient agreement: 'These numbers … suffice of themselves to dispel the idea … that the observation of two lights of different colors, to say which is the brighter, is devoid of all certainty, because they [the numbers] exhibit so much regularity and concordance among themselves' (W3:392).

In another place, some years later, Peirce wrote of an unnamed person – surely himself – who

> … upon hearing a note struck upon the piano was utterly unable to pick out any harmonic by ear. He then went through a course of training with a color-box [discriminating differences of 'luminosity', i.e., brightness, as distinct from color] … until he acquired a good deal of skill. Upon now returning casually to the observation upon the piano-tone he found to his surprise that he could pick out three or four harmonics without difficulty. (7.256)

As he concluded in his 1873 paper, '… it is the general condition of the nerves which it is important to keep in training more than anything peculiar to this or that kind of observation' (W3:137). This is a remarkable conclusion. One would not have supposed that the different orders of sensation could be so easily bridged. It suggests that there must be analogies between, say, color and sound, not only physically – we know that both are wave phenomena – but in our experience of them. In 1910, Peirce repeated, as evidence of this, the story of the man blind from birth who asked 'whether the color scarlet was not something like the blare of a trumpet' (1.312).

That observers may be trained to greater accuracy, that this training may be of nerves rather than of conscious judgment, and that this results in a generalized sensitivity across distinct modalities of sense – all these conclusions were established experimentally and all are to be recalled later.

C

One wonders what Peirce's superiors in the Coast Survey thought of the chapters in *Photometric Researches* that do not bear on the assigned task of determining stellar magnitudes and mapping our galaxy. The first chapter, 'The Sensation of Light' (W3:382–9), pursues questions of psychophysics in some detail, in order to justify the scale adopted in comparing magnitudes. The second chapter, 'On the Numbers of Stars of Different Degrees of Brightness' (unfortunately omitted from W3, but see the editorial note to 389(l.4) at W3:536–38), contains translations of earlier star catalogues and a reduction of their rankings to the scale established in the first chapter. Peirce's own observations and rankings of stars' magnitudes occupies the third chapter. The fourth chapter, 'Comparisons of the Different Observers' (also omitted from W3, but see the editorial note to 475(l.32) at W3:538), compares Peirce's results to those of the earlier astronomers, measures their agreement, and examines the evidences of errors due to various factors, duly distinguished. The fifth chapter maps the galaxy. The interest of the second and fourth chapters may seem less astronomical than historical, but in fact it is epistemological or logical in Peirce's broad sense. They, and the psychophysical first chapter, probe the distinction between the physical and the psychological and establish the accuracy of judgments that one would have supposed were subjective. They bear on the possibilities of empirical methods. We shall now examine those chapters with that same extra-astronomical interest.

Ancient astronomers divided stars into six orders of magnitude; in the second-century AD, Ptolemy subdivided these into thirds, making eighteen orders. Stars – largely the same stars, identified by location – were similarly ranked in Persia in the tenth century, Samarkand in the fifteenth century, and then in the modern period by Tycho Brahe and many others, continuing into the nineteenth century. Progressively finer discriminations were introduced, until the six orders were subdivided into tenths – sixty distinct magnitudes in all. Many hundreds of stars were ordered by brightness – eventually, over a thousand. Peirce himself observed 494 within a narrow segment, between 40° and 50° north, of the night sky.

What, by all these stargazers, was being observed? What is the reality that their rankings represent or misrepresent? In the first chapter of his book, Peirce surprisingly adopted Kantian terminology, naming physical light 'noumenal' and light 'as an appearance, and as a function of the sensation', 'phenomenal'. Kant would have called physical light phenomenal; but Peirce rejected Kant's notion of noumena and apparently felt free to adapt the terminology to an analogous distinction. Noumenal light is a form of physical energy. The energy of a beam of light of given wavelength is the square of the amplitude of that wave. Brightness is a function of sensation and, thus, is phenomenal. Fechner's psychophysical law is that as the energy of the stimulus increases geometrically, the intensity of the resulting sensation increases arithmetically. Not when stargazing but in other conditions, light energy can be measured and Fechner's law tested. 'Various circumstances interfere with the exactitude of this formula in the case of light; but still it is approximately true and this is why we do well to fix our scale of magnitude of stars so that equal increments of numerical magnitude correspond to equal increments in the logarithm of the light'

(W3:388). Having so fixed his scale, Peirce found that the star catalogues of earlier astronomers could be reduced to that scale. As he put it c.1900, 'The old astronomers assigned successive numbers to stars which gave equal differences of sensation, and these … correspond to a geometrical progression of intensities of light measured physically …' (7.258). One astronomer's impressionistic sense of equal differences of his sensations largely agreed with other astronomers' equally impressionistic judgments of the differences of their sensations. And all were confirmed – by Peirce, in the nineteenth century – as corresponding to equal differences in the physical causes of those sensations. Ancient astronomers' distinctions of magnitudes corresponded to equal divisions *of what they knew nothing of*, namely, the logarithm of the energy of light.

The agreement of these judgments, made over many centuries and places by persons of different cultures and races, proves the uniformity of human sensation, hence the possibility of testing one's observations of one's own sensations against observations made by others of *their* own sensations. The agreement is so great that the occasional idiosyncrasy, for example, color blindness, can, by its disagreement with the norm, be identified and set aside.[4] All of this shows that experience is itself capable of being examined empirically. There can be an empirical science of experience, and we know this on empirical grounds.

Furthermore, this knowledge of our own sensations is confirmed by the fact that our sensations correspond in regular fashion to differences in the world experienced. That is to say, the sensations have causes which they, to some degree reliably, map. This conclusion was not new, but it was arrived at in a new way. That sensation is generally reliable is implied by our survival. It is also implied by our success in distinguishing cases where it is not reliable, the familiar catalogue of illusions and delusions. A less familiar example of the same was the experimental proof that differences in color affect judgments of differences in brightness. A red light and a blue light of the same apparent brightness were doubled by superimposing two lights of the red hue on the same spot on the retina and two of the blue hue ditto. The doubled red light appeared brighter (i.e., was so judged by the subject) than the doubled blue light. If Fechner's psychophysical law is correct, the doubled red light could not be brighter than the doubled

---

[4] Just as measurements far from the average are ignored in the method of least squares. How is that consistent with empiricism? The answer is simple: empirical inquiry is not independent of a metaphysic, however tentative. We believe that measurements have causes and that these sometimes produce results wider of the mark than most.

blue light, as the two lights when not doubled were equally bright. It was therefore concluded that the color difference affected judgments of brightness (W3:382, 388–89).

A general moral may be drawn: Once some observations of a given type have been explained, then the causal theory assumed can be used to criticize or refine those observations and others of the same type. That is so, even in cases where the theory is justified by the evidence those same observations provide.

Another moral is to be drawn from Peirce's method in his photometry: Measurement presupposes a scale, and this must first be constructed. Obviously, the scale may be in some respects arbitrary, for example, in English yards rather than Continental meters. But not in all respects. It must be justified by theoretical considerations, as representing real differences, and the theory assumed must be confirmed by consistency among the results of the scale's use. Furthermore, those uses should turn out to be fruitful of additional discovery.

Both of these morals illustrate the fact that inquiry is nonlinear: Results attained are used to criticize, refine, and/or justify the means by which they were attained. Through use, empirical methods grow in strength, reliability, and confidence. Being empirical, this is not circular reasoning.

A third and final moral: Empirical discoveries sometimes revise meanings. An obvious example of this is the distinction between heat and temperature, which did not become common until the latter part of the eighteenth century, when Joseph Black showed how heat could be measured distinctly from measurements of temperature. Peirce's experiments similarly suggest a revision in the concept of observation – not a division of the concept in twain, but its extension to related phenomena. It might have been supposed that observation must always be of what one is conscious of sensing and, hence, of what one has a concept of. But the experiments in subliminal sensitivity challenge that idea in one way, while psychophysical parallelism challenges it in another way. The former established a phenomenon not previously known (unless under such problematic rubrics as 'feminine intuition'). How should that phenomenon be labeled? Should it be called 'observation', or not? The latter experiments concern observations consciously made, but reveal that they correspond to physical quantities the observer may lack any concept of. Should we say, then, that judgments of brightness are observations only of one's own sensations, while measurements of light energy are of objective realities? As brightness is *how* light energy (wave amplitude squared) appears to us, and as color-sensations are *how* wavelengths appear to us, why not say that observations of brightness and of color *are* observations of wave phenomena, even if the observer has no such concept? After all, observations of brightness and color provide data relevant to physical inquiry regardless of whether the persons making those observations have any idea of what light is, physically, or even if they have a false idea of it.

One difficulty reading Peirce is that he defined key terms in surprising ways. It cannot be too much stressed that more often than not these innovations were due to empirical discoveries, and, hence, that they cannot properly be judged in ignorance of the science which he cited or to which he contributed.

D

That Peirce, during his 1875 visit to Paris, had himself tutored in Médoc wines by a French sommelier is well-known and is usually met with a smile, as testifying to a nonscientific interest. He was fond of wine, but in this case, his interest may well have been wholly scientific. For, although not strictly speaking an experiment, that tutelage is akin to the sequence of experiments that he made in training an observer in sensitivity to small differences. Like pre-instrumental observations of stellar magnitudes, wine connoisseurs' judgments require careful attention to their own sensations. But they differ from judgments of stellar magnitudes in being, in essential instances, evaluative. For, that is what wine tasting is all about. The interest in identifying wines, their provenance, and their characteristics – all of that is derivative from an interest in distinguishing the more from the less appreciable, that is, the characteristics or combinations of characteristics that make wine enjoyable, different wines enjoyable in different ways, and some wines more enjoyable than others. That the values in this case are relatively trivial is irrelevant. Peirce's wish to be trained in wine tasting suggests an interest in this important question: whether differences in value are learned by observation of actual instances. In other words, are values a species of positive fact?

A fact is what is represented in a true statement; a positive fact is what is represented in a true statement about actualities (facts of mathematics, for example, are not positive). Without attempting to state a theory of value, something must be said about what distinguishes evaluative judgments from nonevaluative judgments – in such a way as not to beg the question whether such judgments might represent positive facts. This is to be recalled in Chapter 9.

Judgments are what may be expressed by assertively uttering declarative sentences, that is, making statements. Statements and what statements express are what we are inclined to suppose must be either true or false (with some exceptions, for example, some statements about the future). Utterances of sentences in the imperative mood – commands or prescriptions – are not what is at issue; nor are exclamations expressive of attitude. Evaluative statements, however, are closely related to prescriptions and to expressions of attitude, and there have been many philosophers who have argued that such statements are not really either true or false but are properly understood either as prescriptions in disguise or as emotive expressions in disguise.[5] We may draw upon their analyses while cautiously refraining from drawing their respective conclusions.

Their analyses suggest that evaluative judgments may be distinguished by certain predicates occurring (in non-intensional contexts) in their expression, which predicates belong to pro/con pairs having the imperative force of do/don't or being expressive of such attitudes as approval/disapproval, appreciation/disgust, etc. (An intensional context is, for example, '... believes that ...', as in 'Mary believes that it is wrong to lie': Mary's belief is evaluative, but the claim, that that is her belief, is not.) There are many such predicates – we may call them 'value-terms' – the exact list being subject to debate. And there are many such pro/con polarities; for, values are not all of one kind.

This rough sketch will suffice; greater depth or precision will not be needed. However, it should not be taken simplistically. Value-terms have sometimes been said to be distinguished from non-value terms in being action-guiding, for example, 'good' versus 'red'. But if red is what is wanted, then 'X is red' is action-guiding. And 'X is good' is often not action-guiding, for example, not in historical judgments. If moral goodness is meant, 'X is good' may fail to influence the conduct of the morally weak, the immoral, and the amoral. One may even adopt a principle of acting contrary to goodness: 'Evil be thou my good'. However, 'red' does not bear always in one way on action, whereas 'good' functions in our language to approve, recommend, prescribe, urge, etc. and not – normally – to disapprove or proscribe. It is the linguistic norm that matters here. The word 'evil' normally is proscriptive and that is why 'Evil be thou my

---

[5] In the mid-twentieth century, Anglophone philosophers devoted much attention to this topic, particularly with reference to moral language (e.g., Hare 1952, Nowell-Smith 1954). I am not attempting a comparison of Peirce's views to later theories but am using what comes to hand that may help to make his thought clearer.

good' has force, the force of paradox. The pro/con pairs are therefore to be identified by the normal usage of these terms, where normal usage is not merely (and perhaps in some cases is not) the most frequent use but is also (or instead) that use which explains the peculiar meaning or force of deviant uses.

Another warning: We must be wary of abstract words. Values, we noted, are not all of a kind. Even to distinguish moral, aesthetic, and cognitive values fails to do justice to the complexity of values. For example, appreciation is not always approval: We can delight in the charming personality of a known rogue and we can admire the cleverness of an evil genius or the boldness of a villain. Even if we restrict attention to just one dimension of value, say, the enjoyable, the variations are enormous. The pleasures of palate and nose are not the same as the pleasure one takes in music or in solving a chess problem, and all differ from the pleasures of conversation or of doing good deeds. Nor are pains all the same: A stomachache does not feel like a headache and heartache is a pain of another kind. I am not the first to note that many philosophers have mistakenly assumed that pleasure is one feeling and pain is another, whereas in fact neither is a feeling but each is a large class of distinct feelings: feelings we seek are named 'pleasure' and those we try to avoid are named 'pain'. That is, they are what we normally seek or shun, but the human personality is complex: the ascetic shun pleasure and the masochistic seek pain.

The way taken here of distinguishing evaluative judgments, by their expressions containing pro/con terms in non-intensional contexts, does not depend on contrasting them to factual judgments; it does not depend on any dichotomy of evaluation and description. The aim has been to avoid biasing discussion of whether evaluation may be descriptive or, that is to say, factual. For, that is the issue to be discussed.

To defend the assumption, largely due to the materialist and mechanist metaphysics of early modern science, that values never can be facts, philosophers have sometimes cited the fact that moral standards and aesthetic tastes vary markedly among cultures and that even among persons in a given culture there is much disagreement in evaluative judgments. But there is also much agreement, which requires another strategy, viz., to explain that the agreement is due to a common human nature rather than to any values or disvalues discerned in the objects, actions, persons, or policies at issue. The latter strategy is like that of discounting alleged observations of ghosts: it turns on explanation, just as the former strategy depends on statistical analysis. David Hume's view, for example, was that the moral distinctions in which we agree are real – benevolence really is good, cruelty really is bad – but that these characteristics are good or bad only because of the sentiments they evoke in us, due to our common human nature. There are no moral qualities independent of human nature.[6] Sentiment, then, is not observation; it is merely an effect, one that causes us to judge its cause evaluatively. Disagreement is to be explained as due to differences in what we observe and in what we infer from what we observe: so far as we agree about the (nonevaluative) facts, our sentiments, hence our evaluative judgments, will be the same, according to Hume.

There are other ways than Hume's, by which evaluative judgments, or one or another class of such judgments, may be held to be either true or false, without supposing that values have any objective existence. For example, any rule-governed activity entails distinctions between right and wrong, better and worse. If we decide to play chess, then one may not move one's king more than one square at a time and, while it is permissible to advance all one's pawns before moving any other piece, it is wiser not to. So also, promising, conveying information, and the like are, as it were, games defined by rules which may not be violated without undermining the very *raison d'être* of playing (cheating implies extraneous motives). But this, it might be argued, depends on deeper values, such as the goals such games serve.

Hume treated aesthetic taste as he did moral judgment, though he acknowledged that in matters of taste disagreements are more common and harder to resolve. But that is due, he alleged, to differences in sensitivity to those objective features that act on our common human nature so as to produce appreciation or disgust, resulting in judgments of beauty or deformity. In his well-known essay, 'Of the Standard of Taste',[7] he introduced the example, from *Don Quixote*, of two connoisseurs who judged a cask of wine good except for, one said, a slight taste of iron or, the other said, a slight taste of leather; their judgments were derided by the other topers until, when the cask was at last emptied, an iron key on a leather thong was found in it. A standard of taste is a general rule connecting qualities that are not values (qualities assumed to be 'in' the things judged) with sentiments dependent on human nature alone. Perhaps it was this essay which suggested to Peirce the relevance of wine tasting to the more general question, whether observations that result in evaluative judgments are of properties that can be defined in terms not at all evaluative. The alternative is that they cannot be defined except evaluatively, hence that the observation is of a value or a disvalue.

---

[6] See his *Treatise*, Bk.III, Part ii and Part iii, §i, and his second *Enquiry*, §i, §v and Appendix i.
[7] Often anthologized from one or another edition of his *Essays, Moral, Political, and Literary*.

E

As Peirce left no commentary on his experiment in wine tasting, I will attempt to fill in the blank. Lest that effort seem unduly speculative, I aver that it is justified by the sequel, where training by a sommelier will be seen to have been a step on the road, from Peirce's astronomical work, completed in the same year, to the curious experiment at Johns Hopkins, begun eight years later.

Frank Sibley (1959) argued persuasively that there are a large number of 'aesthetic' concepts which cannot successfully be defined by terms not 'aesthetic'. A painting might be called 'delicate' because it has curving contours and pastel colors in subtle contrasts, rather than jagged shapes, colors in bold contrasts, and so on; but these nonaesthetic properties could also be cited to explain why a different painting is judged 'insipid'. Sibley adduced many examples to show that nonaesthetic properties bear in various ways on aesthetic judgment, or taste, but never serve as sufficient conditions for the application of an aesthetic term. He was not arguing that taste is subjective: he noted that, by pointing out features to attend to, a critic can help those less perceptive to see what he sees, to appreciate what he appreciates, and thus to share his evaluation. To do so, Sibley added, the critic uses both nonaesthetic terms, often metaphorically, and also other aesthetic terms than the one at issue. Implicitly against Hume's theory (which he did not mention), Sibley argued that there is no rule, no criterion by which a judgment of taste may be justified by the presence of nonaesthetic properties. Seeing one painting as delicate and another as insipid is seeing what is there, though the quality seen is irreducibly aesthetic.

Not that aesthetic qualities exist distinct from physical, nonaesthetic properties. Rather, the former are irreducible to the latter because they group and divide the latter in ways that cannot be specified abstractly, that is, by rule, but only by the exercise of taste. So also, Bernard Williams (1985) called 'thick' those concepts that apply descriptively but purport morally (he said, 'ethically'), for example, concepts of courage, cowardice, brutality, kindness, courtesy, boorishness. He made the perceptive remark that the fact/value dichotomy is brought to the analysis of language and is not found by analysis (1985, pp.129–30).[8] Thick concepts show this. As against R. M. Hare's theory (Hare 1952), that the descriptive and prescriptive components of such concepts can be distinguished, Williams argued

---

[8] Williams proceeded to reinstate the fact/value dichotomy, which his identification of thick concepts had seemed to undermine. His views receive further consideration in Ch.9.

that the descriptive component cannot be separately identified (Hare 1952, pp.141ff). At what point does boys' roughhousing, which involves intentional infliction of needless pain, cross the line into brutality? Can that line be defined in terms not themselves evaluative? Can it be discerned absent feelings of revulsion?

Sibley did not define 'aesthetic'; instead, he listed a great many examples of terms distinguished either as aesthetic or as nonaesthetic, declaring that those of the former class, unlike those of the latter class, are applied in judgments requiring '… the exercise of taste, perceptiveness, or sensitivity, of aesthetic discrimination or appreciation …' (1959, p.352). In effect, then, he turned into a mark of the aesthetic what Hume took to be a problem needing explanation. For our purpose, what matters is that judgments of taste bear on appreciation, as Sibley called it. The bearing is complex. In Hume's usage, 'appreciation' is one of a pro/con pair, of which the other is 'disgust'. And, indeed, appreciation does ground evaluation. But it may ground negative as well as positive evaluations, the same appreciable quality being in one context positive, in another negative. Whether delicacy in a painting is a positive feature depends on the sort of painting the painting is and on its other features. We can imagine a delicate hue or graceful line in Picasso's *Guernica* that would ruin its effect. So also, a delicate wine is enjoyable sometimes but other times a robust wine is better. Such complications understood the qualities 'appreciated' (i.e., discerned by exercise of taste) are evaluative: Alone or in combination, they account, in given contexts, for evaluative judgments.

Of the qualities, bearing on appreciation, that may be discriminated in wine, some, such as complexity, can be defined in terms owing nothing to appreciation. But when complexity is desired, so also is something called 'balance'; and can the combinations of characteristics that are 'balanced' be identified without being found pleasing? Again, what distinguishes a delicate wine from one lacking character or an earthy wine from one that tastes moldy? Sibley's argument regarding aesthetic concepts seems to apply here: Wine tasting involves the perception of characteristics that cannot be perceived independently of affective response. There is no defining some of these characteristics in value-neutral terms, yet we are inclined to judge them to be real. Of course, there can be chemical analyses of what, in any given instance, produces such-and-so sensations; but these vary from instance to instance, and the grouping of some organic molecules or esters as, say, 'earthy' and others, very similar, as 'moldy', is not reducible to chemical formula.

We do not know what Peirce learned about Médoc or even what he hoped to learn. But his persistent efforts to probe the limits of observation suggest a scientific rather than a bibulous interest. Moreover, the 'great men' study, as we shall next see, was also about evaluative discrimination, albeit non-sensuous. Like wine tasting, that discrimination was not inferred, via rule or criterion, from nonevaluative observations.

F

The 'great men' study was the last of Peirce's experiments on observation, begun at about the time of his and Jastrow's experiment on small differences of sensation and eight or nine years after his tutelage by a sommelier. What was it all about? We get a hint of its point when we notice that the great were placed into six orders of greatness, subdivided by tenths, as early astronomers had divided stellar magnitudes. But greatness, unlike brightness, is a value. Like aesthetic qualities, its perception is appreciation. Or it is something like appreciation: a feeling to which there is a polar opposite. We contemplate the great with a sense of astonishment and awe; others we are less impressed by. As greatness pertains to human endeavor, one might call it a moral value; however, it does not entail moral approval. Approval or disapproval was a prejudice that had to be resisted in judging greatness: 'I think we had a human prejudice against monsters of iniquity and against men of greed' (7.265).

This last is from Peirce's aforementioned c.1900 description of the 1883–1884 study of great men. In it, he revealed that that study was deliberately modeled on observations of stars' brightness. Greatness, like brightness, is a function of an impression made.[9] Its observation requires sensitivity to one's own sensations or feelings: '… one of my main purposes was to train the men to the nice observation of their own sensations, to show them that feelings are capable of direct evaluation with sufficient precision to serve a scientific purpose …' (7.265). Ranking greatness across such classes as poets, scientists, and statesmen, men and women, the good and the evil, is like learning to rank the brightness of stars despite their differences in color. A second purpose, listed in the same sentence, was to show

---

[9] In his 1901 essay, 'The Century's Great Men of Science', Peirce wrote that it wouldn't do to determine greatness by abstract definition; referring to his 'long years of experimentation', he said that one should 'put aside all analysis' and 'estimate the impression'. 'The great man is the impressive personality, and the question whether he is great is a question of impression' (Peirce 1958, pp.266–67).

the students that their impressions could 'admit of mathematical treatment'. After describing how the gradations employed by the 'old astronomers' were found to correspond to equal 'ratios of excitation', conforming to Fechner's law, Peirce concluded, 'The scale of star-magnitudes, having been found to lend itself perfectly to mathematical treatment, was imitated by us in expressing our impressions of the greatness of different men' (7.258).

In this case, however, there can be no independent measure of the strength of the stimulus. Thus the third and final aim listed: 'to demonstrate that they [the students' "sensations" of greatness] do not, for the most part, differ extravagantly among different persons of the same environment'. After the students, having been exposed to uniform biographies of several of the great, individually ranked them by order of greatness, Peirce computed the mean values of each ranking and the variance of the individual rankings from the mean. It turned out that the variation was small: 'extreme variation would not ordinarily exceed two magnitudes' (7.265). Thus, impressions that would have been thought to be personal or idiosyncratic turned out not to be.

An obvious objection is that the students were all from much the same background: they were all able, similarly educated young men, who had been raised in a democratic and predominantly Christian, indeed, Protestant society, and who came to Johns Hopkins because of scientific interests. Of course they judged the great similarly! But that was taken into account: note Peirce's reference to 'the same environment'. The point is that their agreement was greater than could thus be explained. So, at least, Peirce claimed. I think the claim is plausible, though it can only be verified by one's attempting, and failing, to explain their agreement. Do you think that their agreement, for example, that Napoleon is greater than Balzac who is greater than Joan of Arc, could be explained by their being students of science, Christian and democratic in upbringing? Especially as approval/disapproval was to be put aside, could those factors explain that agreement?

Sameness of environment, like the superficiality of the biographical data relied on, makes this agreement to be of no value as an estimate of any figure's true greatness, if there is such a thing as true greatness. Once again, then, greatness is not what the study was about. Its purpose, rather, was what Peirce said it was: '… I cast about for a subject that might afford valuable training in … inductive investigation …'; '… it was desirable to explode the ordinary notions that mathematical treatment is of no advantage when observations are devoid of precision and that no scientific use can be made of very inexact observations' (7.256). What the study showed is that impressionistic feelings can be ranked, examined mathematically, and shown to agree sufficiently to suggest that they have a common cause other than (or in addition to) shared bias.

The passages I have been quoting are from two incomplete drafts of an article Peirce never finished writing. It is not to be taken as a complete and definitive account. But we have to use what is available; other sources (Fisch and Cope 1952, pp.290–91; Jastrow, 1914, 1916) add little. The study's upshot is indicated in a paragraph from one draft and a sentence from another:

> I do not think that there was any man for whom the extreme estimates exceeded two magnitudes.... It is obvious, therefore, that if what we mean by a judgment being 'objectively valid' is that all the world will agree in it, and after all Kant's discussion that is about what it comes to, then there was a satisfactory degree of 'objectivity' in the mean magnitudes we assigned, although they referred, not to the man as he really was, but to the man as he was presented in the account read to the class, and although the marking could not escape a large 'subjective' percentage due to our common, but not thoroughly catholic, culture and environment. (7.259)
>
> This objectivity is, like Mercutio's wound, not as wide as a church door, yet 'twill serve. (7.266)

The objectivity referred to did not pertain to any claim made about the great as they really were – Peirce made that clear: 'they referred, not to the man as he really was'. However, the impressions formed showed a degree of agreement not explained by common culture alone. But what, then, is the explanation?

Is there a quality of greatness, occurring in different degrees, represented in the capsule biographies (accurate or not, penetrating or not) read to the class, and does that quality explain the concordance of the students' judgments of greatness? The quality in question cannot be physical and the explanation of our perceiving it cannot be physical and physiological, like the explanations which connect physical properties to our sensations of them; it cannot be mechanistic. What, then, could the explanation be? If none but mechanistic explanations are possible, then it cannot be concluded, from the students' agreement in judgment, admittedly slight, that they were observing any real quality. It can only be concluded that there is something beyond a shared culture – something, then, common in human nature – that, as in Hume's analysis of taste, causes similar evaluative response to similar nonevaluative facts. Surely the hypothesis Peirce was exploring is more interesting than that.

In Chapter 9, we will explore Peirce's idea, not expressed before the turn of the new century, of a science, or set of sciences, at once empirical and normative. To establish such a realm of possible empirical knowledge, it is necessary not only that the putative observations be made and that they be found to agree more than they would by chance, but also that their agreement (and occasional disagreement) can be explained on the hypothesis that the entities which those judgments purport to represent are real. As the 'great men' experiment accomplished – in a most unpromising realm! – the first two conditions only, it was but a step in the direction Peirce was evidently taking.

CHAPTER 8

Phaneroscopy and Realism

Peirce first wrote of a new science of phenomenology in 1902, in ignorance of Husserl's similar idea broached under that same name c.1900. Each borrowed the term from Hegel, who used it differently. In 1904, Peirce adopted the term 'phaneroscopy', so as to distinguish his science from Hegel's phenomenology. Like 'phenomenology', the new coinage has a Greek root denoting appearances. But appearances are often assumed to be disjoined from reality, whereas, for Peirce as for Husserl, the idea was to study all that is present to mind without judging what is or is not real. Most importantly: it is *not* assumed that reality is knowable only by inference from appearances.

This new science presupposes the expansion of empiricism described in the preceding chapter, specifically, the experiments showing that there can be intersubjective agreement about the character of our respective experiences of the same things. Experience – indifferently yours or mine – can then be made an object of study. So also can memory, imagination, and contemplation; for, as these are related to experience, they may be inferred to be in general features the same among persons. All these constitute 'the phaneron' (EP2:362). Phaneroscopists observe the phaneron and endeavor to identify its universal features. Immediately, a problem: How can appearances be described without assuming anything about what is real? Our descriptive vocabulary, ordinary and scientific, is replete with assumptions about causality and reality. To describe a stick as 'straight' is to imply that it really is straight even if it sometimes appears bent; a rose that is red is so even in the dark, because being red is conceived of as the cause of something's appearing red in good light; and so on. Peirce's answer was to draw his vocabulary from pure mathematics. He always maintained that pure mathematics explores the necessary consequences of the merely supposed (PM:3–9, 25–36). Thus, it assumes nothing about reality.[1]

---

[1] Peirce held that the ideal world of mathematical study is itself real (a subject of some debate: see Tiercelin 1993, 2010), but that is a conclusion drawn from the fact of mathematical discovery; it is not assumed in such discovery.

But which part of mathematics will serve this purpose? Peirce chose that branch to which he himself had made the most signal contribution, the algebra of relations. But how did he know that appearances could success-fully be analyzed in relational terms? And how did he know that this would result in anything of interest? Those questions were answered in Chapter 5, Section G. The possibility of a relational phaneroscopic analysis had to have been discovered – almost, one might say, stumbled upon. It cannot be known a priori. And that such analysis is worthwhile can be known only by applying its results in other inquiries and seeing whether they prove fruitful. His 1867 'New List' paper is important as being where he stumbled into a relational analysis and glimpsed its potential use. The following year he began work on an algebra of relations (*vide supra*, Ch.1, C).

This ordering of diverse inquiries – first mathematics, then phaneros-copy, then applications of phaneroscopy to other inquiries, distinguishable as philosophic – suggested a taxonomy of sciences, arranged hierarchically. For, the very possibility of phaneroscopy depends on mathematics' inde-pendence of it and on phaneroscopy's independence of normative and other realist inquiries. But 'independence' here refers to systematic exposi-tion, and not to discovery, confirmation, or significance, in each of which the order of dependence is reversed (as in the case of relational analysis just noted). It is therefore no accident that in the same year, 1902, that Peirce first wrote of phenomenology, he also introduced a taxonomy structured by relations of dependence. He had earlier proposed other taxonomies of the sciences; this one was the last. We will spend a moment with it, then pro-ceed to an exposition of phaneroscopic method; next, to an exposition of the three phaneroscopic categories and their modal interpretation; finally, to the use of phaneroscopy in defending metaphysical realism, scholastic, modal, and physical. As this chapter attempts much, textual exegesis, in Sections A through E, will be sacrificed to systematic exposition.[2] Beginning in Section F, we reenter exegesis' forbidding thickets.

A

The 1902 taxonomy[3] of the sciences is constructed on the assumption that one science is 'basic' to another in the sense indicated above: viz., that in

---

[2] These sections correspond to Chapter 3 of Short (2007); the repetition is inescapable; however, much said earlier is here condensed, other themes expanded.
[3] 1.231–82 is the text in which the 1902 taxonomy was presented; briefer statements of the same were made in 1903 at EP2:146–47, 196–200, 258–62; cf. Kent (1987).

their systematic exposition, one depends on another but not conversely. The theoretical sciences – in 1903 renamed more accurately 'sciences of discovery' (EP2: 258–9) – are basic to the sciences of review and to the practical sciences, while, of the sciences of discovery, mathematics is the most basic, next the philosophical sciences, of which phenomenology is the most basic, and then the 'special' sciences of physics, economics, philology, etc.

This is subject to misunderstanding. The 1902 taxonomy is not foundationalist. In the first place, it lists itself among the sciences 'of review', from which it follows that it is not laid down a priori. It extrapolates from dependencies found among existing inquiries and it is subject to revision as new discoveries result in new relationships among diverse specialties. That the sciences can be so arranged – and to what extent so arranged – must always remain to be seen. The taxonomy is a hypothesis to be confirmed, or not, by the outcome of future inquiry. So also, any subsequent revision of it is a hypothesis.

Secondly, the idea of one science being 'basic' to another does not imply that those more basic must be completed first. Typically, the less basic sciences develop first and bring more basic inquiries into being as necessary to supply their needs. For example, it was a need of physics that drove the development of the differential and integral Calculus. The Calculus is basic to physics only in the sense that its theorems do not depend on physical discovery, whereas physical theory makes use of the Calculus.

Nor, thirdly, is it implied that the more basic sciences dictate principles to those less basic. The principles provided are not applied mechanically; the less basic sciences take what they need, as if from a tool box. Where and how the physicist uses the Calculus is up to the physicist, not the mathematician.

Finally, the less basic sciences not only motivate but also confirm the more basic; they do so by being applications of the more basic, in which the latter are tested and their significance for further inquiry is shown. This is the opposite of foundationalism.

The sciences of discovery include mathematics. The fact that mathematicians make discoveries, albeit not by observing the actual world, poses a problem for those who suppose that all knowledge not empirical is tautological. Peirce argued that mathematical reasoning is observational: It consists in observing the results of experiments on diagrams, including the linear diagrams of algebra; this is not the same as empirical observation (*vide supra*, Ch.4, D). It is not the diagrams themselves but the possibilities, sometimes ideal only, they represent that matter. Since experiments made on diagrams have results not entailed by one's concepts, non-tauto-logical necessary truths are discovered. The joy of mathematics is in discovering truths at once surprising and necessary.

By placing philosophy among the sciences of discovery, rather than among the practical sciences, Peirce implied the view that he had stated in 1898, that philosophy should be free from all practical, including all moral, considerations; it should make no attempt to edify (EP2:27–41). Philosophy is divided into phenomenology, as most basic, then the three normative sciences – in order: aesthetics, ethics, and logic – and, lastly, metaphysics. It follows that even the normative sciences are meant not to influence conduct but only to discover truths. Hence Peirce's extraordinary doctrine, which implies (not in words he used) that values are facts. I do not mean facts (historical, anthropological, etc.) about what particular people have valued, but, rather, facts intrinsically normative.

All the sciences of discovery are observational and are distinguished by their means of observation, mathematics being by diagrams and the special sciences by such instruments as measuring sticks and pendulums and cell-staining and demographic surveys and historical documents. The philosophical sciences are distinguished from the other sciences by their not requiring any special instruments of observation, but only a training in noticing what confronts us all, all of the time. (Sometimes, Peirce used 'observation' in a narrow sense: philosophy '… makes no observations but contents itself with so much of experience as pours in upon every man every hour of his waking life' (5.13n1, c.1902). The contradiction is merely verbal.)

Apart from mathematics, all sciences are 'positive' (a term Peirce adopted from Comte) in the sense of establishing contingent fact.[4] Phenomenology is the most basic of the positive sciences of discovery. As to the normative sciences, more in the next chapter, where we will see why aesthetics is basic to ethics, which is basic to logic. That logic is basic to metaphysics was an old doctrine of Peirce's, well-grounded in the history of metaphysics, though the way in which he thought it basic kept changing. We have seen that in practice the hierarchy of sciences is jumbled, and thus it will be no surprise to discover that metaphysical considerations not only drove Peirce's phenomenology but also that he tended to pass swiftly from the categories' phenomenological description to their metaphysical application, skipping over the intermediate normative sciences.

---

[4] Peirce may have employed this term rather than 'empirical' because historiography, philology, cultural anthropology, etc., are not empirical in the way the natural sciences are. Their data derive from reading documents or otherwise interpreting symbols.

Peirce mentioned other categories, distinguished as 'particular', that is, as not applying universally, perhaps modeled on the distinction in Kant's table of categories, between quantity, quality, relation, and modality, on the one hand, and the three modes into which each of those is divided, on the other. Though Kant referred only to the latter twelve as categories, it is the first four that count as universal categories in Peirce's lexicon (see, for example, EP2:148). Peirce's idea of 'particular categories' or (equivalently?) 'material categories' remained undeveloped and has been little commented on except by Richard Atkins (2018, pp.140–43, 180–204). Atkins' detailed treatment is persuasive, and it is important to know that that type of phaneroscopic analysis is possible; but I remain of the opinion that it is the universal categories that matter in addressing the larger questions of philosophy.

B

The relevant texts for Peirce's phenomenology/phaneroscopy are from the years 1885–1910 (1.284–544, EP2:145–95, 8.264–9, 327–41). Writings of the years before 1902 are germane, because they contain suggestive phaneroscopic descriptions made before the idea of phaneroscopy had been framed. However, there are many discrepancies among these texts, sometimes merely verbal, other times conceptual; there are discrepancies also among those post-1902, as Peirce's thought never ceased evolving; I shall ignore all these discrepancies in the interest of presenting a consistent doctrine concisely. For example, I shall use 'phaneron' and its cognates rather than 'phenomenon' and its cognates, even when citing writings using the latter term, and I shall speak of 'the phaneron', as Peirce sometimes did, and not of 'phanerons', as he did other times.

What does phaneroscopy require? Like every science, it is an inquiry engaged in by specialists who must communicate their discoveries to one another for confirmation or correction and to other specialists for use in their own, non-phaneroscopic inquiries. This presupposes not only a common language but also the knowledge that there are other persons. Phaneroscopy presupposes, furthermore, that the experience of each can be directly observed only by that person himself: that is part of what distinguishes phaneroscopic observation. In short, no matter how basic phaneroscopy is and no matter that it may presuppose nothing in its analyses, the idea of phaneroscopy presupposes much, as does any statement of its method. In particular, while the language of phaneroscopic description must be drawn from mathematics, so as to avoid realist assumptions, in the identification of the experiences to be described, there must be use of nonmathematical language, ordinary or scientific, in which ideas of physical and social reality are implicit. For it is only in relation to the publicly observable that private experiences can be publicly identified. Thus, for example, one phaneroscopist can ask another whether he agrees that seeing a color differs in relational complexity from the experience of pushing. For these reasons, it is essential to phaneroscopy that it is not a foundationalist exercise like Descartes' 'Meditations', in which nothing is to be presumed. That nothing may be presumed is, if Peirce is correct, impossible.

For the purposes of phaneroscopy, very little of the algebra of relations is needed; let us begin by stating that little formally, using realistic, not phaneroscopic, examples. As earlier (Ch.1, B), a monadic predicate, Rx, is one true of objects taken one at a time; for example, x is blue, x is a man, x walks. A dyadic predicate, Rxy, is one true of ordered pairs of objects; for example, x is larger than y. A triadic predicate, Rxyz, is true of ordered triplets, for example, x means y to z. In some cases, the order among subjects does not matter: if R is being equal, then, for a given x and y, Rxy if and only if Ryx. In other cases, the order does matter: if R is being larger than, then, for a given x and y, Rxy only if not Ryx; and if R is loves, then, sadly, from Rxy nothing follows about Ryx.

We must distinguish predicates from what they represent, which we shall refer to as relations. Relations in the ordinary sense of that term are what dyadic or triadic predicates represent; for convenience, we shall extend the term to what monadic predicates represent. Thus, monadicity, dyadicity, and triadicity are three orders ('adicities') both of predicate and of relation. We shall call 'higher' an order combining more terms and 'lower' one combining fewer.

There often are discrepancies between the order of a predicate and the order of the relation it represents. A relation appears to be of the order of the predicate by which it is represented; it may be of a different order in reality. Consider, for example, the monadic predicate, 'x is a gift'. By conception, there is no gift if there are not two other items, the giver and the recipient: x gives y to z, Rxyz. That is so, even if the giver and the recipient are the same person (if it is possible for one to give a gift to himself), Rxyx, or even if the gift is the giver ('He gave himself to The Cause'), Rxxy. The monadic predicates 'x is a gift', 'x is a giver', 'x is a recipient' are thus *elliptical*: Each is understood as implying a triadic relation. An elliptical predicate is of lower order than is the relation it represents.

Ellipticity has a converse, named *reducibility*. For example, the triadic predicate, 'x benefitted y by doing z' represents, by conception, a logical compound of two dyadic relations: x did z *and* z benefitted y. (A logical compound is formed by combining other linguistic units by means of such logical particles as 'and', 'not', 'if', and 'some'.) There is in that case no triadic relation in reality but merely two dyadic relations. Whereas ellipticity is the characteristic of a predicate, it is more common to assign reducibility to relations: but those are relations as they appear to be, that is, as represented by predicates. An apparent relation is reducible if the predicate that represents it is equivalent (whether logically or in some other way) to a logical compound of non-elliptical predicates of lower order.

Can a relation of higher order be *irreducible* to any compound of relations of lower order? Consider a plausible example, phrased in a familiar notation, in which '$\forall x$' is to be read, 'for any x' and '$\exists x$', 'for some x', and in which '$\&$' abbreviates 'and', '$\rightarrow$', 'only if', and '$\leftrightarrow$', 'if and only if'. To illustrate the notation, the formula,

$$\forall x \ (x \text{ is a gift} \leftrightarrow \exists y \exists z \ (y \text{ gives } x \text{ to } z))$$

represents the ellipticity of being a gift. Now, while

$$\forall x \forall y \forall z \ (x \text{ gives } y \text{ to } z \rightarrow (x \text{ is a giver } \& \ y \text{ is a gift } \& \ z \text{ is a recipient}))$$

is true, its converse,

$$\forall x \forall y \forall z \ ((x \text{ is a giver } \& \ y \text{ is a gift } \& \ z \text{ is a recipient}) \rightarrow x \text{ gives } y \text{ to } z)$$

is false. Were this statement true, it would show that giving is reducible to the three monadic relations represented; its being false therefore shows that giving is not thus reducible. It does not follow, but it is strongly suggested, that giving is reducible to no combination of monadic and dyadic relations.

The idea of irreducibility is key to phaneroscopic analysis. However, the examples considered so far do not illustrate that form of analysis. Not only are they realistic, their analysis is conceptual: In their case, the equivalence, or lack of equivalence, of a predicate to a logical compound of predicates is to be discovered by reflecting on what the concept, that the predicate in question expresses, logically entails; the equivalence is logical. But not every equivalence of a predicate to a logical compound of predicates is itself logical. Instead of conceptual analysis, we might try causal explanation. For example, the monadic predicate 'warm' denotes what in reality is an average of molecular kinetic energies. What the concept of warmth was before the eighteenth century, or what it still is in ordinary usage, does not matter: The equivalence is factual, not logical. Now, in phaneroscopy, the reality of a relation is not at issue, but neither is its conception. Phaneroscopy employs concepts and constructs new concepts, but it is not *about* concepts. It is neither reality nor concepts but experience that is to be analyzed. And in this case, too, there can be a discrepancy of order, namely, between that of a predicate and that of a relation *as experienced*. 'Continuous' is a monadic predicate, but the experience of continuity will be shown in Section D to be triadic. The verb 'push' may be either transitive (dyadic) or intransitive (monadic), but the experience of pushing will be shown in the next section to be dyadic – or, rather, to have a distinguishable component that is irreducibly dyadic.

Peirce asserted on formal grounds that all relations of order higher than triadic could be reduced to logical compounds of relations of lower order, and that not all triadic relations and not all dyadic relations can be so reduced.[5] But that does not settle the phaneroscopic question. What *in experience*, if anything, is irreducibly triadic, what is irreducibly and non-elliptically dyadic, and what is non-elliptically monadic? That all experience is, in content, monadic only is what Locke and the other British empiricists have ambiguously espoused (Locke presented 'ideas of relations' as depending on 'comparison', that is, of items monadic, the act of comparison being dyadic; Hume wrote of 'impressions' having 'force and vivacity' and being 'contiguous', all which imply dyadicity, but that does not pertain to their contents). If so, then all other relations are introduced by our clever minds, as convenient ways of representing congeries of monadic impressions. Kant differed from the empiricists by making our cleverness to be structured innately, grounding non-tautological truths a priori. Peirce, by contrast, held that we have direct experience of relations irreducibly dyadic and others irreducibly triadic. That doctrine depends on an examination of experience – one that contradicts the British empiricists' unstated assumption of monadicity.

This brings us to the heart of the subject. The aim of phaneroscopy is to identify the three irreducible orders of relational complexity in experience. These are the phaneroscopic 'categories': 1stness, the category of the monadic, 2ndness, the category of the irreducibly dyadic, and 3rdness, the category of the irreducibly triadic.

---

[5] Peirce offered some less than rigorous proofs and claimed to have rigorous proofs, but the latter have not been found. Whether his theses can be proved is a matter of controversy: Herzberger 1981, Burch 1991, Kerr-Lawson 1992. My view is that such proofs, while they would be nice to have, are not essential to phaneroscopy.

Before proceeding to a discussion of the phaneroscopic categories, more needs to be said about phaneroscopic method. The categories cannot be discerned by logical analysis of a concept nor by explanatory hypothesis, but only by an analysis of experience. A rough account of such analysis might be as follows. Given an X and a Y that are distinct but experienced together, let the experience of X be drawn as narrowly as possible: Is it still an experience also of Y? If it is, then the experience of X is irreducibly complex: It is not of X alone, but of X in dyadic relation to Y or in triadic relation to Y and some third item. X in that case is experienced *as* a relatum. But how is this narrowing – which is my term, not Peirce's – done, and how is it done in such a way that we can see, with at least some degree of assurance, that further narrowing, leaving out Y, is not possible without leaving out X, too?

Peirce never produced an account of phaneroscopic method with which he was satisfied. We saw (Ch.5, D) that in the 1867 'New List', he introduced a method of distinguishing that he named 'prescision': 'that which arises from attention to one element and neglect of the other'. Something like this is indeed required (De Tienne 1989, 1996); yet, in later writings the term occurs infrequently and, with only one exception that I have found, not in expositions of phenomenological/phaneroscopic method so named.[6] The exception (EP2:367) occurs in a 1905 fragment, in which the noun 'prescision' does not occur but the verb 'prescind' occurs, though only twice, in one sentence and without any explanation. That fragment was intended for an article never completed. As the article was not completed, it is likely that a problem was encountered and not resolved. Might that problem have been with the idea of precision? The fragment as a whole (EP2:360–70) works a chemical analogy, embodied in the phrase, 'indecomposable element', about which I will say more in Section H. There are several references in this fragment to 'logical analysis' and to 'logically indecomposable' elements of experience, but the point is that phaneroscopy describes those elements of experience the concepts of which are *not* subject to logical analysis.[7]

---

[6] Under various spellings and variously defined, not always consistently, the term occurs without reference to phenomenology or phaneroscopy in 1885 at W5.238, 1893 at 2.428, 1902 at 4.235, 1905 at 1.313n1 and 5.449, and 1910 at 2.364. In 1867 prescision was one type of abstraction, but in these writings it is cited by way of contrast to abstraction properly so named (otherwise distinguished as 'hypostatic'), the latter being implied to be more important.

[7] Many have supposed that logical analysis is part of phaneroscopy, for which the textual evidence is limited to this fragment – misunderstood. They have perhaps been unduly influenced by logical analysis in the mode of Frege, Russell et al., which employs the logic of relations in an analysis of concepts, not of experience. Logical analysis can only be of concepts, propositions, and the like.

The second of the 1903 Harvard lectures (EP2:145–59) presents the science of phenomenology without mentioning prescision. In this lecture, the method is vaguely described as consisting of observation, discrimination, and generalization (147–48). Now, observers need to know what they are looking for: It is implicit in Peirce's account that the observation of experience is to be guided by the idea of the three lowest orders of relation; it is not explained how this is to be done. And then, in that and in subsequent lectures, the three categories are adumbrated. Thus the method, though it is inadequately formulated, is persuasively illustrated. Let us follow that strategy, exemplifying rather than formulating the method, and allowing the results attained to testify to its cogency. Its correct formulation remains a problem to be solved.

C

'Go out under the blue dome of heaven,' Peirce said in 1903, 'and look at what is present as it appears to the artist's eye' (EP2:149). We are to ignore all that we know about the physics of light and the physiology of sensation; we are to ignore even the psychology of color-perception, though it involves contrasts within the perceptual field. We are also to ignore the fact that color as experienced combines hue, luminosity, and saturation, if those features are not distinct to the perceiver. Usually, they are not distinct; recall that Peirce had to train himself to observe luminosity distinct from hue. Of course, experience is a function of prior learning. Our ability to attend to color distinct from shape and to be aware of this shade as one shade distinct from other shades depends on past contrasts and comparisons (as Peirce noted in the 'New List'), and on verbalization and conception. But that, too, is not a content of the experience itself. We are to concentrate, like an artist, on the quality itself, as it appears. So identified, it is not what it is in relation to any other; neither is it a relation of two or more. It is monadic, an example of phaneroscopic 1stness.

We call this quality 'blue', but it is not what the word 'blue' denotes, which is a spectrum of shades (either sensed or physical). A spectrum combines many into one and, therefore, it is triadic (see Section D), not monadic. The exact shade of blue seen has no description that distinguishes it from all other shades of blue; 'azure' only denotes a narrower

---

Peirce sometimes drew hints from such analysis of what to look for in phaneroscopy – we shall begin Section D with an extended example – evidently on the assumption that conceptual distinctions normally have experiential roots. But that does not make it part of phaneroscopy.

spectrum. A particular shade experienced cannot be known by description but only by experience. It is ineffable. The ineffable falls under concepts but is not fully comprehended in the concepts under which it falls. That is, perhaps, not the usual meaning of 'ineffable', but it is how I shall use the term. The effable (a word archaic but useful) is fully comprehended by a concept. This distinction between the ineffable and the effable is crucial to the argument made in Section D, in which effability will be illustrated.

But any quality perceived must be of some duration, however brief, and, in the case of colors, of some spatial extent, and within that time and space there is room for variations, possibly continuous (one shade of blue shading into another). To speak of any one instance of 1stness – that is, a 1st – is therefore an idealization, akin to Euclidean lines without width and dimensionless points.

Phaneroscopic 1stness is not monadicity in general; it is the monadic element in experience. Words used to direct attention to that aspect of the phaneron may then be made into a technical term of phaneroscopy, redefined as denoting exactly that aspect. Thus Peirce made 'quality of feeling' a synonym for phaneroscopic 1stness. One cannot understand his use of 'quality of feeling' merely by looking up 'quality' and 'feeling' in Webster; one has to attend to the examples given, with the idea of monadicity in mind:

> Such a consciousness might be just an odor ... one infinite dull ache ... [a] piercing eternal whistle. In short, any simple and positive quality of feeling .... The first category, then, is Quality of Feeling, or whatever is such as it is ... regardless of aught else. (EP2:150)

The words 'infinite' and 'eternal' have to be understood here, not as denoting extent, but as excluding location or extension, spatial or temporal. We can distinguish the ache from any idea we might have about how long it is to be endured. Concentrate on the ache itself; forget that it is in your toe, which you have just stubbed, and that you expect the pain to subside shortly; and then you will understand what Peirce meant by 'quality of feeling'.

Elsewhere, Peirce cited other qualities of feeling than those that are sensory, for example, 'the quality of the emotion upon contemplating a fine mathematical demonstration' (1.304). More obviously than in the case of color-perception, experiencing that emotion depends on a set of relations – from which the emotion may nonetheless be distinguished. Any emotion has its intrinsic quality, or complex of qualities, or qualities swiftly shading one into another, distinguishable from their reference to things, persons, events, and principles. There is the perfidy of a friend who proved treacherous and then there are one's feelings of indignation, giving way to sorrow, waxing into anger, modulating into contempt, and so on.

We have already encountered phaneroscopic 2ndness in two examples. One was pushing. Think of pushing a cart. The experience of the effort made differs from one's intention to move the cart and from any ideas one might have of cause and effect. But it cannot be had without also experiencing the resistance to that effort. The experience of effort and the experience of resistance are the same experience. It is a single but bipolar experience: an experience within which the effort and the resistance are distinguished as mutually opposed. Opposition is, Peirce said, 'a single fact', 'a fact of complexity', and 'not a compound of two facts' (1.526).

Peirce often denoted phaneroscopic 2ndness by 'action and reaction' or by 'struggle'. Neither phrase can be grasped in its phaneroscopic meaning without deleting the reference of the first to Newtonian physics and that of the second to intention. They have to be understood as denoting the dyadic element *within* the sort of experience one has when one is (in the full ordinary sense of the word) struggling to overcome a physical resistance. Phaneroscopic 2ndness, then, does not include every dyadic relation. Rather, it is the dyadic within experience: a felt opposition.

To say that phaneroscopic 2ndness is an experience of 'self' versus 'other' is suggestive but implies too much. It implies a consciousness of oneself as an entity and an idea of entities not oneself. Such concepts go beyond the dyadic element in experience. Yet, it is this dyadic element which grounds the sense we have (once we do come to self-consciousness) that we are interacting with things other than ourselves. Think of an infant, as yet innocent of any concept, reaching and grabbing, pushing and pulling. The behavior is instinctual, the resulting experiences are directional: pushing away or pulling towards. Individuals, self and other, are experienced as located relative to one another in space and time, in dynamic interaction. Phaneroscopic 2ndness is that element in experience that accounts for our sense of things existing or occurring, as located here and now, and, hence, as individual. Our ideas of individuality, location, and existence are all rooted in the same element of experience, phaneroscopic 2ndness; only by metaphorical extension may individuality or existence be pried loose from location.

Direction, however, can only be defined with reference to additional points in space, uniting a variety of experienced oppositions; and it can only be experienced in a continuity of motion. The definition and the experience are each in their different ways triadic. We can speak of 2nds, but, like 1sts, they are idealizations. A 2nd is instantaneous and innocent of combination, whereas experience is continuous. Nonetheless, it is the element of 2ndness within the continuity of experience which grounds our sense of existence. And it is 2ndness felt in directionality that grounds our idea of space.

The concept of the individual is the concept of that which is not conceptual, hence, not general. We can use words to speak of what distinguishes things from words; we can say that it is the dyadic in experience that does this. But the words alone cannot capture that distinction. Obviously, they cannot: for then the distinction would fail. To know what the dyadic in experience is, one has to have experience: and then one has to attend to its dyadic aspect, *a fortiori* with the formal concept of dyadicity in mind. Like 1stness, therefore, 2ndness is ineffable. It is known by experience, not by description. It can be accurately described, namely, as dyadic, but the description does not suffice to convey what it is that is thus described. The dyadic element in experience is not dyadicity in general; it is nothing general.

The other example of 2ndness cited was one's sense of fact, that this *is* blue. Again, we have to put aside all concepts introducing realist assumptions, for example, one's idea of oneself as seeing that color. The word 'fact' is suggestive but treacherous. A fact is that which can be stated in words, some of which must be in meaning general; 2ndness, then, is less than the factual. But it is the element in experience that distinguishes fact from wish, imagination, reverie. It is the insistency of the blue seen that distinguishes it as actual; an effort made to see something different (without closing one's eyes or looking elsewhere) will fail.

A blue as 1st is distinguished from its occurring, from its being here and now. To be sure, it is actual only as the content of a 2nd. But actually occurring does not make it what it is. Its actuality – 2ndness – is added to it. In itself, a 1st is a mere may-be. What may be is not diminished if it is never made actual; it remains what may be. (In the distinction of 1stness and 2ndness we have the root of the distinction between actuality and one sort of possibility; another sense of 'possibility', exceeding the may-be, is discussed in the next section.) So far, however, we are speaking of possibility and actuality only as elements of the phaneron, that is, as contents of experience.

That possibility is not elliptical for some number of actualities is a profound and characteristic conclusion of Peirce's phaneroscopy. Just as not every relationally complex whole is reducible to its parts, so also, not every part is elliptical for the whole. Actuality is irreducibly dyadic; it is not composed of 1sts, one added to another. And the may-be is non-elliptically monadic; thus, there *are* possibilities that never occur.

D

Combination, even of just two items, is irreducibly triadic: x and y make z. Combination is always more than the items combined, since it is also how they are put together. This is conceptual analysis, not phaneroscopy. Let us continue in that vein for a few moments.

How the items are combined may be expressed as a rule, and every rule is general. Peirce defined generality as that which no set of actual individuals can exhaust (e.g., in 1903 at EP2:183): there can always be more examples of a type, more instances of a rule. Take the loosest sort of example, say, a pile of stones. Some have to rest on others, otherwise it is not a pile: that is the rule that defines 'pile'. That rule is general not only as applying to any number of distinct piles but also in the way it applies to just one pile. Stone A rests on stones B and C; stone C rests on stone D; and so on. Furthermore, any number of stones may be combined into one pile, which will retain its identity if some stones are added or a few (not too many) are subtracted. There is no upper limit on the possible changes that can be made in a pile while maintaining its character as a pile and, indeed, as this particular pile (as an organism remains the same while gaining and losing matter). An individual combination, as it consists not only of what is combined but also in a rule of combination, is general: it is a whole of many parts and, indeed, potentially of more or other parts. But it is also an instance of a type. It is general in being of many and it is singular in being one of many.

The fact that an individual thing is general *qua* embracing many is central to much that follows. However, the relation of type to instance, or of a law to its instances, is different from the relation of a whole to its parts. An individual thing has a location, and at that location its parts may be found; types and laws have no locations and their instances may be scattered. (A biological species and some works of art occupy an intermediate category: like individuals, they have origins in time, a history, and initially a location, but like types, they may have any number of instances – members of a species, performances of a sonata – in different places.)

As laws and types are not individual things, it would not be correct to say that a law or a type combines their instances into single wholes: they are not combinations. Nevertheless, like combinations, they are triadic. Anything general is triadic: only in relation to many can it be defined as one, whether the many are actual or possible only.

Continuity is an example of triadicity important to Peirce. Although a continuum is not formed by combination, as its parts have no distinct existence, it is divisible into many. As its parts are not distinct, Peirce once described continuity as the 'perfection' of combination. Continuing with conceptual analysis, we may say that z is a continuum only if it is undivided but can be divided (if not physically, at least mathematically) – at any number of points – into parts. This is a necessary condition of continuity, not its definition (among other considerations, the parts must also be continua). Peirce worked persistently throughout his career on the mathematical analysis of continuity, never satisfied.[8] At least by 1903, he appears to have decided that the concept he wished to make mathematically exact is that of an unbroken expanse – an idea grounded in ordinary experience. An unbroken expanse is everywhere divisible but nowhere divided; when broken, it is broken into parts also continuous. It is that inexact concept on which we will here rely, taking especially to heart Peirce's 1903 statement that a continuum 'contains no definite parts', because any definition of parts 'breaks' the continuity (PM:138–39).

It follows that continuity *consists in* unactualized possibilities. Unactualized possibilities are the actuality of any actual continuum. An actual stick is continuous from one end to the other; otherwise, it would not be one stick. But its continuity consists in what is not – it's not being broken here, there, anywhere that it could be broken. There are more unactualized possibilities than can be actualized: each can be, but not all can be. The possibilities a continuum embraces are inexhaustible; a continuum, therefore, is general in nature, even if it is limited to a single individual thing of finite extent, such as this stick.

And each of the possibilities a continuum contains is something that *would be, were* a certain break made. The rule or law defining a continuum connects counterfactual condition to type of result. Being determined by law, what would be is not merely what may be. There is a way in which it can be brought about: it is a potentiality. As laws are of many kinds, for example, mathematical, physical, moral, civil, so also potentialities are of

---

[8] After 1884, Peirce was influenced by Cantor but soon rejected Cantor's identification of continuity with the real number system. Cantor proved, and so did Peirce independently, that the cardinal number of the set of subsets of a set, A, is always higher than the cardinal number of A, even if A is infinite; from which Peirce, but not Cantor, concluded that a continuum is divisible at more points than the real numbers, or any set of numbers, can represent. See the writings from 1884 to 1908 collected in PM:135–225; also 6.177–82 of 1911. Potter and Shields (1977) and Putnam (1995) are helpful. Peirce's later mathematical definitions of continuity might be described as topological (Havenel 2008).

many kinds. I would be obligated to you were you to make me the loan I request. What would be mathematically might not be possible physically; thus continuity is a mathematical notion, not one of physics though employed in physics.

So much for conceptual analysis; let us return, now, to phaneroscopy. The major texts that bear on what I shall say about the phaneroscopy of 3rdness are from the seven 'Lectures on Pragmatism' delivered at Harvard in 1903 (EP2:133–241). As it is primarily to these lectures that I shall refer in the remainder of this chapter, citations to them will be by page number alone (of EP2).

Thought is part of experience, but continuity not only is thought of; it is also experienced independently of thought. For, continuity is present to us everywhere in sensation. It could not be otherwise, as we cannot sense a mathematical point. Colors seen, sounds heard, motion felt must always be of some continuous extent, spatial and/or temporal, whether or not their physical reality is continuous. As continuity is irreducibly triadic, it follows that irreducible triadicity is a universal feature of sensory experience. 'Thirdness pours in upon us through every avenue of sense', Peirce said in Lecture VI (211). And this, we have seen, consists in generality, law, and potentiality, ergo, unactualized possibilities. All this is given in sensation.

However, to apprehend 3rdness as 3rdness is another matter. To apprehend the stick we see or feel as being continuous from end to end, we must *think of it* as *not* broken – that is, not broken at any point where it could be broken. And we can think of it as not broken only if we have ideas of breaking and of parts. Such ideas are general: like types and laws, they apply to any number of instances, actual and possible. Having an idea in mind, we can judge that there is *nothing of that type* in what we sense, for example, no breaks. Only then is the stick's continuity apprehended.

One might object that all apprehension is thought, and that it is therefore a trivial truth that the apprehension of 3rdness requires thought. But the role of thought in the apprehension of 3rdness goes deeper than that. Peirce often remarked that 3rdness is of a 'mental' or 'intellectual' character or that it is of the nature of a 'representation'; in Lecture III, 3rdness is said to be '*Representation* as an element of the Phenomenon' (160). Now, if 3rdness pours in on us through every avenue of sense, how could it be of the nature of a representation? There is no explanation of this in the text. I suggest this: a 1st or a 2nd, while it falls under the concept through which it is apprehended, is ineffable (*vide supra*, Section C), whereas a 3rd, apart from any 1sts or 2nds it incorporates, is exactly as it may be represented to be: its representation leaves nothing out. Newton's law of universal gravitation, for example, is exactly what Newton's inverse square formula represents it to be. It is not that representation, since the same law may be otherwise represented, in different words or other mathematical symbols. And it is not its instances, since the law would be the same if, for example, there were no solar systems; it would also be the same if no events conformed to it, although then we would say that it is not a real law (about which, more in the next section). The law is neither the representations through which it is grasped nor the events through the observation of which it is known to be real. The law is nothing particular, concrete, physical, existent, sensible. There is nothing more to the law than is expressed in any of its representations. It follows that 3rdness is, so to speak, the eminently effable. Which is to say: not only is it apprehended, it also is comprehended. I think that is what Peirce meant by calling it 'mental'.

It should not be concluded that 3rdness, continuity, generality, law, potentiality, and what-is-not reside only in thought, that is, the thoughts of particular persons. That would be to reduce 3rdness to particulars. And it would be to deny that laws can obtain unknown. Besides, the spatial and temporal continuities are sensed independently of being apprehended as such in thought. When Peirce identified 3rdness as representation, he defined the latter as any mediation between two others (171), and then, in the next lecture (IV), declared that he preferred the word 'Thirdness' because 'its suggestions are not so narrow and special' as those of 'representation' (184).

Unlike laws manifest in sensed continua, laws of nature and many other 3rds are known to us only by inference. But processes of inference are themselves immediately present to us. As already noted, we experience ourselves thinking. Human experience is permeated by conception, judgment, inference, and inquiry – in short, by thinking. And that is inherently triadic. Thinking is putting things together (symbolically rather than existentially): judgment subordinates the particular to the general, inference combines judgments, and inquiry combines inferences. Or perhaps the process of thinking is primary: a continuum analyzable into such virtual parts as inferences, judgments, and concepts (as Peirce appears to have argued in 1867–1868: *vide supra*, Ch.5, B).

In all these ways, 3rdness is a universal feature of the phaneron. It is present in sense, comprehended in thought, and exhibited by thought. It – and all that it entails of lawfulness, generality, and potentiality – is something with which we are directly acquainted ('directly perceived' Peirce said in Lecture VII, where he gave an exact account of what this consists in: *vide infra*, Section G). Thus we are directly acquainted with nonbeing: possibilities not actual, nonexistent breaks in a continuum, the absence of gaps in a spectrum, what could be that isn't. That we are directly acquainted with all of these is a fact disclosed through phaneroscopic observation. Phaneroscopy therefore contradicts British empiricism: it shows it to have been hobbled by assumptions not themselves empirically justified.

E

Direct acquaintance is not intuitive cognition: there is not, in it, a disclosure of reality as distinct from appearance. Phaneroscopic 3rdness does not attest to law's reality. It is, nevertheless, the source of the idea of law and, hence, of reality. It is so, however, only as implicating the other two categories. In Chapter 4, we saw that Peirce defined the real as that which is what it is independently of what it is thought to be, and that he further identified it as the object represented in a final opinion that would be formed were inquiry pursued sufficiently far under adequate conditions (including counterfactual conditions). What is known is known to be independent of its being known, and what is independent of being known is nonetheless knowable. Phaneroscopic 2ndness is the source of this idea of independence, and phaneroscopic 3rdness is the source of the idea that what exists independently is nonetheless knowable. For, things are known when they are comprehended under laws introduced by hypothesis.

That which fits into what we think lawful is judged real; that which does not fit directly is made to fit another way, by being judged illusory or an hallucination, etc. The gray rock that suddenly spreads its wings and flies away is judged not to have been a real rock, as it violates the law of rockiness; it fits, instead, into the law of avian camouflage. The purple spiders that no one else can see must be Sam's hallucination; real spiders are visible to others. The hallucination is nonetheless forceful: it actually occurs (Sam wishes it didn't). The problem is how to locate that actuality within the lawful. To which reality does it belong: that of arachnids or that of dipsomania? In this way, phaneroscopic 3rdness is at the root of our distinguishing reality from appearance. We conceive of the real as the lawful.

But what, then, of law's reality? This is awkward. If the real is the lawful, then a real law is a lawful law – a formulation at best redundant. But we can ask: what is it that, not being a law, might be mistaken for a law? The answer is found in what we earlier recognized, that a 3rd is the eminently effable: it is exactly – neither more nor less – as it can be represented to be. Thus, what can be mistaken for a law is something stated as a rule, a purported law. It is something that can be thought of. It might be a law, but it is not a law of nature if actual events do not conform to it; it is not a law of society if it is not enforced; and so on. Events occurring and acts of enforcement are matters of 2ndness. They are something forceful that is in addition to the rule represented or thought of. It is our experience of apples falling or of sheriff, judge, and jailer that convinces us of the reality of a law. Let us restrict attention to laws of nature, putting civil laws, moral laws, laws of mathematics, rules of chess, etc., aside. Events are real so far as they fall under laws, but a law of nature is real only so far as events conform to it. 3rds are real as embracing 2nds; 2nds are real as so embraced. The lawfulness with which we identify reality is that of real laws: it is 3rdness plus 2ndness. This accounts for our idea that the knowable is independent of us and also for our idea that that which is independent of us is knowable.

Having introduced the idea of reality, we have made the transition from phaneroscopy to metaphysics. The phaneroscopic categories are now to be generalized beyond the immediacies of experience. 2ndness is to comprise all of actuality and not experienced dyadicity only, 3rdness all of reality and not experienced continuities only. Metaphysical generalization of the phaneroscopic categories entails a corresponding generalization of their modal interpretation, bringing it into closer alignment with ordinary usage, for example, of 'may be'. What may be is no longer restricted to phaneroscopic 1stness or qualities of feeling, as we can also speak of possible individuals and possible laws. There is, then, modally speaking, a 1stness of 2ndness and of 3rdness.[9] Similarly, there is a 2ndness of 3rdness: The actuality of a law of nature consists in its governing reactions that actually occur. Thus we can say that it *is* the case that such-and-so *would be*.

Those are applications of lower to higher categories; the converse applications may also be made. For example, experiments on diagrams reveal forcefully that there are laws – the laws of mathematics – that apply to what may be. And therefore we find that some things, though they are not actual, really are possible, while other things, such as a circle whose circumference is double its diameter, really are impossible. But when Peirce spoke of 'the reality of some possibilities' (the motto

---

[9] There is also a phaneroscopic 1stness of 2ndness and of 3rdness: the quality of an experience of 2ndness or of 3rdness, respectively. All applications of the categories to one another occur at every level, phaneroscopic, metaphysical, and modal – and even in the purely mathematical theory of relations, where, for example, 'dyadic' and 'triadic' are monadic predicates.

of Chapter 4), he meant more than mathematical possibility. He meant that some, not all, of what may be is potentiality. Something is potentiality when there is a way in which it can be brought about, that is, when there is a law applying to actual things that determines that that it would be were certain conditions realized. The latter conditions must also be potential, and therefore potentiality is a realm unto itself, distinct from the possibilities represented in, for example, myth. What can be made actual is really possible, as distinct from possibilities only conceived of.

The word 'possible' turns out to be equivocal: It can refer to what may be or to what would be. And the words 'real' and 'really' can be confusing: it really is possible for me to loan you a dollar, as I have one in my pocket, but the loan is not a real possibility, as I am not such a fool. We notice that the word 'real', in these various – quite ordinary and thoroughly intelligible – uses of it, displays an acrobatic facility for operating at different levels: what is really possible, what is really actual, what is really a law. But all of its applications derive from its relations, which prove to be multifarious, to law. And law, when real, is such by virtue of its relations, also multifarious, to 2ndness.

F

Phaneroscopic 3rdness, I have said, does not attest to law's reality. The lawfulness experienced might be a figment. Early in Lecture IV, Peirce announced, 'I proceed to argue that *Thirdness* is operative in nature' (181). By 3rdness being operative he evidently meant that there are laws that determine probabilities of events of specified kinds in specified conditions, and that these laws, once formulated, ground predictions that are somewhat reliable. Putting aside the questions, 'How is it that laws determine anything? How is it that they ground reliable prediction?', we can agree that laws having these characteristics are real, in contradistinction to fanciful laws, for example, that virtue is rewarded, which do not ground reliable prediction.

Peirce then held a stone aloft, predicting that were he to let it go, it would fall (181; the argument continues to 183). In the secondary literature, this passage has not been sufficiently commented on: what sort of argument was being made? *Obviously*, dropping the stone was not a genuine experiment. Peirce admitted as much: '… I see by your faces that you all think it will be a very silly experiment. Why so? Because you all know very well … that the fact will verify my prediction'. His audience knew this the way he knew it: 'Experience has convinced me that objects of this kind always do fall'. This is unreflective experience: A child before acquiring language sufficient to form an argument knows that the released stone will fall, and most people know this same fact in the same way, without ever having had recourse to argument. We know much more than we can give reasons for: '… our logically controlled thoughts compose a small part of the mind …' (241).[10]

Granted that experience *explains* the conviction that the released stone will fall and that this is distinct from there being an argument from experience that *justifies* the conviction might Peirce have been attempting nonetheless to give an argument from experience for the reality of 3rdness? One may seek to justify a claim to know, albeit the knowledge obtains *sans* justification. After all, he *said* that he was going to argue that 3rdness is operative in nature, and the pretend 'experiment' suggests that the argument will be inductive. But an inductive justification presupposes the validity of induction, and in 1878 Peirce had argued that inductive argument has no demonstrable validity. In 'The Probability of Induction' (EP1:155–69), he showed that induction has no probability of resulting in true conclusions from true premises, and he concluded that induction's validity, if it is valid, consists in a fact, viz., that if we continue to make inductions, then belief will tend over the long run to become fixed on a certain set of answers. (This assumes a definition of induction at odds with the idea that it is a generalization from a finite sample; at 205, it is defined as 'the experimental testing of a theory', elaborated at 216; thus, induction includes discarding theories disconfirmed.) As Peirce argued elsewhere, those destined beliefs are the truth and what they represent is the real (*vide supra*, Ch.4, F). But a justification of the claim to know this fact, in which the validity of induction consists, would have to be inductive and, hence, circular. Thus the belief that 'induction will hold good in the long run' is one 'with which logic sets out' (EP1: 169). Any belief with which the science of logic sets out must have resulted from experience before inference became deliberate (i.e., controlled by reference to some idea of good reasoning: 188, more fully at 2.186, of 1902), and therefore before justification became possible. In short, that induction is valid and that the released stone will fall are known in the same way, by the accumulated weight of

---

[10] The definition of 'knowledge' as 'justified true belief' has often been claimed by analytic philosophers (notoriously neglectful of history) to be traditional; but it is not traditional. Proposed in Plato's *Theatetus*, it had little influence before the 1960s. It is neither mentioned nor implied in Peirce's definition of 'knowledge' for the 1901 Baldwin dictionary (5.605–6).

unreflective experience. The reality of 3rdness and the validity of induction are equivalent.

It follows that the argument Peirce proceeded to make was not *to* the proposition that there are laws grounding reliable prediction but *from* that proposition. It was a dialectical argument, a conclusion drawn from what we already believe to something further to which that belief commits us. What is believed when we believe that the released stone *will* fall? The proposition entailed is that something general – 'which is of the nature of a representation' (181) – is 'operative' among actual events. But what does 'operative' mean?

After holding the stone aloft for several minutes, Peirce did drop it. Had he walked off the stage with the stone in his pocket, that would have dramatized something more that we believe: viz., that the stone *would have* fallen *had* he let it go. That is to say, to believe that 3rdness is real or, which is the same thing, that law is 'operative' is to believe something not only about what actually happens but about what would happen were such-and-so done and what would have happened had it been done. Peirce implied as much when, after having dropped the stone, he said, '… the idea of a general involves the idea of possible variations which no multitude of existent things could exhaust …' (183). This brings us to the real issue, the one addressed in the last of the 1903 lectures. As Peirce wrote in 1907, '… no agglomeration of actual happenings can ever completely fill up the meaning of a "would be"' (EP2:402). The real issue is one of meaning.

The real issue is one of meaning, for, in the modern period, beginning in the fourteenth century with William of Ockham, metaphysics has been upended by a question about metaphysics: is it meaningful? The issue of meaning was raised by Ockham about universals, not laws.[11] That does not preclude its being extended, as Peirce did extend it, to laws, but then it becomes more complicated: a universal (distinct from a natural kind, which is framed by causal laws and/or has a history) is a may-be and, as such, is more than its instances, while a law determines what would be, which is in a different way more than its instances. In either case, the question is normally framed on the assumption that meaning is empirical and consists of references to observable things and events, which are material and particular, while metaphysical talk pretends to be about something

[11] This, despite the fact that Ockham made some contributions to the modern idea of laws of motion (kinematics, those of dynamics came later) that emerged at the universities of Oxford and Paris during the time he was at the former (Clagett 1959, *passim*).

else. Ockham's nominalism has thus been taken, more often than not, to be an assertion of empiricism contra metaphysics.[12]

But did we not, in Section D, see that phaneroscopy shows that we *do* experience 3rdness in its fullness, even including what would be that is not? Does it not follow that nominalism is refuted on empirical grounds, viz., by the empirical science of phaneroscopy? The empirical science of phaneroscopy shows that modal realism and scholastic realism, call them metaphysical doctrines if you will, have empirical meaning.

Alas, matters are not so simple. For the nominalist argument has a force paradoxically a priori: that it is impossible to perceive what is not. This argument is enshrined in the verification theory of meaning, according to which the meaning – the entire meaning – of an assertion or belief consists in its verification conditions, which, when fulfilled – and, hence, when perceived – consist of actualities. The real issue, then, is not one of meaning simpliciter. The real issue is one of *theory* of meaning. Is there a theory of meaning that will permit us to acknowledge the plain fact that claims about what would be are meaningful, indeed, empirically meaningful? (You might say, if a theory is contradicted by the facts, so much the worse for the theory. But the fact is, we are not so confident about either our facts or our theories as to be content with either *sans* support by the other.)

At the end of Chapter 4, we looked briefly at the concluding section, Section V, of the last of Peirce's 1903 Harvard lectures, Lecture VII, in which he implied a non-verificationist yet empiricist idea of meaning: a Lockean element of meaning added to verification conditions. We shall now return to that section. The added element is Lockean in being backward-looking, to the origin of ideas in sense experience; but we will find that this was glossed by an account of sense experience that is anti-Lockean. This Lockean/anti-Lockean notion of meaning is the bridge we need from phaneroscopy to scholastic realism (extended to encompass laws), modal realism (implicit in the idea of law as more than regularity), and physical realism (as implying the reality of law). To cross that bridge is to declare that metaphysical theory has empirical meaning and that nominalism is itself a metaphysics. Nominalism is an impoverished metaphysics based on a truncated empiricism. That, in outline, is the argument of the next two sections.

---

[12] Ockham did not deny the meaningfulness of theological doctrine, but he was perhaps most important for having radically divided the realm of knowledge from that of faith. Here, we are less interested in Ockham than in his influence on modern philosophy.

I do not claim that we will have refuted nominalism, but only that, by examining some difficult passages, we will have clarified Peirce's realist alternative. If clear, it is plausible – or more than plausible.

G

The final section of the final lecture of the 1903 lectures on pragmatism begins this way:

> There are two functions which we may properly require that pragmatism should perform ... in the first place, to give us an expeditious riddance of all ideas essentially unclear. In the second place ... to ... help to render distinct, ideas essentially clear but more or less difficult of apprehension; and in particular, it ought to take a satisfactory attitude toward the element of Thirdness. (239)

Pragmatism, then, has the function not only of eliminating nonsense but also of making clear some 'difficult' ideas, specifically, the idea of 3rdness. But in Lecture II, Peirce had said that 'The third category of which I come now to speak is precisely that whose reality is denied by nominalism' (157); it follows that by 1903 pragmatism, far from being anti-metaphysical, had acquired the 'function' of defending a metaphysical doctrine against nominalism. Nominalism denies the reality of 3rdness – scholastic realism, modal realism, etc. – on the ground that it is meaningless; pragmatism defends realism in the only way it needs defending, by making its meaning clear. But that is not what the pragmatic maxim of 1878 can do. Only if we include in pragmatism the Lockean/anti-Lockean addition of 1903, can pragmatism defend realism, viz., by showing that its meaning can be made clear by phaneroscopy.

To see how the Lockean addition achieves this, we must first spend some time – all of the present section – on Peirce's anti-Lockean theory of perception. One difficulty may be cleared away now, though more will be said about it later: by 'direct perception' Peirce meant a perception which does not depend on inference (195); as it may be (and indeed is) mediated in other ways, it is neither intuitive cognition[13] nor infallible. We shall begin with the passage following the one just quoted, then draw on other passages in the Harvard lectures and in related writings.

Peirce proceeded (after summarily rejecting some other views) to argue against the thesis, hereafter T, that 'Thirdness is experimentally

---

[13] *Vide supra*, Ch.5, A.

verifiable, that is, is inferable by induction, although it cannot be directly perceived' (240). The brief paragraph (also 240) intended to refute T is obscure.[14] I take its upshot to be as follows.[15] Firstly, a law, understood as a 3rd, cannot be a simple generalization from an observed regularity. Such a generalization – 'All swans are white', believed when none but white swans had been observed – does not have the force of a law: it does not imply anything about what would be and does not ground reliable prediction. Thus, secondly, if a law, *qua* 3rd, is to be supported inductively by an observed regularity, it has first to be introduced, by abduction, as a hypothesis that explains that regularity. And therefore there has to be a source for the idea of 3rdness distinct from the observed regularity. T recognizes that inductive evidence for the law is not a source of the idea of lawfulness, but it adds that there is no source of that idea in anything 'directly perceived'. But to suppose that 3rdness can be real without being directly perceived implies, Peirce said, an idea of reality '… such as completely to sunder the real from perception' (240). Now, how does the denial that 3rdness is *directly* perceived sunder its reality from perception? And why is that an objection to the doctrine? He did not say. We have to fill in the blanks.

Take the second question first. If 3rdness is sundered from perception, then it must be either a creation of our own minds, a construct of culture, or an artifact of language; but then, as dependent on its representation, it is unreal. That was the view of Hume, who held that our idea of a 'necessary connexion' between cause and effect derives not from our perception of those events but from our subjective expectation (a 'custom' of the mind) that one will follow another, due to our having experienced like successions in the past (*Treatise*, Book I, Part III, Section XIV). Hume's heirs, the logical positivists and logical empiricists, held similar views; one of their variants was to define a law as any regularity the statement of which is deduced from a theory (e.g., Hempel 1966, p.58) – which is to make law a mental or even a linguistic construct, something we do not find in nature but impose on it. Thus, to declare that 3rdness is real yet sundered from perception is a contradiction.

---

[14] Patricia Ann Turrisi informs us that Lecture VII was an afterthought occurring after delivery of Lecture V (Peirce 1997, p.13); necessarily, then, its composition was hurried, which accounts for its defects. I have not found in the secondary literature any attempt to explain why Peirce thought Lecture VII essential and little attempt to penetrate its obscurities. The view I take is that Lecture VII is necessary to explain why phaneroscopy shows modal realism to be meaningful; to this, the passage in question is crucial.

[15] This reading of EP2:240 is defended in Short (2021).

The first question is more difficult. Verification is by events that are perceived. So, why does the inductive argument for a law, that is, from its verification, *not* suffice to link the law to perception? Oddly, this question has not been raised, even by the few, like Fitzgerald (1966, pp.133–34), who have commented on this passage. But to frame the question is to see, in outline, the answer. The answer must be that laws comprise more than can be specified in verification conditions. As T recognizes, this is something – 3rdness – that is not found in the observed regularity that is the law's inductive support. If the idea of 3rdness is not found in verification conditions, then it must have another source. But if that source is not a direct perception of 3rdness – hence, if it is only an inference, of whatever sort, from the perception of something else – then the same problem arises. Peirce concluded that, if we can know that 3rdness is real, then it must be directly perceived.

Not that 3rdness must be directly perceived in each instance of inductive confirmation of a law. The claim is only that, if we are to have a conception of law, 3rdness must at some time be directly perceived. The reasoning is familiar: one need not have perceived a pink-striped zebra to conceive of a pink-striped zebra, since concepts acquired from varied experiences may be combined. The novelty in what Peirce was arguing is that 3rdness (combination, continuity, lawfulness, the would-be) is an element of experience, somewhat more subtle than being pink or being striped, and that a concept of it must be combined with a concept of a regular correlation (of events or of characteristics) if a concept of a law is to be formed. Once possessing the concept of lawfulness, we can frame a hypothesis of a particular law, that is, one entailing a specific regularity, even if we do not in that case directly perceive the law's operation. And then, events observed conforming to that regularity are evidence for the law.

But how can 3rdness be directly perceived? In Section D, I claimed that the contents of sensation are continua and are recognized in thought to be continua; but continua are 3rds. Hence, 3rdness is directly given in sensation though apprehended as such only in thought.[16] Here we have both sensation and conception, and the question arises: With what did Peirce identify direct perception?

Not, certainly, with sensations *qua* physiological events, as of these we normally have no awareness. The contents of sensation become objects of

---

[16] There is sometimes a reluctance to accept that Peirce held 3rdness to be in sensation and not in thought only, for example, Houser (2011), p.67 and Wilson 2012, pp. 172, 177. Curiously, Wilson inconsistently also puts the correct point very well, that in the perceptual judgment '… generals are *discerned* in the perceived object, and not imposed on it …' (*Ibid.*, p. 172, Wilson's emphasis).

awareness within the sensory images which our nervous systems construct out of physiological sensations. In 1901, Peirce named these images 'percepts' while denying that they are images in the sense of being *of* something distinct from the percepts themselves: '... the parish of percepts ... is not inside our skulls .... It is the external world that we directly observe' (EP2:62). The percept is 'directly observed' in that it is not inferred from something else we are aware of; it is, however, a construction of the nervous system. But also it is reality. Think of the infant looking around, crawling about, reaching for and grasping objects – all before learning their names. The infant's world – the world it perceives – is also the world within which it is acting. The same is true of the housefly, though the latter's perceptual apparatus structures that world differently. And the infant, like the fly, acts with some success, as it sometimes manages to grasp what it was reaching for. The infant's nervous system is continually modified by experience so that its percepts become progressively better organized; its world, the percept, is structured by space, time, and causality before conceptual thought is possible. As we, children and adults, often enough grasp what we reach for, the perceived world must be counted real. This happy fact is not negated by scientific discovery of respects in which percepts systematically misrepresent reality. The percept is like a hypothesis that might not be correct in all respects but that explains a variety of data and reliably guides action for most practical purposes. Only, it is not a hypothesis, as it is not verbal, and the sensations which it organizes are not data, as we are unaware of them independently of the percept itself.

In the 1901 passage quoted (EP2:62), percepts are said to be 'our logically initial data'. As data are facts, ergo, propositional, that was a mistake, corrected several months later in 1901 (EP2:92) and, again, in 1903, in Lecture II:

> The whole question is what the *perceptual facts* are, as given in direct perceptual judgments. By a perceptual judgment, I mean a judgment asserting in propositional form what a character of a percept directly present to the mind is. A percept is not itself a judgment, nor can a judgment in any degree resemble a percept. (155)

In Lecture IV, a perceptual judgment is said to be '... the first judgment of a person as to what is before his senses ...', hence, such judgments are '... the first premises of all our reasonings ...' (191). The purported facts perceptual judgments represent are our 'logically initial data'.

In not being inferred, a perceptual judgment is 'direct perception' (195). Clearly, it is not direct in the sense of being intuitive, since it is mediated by complicated processes of sensation and prior learning (of words and concepts). Nor is it infallible; for any judgment about reality is subject to correction. True, Peirce declared that percepts and perceptual judgments are beyond control and criticism and 'cannot be called into question' (191). But he meant that they cannot be questioned at the time of their formation (Bernstein 1964). More precisely, it is the process that at the moment is not subject to control or criticism: '… a perceptual judgment is a judgment absolutely forced upon my acceptance and that by a process which I am utterly unable to control and consequently am unable to criticize' (210). The judgment can be questioned later in light of further information.[17]

The perceptual judgment does not resemble the percept (this is repeated at 191), since the percept is nonconceptual and sensuous while the judgment is verbal and conceptual (210, 223–24, 227). Later in 1903, in a manuscript Peirce did not publish, he wrote that, as the perceptual judgment is neither inferred nor resembles a percept,

> There remains but one way in which it can represent the percept; namely, as an index, or true symptom …. There is no warrant for saying that the perceptual judgment actually *is* such an index of the percept, other than the *ipse dixit* of the perceptual judgment itself. (7.628)

This is a crucial passage. The perceptual judgment is rational in content (thus the *dixit*). The proposition it expresses could be either a premiss or the conclusion of an inference. But this judgment does not occur rationally; so far as one is aware, it merely occurs. As a symptom, it is an effect of mechanical causes, in this case, of a physical stimulus on the nervous system of one whose nervous system has been modified by acquisition of words and concepts. Thus it occurs without warrant. Only so, could reasoning get started.

That does not mean that we do not *subsequently* confirm the accuracy (up to a point) of the majority of our observations. We do so by forming hypotheses that represent and explain their coherence. Their coherence, notice, does not depend on their rational content alone, but also on the occasions of their occurrence; for their content refers to what is

---

[17] In the passage from 155 perceptual judgments are said to describe percepts (so also in 1901 at EP2:92 and later in 1903 at 7.626–8), that is, reality as it appears. Where does the emphasis fall, on reality or on appearance? Peirce seems sometimes to have thought the latter. An example of a perceptual judgment given at 7.626 is: 'That *appears* to be a yellow chair' (my emphasis); but that expresses hesitation, a second thought, a fear that the percept is misleading. A more typical, or accurate, example of a first judgment of what is before one's senses would be this: 'That *is* a yellow chair'. Although responding to a percept, it is about reality, not appearance. That is why it is subject to correction.

here and now. Thus our success in finding coherence among them testifies to their being reliable symptoms. These hypotheses, which are made more specific and detailed in scientific theory, also explain occasional failures to cohere. But all such hypotheses begin with the perceptual judgments themselves! To judge that the chair *is* yellow is to explain (albeit in a very vague way) why it appears yellow and why, when looking at it, we continue to agree that it is yellow; it also explains why it appears orange when flooded with a red light and may mistakenly be judged to be orange. As perceptual judgments are explanatory, Peirce viewed them as hypotheses, like the conclusions of abductive inference: '... our first premisses, the perceptual judgments, are to be regarded as an extreme case of abductive inferences ...' (227). They are an extreme case of abductive inference in not being inferred.

Later in the same manuscript of 1903, Peirce coined the term 'percipuum' to denote the percept as conceptualized in a perceptual judgment (7.629, 643).[18] Thus it is that 3rdness, which is of the nature of a representation, can be directly perceived: it is an ingredient of the percipuum, both in its sensuous contents so far as continuous (and, as we shall see in Section H, in some other respects) and in their conceptual representation, so far as that is non-inferential. In both respects, sensuous and conceptual, 3rdness is directly present to mind.

But there is a problem. Just as a judgment would not be intelligible to anyone who did not know the concepts employed, so also it could not have been formed by a person who did not possess those concepts. Thus, on the one hand, a perceptual judgment applies concepts already understood to particulars present to sense, that is, in a percept, while, on the other hand, Peirce held that every concept applicable to reality must have first occurred in 'direct perception', *a fortiori* not in a percept but in a perceptual judgment. How can a concept be introduced in a judgment which presupposes that that concept is understood? The answer must be that the introduced concept is understood at the moment it is introduced. But how is that possible?

The solution to this problem is implicit in much that Peirce said in the Harvard lectures and is suggested by his frequent use of the idea of continuity, eventually affirmed in the doctrine of synechism. It is suggested also by the 1878 pragmatic maxim, properly understood as a rule for growing

---

[18] All of 7.618–79 deserves close study: it is a subtle analysis of perception. Typical of Peirce, it is misleadingly embedded in a discussion of a much narrower topic, telepathy.

concepts. Very briefly, a concept grows in being applied: it acquires additional meaning. It becomes what may in some cases be distinguished as a new concept, though it is not entirely new. This concept is understood *in* making the judgment, and not previously. To be understandable, a concept introduced in a perceptual judgment requires only to be a *development* of a concept or concepts already understood. This is illustrated by phaneroscopic method. Purely mathematical conceptions of orders of relation, applied to the analysis of the phaneron, yield new concepts, which are not purely mathematical. They remain orders of relation, but orders more specific and empirical. Without observation of the phaneron, the concepts of 1stness as qualitative content, of 2ndness as effort/resistance, and of 3rdness as lawfulness could not have been formed; but neither could they have been formed had the phaneroscopist not brought to his task mathematical concepts previously acquired. The history of science is replete with examples of the same. To take one such example, the concept of a ray of light emerged from using straight lines to diagram optical phenomena (Toulmin 1953, pp.21–28): One needed both the geometric idea of a line and the experience of shadows cast.

There remains one last point to make about this theory of perception. At the conclusion of Lecture VI Peirce summed it up in three propositions: '… *first*, that there are no conceptions that are not given to us in perceptual judgments …', '… *second*, that perceptual judgments contain elements of generality, so that Thirdness is directly perceived …', and '… *third*, that the abductive faculty … is … a gradation of … perception' (223–24). In Lecture VII, the first of these three propositions is restated by affirming the scholastic formula, *Nihil est in intellectu quin prius fuerit in sensu* (226). Peirce proceeded to explain that he takes *in sensu* to refer to what is contained in a perceptual judgment, 'the starting point or first premiss of all critical and controlled thinking' (226). This is another difficult and surprising passage that has received insufficient discussion (not, so far as I know, in any of the secondary literature). As Peirce well knew, *in sensu* had always been understood as referring to sensation, not judgment. Why, then, did he cite the scholastic formula at all? Why affirm it, only, immediately afterward, to contradict it?

Recall the 1906 gloss on the 1878 pragmatic maxim (quoted in Ch.4), where Peirce said that his repetition of 'derivatives of *concipere*' was intended 'to avoid all danger of being understood as attempting to explain a concept by percepts, images, schemata, or by anything but concepts': thus he could not have accepted the scholastic formula without redefining *in sensu* so that it did not refer to sensation simpliciter. I suggest that the reason why he affirmed the formula anyway is that he retained, and wished to emphasize that he retained, a truth embedded in that otherwise mistaken doctrine, viz., the fact that sensation is essential to forming new concepts.[19] For, without the sensuous content of the percept (or of the percipuum) to which familiar concepts are being applied, no new concept would result. Thus the Lockean aspect of meaning: all ideas derive from sense experience, albeit, contra Locke, not from sensation simpliciter. A concept cannot be cut off from its sensory roots without withering. Conversely, to establish the meaning of a word or phrase, it is necessary to identify not only its implications for action but also its origins in perception. Hence the 1903 maxim.

H

Let us quote again the 1903 maxim, the concluding passage of the seven Harvard lectures:

> The elements of every concept enter into logical thought at the gate of perception and make their exit at the gate of purposive action; and whatever cannot show its passports at both these two gates is to be arrested as unauthorized by reason. (241)

Recall Chapter 4, Section H, where we noted how this 1903 maxim differs from the 1878 maxim. The exit gate corresponds to the latter; the entry gate adds something new, a Lockean demand that concepts must originate in perception. Another difference is that the 1903 maxim refers to 'elements' of concepts: it is not only concepts as wholes but each of their 'elements' that must originate in perception and have practical bearing. I say 'practical bearing', since the exit gate's 'purposive action' may remain merely potential.

We can now understand 'elements' as referring to or at least as including those aspects of experience distinguished as 1stness, 2ndness, and 3rdness. In a preceding paragraph, Peirce repeatedly referred to 3rdness as an 'element' (240), and in Lecture II he referred to 2ndness as an element (150–51). More importantly, earlier in Lecture VII, he declared that '… every general element of every hypothesis, however wild or sophisticated it may be, [is] given somewhere in perception …' and, indeed, '… every general

---

[19] Reading Peirce is made easier if we recognize that he always retained as much as he could of earlier doctrines, including their names and much of their expression, even if, to secure what is true in them, he had to reinterpret them radically. We have seen this before, in his affirmations of scholastic realism and of final causation, neither of which he defined as those doctrines were originally defined.

form of putting concepts together is, in its elements, given in perception' (229, Peirce's emphasis). *Every* general form of combination of concepts is given 'in its elements' in perception.

Several different forms of combination of concepts are expressed by conditional statements, for example, 'If this stone is released, it will fall', 'Were I to release this stone, it would fall', 'Had I released this stone at any time in the minutes past, it would have fallen'. The latter two conditionals are expressly modal and the last is counterfactual. What are the 'elements' of modal, even counterfactual, conditionals that are 'given in perception'? The elements given in perception may be given in perceptions other than those which bear directly on the conditional in question. One observes released stones falling, but the idea of what would be that is not yet, and also the idea of what would have been, must be traceable, if traceable at all, to other observations. Which? We noted above that to perceive something continuous is to perceive unactualized possibilities: an absence of breaks where breaks could have been made. This perhaps suffices to provide concepts of the 'would be' and the 'would have been', though not as expressly causal. But continua are of many kinds, including continua of effort overcoming resistance or of resistance thwarting effort, represented in such conditionals as 'Had I stopped pushing earlier, the boulder would not have gotten as far up the hill' and 'Had I continued pushing it (or been able to continue pushing it), it would have gotten further up the hill'. Here we seem to have an idea of 'making happen'. That idea can be applied to where there is no direct perception of one thing's making another happen.

These locutions – modal, causal, etc. – are the sort that cause many philosophers, but not other people, difficulty. What is their meaning? We cannot here venture a theory of meaning.[20] However, Peirce's metaphor is suggestive. It can also mislead: the two gates are closely connected; for, in one and out the other is but a single step, from perception to practical bearing. Perhaps the moral of the metaphor is that, to understand a locution, we must go back and forth between its bearings on practice and its roots in perception.

---

[20] So far as Peirce had a theory of meaning, it is to be found in his theory of signs or semeiotic, according to which a sign mediates between an object (in the most general sense of that term) signified and an actual or potential response or 'interpretant'; in many passages, he associated meaning with one or another, or several or all, of the various sorts of interpretant that he distinguished, but reference to an object is implicated. This semeiotic, though elaborate, was exploratory and unfinished (pragmatism is a small part of it, pertaining to one kind of interpretant of one kind of sign); it was not a system but an inquiry (Short 2007, *passim*).

Take the exit gate first. To be sure, a supposed law is verified (or disverified) by observing what actually happens; but, as what is verified is more than what verifies it, one may ask, 'How much more?'. No more than additional events of the same kind? No; for, what actually happens is not the whole of practical bearing. There are many ways in which concepts bear practically. For example, in Chapter 4, we witnessed your narrow escape from the falling anvil and rejoiced that what could have been – and would have been, had you not stepped nimbly aside – was not. To suppose that there are no facts about what would have been is to deprive what actually happens of the greater part of its significance. Practical bearing, then, is not limited to actual outcomes.

Let us make the same point in another way. To suppose that there are no facts about what could be but need not be is to deprive the practical decisionmaker of any possible basis for making a decision. Here is how practical decisions are made: 'Were I to do A, X would happen and Y wouldn't happen; were I to do B instead of A, Y would happen and X wouldn't happen; I prefer Y to X; therefore, I will do B'. The practical bearing of law cannot be reduced to a regularity in what actually happens. What would be is broader than what will be, and that greater breadth matters. Law, as more than regularity, matters, because it determines not only what will be but also what could be and what would have been.

And yet, we would not be able to understand this talk of what would be, could be, might be, could have been, and so on, were there no entry gate. Here, some care must be taken. The entry gate is not in this case the passive observation of a regularity, as of released stones falling. It is, rather, such active experiences as that of effort overcoming resistance or resistance overcoming effort. This idea is nothing new; it is almost a commonplace. W. V. O. Quine, for example, once conjectured that the idea of causality '... may have had its prehistoric beginnings in man's sense of effort, as in pushing'; but then he dismissed the possibility as of no importance (1974, p.5).[21] So, the issue is whether such a source *is* of importance. There are many who thought so: for example, DuCasse 1924/69, Whitehead 1929; I shall mention a more recent work (Woodward 2003) in a moment. Peirce's metaphor of an entry gate differs from the similar claims of DuCasse et al. by its connection

[21] Quine held that the concept of causality is replaced in physics by functional relationships or laws; but the latter were also Peirce's focus and, in any case, about them the same questions arise. Quine in the same place (pp.1–4) argued that continuities in the world as perceived (he referred to Gestalt psychology) prove nothing, since in fact (as Peirce also knew) stimulations of nerve endings are discrete. That would destroy any argument that we know laws by direct perception. But Peirce implied only that phaneroscopy grounds meaning, not truth.

to phaneroscopy. This is not the place to attempt an analysis of the idea of causality (there might be no precise definition of a term that has such an unruly family of uses); I am attempting only to establish the relevance of Peirce's new science of phaneroscopy to his defense of metaphysical realism and of that realism to his pragmatism and his account of scientific inquiry. But we may take a moment to notice that phaneroscopy's relational analysis of experience provides what is needed to identify the experiential roots of causal talk.

Part of what is at issue here is a difference in method and aim between analytic philosophy on the one hand and phaneroscopy on the other. Whereas conceptual analysis employs relational predicates to explicate concepts (those, like that of causality, deemed problematic), phaneroscopy predicates orders of relation to describe experience (e.g., the experience of making happen). The aim of analytic philosophy is precise definition, whereas phaneroscopy aims to draw attention to aspects of experience – to make us see what's there, even if we have some difficulty putting what we see into words.[22] Those aspects ('elements') are relations that must be correctly characterized by their irreducible order. Such characterization, however, falls short of definition; and further description of these elements ('qualities of feeling', 'effort and resistance', etc.) is merely suggestive, a way of directing our attention to what is being referred to. But that, too, is clarification: it is entry-gate clarification.

Peirce (recall that he was trained as a chemist) intended an analogy of phaneroscopic elements to chemical elements. In a later manuscript (of 1905, EP2:360–70), he declared that the phaneroscopic elements are 'logically indecomposable' (EP2:366), that is, 'incapable of being separated by logical analysis into parts' (EP2:362).[23] As far as chemical reactions (as distinct from nuclear reactions) are concerned, the chemical elements are indecomposable; any difference in the internal structure of distinct elements is revealed *only* by differences in how they combine with other elements – their 'external form' as Peirce expressed it (EP2:363). The logic of 1sts, 2nds, and 3rds is in that same sense 'external'. The concept of a 3rd cannot be analyzed into a logical compound of other concepts. Its complexity is recognized in its being a relation of three items, separately

---

[22] Observing, seeing, taking note of relevant facts is as much a part of philosophy as is argument and definition: this is indeed the method of the later Wittgenstein (1953, para.127), even when what he was 'reminding' us of were facts about language and its uses.

[23] Others also have argued that the concept of causality is not analyzable into a logical compound of other concepts, for example, Taylor 1966, pp.35–39.

conceived; but that triadic relation is irreducible. This, however, does not preclude an 'external' logic of inferential relations among modal conditionals and other statements. Such a logic is obvious. For example, the irreducibly dyadic fact that B is (or, depending on temporal parameters, that B will be) is inferable from the irreducibly triadic fact that B would be if A were, plus the dyadic fact that A is. Conversely, the triadic hypothesis, that B would be if A were, is refuted by a pair of dyadic facts that A is and that B is not.

As an example of the power of phaneroscopy to address philosophical problems, consider this use of it to refute an argument that Harré and Madden (1973, pp.58–62) make, that restricting direct perception of causality to one's own activity commits one to panpsychism. Their argument is that if the concept of causality derives from such perception, then ascribing causality to other processes implies that these, like our actions, must have a psychic element. To this, we can object that phaneroscopic 2ndness is the direct experience of an opposition of self and other. In that experience, the other is not experienced as, like oneself, conscious, etc. It is not reduced to oneself: it is experienced *as other*. And, so far as the experience is of a continuum of 2ndness, that is, as a 3rd, the force opposing our intentional effort is experienced as having direction and being of measurable degree, but not necessarily as intentional.

Despite Peirce's influence on analytic philosophy via his historically important contributions to the logic of relations, the difference of aim and method is fundamental. But analytic philosophy, like Peirce's work, is in spirit scientific; that is, it sees itself as an inquiry, not a body of doctrine. In consequence, it has progressed by corrections seriatim of its own assumptions, as when the failed program of logical positivism was made looser and renamed 'logical empiricism'. Perhaps the most significant of these corrections was Quine's 1951 essay, 'Two Dogmas of Empiricism' (Quine 1961, Ch.II), wherein he argued against the analytic/synthetic distinction. For this had the implication that conceptual analysis cannot fruitfully be divorced from empirical discovery. Methodological inertia nonetheless prevails, and it is only very slowly that analytic philosophers have begun to pay attention to facts. An example is the well-regarded recent book, *Making Things Happen: A Theory of Causal Explanation*, by James Woodward (2003).

Woodward is still focused on defining the word 'cause', but he denies that he is doing conceptual analysis: this on several grounds, of which two are that he examines the practices – of manipulation and control – involved in applying causal language, and that, by fitting it to the purpose of causal talk, his definition of 'cause' is normative, possibly entailing revision of our linguistic habits (p.7). Woodward relates his 'manipulationist' view more to the purpose than to the source of the idea of causation, but the latter is mentioned: 'If we had been unable to manipulate nature – if we had been … capable only of passive observation – then it is a reasonable conjecture that we would never have developed the notions of causation and explanation … that we presently possess' (p.11). In order to free this concept from limitation to manipulations actually within our reach, he has recourse (Chapter 5) to formulations 'understood modally or counterfactually' (p.10). Though he does not assert the irreducibility of the counterfactual, neither does he rely on its being reducible. Peirce's thought, once spurned by analytic philosophers as embarrassingly 'metaphysical', is now the unacknowledged horizon toward which their ship is sailing, fearful though many remain of falling off the world's edge.

The distinction Woodward makes of 'passive observation' from active experience is crucial. The tradition of British empiricism tacitly assumes that the mind is a passive recipient of sense impressions, intellectual work taking place after these 'data' are in hand; Kant followed Hume in this regard and the twentieth-century 'sense-data' theorists ditto. Peirce, William James[24], G. H. Mead, and John Dewey all denied that assumption; in Dewey's late phrase, experience is 'transactional' (Dewey and Bentley, 1949, p.69 and *passim*). Once accepting their view, it is no longer absurd to suppose that one may directly experience making-happen and what would be.[25]

Consider infants. An infant can only learn the meaning of the word 'block' because it has already learned to grasp blocks and move them about. A diversity of sensations, visual and tactile, are united in its preverbal 'idea', which, as guiding behavior, classifies: for one block is much like another in the uses to which it may be put, and all blocks are in some

---

[24] A dominant theme of James' last two books (1909 and 1912) is that we have direct experience of relations. Referring to T. H. Green, he wrote, 'But the atomistic and unrelated sensations which he had in mind were purely fictitious products of his rationalist fancy …. Every examiner of the sensible life *in concreto* must see that relations of time, space, difference, likeness, change, rate, cause, or what not, are … integral members of the sensational flux …' (1909, p.279). Still earlier, he wrote at length about why philosophers of various schools have ignored the fact that we have immediate feelings of relation (1890, vol.I, pp.243–56), and in that work's abridgement (James 1892), while omitting most of the material quoting and criticizing the 'sensationalists' and 'intellectualists', he condemned their willful blindness.

[25] The hold that Hume and Kant continue to have on the minds of philosophers is illustrated by the fact that even the best of Peirce scholars have found problematic Peirce's claim that 3rdness is directly perceived (Murphey 1961, p.373, Hookway 1985, p.179).

of those respects unlike a rubber ball or a puppy. The infant's movements, beginning in the womb, are either mechanical and random or instinctual but become in time subject to self-control, that is, subordinated to a purpose becoming conscious: thus habits are modified when failing their purpose. Control is extended and strengthened once a language is acquired; for then one can represent possibilities to oneself and reason about them. Viewing the genesis of ideas in this light, we see that from the beginning they mediate between perception and action. There is in the infant's first ideas no gap at all between perception and potential action: a block is perceived as that with which certain things can be done. There is no gap, but there is still a distinction between sensing and doing, a passage from one to the other. The two gates are the two sides of one gate.

What we know of physiology deepens this account. Even when, in perceiving, we are not consciously active, our nervous systems are busy integrating sensations. There is constant feedback from the brain to the sense organs, making them seek out additional sensations (e.g., eye movements and focusing) to complete a story that is beginning to be told. Thus we become conscious of things and events. In addition to these facts, we know from evolutionary theory that our sense organs and nervous system have evolved in order that we may, for purposes of survival, deal effectively with the world around us: eating, not being eaten, procreating. However tenuous those connections between sensation and action later become – in, say, the more sophisticated theories of astrophysics – they are never altogether lost: the world is still perceived as that with which we are engaged – as something that can affect us and that we can sometimes affect.

Was there ever a good reason to deny this robust doctrine? Despite conceiving of the contents of experience as passive, Locke wrote of 'receiving impressions' and Hume spoke of the 'force and vivacity' that distinguishes sensation from memory. How does forcefulness of impression differ from the content impressed? The difference is order of relation. Here again we witness the power of phaneroscopy: it provides a decisive argument against British empiricism. Passive contents are monadic whereas 'force' denotes a dyadic relation, an opposition of self and other: one thing imposed on another. But the fact that we are aware of forcefulness indicates that dyadic phenomena are also contents of experience. So, now, we have two categories of content of experience, the monadic and the dyadic. But continuities of effort and resistance – our active engagement with the world – also are contents of experience: we feel ourselves acting and being acted on. These contents are distinguished as irreducibly triadic. By what principle must the triadic be attributed to the way minds think about what is experienced, while what is experienced is limited to the monadic and dyadic? If no principle can be cited, then we must agree that continuities of effort and resistance – and indeed many sorts of continuity, combination, and what would be – are just as directly perceived as are yellow and forcefulness.

It is true that Peirce often described the triadic as 'mental' or 'of the nature of representation'. But that was not to say that mind imposes triadic order on a world otherwise devoid of 3rdness. In Lecture VII, as we have seen, he rejected any such notion. It was, rather, to say that the triadic element of experience is that out of which grow concepts, judgments, knowledge, and understanding.

CHAPTER 9

Normative Science

Peirce's idea of normative science – as theoretical, not practical, and as positive, that is, about the actual – seems absurd. It contradicts a dogma of modern life, that values are not facts (though there are facts about what people value). Evaluation would seem to be inherently practical, not theoretical. And, surely, the ideal, by definition, is distinct from the actual. Worse yet, Peirce introduced this apparent absurdity only rather late in his career, c.1902, and never more than sketched it. It might therefore seem prudent to ignore it.

However, the idea of normative science, whether it makes sense or not, is inescapably part of our topic. It is so, given Peirce's proposal that philosophy be made scientific (Chapter 8, A), together with his assumption that philosophy addresses normative questions. As a branch of the sciences of discovery, philosophy does not aim to improve practice or people; but that alone does not prevent it from being normative. If good and evil are objects of possible knowledge, then that knowledge would be inherently normative, even if sought out of theoretical, not practical interest.

Furthermore, knowledge that is both positive and normative must be possible if the empirical sciences – sciences based on observations of actual things and events – are responsible for their own methods and goals, as Peirce claimed they are (Chapter 2). For, methods and goals are normative, and if they are to be a justified result of empirical inquiry, then their adoption must have grounds discovered empirically. Indeed, the history of modern science shows that its ideals and values have in fact been factual discoveries (Chapter 3). It remains to try to understand how that was possible and whether that possibility extends to other values, for example, moral. Insofar as Peirce addressed those issues, it was in his account of normative science as divided into three inquiries, aesthetics as basic, next ethics, and then logic.

I will not presume to improve on what was sketchy and tentative in Peirce's thought. We shall see that he could not have meant that normative inquiries become the province of specialists – contrary to his own idea of science. Nevertheless, any reason to suppose that knowledge both norma-tive and positive is possible is reason to question the alleged dichotomy of fact and value. And thus all the pernicious doctrines, of relativism, subjec-tivism, and cynicism, which that dichotomy supports, would be subverted.

After some preliminary ground-clearing, I will describe Peirce's scheme of the normative sciences and then consider the sources, in his experiments and writings earlier examined, of such plausibility as it may be said to possess.

A

Peirce's idea of normative science has been little studied; when mentioned at all, it has usually been in the context of discussions of his substantive moral views. Vincent Potter's pioneering early work is a good example; it has the virtue of exhibiting the basis of normative science in Peirce's phaneroscopy and of establishing the relation of his moral claims to his realist metaphysics (Potter 1967). Unfortunately, conflating Peirce's moral views with his idea of a normative science distorts both. It leads one to conclude that he had a comprehensive ethical system; but the search for that system in his literary remains proves elusive. And, as he identified science with inquiry, not with conclusions, it is a mistake to frame his idea of normative science in terms of his moral views: it begs the questions normative science was meant to answer.

It cannot be too much emphasized that we are not here concerned with Peirce's moral views or with any system of ethics he might have had or have sought. It may nevertheless be helpful to devote a few paragraphs now to aspects of Peirce's ethical thought which it is important for us to distin-guish from his idea of normative science. In the lead essay in a recent vol-ume of essays on Peirce's 'normative thought', Vincent Colapietro declares that 'The normative dimension of Peirce's thought is not reducible to his explicit doctrine of the normative sciences' (de Waal and Skowroński 2012, p.2). Indeed it is not: Colapietro proceeds to mine several aspects of Peirce's thought for its normative content, and other contributors to this volume mine other aspects similarly – a valuable resource for what in the present book is none of our business.

The one essay in that volume that is primarily about normative sci-ence, or that branch of it Peirce named 'ethics', by James Liszka, pro-vides many details and textual citations omitted here, which the interested reader should consult (pp.44–82).[1] Liszka, however, assumes that what is at

---

[1] Expanded in Liszka (2021), a volume that appeared too late to be made use of here.

issue is a system, rather than an inquiry, and thus laments that Peirce was not able to 'complete' his ethics 'in any systematic fashion' (p.46). And, like other authors in this volume (Cornelis de Waal, pp.83–100, and Mats Bergmann, pp.125–48) and earlier writers (Hookway 2000, p.23 and Misak 2004, p.164), he exhibits angst regarding the 'sentimental conservatism' Peirce espoused in 1898 (*vide supra,* Ch.3, C). Liszka tries to domesticate that dread beast by identifying it as 'practical ethics', in conformity with Peirce's general distinction between 'theoretical science' and 'practical science' (p.48). But that misses the point. Practical science is to theoretical science as rocketry is to physics: it assumes theory, which it applies by drawing inferences and making calculations. Thus it relies on our powers of reasoning. Relying on sentiment (or instinct or tradition) is an alternative to relying on reason, though Peirce urged it with respect to 'vital matters' only. Rosa Mayorga provides an antidote to angst in her essay: she points out that Peirce's conservatism does not apply to the long-run pursuit of truth (pp.101–24).

In a more recent volume, Richard Kenneth Atkins defends Peirce's 'sentimental conservatism' at considerable length (Atkins 2016, pp.14–27, 34–82), improving on Mayorga's account, in part by drawing on Mark Migotti's distinction between two senses in which Peirce used the term 'belief' (Migotti 2004 and 2005). As if taking Colapietro's advice, Atkins when discussing Peirce's ethics rightly ignores his sketch of the normative sciences – except for some sensitive and probing pages on the normative science of aesthetics (141–53), citing a number of passages that reveal Peirce's uncertainty about aesthetics. Now, as Peirce took aesthetics, as he defined it, to be the basic normative science, his uncertainty about it proves that the entire scheme of the normative sciences was a less than fully developed conjecture. Like Liszka's essay, Atkins' pages on aesthetics should be consulted by any who want a guide to the labyrinthine developments and variant texts that I blithely ignore.

My aim in this chapter is not to trace Peirce's thinking but is to make the best sense I can of his conception of normative science. Two authors who have also discussed that conception with an interest in whether it makes sense are Richard Robin (1964) and Cheryl Misak (1994, 2000). I will take issue with Misak later in this chapter. Robin's basic idea, that Peirce's doctrine of the normative sciences derived from his study of the norms governing scientific inquiry, provides the framework for my own account. However, it is not the norms of science *per se* but, rather, it is how in historical fact those norms developed that arguably inspired the idea of normative science.

A word needs to be said about the words 'norm' and 'normative', 'value', and 'valuable'. 'Norm' originally meant something adopted or established as a standard (from the Latin, *norma*, for a carpenter's square). It could be a particular exemplar or a general rule, but in either case a norm depends on a decision, a convention, or a custom – in short, something is a norm only if it is made a norm. A norm, then, may be arbitrary, ill-advised, or no longer useful. The OED dates 'normative' to 1880, defined as 'establishing a norm or standard'. Whatever it is that normative science is supposed to discover, it is not norms already established (a matter for history or cultural anthropology, etc.). Peirce would seem to have meant by 'normative' any consideration – of what is better or worse, valuable, truly ideal, etc. – that may bear on establishing a norm: a broad inquiry. (It need hardly be added that 'norm' has uses lacking normativity, as in 'statistical norm' or as in 'normal' as denoting the typical or average.)

Valuing is something persons or societies do; it is less formal or deliberate than is the adoption or institution of norms. 'Value', as a noun taking a plural has many uses, not all of them normative (e.g., 'values of a variable'); in the sense germane to normative science, a value is a *type* of attribute, thing, action, etc., that is valued. But we also refer to types of thing (and to individual things) as 'valuable' when they are not actually valued, if we think that they ought to be valued or, at least, that one might come to value them (compare 'desired' and 'desirable'). Recall Chapter 7, D, where 'value' was defined as represented by a predicate that makes a judgment an evaluative, or pro/con, judgment. As a fact is what is represented in a true judgment, values are a species of fact if and only if evaluative judgments are either true or false. In that case, there would be facts about what is valuable, regardless of any evaluation actually made. That there are such facts, and in particular ones waiting to be discovered, is presupposed in the very idea of a normative science.

B

Peirce's scheme of three normative sciences[2], logic, ethics, and aesthetics, one based on another, appears perverse: that logic is empirical, that it is normative, that it is based on (or is a branch of) ethics, that ethics is based on aesthetics, and that aesthetics can be a science – all of this looks wrong.

[2] The sources upon which I will draw are from the years 1901–1911. To minimize citation anon, I list them now: 1.281, 573–615; 2.46, 65, 195–204; 5.3–4; 8.158; and EP2:59–61, 142–43, 147, 196–207, 258–60, 272, 343–44, 371–97, 459–62.

It looks wrong for many reasons. A few misimpressions may be quickly corrected, only to bring more difficult questions to the fore.

Let us begin from the bottom up. By aesthetics, Peirce did not mean the philosophy of art or the study of beauty; he meant the study of 'ultimate ends', that is, those ends that are not means to a further end (EP2:200). The aim, however, appears to be to establish ends ultimate also in another sense, that of being what we would ultimately adopt as ultimate ends, all things considered (EP2:260). These ends, Peirce supposed, are determined not by reason but aesthetically, that is, by feeling. That meaning of 'aesthetic' was probably derived from Friedrich Schiller's *Über die ästhetische Erziehung des Menschen*, which, except for a treatise on logic, was the first book of philosophy that Peirce studied, even before he encountered Kant. See especially Schiller's long footnote to the twentieth 'letter' (of the twenty-seven of which his book is composed), in which he defined the aesthetic as pleasure taken in contemplating something and then wrote, in a parenthesis, that the entire purpose of these letters was to correct the error of supposing that the aesthetic must be arbitrary (Schiller 1801/1967, pp.140–43).

The word translated as 'the arbitrary', *Willkürlichen*, connotes being voluntary. The suggestion, then, is that the error consists in supposing that pleasure in contemplating varies wholly with the individual, even with his choice, and not with the object contemplated, as if one could never be obtuse or otherwise mistaken in his feelings or lack of feeling. The error that Schiller meant to correct is that evaluative judgments based on feelings, unlike nonevaluative judgments based on sense experience, are never either true or false. The crux of Peirce's scheme also is the assumption that feelings, like sensations, are representational *qua* eliciting judgment, hence, that they sometimes misrepresent, by eliciting judgments that are false. Many feelings may be germane to the determination of ends, but those of esteem or approval would seem to sum them up. Peirce's word was 'admiration': he defined aesthetics as seeking to determine what is admirable unconditionally, that is, for its own sake.

By ethics, Peirce did not mean the study of moral right and wrong or of duty or justice or how best to live; he meant any determination of means to any ultimate end established aesthetically. Thus the studies of moral duty, political justice, etc., are special departments of ethics. This definition is idiosyncratic (as Peirce admitted: EP2:377, 1.573–4), but it need not mislead us.

And by 'logic' Peirce did not mean what logic is often taken to be today, viz., a branch of algebra. That branch of algebra, to which Peirce had contributed so much, he located in mathematics. The transition from algebraic studies in mathematics to logical algebras requires the assignment of aim, specifically, a cognitive aim, roughly, knowledge and understanding. With that addition, some parts of algebra become logic because they represent means to cognitive ends: to preserve truth, you must reason this way (deductive validity), to extend knowledge, you must reason that way (inductive and abductive validity). Inference, however, is not the only means to cognitive ends. Peirce at different times defined logic in different ways; at its broadest, it is the study of all means to cognitive ends, ergo, how best to inquire. Thus, methods of observation and modes of representation also are topics of logical study. So is 'the economy of research', pertaining to which lines of inquiry should be pursued first if progress is to be made (the end assumed *is* progress, that is, endless growth of knowledge).

Logic, then, is not based on ethics (though that is suggested by some statements) but is a department of ethics in Peirce's broad sense: it is the ethics of inquiry. This does not imply that logic is to be trammelled by moral concerns. In 1898, Peirce had emphatically maintained that science, presumably including logic, is and morally ought to be amoral (*vide supra*, Ch.2, G). Morality belongs to another department of ethics than that occupied by logic, though there is a logic of reasoning about moral issues and a moral imperative to be logical.

The preceding is one way in which the three normative sciences were distinguished in 1903 (EP2:260). In another passage of the same year the divisions were drawn differently. There the normative sciences were said to be about 'conformity … to ends': 'esthetics considers those things whose ends are to embody qualities of feeling, ethics those things whose ends lie in action, and logic those things whose end is to represent something' (EP2:200). But this was a passing thought; despite its obvious virtues, it was not repeated. Why not? This, I think, is the reason: Some ultimate ends may lie in action and others in representation, but their discovery, in Peirce's view, must nonetheless be aesthetic, by our feeling admiration for them; and, therefore, *qua* mode of inquiry, aesthetics pertains to all ends. Then, all inquiry pertaining to means to ends must be distinct from aesthetics; Peirce named it 'ethics'. Logic, alone, is restricted to inquiry concerning just one type of end, that of representation (indeed, propositional representation only), to which it determines means; and that is why logic is a division of ethics.

In either version, the trio of normative sciences generalizes – almost beyond recognition – the traditional triad of the True, the Good, and the Beautiful. It is typical of Peirce that this generalization is extraordinarily bold yet made tacitly (for the most part, but explicitly in 1903 at EP2:143,197). Typical also is that it is revolutionary yet preserves tradition – in a new form. And, most typically, this preservation is achieved by transmuting the substantive into the dynamic: in this case, supplanting conclusions by inquiries.

C

Of the three normative sciences that Peirce projected, the only one to which he devoted much attention was logic. One might question whether logic could be dependent on other studies. Does not every inquiry involve reasoning and is not every inquiry therefore dependent on logic? Yes, on a *logica utens,* necessarily vague, tacit, mostly instinctual; but not on an explicit, deliberately formulated science of logic, a *logica docens* (these two logics are distinguished at 2.186–95 and elsewhere). The science of logic must itself employ a *logica utens* (as in Hilbert's idea of metamathematics). And there is no reason why a *logica docens* may not depend also on some other sciences (each of which employs a *logica utens*).

The dependence of ethics on aesthetics raises other questions. It may seem to entail a consequentialist view of right and wrong, such as utilitarianism. That is a controversial position, one that ought not to be begged from the outset in the way these inquiries are structured. Moreover, by making ultimate ends to be determined by how we feel, Peirce seems to have committed himself, contrary to his expressed views, to hedonism or even to a most unscientific subjectivism. But these appearances are deceptive. We shall address the question of subjectivism later (Sections D–F), those of hedonism and consequentialism now.

Consequentialism is best understood as opposed to deontology. Kant's ethics is the *locus classicus* of the latter and Mill's utilitarianism a favorite example of the former. Let us take a moment to formulate consequentialism with some care and then more than a moment to examine Kant's deontological alternative. I shall argue that Peirce's account of the normative sciences does not preclude deontology, that his development of these sciences strongly suggests deontology, and, finally, that his idea that ethics must be based on aesthetics probably derives from Kant's own 'metaphysics of morals' and is, like Kant's view, very far from being hedonistic.

According to some versions of consequentialism, acts are morally right or wrong depending on their consequences (actual or perhaps only intended or perhaps merely anticipated or anticipatable); according to other versions, acts are right or wrong as determined by moral rules justified by the (usual) consequences of obeying them or (the most sophisticated variant) by the consequences of there being such rules that most people obey. The crux of the matter is that these are consequences desirable independently of moral considerations: as it is often expressed, they are 'naturally' good. What such consequences may be is an issue; utilitarianism, which has been formulated in all of the preceding ways, specifies that happiness is the aim of being moral – not one's own happiness but that of all persons considered equally. How is the transition made (if by an argument, what is the logic of the argument?) from the natural desire for one's own happiness to the moral end of maximizing happiness for all? We need not be detained by that problem, nor by the also much-discussed problems of defining happiness (is it only pleasure and absence of pain, or is it, instead, contentment, or is it …?), of measuring it (behaviorist measures have been suggested), and of determining its preferred distribution (is a more equal distribution of less happiness to be preferred over a less equal distribution of more happiness?).

In the deontological view of Kant, by contrast, an act is right or wrong as it conforms to the moral law, regardless of its consequences, and that law is not itself justified by any calculation that it promotes consequences naturally good. Being moral is an end in itself: it is an end in itself from the moral point of view, and not as satisfying our natural desires. It is one's moral duty to take consequences into account, but those are consequences of types ordained by moral law to be taken into account; they might but need not be what we naturally desire, and the way in which they are to be taken into account often results in imperatives opposed to our natural desires.

Kant's distinction between hypothetical and categorical imperatives is clarifying. An imperative is hypothetical if it is of the form, 'If you want Y, do X'. The force of the imperative derives from one's desire for the end, Y, mediated by a purported instrumental connection of X to Y. Moral obligation for Kant is categorical: 'Do X'. It does not make any difference what you want: you should be honest. You should be honest even were it not, from a natural point of view, the best policy. The force of the imperative derives from our respect for the moral law and not from any inclination for one consequence rather than another. As consequentialism is limited to hypothetical imperatives, it has, from Kant's point of view, nothing to do with morality. Since Peirce defined ethics as determining means to ends, all of its imperatives are hypothetical. This would seem to be consequentialist and opposed to Kant's view.

However, consequentialism is not entailed by Peirce's having limited ethics – in his idiosyncratic definition of it – to hypothetical imperatives.

Kant did not deny that means/ends calculations are morally required – given moral ends. As Peirce placed the determination of ends within aesthetics, it is there that we must look to see whether being moral, as defined by Kant's idea of moral law, is a possible candidate for being an end in itself. And there is nothing in Peirce's conception of aesthetics which precludes our finding a certain form of conduct admirable in itself, regardless of its consequences, and, indeed, more admirable than conduct good by utilitarian or other consequentialist criteria. To drive this point home, let us first illustrate it and then explain it.

Although Peirce's substantive moral view is not our topic, what he said about ultimate aims illustrates the claim just made: his sentiments were markedly Kantian. Kant, I assume the reader knows, rooted the moral law in pure reason, in the practical demand a rational being makes on himself to act only in ways that he would be willing for all others to act. Whatever naturally desired ends one pursues, they and their pursuit must be so limited as to be consistent with an ultimate harmony of ends and of actions possible for all rational agents: that harmony is the *summum bonum* – a goal legislated by pure reason.[3] This goal prospectively joins all rational agents into a single community, a subordination of individuals to a universal order that each himself, as rational, freely wills. That we should so constrain ourselves is what the moral law demands of us in each choice we make, regardless of whether others act morally and therefore regardless of whether the *summum bonum* will be achieved. According to Kant, this idea is the practical equivalent of the scientific goal of unified, comprehensive theory.[4]

Similarly Peirce in the years 1902–1903: 'The object admirable that is admirable *per se* must, no doubt, be general' (1.613); 'The one thing whose admirableness is not due to an ulterior reason is Reason itself …' (1.615); '… this Reason … can never have been completely embodied' and yet '… the very being of the General, of Reason, is … actually governing events' (1.615), that is, being embodied. Thus, the ultimate good is not reason's actually being embodied. It is the unending process of embodying reason: '… the only ultimate good … is to further the development of concrete reasonableness …'

---

[3] For Kant's conception of the good, see Silber (1959).

[4] Perhaps it needs to be said, since Kant has so often been misunderstood in this respect, that he did not make the absurd attempt to ground moral law in the idea of logical consistency. According to Kant, reason in both its practical and theoretical employments posits an end peculiar to itself, named in the first Critique (A567/B595 ff) the 'ideal' of pure reason and characterized, among other ways, as completed perfection; this perfection exceeds what is empirically possible in theoretical science and actually possible in practical conduct.

(5.3); '… the coalescence, the becoming continuous, the becoming governed by laws, the becoming instinct with general ideas, are but phases of one and the same process of the growth of reasonableness' (5.4). Reasonableness, then, is not good as a means merely, that is, as a tool for calculating how best to satisfy our desires. It is, as it was for Kant, an end in itself. But, for Peirce, it was so as process, not as result, just as, for Peirce, science is inquiry, not knowledge.

Peirce's views were as much deontological and as little hedonistic as were Kant's views. But how, exactly, can feelings determine ends without feelings being our ultimate ends? A further comparison to Kant's philosophy sheds a surprisingly vivid light on that question.

Although Kant denied that there can be a causal explanation of our acting morally[5], he did not leave such action wholly inexplicable. Earlier, I said that in Kant's view the force of the categorical imperative derives from our *respect* for the moral law and not from any *inclination* for one consequence rather than another. This language is drawn from Lewis White Beck's translation of the *Grundlegung zur Metaphysik der Sitten* (Kant 1785/1959); in H. J. Paton's translation, respect is 'reverence' (Kant 1785/1948); Kant's word was *Achtung* and it might also be translated 'esteem' (its use as an interjection, 'Attention!' is different though related: it assumes esteem for law); 'admiration' is not far off from 'esteem'. The problem of accounting for morality is addressed most directly in the long second footnote in the first part of the *Grundlegung* (the ideas broached in this note do not otherwise appear, except twelve years later in the introduction to the *Metaphysik der Sitten*; see Ladd's translation, Kant 1797/1965, pp.10–14). In Beck's translation, part of that footnote reads:

> It might be objected that I seek to take refuge in an obscure feeling behind the word 'respect' … But though respect is a feeling, it is … self-wrought by a rational concept; thus it differs specifically from all feelings of the former kind which may be referred to inclination or fear …. The direct determination of the will by the law and the consciousness of this determination is

---

[5] Kant distinguished the theoretical employment of reason, which is to produce knowledge and understanding, from its practical employment. He limited the theoretical employment of reason to experience and hence, in his view, to appearances; we can have no knowledge of what things are 'in themselves'. That applies as well to what we are in ourselves. Reasoning about appearances is in terms of the categories of the understanding, including the category of (mechanical) causality: we understand – indeed, we apprehend – events as causally connected. Our own behavior, so far as we understand it, is understood as causally determined, namely, by what we most desire. But we cannot know that we, as we are in ourselves, are causally determined. And when we act morally, we act under the idea that we are free to conform to the moral law, hence, free of determination by mechanical causes.

respect: thus respect can be regarded as the effect of the law on the subject and not the cause of the law. Respect is properly the conception of a worth which thwarts my self-love. (Kant 1785/1959, p.17n2)

Inclination, or desire, was assigned by Kant to an 'outer' influence, that is, outside the rational faculty, presumably in our physiology (hunger, lust). The mere idea of bread does not account for one's eating bread: one must be hungry. But the mere idea of being moral does account for the hungry man's refraining from stealing a loaf of bread. As it is the rational faculty that makes decisions, respect, being determined by reason alone, is 'self-wrought' by that faculty, or by its principle (thus Kant satisfied the Enlightenment ideal of individual autonomy: recall that the *summum bonum*, or harmony of ends, is willed by each of us insofar as we are rational). Respect and inclination are alike feelings (*Gefühlen*), but they differ in source. The source of respect is in our consciousness of the moral law and its 'direct determination' of our will. Determination (*Bestimmung*) is here not clearly causal: Perhaps the law determines the will by defining its object, as a game is determined by its rules. However, causal language is not altogether avoided: Respect (a conception of a worth that 'thwarts' my self-love) is an 'effect' (*Wirkung*) of the moral law.

Can this be made consistent with the doctrine that moral conduct has no causal explanation? The bifurcation of ethics and nature is one of the most fundamental problems in Kant's philosophy; we will see in Section F that Peirce overcame that bifurcation. In the meantime, it is clear that, however problematically, Kant connected motivation to feeling. In moral conduct, that feeling is a respect engendered either by the mere idea of law or by a consciousness of one's will being determined by that idea. Whereas Hume et al. supposed that reason is the 'slave of the passions', Kant held that passion can sometimes be the servant of reason. This footnote might be the source, *via* Schiller, of Peirce's doctrine that ultimate ends are established aesthetically, by feelings of admiration.[6]

---

[6] It is irrelevant that in the first Critique Kant used the word 'aesthetic' differently from Peirce and Schiller; he used it in a third way in the third Critique. In the second part of his 1797 *Metaphysik der Sitten*, he seems to have used it in the Peirce/Schiller way, by extending it to cover moral feelings (see Gregor's translation, Kant 1797/1964, pp.59, 68), but this obscure occurrence is unlikely to have been Schiller's source. None of these authors used it as did Baumgarten, who introduced the term into modern philosophy – from classical Greek, where it had yet another meaning. Contemporary usage, and Kant's in the third Critique, is closest to Baumgarten's, viz., aesthetics as a philosophy of art or a receptivity to beauty in art and in nature. Kierkegaard used the term to denote refined hedonism. All of these usages are of course related, and the fine arts and natural beauty are germane to aesthetics in Peirce's and Schiller's sense, as the latter made clear.

Neither hedonism in particular nor consequentialism in general is a corollary of Peirce's having made aesthetics the basic normative science.

D

Whether aesthetics, so understood, can be made a science is another question. In Chapter 7 it was argued that any science, if successful, confirms its own observational base: it does so by finding that its putative observations tend to agree and by showing how that agreement may be explained by what is putatively observed. Anti-foundationalism follows: any explanation of scientific methods and any justification of those methods must depend on the use of those methods and cannot be attempted before inquiry is well advanced. Thus our present problem is threefold: (1) to identify aesthetic feelings in scientific inquiry and in other realms where normative judgments are made; (2) to show that the normative judgments those feelings elicit tend to agree; and (3) to show how that agreement might be explained on the hypothesis that what these judgments represent is real and is a cause (*a fortiori* nonmechanistic) of those feelings. This section addresses the first two problems, drawing on Chapters 3 and 7. The third problem is addressed in the next two sections, drawing on Chapters 2 and 6.

It is a mistake to suppose that agreement must always be of the impressive kind exhibited by progress in the natural sciences: viz., a convergence of opinion, arrived at by diverse methods, on single answers to single questions, where the questions continue to grow in number and the answers in depth and precision. Normative judgments have a history in which there is much agreement but not that kind of growth. Nor has normative agreement been achieved by a convergence of the results of diverse methods, or, indeed, by any methods consciously adopted. In the fine arts, morals, and politics, agreement has been overshadowed by vehement and/or persistent disagreements; but this must not prevent us from noticing the large and important bodies of agreement.

Let us begin with the natural sciences. There has been agreement, often after initial disagreement, on methods of inquiry, including inquiry's social organization, the sorts of problem deemed significant, criteria of theory-choice, what counts as a good explanation, what counts as relevant data, subordinate desiderata of reproducibility of results, simplicity, accuracy, honesty, etc., and also the aims thus served. So far as the aims are purely cognitive, they are found in the types of theory and explanation that are to be sought, as these types define what knowledge or explanation or understanding is. Theory may be, for example, either taxonomic or pre-dictive – two different forms of understanding. The taxonomic is a resting place for thought while the predictive is an engine of further discovery – two different aims. We have seen in Chapter 3 that all of this has had a history, that the aims and organization of modern science were a product of earlier inquiries.

But whereas progress in theory is in part by the elimination of mis-taken conjectures, the discovery of cognitive values tends to be additive: in most cases, the new does not eliminate the old but only demotes it in importance. For example, the taxonomic ideal of understanding never was refuted: it endures though subordinated to dynamic theories, either pre-dictive (as in the Periodic Table of chemical elements) or historical (bio-logical taxa, formerly static forms, are now arranged by descent). Similarly, wave mechanics did not refute the earlier (cogwheel and billiard ball) ideal of mechanistic explanation; it merely added to it, introducing a more mathematical form of understanding. The quantum revolution defeated determinism but did not reject deterministic explanation where it remains possible. The major apparent exception was the denial of teleology in early modern science, which was made to seem an empty sort of explanation; but, as we have seen, Peirce argued that that ideal reëmerged in the nine-teenth century, along with the discovery of statistical forms of explana-tion that proved fruitful. Changes in the subsidiary values of accuracy, etc., also occur additively: for example, quantitative accuracy supplanted qualitative accuracy in importance but did not eliminate it (*vide supra*, Ch.3, H). (This is not to deny that some methods have been decisively rejected or are still disputed: for example, introspection versus behaviorism in psychology, Weber's method of *Verstehen* in the social sciences, and the rational-actor model in economics. In at least some of these cases, norms of accuracy, testability, and fruitfulness are assumed and it was or is a fac-tual question whether the method at issue could satisfy them.)

The dimension of experience that accounts for the emergence of new cognitive values has been little noted. Peirce was original in addressing this neglected yet fundamental question, and he was brilliantly original in devising experiments that bore on it: in particular, the 'great men' experiment at Johns Hopkins. That experiment pertained to a minor and noncognitive dimension of the normative, viz., the relative 'greatness' of persons; but what it showed would seem to apply also to other dimensions of the normative. It showed that judgments of greatness formed 'impres-sionistically' – that is, on the basis of feelings and not by application of criteria – agreed more than could be explained by shared prejudice. Those feelings are, of course, a form of admiration – one expressly not moral. But if it is through admiration that values are formed, then we can explain why the evolution of values tends to be additive: for, what has been found admirable would normally remain admirable, even if it is later found to be less admirable than something not earlier encountered.

Normative questions, often invisible in histories of science, are featured in histories of the fine arts, morals, and politics, where changes and conflicts of values and disagreements about values monopolize attention. However, in those areas there also is significant agreement. That is an obvious fact. The agreements need only to be properly identified, and then the patterns of agreement and disagreement must be noted. They are not the same in morals and politics as in the arts, nor in the arts as in the sciences.

In the fine arts, values are, or are found in, the forms, styles, qualities, and types of effect that artists create, that the public learns to appreciate, and that critics attempt to define. What in the arts we enjoy or appreciate or admire is of vast variety and cannot be reduced to a simple formula. 'Giving pleasure' covers many different feelings and only restates what is to be explained. We enjoy, for example, novels that depict the sordid aspects of life (think of Conrad's *The Secret Agent*) – but only if the depiction is precise and revelatory. We appreciate Picasso's horrifying painting, *Guernica*. Aristotle already noted that '... though the objects themselves may be painful to see, we delight to view the most realistic representations of them ...', which he explained this way: '... the reason of the delight ... is that one is ... learning – gathering the meaning of things ...' (*Poetics* 4, Bywater trans.). But there are other causes of delight as well.

As in science, a novel type of value, introduced by a new way of doing things, typically meets initial resistance; genius is recognized belatedly. Also as in science, an innovation met with acclaim often proves to have no staying power: like scientific theories, the artistic forms or styles most valued are those that prove to be most subject to development. What can be done in another area of science with a new type of experiment or new mathematical technique? (Harmonic analysis originated in thermodynamics, then was adopted in optics, acoustics, and seismology.) What more can be done in music with counterpoint or the sonata form? (Bach and Mozart are celebrated mostly for having done so much more with forms already created.) In painting, impressionism and cubism have run their course, though the works that established those styles are still admired. And so on.

It is essential to our purpose to recognize that each new development in any of the arts introduces a new value or new set of values: it is not the case that cubism or jazz did differently, much less did better, something already done by Delacroix or Brahms; rather, they expanded what may be done with pigment or notes, creating new kinds of awareness, experience, or enjoyment. In other words, they taught us new values – new types of thing or effect to value – expanding our ability to appreciate. Those values were discovered by the artists who created the works that impressively exhibited them. As with cognitive values, older artistic ideals are not refuted, though they are sometimes eclipsed by the new. When emerging from occultation, they are placed in historical perspective: we admire the baroque but recognize that it belongs to an earlier age. A difference from science is the proliferation of values in the arts; a related difference is the value placed on novelty itself – the discovery of new forms of appreciation, new joys in learning or in feeling. One might almost say that the discovery of values is what the fine arts are all about.

In the arts, disagreements are rife; however, they often are about the relative importance of agreed-upon values. Frost's objection to free verse, that it is playing tennis without a net, does not mean that he was unaware of the poetic qualities, achieved net-less, in the best examples of free verse. Because it is our best example of how values are learned from experience, aesthetics *qua* judgment in the fine arts is the model of aesthetics in Schiller's and Peirce's sense of the term. Agreement among such judgments is not perfect but is sufficient to be evidence that the feelings that elicit them *are* evidence: viz., of what is truly appreciable or truly admirable.

The agreement does not need to be perfect: it matters little to me that you are tone deaf or to you that I refuse to take pop art seriously. It is quite otherwise when we disagree morally or politically, as we are not free to live in different societies, and a society is shaped by its moral values and political ideals. Values in the fine arts invite; in morals and politics they command. Moral or political disagreement therefore compels attention. But here, too, there is agreement – indeed, more agreement than elsewhere. For, while the practical issues are many, the conflicting ideals that underlie them are few. We agree in ignoring an infinitude of logically possible ideals, and therefore we agree more than we disagree. And even where two ideals conflict and we come to opposite conclusions, we typically share both ideals and disagree only about which, at least in that instance, is the more important one. We agree that people should be honest and that they should be kind; it is over the cases where kindness and honesty are incompatible that we are likely to disagree.

In our society, freedom and equality are ideals widely shared, and few would maintain that either can be achieved in total neglect of the other.

But we disagree vehemently when circumstances require a sacrifice of one for the sake of the other: we disagree about which is the more important, either in general or in that particular case. Thus we distinguish between different meanings of 'freedom' or different kinds of equality, so as to be able to deny that we are sacrificing either, where it really matters, to the other; only, we do not make these distinctions the same way. Our agreement, it turns out, is ambiguous. And yet, the ideals vaguely defined that we do share matter: they are why we argue with one another, for example, over definitions of 'freedom'. Disagreement presupposes a common ground, an agreement about what it is that we are disagreeing about.

Often, those who disagree most vehemently are alike in assuming that whatever is ideal in one respect should be compatible with whatever is ideal in any other respect. This leads to much mental effort and dialectical subtlety; it leads ideologues to distort the facts so as to make them fit their respective utopian visions. Somehow, they think, there must be satisfactory solutions to all our problems! The alternative assumption is that no systematic unity of ideals, genuine as those ideals are, is possible, that goods often conflict, and, hence, that in our lives and in human history there must always be failure, injustice, evil, and guilt. In that tragic view of life, an incompatibility of values does not prove that not all are real; indeed, it presupposes the reality of each. And since the tragic view is a possibility, it follows that irresolvable disagreements in morals and politics do not prove that values are merely subjective.

Because moral and political values organize our social existence, they must change as the material and economic conditions of society change. But this – the historical relativity of values – should not be confused with the doctrine of moral relativism, that right and wrong vary with subjective opinion or social convention or the interest of the stronger. It is simply a fact that neither freedom nor equality would have been desirable or so much as conceivable in a tribe of hunter-gatherers living always on the edge of starvation, where all depends on the unquestioned authority of the strongest individual. Conversely, when circumstances change, that change does not refute the values that earlier reigned, which we can still admire even while deeming them now irrelevant. We can appreciate Athenian democracy while admitting that direct democracy is impossible in the large nations that an industrial economy requires. Similarly, we can appreciate the values that were achieved, and perhaps could only have been achieved, in a form of society of which we otherwise disapprove. Medieval feudalism and the Ming dynasty had each their virtues. Athenian society was slave-owning and perhaps the leisure that made democracy and philosophy possible would otherwise have been impossible at that pre-industrial time. The necessity of painful choices attests to our agreement about what is valuable, even when we disagree about which of two values is the greater.

In this section, I have only pointed out the obvious, that there is significant agreement about values in the sciences, in the fine arts, and in morals and politics. Some of that agreement can be explained consistently with physicalism, that is, without assuming that values have any reality beyond facts about what people actually value. Physiological needs and drives account for much that is common among human societies; for example, the sexual drive cannot be denied and therefore it must be channeled – in one way or another – so as to preserve the social cohesion on which our survival depends. We seem, however, to prize freedom and equality beyond their utilitarian value. What explains that? And what explains our appreciation for all the diverse values displayed in the fine arts? Or for the pursuit of knowledge and understanding for their own sake, beyond their utilitarian value?

Peirce's suggestion was that some normative judgments are observations, elicited by feelings of admiration (we must add: approval, disgust, etc.), much as observations of the physical world are elicited by physical sensations. Other normative judgments then depend on these just as physical theories and other inferences about the physical world are grounded in observation of the physical. In other words, we learn of good and evil – we learn of the better and the worse in any realm, including art and science – by experiencing them. The preponderance of agreement among these judgments is strong evidence that the values discovered in that way are real.

This evidence must however be discounted if we cannot imagine any way in which values could cause normative judgments and explain their agreement. There cannot be evidence for what is inconceivable.

E

To argue from the fact of normative agreement to the reality of the values agreed upon, as being the only way (or the best way or, at least, a way) to explain that agreement, presupposes that we can conceive of a non-mechanistic mode of causation. For, mechanistic causation, even broadly defined, limits causes to spatiotemporal particulars producing particular effects or making them to be in one or another degree probable or possible. These particulars may be properties, conditions, entities, fields, forces, events, or processes, but none are causes unless they actually exist or actually occur. They are identified by type, but they are not types. Whereas, values and ideals, etc., are types; as such, if real, they are real independently of being made actual. (However, values are not independent of the actual constitution of the world: any political ideal presupposes the existence of a community of rational agents; fairness presupposes a limited supply of a distributable good; and so on.) It follows that a metaphysics exclusively mechanistic denies the possibility that values may be causes. But if values are products of valuation merely and never are causes of valuation, then they are not independent of opinion; that is, they are not real. And then normative judgment can never be factually true or factually false. Thus the famous fact/value dichotomy: it is a corollary of mechanicalism.

Before considering what little Peirce had to say about a metaphysics that embraces nonmechanistic causes, I must defend the assumption that normative science requires such a metaphysics. For, the fact/value dichotomy, long a dogma of analytic philosophy, has recently been denied by prominent analytic philosophers – who, at the same time, deny that their arguments depend on metaphysics. By metaphysics (or 'ontology'), however, they mean any metaphysics other than physicalism, understood as admitting none but mechanistic causes. These philosophers are not in fact innocent of metaphysics: their metaphysics is that which they assume to be implied by physical theory.

Let us begin with John Rawls' influential 1971 book, *A Theory of Justice*. Rawls' method was to ask what social arrangements would be chosen by persons who, behind the 'veil of ignorance', do not know what their place in that society would be. This is not a matter of judgment about right and wrong; it is a matter of self-interested but rational choice under a condition of ignorance. The moral judgment is that what is so chosen would be just, that is, that Rawls' method defines the concept of justice. What is the ground on which that judgment is made? In the first edition of his book, Rawls wrote that his 'theory of justice' is to be tested against the moral judgments that 'normal', that is, average or typical, adults make in a condition of 'reflective equilibrium' (pp.40–46). Such adults are assumed to have developed a 'sense of justice'. As the general theory is to be tested against particular judgments, 'A theory of justice is subject to the same rules of method as other theories' (p.44).

The idea that all theories are subject to the same rules of method reflects the pre-Kuhnian philosophy of science that prevailed at the time Rawls wrote (it was fading by the date of publication). Theories in the natural sciences were supposed to ground predictions of particular events under particular conditions, which permitted them to be tested against observations of what in particular occurs under those conditions: in that way, the general is tested against the particular. But such observations are of what in fact is, not of what ought to be. Rawls therefore compared a theory of justice more specifically to linguistic theories that are tested against native speakers' 'intuitions' distinguishing correct from incorrect speech (obviously, these are not intuitions in the original philosophical use of that term). Native speakers, as they usually speak correctly (or correctly enough for their purposes), know the grammar and semantics of their language, that is, its rules of usage. But seldom are they adept at stating those rules; they are much more accurate and confident in making judgments about which particular uses of words are correct. Their knowledge of the rules is therefore tacit. So also, the suggestion is 'normal' adults' sense of justice is a tacit knowledge of general rules: the typical is here made the norm. Philosophers, testing their hypotheses against the particular judgments 'normal' adults make, attempt to formulate this tacit knowledge. Rawls' ultimate appeal was to the moral 'intuitions' of his readers. He hoped that those intuitions would confirm his proposed definition of 'justice'.

There are obvious difficulties in that view, which perhaps explains why, in the second edition of his book (1999), Rawls omitted entirely his 1971 discussion of theory and method. Firstly, on what basis, not begging any moral questions, are we to determine who is a normal adult? Does a typical adult member of a tribe of cannibals count? Secondly, do the views of moral reformers – manifestly not 'normal', that is, average or typical – not count? Jesus of Nazareth comes to mind and also Bishop Wilberforce, who was the most prominent early opponent of the African slave trade, at a time when few Europeans questioned its morality. They seem beyond average (rather far beyond average in the case of Jesus), but not for that reason normatively incompetent. Thirdly, if knowledge of justice is like knowledge of grammar, then justice would seem to be merely conventional and, as such, relative to different societies' different conventions. So, 'normal' cannibals have a say, after all, though only about cannibal justice. Indeed, by combining utility (defined as what individuals desire) with (a version of) its fair distribution, Rawls' method is well tailored to modern liberal democracies: by a clever device, it supports a view that, in those societies, might be said to be conventional. But do utility and fairness exhaust all that we might, were we to inquire further, find admirable in social arrangements?

Causal assumptions are tacit in Rawls' account. Hypotheses about physical laws are tested against observations of physical events, because those events are assumed to be governed by physical laws. Such observations, of course, are not made by 'normal' adults but by the specially trained. 'Normal' adults are the qualified observers of what by convention is right or wrong (grammatically or morally), because it is assumed that their judgments are governed by social conventions internalized. As Rawls did not consider whether moral judgment might have any cause other than convention, the possibility of moral reformation was not considered, nor from what sources a moral reformer might draw.

Bernard Williams (1985, Ch.5), among many penetrating observations about Rawls' theory that are less germane to our topic, noted some differences between linguistic and ethical 'intuitions' but concluded, in any case, that, as Rawls' method is extended 'outward' to societies other than our own, 'We can less and less appropriately rely on those intuitions that belong distinctively to the local *we* …' (1985, Ch.5, p.103, Williams' italics). The 'local we', in Williams' view, is defined less by conventions than by a 'form of life' (Wittgenstein's phrase that Williams embraced gingerly and used little), that is to say, the ways we have of living together, the sort of society we live in, its institutions and customs, etc. A form of life is not reducible to conventions, but is more substantive, subtle, and perception-shaping, accounting in other ways than conventions do for what we think right or wrong. Even the possibility of there being conventions depends on a form of life. Indeed, in what kinds of society are questions about 'justice' intelligible? The limitation Williams noted is a serious fault in Rawls' theory, given the kind of theory it is meant to be; but such limitations are not a fault from Williams' own perspective. The entire thrust of his book, *Ethics and the Limits of Philosophy*, is that it is a mistake to suppose that an ethics must be a universally valid system of obligations ('morality' in Williams' usage) established by reason, or that it must be a universally valid system of any sort, or that the richness of ethical concepts may be reduced to a few basic principles, or that philosophy can establish any ethics not already the ethical perspective of an existing society. Williams' thesis is that a given ethics is inseparable from a given form of life.

There is in Williams' conclusions much that agrees with the implications of Peirce's conception of normative science. For example, from an empiricist account of the normative, we would expect the irreducible variety and localism that Williams emphasizes. Experience is concrete; thus it varies with different conditions, for example, the sort of society one is born into. Therefore, normative concepts are many and usually 'thick' (in Williams' sense: *vide supra*, Ch.7, E). Also, like Williams, Peirce did not define ethics narrowly as limited to a Kantian sort of system. However, a

Kantian ethics is not ruled out a priori (*vide supra*) and, hence, an eventual triumph of universal principles over local variations is not ruled out a priori. The most we can say is that Peirce's idea of normative science does not require that continued inquiry would eventually result in a universal ethics, any more than we can say a priori that the final opinion in physics is a 'unified' system. Finally, Williams and Peirce agree that conflicts of values cannot be adjudicated by reason alone. Where they disagree is in the reasons given for that conclusion and in the implications they draw from it.

In place of Peirce's empiricism, Williams introduces sociology. While he admits (what we are calling) normative observation – and therefore he rejects the fact/value dichotomy – he does not suppose that these observations reveal values not already embraced in a form of life. For, the normative observations he admits are judgments employing 'thick' concepts and, in his view, it is a society and its ethical perspective that give thick concepts their meaning. The form of life comes first, observation second. More could be said about this: Williams' view is not simple. However, it is not wrong to say that, in his view, our reasons for rejecting, say, cannibalism or a slave-based economy, are simply our reasons; we have no argument that we can expect would persuade others who do not already share our ethical perspective. And that is not only because habit and self-interest would curb their reason and blinker their perception, but also and more fundamentally it is because they, like we, possess no power of reasoning that is both ethical and universal and no power of observation that is both ethical and independent of a form of life. There is, in the figure Williams uses (1985, Ch.2), no Archimedean point external to all ethical systems, either in pure reason or in observation, from which basic ethical views can be justified or refuted.

The reason Williams cannot allow normative observation a more fundamental rôle in the formation of ethical views is that he is committed to physicalism *qua* mechanistic ('the absolute conception' he calls it: 1985, pp.111, 138–40, but originally and in more detail in Williams 1978). If reality is, and is exclusively, as it is represented to be in mechanist theory, then no explanation of the normative aspect of observation is possible other than the influence of an already formed ethical perspective. It is evident that Williams prefers Aristotle's empiricist ethics to Kant's rationalist ethics (see his Chapters 3 and 4), but Aristotle's method '... borrows from a teleological account of nature that we cannot now accept ...' (1985, p.120). That is the key. For it is teleological explanation, and its invocation of what has come to be called 'final causes', that is required if normative observation is to be accepted as genuinely a revelation of values, as opposed to being merely a value-laden response to nonnormative reality. The metaphysics of normative science is teleological. Or so I shall argue in the next section. For the present, my only point is that his physicalism leaves Williams no alternative but to affirm without argument the ethics of his own society.

Hilary Putnam, a leading analytic philosopher sympathetic to Peirce's thought, wrote late in his career two books, *The Collapse of the Fact/Value Dichotomy* (2002) and *Ethics Without Ontology* (2004), the titles of which make clear why they are next to be examined. To show that the fact/value dichotomy has collapsed, Putnam drew from several sources, including two with which we are familiar: Williams' idea of 'thick' concepts and Kuhn's historical studies showing that factual knowledge is informed by cognitive values (discussed also in Putnam 1981, Chs.5–6). However, unlike Kuhn and contrary to our use of Kuhn, Putnam claimed that cognitive values 'are arbitrary considered as anything but part of a holistic conception of human flourishing' (1981, pp.136–37). The idea of 'a holistic conception of human flourishing' borrows explicitly from Wittgenstein's idea of a form of life (Putnam 1981, pp.107–8). Like Rawls and Williams, Putnam is unable to identify any basis for values other than that they are part of what we already value.

Putnam's gloss on Kuhn raises a question: How will scientific theory be defended against someone such as a religious fundamentalist, whose conception of human flourishing differs from Putnam's? Such a person might hold that human flourishing depends on resolute belief in the creation story of *Genesis*. He might even reject the importance that Putnam assigns to human flourishing, preferring to do God's will at whatever cost and looking to a later, angelic existence for recompense. Nor can this alternative be simply laughed away by we who share Putnam's form of life and fancy ourselves enlightened; for even we must admit that fundamentalism has its comforts in contrast to the moral barrenness of modern science. We might observe, further, that deeply religious societies, for example, the Amish, Mormons, Orthodox Jews, have flourished, while secular societies have their discontents – discontents that seem only to grow with increasing affluence. Making cognitive values to depend on ideas of human flourishing puts science at risk of easy rejection – surely not Putnam's intent. But the problem is not so much that of convincing the fundamentalist as it is of convincing ourselves in response to fundamentalism. Rather than showing values to be as knowable as facts, Putnam's way of collapsing the fact/value dichotomy makes facts seem as arbitrary as, in the modern view, values are said to be.

This problem is even clearer in what Putnam says about moral issues. He says so little in that vein that it may be unfair to put much weight on his *obiter dicta*; the point, however, is that the little said omits what most needs saying. It shifts the burden of the argument, once again, onto one's form of life. Putnam declares an ethic 'of compassion', of 'alleviating suffering' – he is careful to add, 'regardless of the class or gender of the sufferer', as if alleviators of suffering often make those discriminations; surprisingly, he omits species of sufferer – and opposes this 'concern for the welfare of others' to '... an "ethics" (note the shudder quotes!) that sees ... courage and "manly prowess" as the chief virtues' (2004, p.23). The parenthetical injunction to notice the 'shudder quotes' is Putnam's. Unfortunately, it appears that, beyond shuddering, Putnam has no argument against any ethic that is alternative to his own.

Indeed, he expressly declares that 'I do not believe that someone who stands outside the whole circle of related concerns I have described as constitutive of ethics can be brought to share any of them by argument alone' (p.29). Two pages earlier, he listed democracy, toleration, and pluralism among these related concerns. As Cheryl Misak notes, '... most of the norms identified by Putnam come from the liberal democrat's stable' (2013, p.244). It looks very much as if the circle of concerns with which Putnam identified ethics (*sans* shudder quotes) are those of a liberal democracy – the same community within which one suspects that Rawls found his 'normal adults'. Or perhaps they found them among their elite academic community. Is there no argument for those values apart from the self-satisfaction of that community?

But surely Putnam is right that *argument* – if an argument is exclusively verbal – presupposes a set of shared assumptions; and then he is surely right also that *argument* can be effective only within a community committed to a particular form of life – a form of life in which there is adherence to principles capable of being formulated (whether or not actually formulated) and thus capable of serving as premises (possibly unstated) for argument. That is right, but Putnam also said something else, easily missed: that 'argument *alone*' (my emphasis) is ineffective when addressed to those outside the community. This suggests that there is something other than verbal argument that might be effective with – what shall we call them? – the barbarians. That could only be some sort of experience. Experience – which includes not only its famous 'hard knocks' but also the lessons of history and imaginative explorations in poetry, drama, fiction, and other arts – is the only thing other than verbal argument that can inform opinion (as distinguished from forming opinion, which might be by such arbitrary means as authority). Argument from shared principles is limited to working out their implications consistently, sometimes as applied to data provided by experience. But experience sometimes leads us to revise our principles: the experience of living by one's principles, though often satisfying, sometimes leads to disappointment, unexpected frustrations, even disaster.

Experience, then, can break in upon the flow of argument, providing novel premises, new principles. We have seen an example of this in the history of science, wherein ideals of explanation were modified by the very inquiries they guided, as their limitations were revealed and the virtues of alternatives were discovered. A community is always evolving in consequence of the experience of living by its principles or customs. And we can also be informed by others' experiences, for example, by observing the happiness of people who have adopted other forms of life. For, communities are not hermetically sealed off from one another. The kinds of experience that can civilize the barbarian may also modify a civilization.

But what, in the moral realm, might those experiences be, and on what grounds can we argue that such experiential lessons are legitimate? Putnam (2004, pp.23–27) mentions the philosophy of Emmanuel Levinas (e.g., his 1991); the reference is intriguing for its suggestion of one kind of experience that is germane to moral inquiry. Levinas, in Putnam's accurate telling, denies that obligation derives from abstract principle, *à la* Kant, and instead grounds it in encounters with other persons, in the imperative we feel to alleviate another's suffering. Putnam does not accept this as the whole truth, but suggests that these encounters work in fruitful tension with Kant's formalism and Aristotle's observations of the forms of life that are most admirable (pp.24–28; the reference to Aristotle would seem better made to Peirce). We have here the beginning of a nuanced account of moral inquiry. But it is only a beginning; what is being experienced in our experiences of 'the other' and why should it influence our moral views?

These questions are not addressed. Instead, Putnam identifies his project of 'ethics without ontology' with Levinas' refusal 'to reduce ethics to a theory of being or to base ethics upon a theory of being' (pp.23–24). Let us agree not to reduce ethics to ontology or to attempt to deduce it from ontology, that is, from abstract ontological postulates. But those proscriptions overlook the non-reductive and non-foundationalist possibility that metaphysics may be *a posteriori* and that it may be needed post hoc to explain how experience produces a modicum of agreement. Putnam's view leaves admiration, moral sensitivity, and feelings of obligation to seem arbitrary, as if they depend on nothing more than having adopted a form of life – say, the form of life of liberal democracy versus that of Islamic radicals.

We in liberal democracies espouse toleration and do not admire suicide bombers. Islamic radicals have contempt for secular society and view the ideal of religious toleration as a rationalization for weakness and loss of faith. Admittedly, liberal democrats might not be able to win Islamic radicals over to their own view. But is there nothing that one liberal democrat can say to another liberal democrat in defense of their convictions, other than that they are 'ours', that is, that this is how our gang feels and thinks? Before we can think of convincing Islamic radicals, by whatever means, that tolerance is better than bloodshed and that science refutes fanaticism, or merely, if it comes to this, to defeat them by force of arms, we need to convince ourselves of these truths. Simply repeating, 'That's what *we* believe!' is quite unconvincing – especially to those of us who pride ourselves on our freedom from dogmatism. It has become a serious question whether faith in liberal democratic values is strong enough to defend itself.

Putnam's assumption that 'ontological' grounds must be reductive and foundationalist is of a piece with his earlier reasons (in Putnam 1978 and 1981) for rejecting what he then named 'metaphysical realism' or 'external realism'. That assumption is contradicted by Peirce's conception of metaphysics (*vide supra*, Chs.4 and 8), but this is not the place to argue the matter. The present point is only that Putnam's view of metaphysics or ontology has prevented him from defending his moral views other than dogmatically.

I am not the first to remark that Rawls' and Putnam's attempts to evade relativism have failed. Cheryl Misak in 1994 ('A Peircean Account of Moral Judgments') cited the same passages in Rawls 1971 as I cited above, and to the same effect, as well as some related passages in Putnam 1981. The 1994 article is brief; Misak develops her view at greater length in a subsequent book (Misak 2000), in which she argues for a 'democratic' form of moral inquiry: one that considers as many opinions and as wide a variety of experiences as possible. The book's argument is based on a 'phenomenology of moral judgment': a review of the variety of ways in which moral judgments are in fact formed and debated. This is in express conformity to Peirce's dictum, that we must begin with inquiry as we find it, that a Cartesian wiping of the slate clean would leave us with nothing to go on. No use is made of Peirce's scheme of three normative sciences; Misak draws instead on his general idea of inquiry, (a) as depending on a compulsive aspect of experience (phaneroscopic 2ndness) and (b) in which one's own experiences are not the only experiences germane to the test of one's beliefs. Those engaged in such an inquiry take disagreement as indicative of error, while agreement attained by reasoning from experience is taken as evidence of truth. Misak goes further than Peirce does in distinguishing moral inquiry from inquiry in the natural sciences; not only does she emphasize, as did I in the preceding section, that some moral disagreements may persist regardless of how far inquiry is pursued, but she also suggests that moral inquiry may have other aims than truth (e.g., a 'deeper understanding' of others or of one's self, p.145, or a 'balancing the human need to belong – to share a past, language, and set of values with others – with abstract principle', p.167n51).

Moral inquiry is portrayed, as in Rawls' initial methodology, as testing general propositions against the judgments of particulars that individuals make. But Misak does not limit the participants in this discussion to 'normal adults' or to those sharing the liberal-democratic concerns Putnam identifies as ethical: she stresses the diversity of persons and the diversity of what they bring to the discussion. Nor does she suppose that relevant judgments are those made behind a 'veil of ignorance' of conditions affecting one's self-interest. Rather than attesting to an idea a priori of justice or other moral principle, these judgments are the fruit of experience, of what individuals have found in fact to be good or evil. Hers is, then, a version of moral inquiry that is empirical.

In a subsequent article (2008), Misak deepens her phenomenology of moral inquiry, distinguishing moral responses from other reactions, narratives of either of which may affect another person's normative views. This, in two, quite different ways. By one's own moral lights, one can take others' nonmoral reactions into account as data. If my principle is to not cause others pain and you say, 'Ouch!', that is a datum I will take into account. Whereas, the principle itself might be amended when confronted with someone's contrary moral response. If you are offended at my being over-solicitous, your account of what made you so respond may lead me to realize that there is more to the moral treatment of others than saving them from pain, for example, it may also require a respect for their autonomy. But this is my example. Misak's example is the judgment, 'That's odious!' made in response to the witnessed or reported sexual abuse of a child. 'Odious!' unlike 'Ouch!' is a moral response and, as such, addresses us regardless of our own principles or lack thereof. To make the latter point, a more controversial example than pedophilia would be better. Corporal punishment of misbehaving children used to be standard but now is by many condemned. If I am administering a spanking that I think is well-deserved and you exclaim, 'That's odious!', you will have at least made me reflect on my practice.

But what makes the diverse experience of diverse persons at all relevant to what you or I should believe about how we and others should act? Misak bases her argument on the principle that belief, if it is genuinely belief, must be 'responsive to experience' or 'sensitive' to the evidence (2000, p.51 and *passim*; also 2008 *passim*). This rules out a prime example of belief, namely, religious belief, which, while it may be responsive to experience in some way, does not subject its articles of faith to empirical test. Nor is it clear what place, if any, belief should have in scientific inquiry. But we can agree with Misak if we understand her to be referring to the conclusions scientists tentatively draw and/or to the beliefs we rely on in practical matters. Yes indeed, either of these must be sensitive to the evidence. But what counts as evidence? Like Putnam, Misak provides no explanation of moral experience that would show why it, and especially others' moral experience, should matter to us. Experience is compelling: we take our own seriously. But that is not a sufficient reason for us to take seriously others' experience. The dipsomaniac's experience of purple spiders is compulsive (he is shaking with fright), but we are right to dismiss it as evidence of what is there, in that well-swept corner.

Purple spiders are easily dealt with if to compulsiveness we add, as surely Misak would agree to do, a demand for coherence: we learn from experience which kinds of experience are reliable, that is, which kinds generally yield judgments that cohere with one another; in the same way, we learn who is a reliable observer. Coherence of beliefs with one another winnows lessons drawn from experience. But in natural science and in our commonsense view of the natural world, this leads to and is supported by explanations (very vague in the case of common sense) of how observation works; and these presuppose the reality of causation, the reality of physical bodies, space and time, etc., in short, a metaphysics. It is that metaphysics, including an assumption that different persons observe the same physical world, which entails that I should test my beliefs against your experience as well as against my own experience. Purple spiders, if real, are the sorts of things we should all be able to see, even or especially those of us who are sober. That is just common sense, though the physics of light, the physiology of vision, etc., provides a more detailed account of the causal relations involved in seeing. The coherence that matters therefore includes explanation of our data by the theories they support. But can this idea be extended to moral experience?

If you find the spanking of children odious and I adhere to the old maxim, 'Spare the rod and spoil the child', why should I find your sensitivity germane to my responsibility as a parent? What makes your response evidence, even weak evidence, of right or wrong? Can we in any way suppose that there is an objective rightness or wrongness that is a contributing cause of your emotional reaction and that makes our seeing things differently a reason for me to hesitate? If not, then a large measure of agreement among people so reacting might be explained, *à la* Williams and Putnam, as due to a shared form of life – which would allow me to shrug my shoulders and dismiss your concern as deriving from a different form of life than that one within which I happily live (and wherein, I might belligerently add, children are raised properly).

The values, of tolerance, pluralism, etc., from 'the liberal democrat's stable' that Misak noted in Putnam's ethics, reappear in her theory, not as explicit dogmas, but as required by the method of moral inquiry, which mandates taking everyone's experience into account. Those values are thus made to seem required by scientific objectivity itself: surely it is unscientific to ignore someone's experience, just because it conflicts with one's own convictions! But this clever gambit fails. For, it lacks a causal account of why someone's experience might attest to moral truths, much less why everyone's experiences do. Science regards as evidence only those observations that are of a kind that have been found to be both reliable and explicable, and only when they have been made carefully, which often is possible only for specially trained observers. It does not give a vote to someone who earnestly insists, 'By golly, I can *see* the Sun going around the Earth!'. Science is not democratic. In fairness to Misak, this perhaps explains why she suggests that moral inquiry may have social goals as well as cognitive ones; for, by that means, she can defend its being 'democratic'. But social goals for moral inquiry beg the moral question.

In all four of the examples here considered, due to Rawls, Williams, Putnam, and Misak, it is the evasion of metaphysics that accounts for a failure to evade dogmatism. These authors do not mean to be dogmatic; they espouse pluralism, tolerance, and reasoned discourse. But they fail to identify any basis on which someone who disagrees with those values might be led to accept them. And if there is no basis on which to convince others, then there is no noncircular basis on which one can convince oneself. Naught remains but the method of tenacity.

F

If values can be causes, types must be capable of being in some cases causes. Recall Chapter 6, Section G: we will now put what was said there to work. The forms of statistical explanation that Peirce discerned in nineteenth-century physics and biology (Chapter 2, C–E) make types of outcome to be what explains there being outcomes of those types. If what must be cited to explain a phenomenon is a cause of that phenomenon, then those types are causes. Even physicalism, then, does not preclude types from being causes, though most physicalists, because they assume that all causes must be mechanical and/or that physics permits only mechanistic explanation, would deny this.

However, the types of distribution that in statistical mechanics explain such phenomena as the ideal gas laws have no normative bearing; they are merely the types that embrace the vast majority of alternative mechanical possibilities. In biology, the theory of natural selection makes some types of outcome causes in another way, entailing a distinction between means and ends. Peirce held that it reintroduces a nontheistic form teleological explanation, modifying Aristotle's equally nontheistic idea in one fundamental respect. This bring us a step nearer to what is needed for normative science: let us see how it nonetheless falls short.

Mechanical causation is essential to all biological phenomena, including the chance occurrence of genetic mutations. Within a population of organisms, a mutation may eventually occur that favors the reproductive success of the individual that possesses it. It is a tautology that such a mutation, unlike most mutations, will tend to be retained in subsequent generations of the population: this is named 'selective retention'. Over much time, a series of many selective retentions results in a form of life otherwise improbable, for example, an animal with eyes and legs. A form of life cannot be explained by mechanical causation alone, as mechanical causation alone does not create novel forms of order. It cannot be explained without reference to the types of outcome, such as visual acuity and speed, for which selection had repeatedly been made. Those types are therefore causes; as they are not mechanical, we may call them 'final causes'.

A final cause is any type for which there is or has been selection. The process of selection may be in Darwin's word 'natural', that is, agentless, or it may be by an agent making choices consciously and deliberately. In the latter case, error is possible, as the selection is by appearances and appearances deceive. The type selected for, whether the selection is agentless or by an agent, may be either a type of the thing selected (its pattern explains why the rug was purchased) or a type of (some of) its consequences (greater speed explains why a gene for longer legs was selectively retained). Either way, the type is a cause of the selection. The ordinary English word for a final cause is 'purpose', which is a term of explanation: for example, 'I picked up that rock for the purpose of pounding in the tent-peg'. We ordinarily speak of seeing as the purpose for which eyes exist, of locomotion as the purpose of legs, and so on; for, these types of effect explain why those organs exist and are as they are. Even dogmatic materialists find it difficult to avoid this teleological way of talking. Darwin's theory justifies that language without recourse to theology.

However, purpose in biology is circumscribed. Biological purposes do not exist independently of the process of natural selection; they are a function of the process.[7] That greater speed would be advantageous in a given population does not by itself make greater speed a purpose; for, that alone does not result in there being selection for outcomes of that type. There is no natural selection *of* a genetic modification *for* a type of outcome if there are no alleles – already existing – differing in the degree to which they promote outcomes of that type. So, existence precedes essence! Nor does natural selection occur for any purpose. Given the conditions that define the biosphere, it is merely a tautology that in the biosphere natural selection tends to occur.

Distinctions of success and failure, of better and worse, follow nonetheless. For, what has a purpose does not always succeed in achieving that purpose: a different adaptation might have functioned better; nor does every instance of an adaptation function properly. With respect to the purposes of legs and eyes, speed and acuity of vision are virtues, while lameness and blindness are defects. This and similar normative language applies factually. It is a fact that it applies factually. However, these facts do not represent what is normative *for us*. The purposes assumed are not necessarily our purposes. What is good for scorpions is not a good we are obliged to promote.

Furthermore, we are free to deny the purposes of our own biology, for example, by choosing a celibate life, by deliberately blinding oneself, by suicide. And certainly we can adopt purposes – for we do adopt purposes – that are not subordinate to biological survival. These are human purposes in contradistinction to biological purposes. One might say that human freedom *is* this capacity to adopt and to act for purposes of our own choosing.

How are such choices made? They can be made arbitrarily. Arbitrary choice is not causeless: there are reasons why a willful child insists on getting its arbitrarily chosen way. Other choices may be driven by human physiology even when they run contrary to biological ends, as in gluttony

---

[7] A point Dennett also makes (e.g., in his 2017, pp.37–38). Dennett, however, insists that the purposes that result from natural selection are explained mechanistically.

and lust. A third possibility was explored at length above, in Section D: cognitive values, artistic values, moral values, and political ideals are found in human history. In these realms, that which comes eventually to be valued occurs first by accident or by what with hindsight we label acts of creative genius. We might compare history's discarded accidents and trials to the non-advantageous genetic mutations that did not survive. But in human history the selective retention of relatively few novelties cannot be explained tautologically on the ground that they confer reproductive advantage; for they do not confer reproductive advantage.

What explains the triumph of new forms of knowing or of art or of ordering human relations? When what is new is repeated, developed, and experienced by more people, its true character is revealed: as its limitations become manifest, it may be discarded, but otherwise appreciation of it may deepen and spread. This means that new pleasures are learned, new desires formed. The values exemplified become or otherwise shape the purposes we adopt. And we are shaped in the process: again, existence precedes essence. Novel types of personality emerge, as do new social institutions. This was illustrated in Chapter 3, in the case of modern science, by the advent of what came to be named 'scientists' – persons dedicated to specialist lines of research – and their institutions. But it could have been illustrated as well by the spread and institutional development of Christianity, from its origin in the Near East to its late arrival in Scandinavia, taming those rude tribes: the civilization otherwise rooted in classical Rome and Greece was thus reshaped. Or it could have been illustrated by the emergence within democracies of the distinctively democratic personalities and voluntary associations that Tocqueville described after his visit to the young American republic.

We have difficulty believing that these distinctively human purposes are arbitrary. Yet, there seems to be no way to deny it, except on the hypothesis that some possibilities become our purposes because of what they are in themselves. That hypothesis was suggested by Peirce in 1902. In the following passages (EP2:122–23), he used the word 'idea' (recalling Plato's similar use of ἰδέα) to refer, not to what a person has in mind, but to a possibility that has a power to make itself conceived and to move us to attempt its actualization:

> … the idea does not belong to the soul; it is the soul that belongs to the idea. The soul does for the idea just what the cellulose does for the Beauty of the rose; that is to say, it affords it opportunity.
> … it is a perfectly intelligible opinion that ideas are not all mere creations of this or that mind, but on the contrary have a power of finding or creating

their vehicles, and having found them, of conferring upon them the ability to transform the face of the earth.

What I do insist upon is … that every idea has in some measure … the power to work out physical and psychical results.

Unlike the types of outcome for which in biological evolution there is selection, these ideas or possibilities, that is, types, do not become purposes merely as functions of processes of selection; for, they account for the occurrence of those processes. They are, as it were, purposes-in-waiting: they are purposes before being adopted as such. Of course, such types could have no effect on us if they did not answer to human nature as already constituted. Their power cannot be manifest without the right conditions obtaining. But their effect cannot be explained by human nature alone. For, as we have seen, they reshape that nature.

This must not be mistaken for the totalitarian fantasy that human nature is infinitely malleable; it is very little malleable; it is subject to shaping along a few alternative lines only. Consider one example. Laws, unneeded in primitive societies, would have been inconceivable in them. In the Chinese empire and elsewhere, there was rule by laws but not rule of law: emperors and their like laid down the law for others. The rule of law had its first, very limited, instances in ancient Athens, the Roman republic, the feudal system of the late Middle Ages. The Magna Carta that English barons, by their military might, forced King John to sign established a rule of law for themselves and their king. But the ideal thus introduced grew in power and scope: other classes of English society won protection from lawless power. And by English, Roman, and Greek example, that ideal has now spread throughout the world, restricting the scope of power arbitrarily exercised and conferring equal dignity on all subjects of state.

So far as Peirce developed the notion that certain possibilities will find or create their vehicles, transforming the world, it was in his account of the science of aesthetics: the idea that feelings of admiration reveal the objectively admirable. But this science provides only such explanations as are internal to the point of view at issue. What is admirable about the theories and methods of modern science can be explicated in terms of the aims and values of that enterprise – testability, concreteness, fruitfulness, etc. – but this will not move anyone who has not already felt the attraction of those aims and values. What is admirable about counterpoint or about impressionism can similarly be explicated by theorists of music and painting, wholly in terms of those forms. That may define, refine, or enhance appreciation but it cannot instill appreciation in those who are not already responsive. There is, then, no definition of admirability other than that it is what feelings of admiration represent. The admirable in all its dimensions – moral and amoral, including what is good in explanation, good in art, good in human behavior and social institutions – is simply that which would be admired for itself, once a clear vision of it is obtained.

Given that (hypostatically abstract) definition of it, the evidence that goodness is an objective quality is limited to that which was reviewed in Section D: the fact that there is widespread and enduring agreement on relatively few values, whether scientific, artistic, moral, or political. The metaphysical support needed for that inductive argument is not available except in the slenderest way: types have been found to be causes in physics and in biology, and therefore it cannot be maintained a priori that types may not be causes in human history.

How far does this take us? Consider just one consequence of Peirce's idea of normative science. Above, I suggested that human freedom is the capacity to adopt and to act for purposes of our own choosing. Now we can amend that definition in this way: true freedom is adopting and acting for purposes chosen because they are seen to be good – or, so as to allow for honest error (subject to correction by further experience), because they appear to us to be good. True freedom is choice neither arbitrary nor mechanically determined, for example, by our physiology, though our physiology must make us capable of being influenced by ideas. True freedom is choice determined by the goodness of what is chosen.

Kant defined freedom ('autonomy of the will') as acting out of respect for the moral law. But Kant placed moral law outside of nature and denied that freedom and moral behavior can be explained by natural science. That made morality a mystery. By recognizing that types can be causes and that teleological explanation reëntered modern science, Peirce overcame the bifurcation of ethics and nature. In his Third Critique, Kant himself tried to bridge the chasm by teleology, but he made teleology to be rooted a priori in human judgment – something that our minds impose on nature. Kant's idea of nature remained mechanistic. Though he did not mention it, Peirce must have been aware that he was saving Kantian ethics in the same way he had saved Aristotelian teleology: by revising it consistently with modern science correctly understood.

G

Did Peirce suppose that the normative sciences could become distinct scientific specializations? Recall that his taxonomy of the sciences is not foundationalist: it is not a prescription for how to inquire but is a retrospective systematization of strands of inquiry that emerged unplanned. Precisely because it depends on experience gained within other inquiries and enterprises, which experience is ongoing, it seems that normative inquiry cannot be assigned to scientific specialists; it must remain the work of each of us. The value of the idea of a system of three normative 'sciences' lies not in its being a practical proposal but in its identifying the sources of normative knowledge.

The idea of normative science remains sketchy: it depends on a teleology that is speculative; it poses questions as yet unanswered; it is in need of much work. That late in his life Peirce was willing to make such a conjecture public, for example in his Harvard lectures, illustrates his scientific spirit. He did not think of himself as possessing final answers but as making contributions – refutable hypotheses and calculations germane thereto – to what others may continue. He was not a philosopher with a system; like Galileo, his intention was to open 'a gateway and a road'.

CHAPTER 10

Modern Science Contra Modernity

But as you know ... my style of 'brilliancy' consists of a mixture of irony and seriousness, – the same things said ironically and also seriously. (letter from Peirce to William James, 1898)[1]

The preceding chapters attempt, first, to explicate and defend Peirce's concept of science as inquiry *sans* foundations and *sans* completion, wherein knowing is discovering more and the goal is to be on the way (Chapters 2 and 3); then to show that this idea of science is assumed and explained by Peirce's so-called pragmatism, which identifies meaning with growth, truth with what would eventually be concluded, and the reality truth represents as that which explains inquiry's progress (Chapter 4); next, to argue that Peirce's philosophical style was neither system-building nor conceptual analysis but was to inquire in the preceding experimentalist sense, wherein finality is not sought and ideas, including ideas of system, are conjectures, more or less vague, that are intended to be developed along diverse lines and thereby tested (Chapters 5 and 6); and, finally, to show that his psychological experiments, related to his work in astronomy, established empirically that empiricism may be expanded beyond its assumed limits (Chapter 7), making possible an idea of philosophy as a network of empirical inquiries, beginning with phaneroscopy (Chapter 8) and proceeding to a trio of normative sciences (Chapter 9).

Metaphysical themes run throughout those chapters. One such theme is that observations in general, and scientific inquiry in particular, always have metaphysical presuppositions, at first instinctual but then tested by the observations they make possible and revised as inquiry proceeds (Chapter 7). Metaphysics, then, is not foundational: present from the beginning, it becomes, via revisions made, a product of inquiry.

---

[1] Quoted in Perry (1935), vol.2, p.420

At some point in that process, metaphysics can be made scientific: that is, it can be made a branch of inquiry pursued under (evolving) ideas of proper method. In Peirce's tentative scheme of the philosophical sciences, metaphysics depends on logic (the study, at once empirical and normative, of methods of inquiry), but, like logic, remains subject to revision in light of discoveries yet to be made in the nonphilosophical sciences (Chapter 8).

A second metaphysical theme is modal realism, the doctrine that reality embraces what may be, would be, would have been, and so on, as well as what is and was. Viewed with suspicion in modern philosophy, modal realism is nonetheless essential to modern science, most obviously in its idea of laws of nature and in its demand that theories ground testable predictions. It is implicit in the 1878 'pragmatic maxim' for clarifying ideas, even though Peirce rejected modal realism at that time and despite the maxim's not indicating how modal ideas may be clarified. That maxim was supplemented in 1903 (Chapter 4), permitting a phaneroscopic explication of the meaning of modality (Chapter 8).

A third metaphysical theme is final causation, a nontheistic teleology. Such an idea was introduced in classical philosophy but rejected in early modern science, only to be reintroduced, unrecognized and in a different form, in nineteenth-century science (Chapters 2, B–E; 6, G; 9, F). But for final causation, the normative sciences would not be objective (Chapter 9). Nor would the natural sciences be objective, as their own discoveries of method, essential to them, are normative (Chapter 3).

A fourth metaphysical theme, inseparable from the others, is that which Peirce named 'scholastic realism', as it is akin to the doctrine, espoused in medieval universities, that 'universals' are real (Chapter 4). Peirce's emphasis, however, was less on universals (or what can be represented by monadic predicates) than on other sorts of 'generals': relations, laws, continua, and wholes irreducible to their parts, human communities especially. Modern science, as it is an evolving network of specialized inquiries, is essentially a communal enterprise, where the community of scientists is unlimited and its task is unending. It follows that scholastic realism, in Peirce's generalized sense, is presupposed by modern science not only in the laws it discovers but also in its very existence as a communal enterprise. Scholastic realism is thus a corollary of logic, that is, the full and correct account of what is required for scientific inquiry.

The reality of the scientific community brings us to a last aspect of science in Peirce's philosophy, which is the theme of this chapter. It suggests a single focus to which the preceding chapters may be brought.

A

We must first develop, briefly hence dogmatically, the idea that a community is more than its members. All relations are general, yet particular individuals – individual things and persons – incorporate relations. That is to say, they are what they are in virtue of relations: relations of their parts to one another and relations of the whole to other things or persons. What, for example, is a stone apart from its having mass? Yet, inertial mass is a dispositional property the stone has in relation to possible others: it is how much it would resist a force on it. A stone's mass is a would-be-if. And the relations of an individual's parts obtain continuously over the small space and span of time that the individual occupies: these are other would-be-ifs, since any continuum is divisible but undivided. A stone, then, is more than the atoms that compose it, as it is also their composition. A standing wave in a mountain torrent is a reality, but it cannot be identified with its material constituents, since, as Heraclitus knew, it consists in their constant flow. Organisms, similarly, sustain themselves by a flux of material constituents: grass is made beef, birdseed birds. In organisms, matter is made to serve ends not its own: to sustain one or another organic form. So also communities: they are their members but are more than their members. Old members depart and new ones are recruited or born whilst the community remains the same community albeit with changed features. More importantly, much that the members of a community are would be impossible outside of that community. The kind of person a farmer, a laborer, a shopkeeper, a professional, a politician, a boulevardier, a courtesan, a con man or thief is, each with his peculiar ambitions, joys, anxieties, and defeats, is determined by that person's rôle in or against society. Societies of different kinds make different kinds of person possible. We saw this most dramatically in the case of the sage versus the scientist, the latter being a creature of a new sort, with purposes and pleasures inconceivable before the advent of modern science and before the advent of those institutions which that form of inquiry created for itself (Chapter 2, G).

Personhood itself is impossible apart from the use of a language in which to represent oneself to oneself, thereby acquiring self-consciousness, and also its use to represent oneself to others, for example, in making promises, thereby acquiring rights and responsibilities. But language is a social product and, therefore, personhood is a social product.[2] The

---

[2] That selves are social is a well-known theme of Peirce's, which he at first expressed in one-sided form (e.g., in 1868 at EP1:20), later more fully (e.g., in 1905 at EP2:337–38 and 347–48): see

freedom that distinguishes persons from other animals is a social product. For, the capacity of a person to deliberate, to ask himself, 'Should I do this when I can do that instead?', depends on having a language. Conversely, the health and vigor of a society depends on the freedom it accords its members to make choices. But that freedom, the freedom to choose, is inseparable from the deeper freedom, the freedom to be, that consists in ways of being – varieties of social rôles and types of person – that society makes possible.

In particular, the education of a scientist is not an indoctrination or even instruction in a system of philosophy. Rather, as noted above (Chapter 2, G), by imparting a knowledge of present-day theory and a mastery of existing techniques, it empowers one to refute received ideas, form new conjectures, and make new discoveries, including normative discoveries of technique, method, and purpose. It frees one to make a contribution that could not otherwise be made and to be something that could not otherwise be. Nor could the community of scientists exist, or be what it now is, without thus freeing its members.

Hence a persistent theme of Peirce's (see, again, Chapter 2, G), that modern science is a form of life distinctively moral, one in which egoistic desires are subordinated to a goal transcending one's self. That goal is the growth, forever incomplete, of a form of knowledge that is essentially social. The locus of knowledge is thus no longer an individual mind but is the community, potentially infinite. To adopt that goal, one is as it were born again, acquiring a new and perhaps happier identity, as part of a larger, indeed illimitable, whole. The specialist's joy is in contributing to the growth of a knowledge of which he can possess only a small and uncertain part. That goal is vague, seen as it were through a glass darkly: for, what is finally to count as knowledge, explanation, and understanding remains to be determined by future inquiry. Faith in that goal, supported but not proven by the history of inquiry's progress to date, binds specialists into a communion not wholly unlike other communities of the faithful. That idea of faith is Peirce's: his writings on religion relate inner spirit to communal worship and distinguish both from doctrine, that is, theology, for which he frequently expressed contempt (see especially 6.429–451, dated 1893 and c.1895). Scientific theory and method are meant to evolve as a function of experience,

Colapietro (1989) for correction, in light of Peirce's later writings, of his initial overstatement, and Short (1997) for development of Peirce's implied idea of selfhood as linguistic act; also, Singer (1980).

and that distinguishes science from theology – which also evolves with experience, but is not meant to.

How ironic! Has not science been the enemy of faith? Surely Peirce intended the irony. He could not have missed it. Besides, his descriptions of science often were ironic. In almost his first writing, he characterized science in terms of that which modern science is supposed to have rejected from birth, or even to have been born in rejecting, namely, medieval scholasticism (Chapter 5, A). He could have made the same points about science without employing that comparison; the point of making the comparison was perhaps to force one to note also the differences between science and scholasticism. The same applies to his retention of the term 'scholastic realism' for a metaphysics that became, under his hand, far broader and deeper than scholastic realism originally was. His use of the language of Christianity to describe the life of science is similarly hyperbolic. In all these cases, hyperbole serves to draw attention to ironic intent, so as to drive the point of the irony home. But what was that point?

B

Second only to the Protestant Reformation, modern science is thought to have been the font of modernity, that restless condition of aimless individualism, with societies always in turmoil and no settled conviction about what is best. The story is familiar but must briefly be repeated. Despite their personal theism, early modern scientists, from Kepler and Galileo to Boyle and Newton, presented a view of the universe as matter-in-motion, where the motions are to be explained by mechanistic principles alone. Neither freedom nor purpose has a place in that universe. So far as there are values and a distinction of right from wrong, those values and that distinction transcend what can be known empirically; for purpose, if any exists, is God's, the creator of this machine, and God and His purposes can be known only by revelation. Not only moral values but even colors as we experience them and also sounds, scents, and tastes, the so-called secondary qualities, are absent from the world portrayed in modern physics. No longer at the center of a cosmos, we feel ourselves to be homeless in the universe. There is in it no purpose for us and nothing that answers to our feelings, moral or aesthetic. Revelation aside, there is no guide to action. We act mechanically as our desires drive us, which puts moral responsibility into question. What we call 'good' is merely what we happen to desire; hence, we can desire nothing *because* it is good. Political rule, therefore, is arbitrary: a mechanism by which some make their desires prevail over others. Revelation aside, political science has no basis on which to distinguish better from worse regimes; it can only be a study of the mechanics of power. So, at least, is the view that seems to be forced on us by modern science.

Peirce, to the contrary, by defining science as inquiry and by rejecting what later came to be known as foundationalism, was able to separate science from any particular doctrine, no matter how important it was in early modern science. Thus, he always denied that science is wedded to a materialist metaphysics and a mechanistic ideal of explanation (Chapter 2). As to mechanicalism: after some vague hints and false starts (the 1890's cosmogony: Chapter 6), Peirce argued that nineteenth-century science reintroduced the classical idea of final causation or teleological explanation, albeit in modified form. The question of materialism is more complicated: in addition to the fact that the idea of matter has been successively transformed with each major advance in physics, there is also an argument to be made that matter is defined by the laws of mechanics which must therefore be real if matter is, though unlike matter they do not exist at any place at any time. But, then, it is a mistake to suppose that modern science is responsible for the idea that nothing but individual things and persons are real. Peirce traced that idea, which supports the moral (or immoral) doctrine of egoism, to Ockham's fourteenth-century nominalist attack on scholastic realism, and he argued that its association with modern science, even in the minds of scientists themselves, is a mere confusion due to historical accident (6.348).

The rediscovery of final causation yields a cascade of consequences. The theory of natural selection, as Peirce glossed it, enables us to explain and to defend what we never were able consistently to deny, even when subscribing to the mechanistic ideal of explanation: namely, that eyes exist for the purpose of seeing, teeth for the purpose of chewing, and so on. Such purposes are known not by revelation but empirically, by induction and hypothesis: we observe a persistent pattern of events, one naturally conceived of as means sustained by the ends they serve. But that explanation is vague and begs to be made more definite. One might suppose intentional creation by a supernatural Creator, but explanation by natural selection makes that hypothesis unnecessary. Purpose, immanent rather than transcendent, thereby re-enters our idea of nature. And, as purpose grounds value, the values so grounded are real also. The purposes that ground those values explain the persistence of moral judgment. Thus we can explain and defend something else we never stopped believing, that we learn of good and evil through experience. As noted in Chapter 9, the supposed dichotomy of fact and value – the foundation of modern relativism, subjectivism, and cynicism – is thus demolished. Step by step, Peirce saw modern science reintroducing what it is supposed to have destroyed.

The same applies even to secondary qualities: Peirce persistently attempted to rescue the reality of the world as we experience it, its colors and sounds and scents, from reductive materialism. In the 1890s he did so in a way that proved abortive, via the hypothesis that feelings, freed from their being felt, are the basic constituents of matter (Chapter 6). Before and after the 1890s, he reaffirmed on other grounds the old doctrine of direct or immediate perception. The grounds were less clear in 1871 (EP1:91) than they later became, for example, in his 1903 Harvard lectures (Chapter 8, G). What happened in the meantime was his experimental work of the 1870s, establishing the scale he used in classifying stars' magnitudes. Those experiments showed that the slightest differences in color-sensation correspond to differences in the physical properties of light – hue to wavelength and brightness to wave-amplitude (Chapter 7, A and B). What then is left of the idea that secondary qualities are 'merely subjective'? Needless to say, in reaffirming the doctrine of direct perception, Peirce also transformed its meaning.

To all of this, we may add what we earlier noted: that Peirce made the life of science to be a model of morality, opposed to selfish individualism, and even to be a form of devotion nearly or quite religious. Thus, almost everything he said about science (one major exception is noted below) was to the effect of opposing it to that for which modern science is usually thought to bear some responsibility, namely, modernity. This was deeply ironic even when not expressed in the rhetorical mode of irony. When that mode was employed, it was evidently for the purpose of drawing attention to the irony. This suggests – see this chapter's epigraph – that it was his view of the relation of modern science to modernity that Peirce was most serious about.

C

Nothing is more characteristically modern than to deplore modernity. Nor was there anything original in Peirce's contrasting the modern world to medieval society. By the middle of the nineteenth century, it had become a commonplace to worry about the decline of religious faith (Mathew Arnold's 'Dover Beach' was published in 1867), and to indulge in a romantic fantasy of the High Middle Ages as an idyllic time of social harmony and universal peace lived amidst the beauty of Gothic cathedrals and ritual worship. Medievalism (a term coined in the 1850s), which took many forms, had begun a hundred years earlier in the Romantic reaction to the Enlightenment.

Peirce's originality does not lie in his attacking modernity but in his attacking it in the most modern way possible: on the basis of modern science itself.[3] That judo trick is advertised by his ironic turns of phrase. It has the virtue not only of originality but of force. How better to counter the deplorable features of modernity than to show that they are contrary to their supposed source and justification? Reactionary attempts to combat modernism, by sidelining modern science as 'merely instrumental', fail (Chapter 3). They do so, because the instrumental success of science proves that its theories, fallible and incomplete as they are, reflect reality. The philosophical significance of modern science cannot successfully be denied. Instead of denying that significance, Peirce argued that it is the opposite of what it has been taken to be.

There is, however, one feature of modernity, perhaps the one most often deplored, that Peirce did not oppose. Instead, he embraced it, making it, with a crucial amendment, the crowning virtue of modern science. The feature I mean is the one that throughout this book I have most emphasized, namely, restlessness – permanent dissatisfaction with what is already known, a never satisfied desire to learn more, a readiness to overturn received views. And in that restless endeavor, individualism of a kind is also embraced; for, scientific inquiry depends on individuals thinking things through for themselves, making novel observations, and introducing new hypotheses. But this is a restlessness that is not aimless and an individualism that is not egoistic. It has an aim, dimly perceived, and that aim, even though purely intellectual and not at all concerned with utility, is social, not selfish.

If we seek a unifying perspective on Peirce's thought, then 'modern science contra modernity' is perhaps the rubric least objectionable. But I think we should not seek to reduce to unity his persistently experimental philosophy. The inquiries he initiated, astounding in number and originality, are subject to development along diverse and not always compatible lines. Those that will prove most fruitful are the ones presently furthest from completion.

---

[3] The only other writer to take this line that I can think of was Peirce's school friend, Francis Ellingwood Abbot, whose 1885 book, *Scientific Theism*, similarly related modern science to scholastic realism; but that book and its author would now be forgotten but for Peirce's mention of them. Which of the two friends most influenced the other? It is not now possible to know.

Bibliography

TCSPS is the *Transactions of the Charles S. Peirce Society*. The letters 'U' and 'P' stand for 'University' and 'Press', respectively. Where date of original publication was deemed significant but differs from the date of the publication (sometimes a translation, sometimes a later edition) cited, the two dates are given in that order, separated by a slash (/).

Anderson, Douglas. 1995, *Strands of System: The Philosophy of Charles Peirce*, Purdue UP.

Apel, Karl Otto. 1980, *Towards a Transformation of Philosophy*, Adey and Frisby, trans., Routledge & Kegan Paul.

    1981, *Charles S. Peirce: From Pragmatism to Pragmaticism*, Krois, trans., U Massachusetts P.

Atkins, Richard Kenneth. 2016, *Peirce and the Conduct of Life*, Cambridge UP.

    2018, *Charles S. Peirce's Phenomenology: Analysis and Consciousness*, Oxford UP.

Ayer, A. J. 1968, *The Origins of Pragmatism*, Macmillan.

Baker, Victor. 2009, 'Charles S. Peirce and the "Light of Nature"', in Gary D. Rosenberg, ed., *The Revolution in Geology from the Renaissance to the Enlightenment*, Geological Society of America, Memoir 203, 259–66.

Bellucci, Francesco and Pietarinen, Ahti-Veikko. 2016, 'Existential Graphs as an Instrument of Logical Analysis: Part I. Alpha', in Andrew Arana et al., eds., *The Review of Symbolic Logic* (published online by Cambridge UP), 209–37.

Bergman, Mats. 2012, 'Improving Our Habits: Peirce and Meliorism', in de Waal and Skowroński, eds., 2012.

Bernstein, Richard. 1964, 'Peirce's Theory of Perception', in Moore and Robin, eds., 1964.

    1965a, 'Action, Conduct, and Self-Control', in Bernstein, ed. 1965.

Bernstein, Richard, ed. 1965b, *Perspectives on Peirce*, Yale UP.

Boler, John. 1963, *Charles Peirce and Scholastic Realism*, U Washington P.

    2004, 'Peirce and Medieval Thought', in Misak, ed., 2004.

Boorse, Henry and Motz, Lloyd, eds. 1966, *The World of the Atom*, 2 vols., Basic Books.

Brandon, Robert N. 1996, *Concepts and Methods in Evolutionary Biology*, Cambridge UP.

Brent, Joseph. 1993, *Charles Sanders Peirce: A Life*, Indiana UP.

Brunning, Jacqueline and Forster, Paul, eds. 1997, *The Rule of Reason: The Philosophy of Charles Sanders Peirce*, U Toronto P.

Burch, Robert W. 1991, *A Peircean Reduction Thesis*, Texas Tech UP.

Burch, Robert W. and Saatkamp, Herman J. Jr., eds. 1992, *Frontiers in American Philosophy*, Texas A&M Press.

Butterfield, Herbert. 1957, *The Origins of Modern Science*, rev. ed., G. Bell & Sons.

Buzzelli, Donald. 1972, 'The Argument of Peirce's "New List of Categories"', TCSPS.

Bywater, Ingram. 1909, *Aristotle on the Art of Poetry*, Oxford at the Clarendon Press.

Clagett, Marshall. 1959, *Science of Mechanics in the Middle Ages*, U Wisconsin P.

Cohen, I. Bernard. 1985, *The Birth of the New Physics*, rev. ed., W. W. Norton.

Colapietro, Vincent. 1989, *Peirce's Approach to the Self*, SUNY P.
  2012a, 'The Proof of the Pudding', TCSPS.

Colapietro, Vincent. 2012b, '*Traditions of Innovation and Improvisation: Jazz as Metaphor, Philosophy as Jazz*', in de Waal and Skowroński, eds., 2012.

Crombie, A. C. 1952/1969, *Augustine to Galileo*, 2 vols., Penguin Books.

Davidson, Donald. 1984, *Truth and Interpretation*, Oxford UP.

Delaney, C. F. 1993, *Science, Knowledge, and Mind: A Study in the Philosophy of C.S. Peirce*, U Notre Dame P.

De Morgan, Augustus. 1846–68/1966, *On the Syllogism and Other Writings*, Heath, ed., Routledge & Kegan Paul.

Dennett, Daniel C. 2017, *From Bacteria to Bach and Back: The Evolution of Minds*, Norton.

Descartes, René. 1954, *Descartes: Philosophical Writings*, Anscombe and Geach, eds., Thomas Nelson and Sons.

De Tienne, André. 1989, 'Peirce's Early Method of Finding the Categories', TCSPS.
  1996, *L'analytique de la représentation chez Peirce: La genèse de la théorie des catégories*, Publications des Facultés universitaires Saint-Louis (Bruxelles).

de Waal, Cornelis. 2012, '*Who's Afraid of Charles Sanders Peirce?*', in de Waal and Skowroński, eds., 2012.

de Waal, Cornelis and Krzysztof Piotr Skowroński, eds. 2012, *The Normative Thought of Charles S. Peirce*, Fordham UP.

Dewey, John and Arthur Bentley. 1949, *Knowing and the Known*, The Beacon Press.

Dijksterhuis, E. J. 1938/1987, *Archimedes*, Dikshoorn, trans., Princeton UP.
  1950/1986, *The Mechanization of the World Picture*, Dikshoorn, trans., Princeton UP.

Drake, Stillman. 1957, Introduction and notes to Galileo 1610–23/1957.
  1974, Introduction to Galileo 1638/1974.
  1978, *Galileo at Work: His Scientific Biography*, U Chicago P.
  1990, *Galileo: Pioneer Scientist*, U Toronto P.

Ducasse, C. J. 1924/69, *Causation and the Types of Necessity*, Dover.

Duhem, Pierre. 1954, *The Aim and Structure of Physical Theory*, Wiener, trans., Princeton UP.

  1969, *To Save the Phenomena*, Doland and Maschler, trans., U Chicago P.

Esposito, Joseph L. 1980, *Evolutionary Metaphysics*, Ohio UP.

Feyerabend, Paul. 1962, 'Explanation, Reduction, and Empiricism', in *Scientific Explanation, Space and Time*, Feigl and Maxwell, eds., U Minnesota P.

  1965, 'Problems of Empiricism', in *Beyond the Edge of Certainty*, Colodny, ed., Prentice Hall.

Fisch, Max. 1986, *Peirce, Semeiotic, and Pragmatism*, Ketner and Kloesel, eds., Indiana UP.

Fisch, Max and Cope, Jackson I. 1952, '*Peirce at Johns Hopkins University*', in Weiner and Young, eds., 1952.

Fisher, R. A. 1930, *The Genetical Theory of Natural Selection*, Oxford UP.

Fitzgerald, John J. 1966, *Peirce's Theory of Signs as Foundation for Pragmatism*, Mouton.

Freeman, Eugene, ed. 1983, *The Relevance of Charles Peirce*, Monist Library of Philosophy.

Galileo Galilei. 1590–1600/1960, *On Motion and Mechanics,* Drabkin and Drake, trans., U Wisconsin P.

  1610–23/1957, *Discoveries and Opinions of Galileo*, Drake trans., Doubleday.

  1632/1953, *Dialogue on the Great World Systems*, Salusbury/ de Santillana trans., U Chicago P.

  1638/1974, *Two New Sciences*, Drake trans., U Wisconsin P.

Gallie, W. B. 1952, *Peirce and Pragmatism*, Penguin Books.

Girel, Mathias. 2003, 'The Metaphysics and Logic of Psychology: Peirce's Reading of James' Principles', TCSPS.

Goodman, Nelson. 1965, *Fact, Fiction, and Forecast*, 2nd ed., Bobbs-Merrill.

Haack, Susan. 2007, *Defending Science – Within Reason*, Prometheus Books.

Hacking, Ian. 1965, *Logic of Statistical Inference*, Cambridge UP.

  1975, *The Emergence of Probability*, Cambridge UP.

  1980, 'The Theory of Probable Inference: Neyman, Peirce, and Braithwaite', in *Science, Belief, and Behavior: Essays in Honor of R.B. Braithwaite*, Mellor, ed., Cambridge UP.

  1983, *Representing and Intervening*, Cambridge UP.

  1990, *The Taming of Chance*, Cambridge UP.

Hall, A. Rupert. 1981, *From Galileo to Newton*, 2nd ed., Dover.

Hardy, G. H. 1940/1967, *A Mathematician's Apology*, Cambridge UP.

Hare, R. M. 1952, *The Language of Morals*, Oxford UP.

Harré, R. and Madden, E. H. 1973, *Causal Powers*, Basil Blackwell.

Hausman, Carl R. 1993, *Charles S. Peirce's Evolutionary Philosophy*, Cambridge UP.

Havenel, Jérôme. 2008, 'Peirce's Clarifications of Continuity', TCSPS.

Hempel, Carl. 1966, *Philosophy of Natural Science*, Prentice-Hall.

Herzberger, Hans. 1981, 'Peirce's Remarkable Theorem', in Sumner et al., eds., *Pragmatism and Purpose: Essays Presented to Thomas A. Goudge*, U Toronto P.

Hintikka, Jaako. 1983, '*C.S. Peirce's "First Real Discovery" and Its Contemporary Relevance*', in Freeman, ed., 1983.

   1997, '*The Place of C.S. Peirce in the History of Logical Theory*', in Brunning and Forster, eds., 1997.

Hookway, Christopher. 1985, *Peirce*, Routledge & Kegan Paul.

   2000, *Truth, Rationality, and Pragmatism: Themes from Peirce*, Oxford UP.

   2012, *The Pragmatic Maxim*, Oxford UP.

Hoover, Kevin D. and Wible, James R. 2020, 'Ricardian Inference: Charles S. Peirce, Economics, and Scientific Method', TCSPS.

Houser, Nathan. 2011, 'Action and Representation in Peirce's Pragmatism', in R. Calcaterra, ed., *New Perspectives on Pragmatism and Analytic Philosophy*, Editions Rodopi.

   2013, 'Peirce's Neglected Views on the Importance of the Individual for the Advancement of Civilization', *Cognitio* (Sao Paulo) 14(2), 163–77.

James, William. 1890, *Principles of Psychology*, 2 vols., Henry Holt and Company.

   1892, *Psychology: Briefer Course*, Henry Holt and Company.

   1909, *A Pluralistic Universe*, Longmans, Green, & Co.

   1912, *Essays in Radical Empiricism*, Longmans, Green, & Co.

Jastrow, Joseph. 1914, Letter to the Editor, The Nation, May 14, p. 571.

   1916, 'Charles S. Peirce as a Teacher', *The Journal of Philosophy, Psychology, and Scientific Methods* 13(26), 723–26.

Kant, Immanuel. 1785/1948, 3rd ed. 1956, *Groundwork of the Metaphysics of Morals*, H. J. Paton, trans., Hutchinson & Co.

   1785/1959, *Foundations of the Metaphysics of Morals*, Lewis White Beck, trans., The Liberal Arts Press.

   1797/1965, *The Metaphysical Elements of Justice*, John Ladd, trans., Bobbs-Merrill.

   1797/1964, *The Doctrine of Virtue*, Mary J. Gregor, trans., Harper & Row.

Kasser, Jeff. 2016, 'Two Conceptions of Weight of Evidence in Peirce's *Illustrations of the Logic of Science*, Erkenntnis 81(3), 629–48.

Kennington, Richard. 2004, *On Modern Origins: Essays in Early Modern Philosophy*, Lexington.

Kent, Beverly. 1987, *Charles S. Peirce: Logic and the Classification of Science*, McGill-Queens UP.

Kerr-Lawson, Angus. 1992, 'Stripped Down Burch', TCSPS.

Ketner, Kenneth, et al., eds. 1981, *Proceedings of the C.S. Peirce Bicentennial International Congress*, Texas Tech P.

Ketner, Kenneth Laine, ed. 1995, *Peirce and Contemporary Thought*, Fordham UP.

Kim, Jaegwon. 2005, *Physicalism, or Something Near Enough*, Princeton UP.

Koyré, Alexandre. 1943, 'Galileo and Plato', *Journal of the History of Ideas* 400–28, reprinted in Koyré 1968, Ch. 2.

   1957, *From the Closed World to the Infinite Universe*, Johns Hopkins.

1965, *Newtonian Studies*, Chapman and Hall.

Koyré, Alexandre. 1968, *Metaphysics and Measurement*, Chapman and Hall.

Kuhn, Thomas. 1957, *The Copernican Revolution*, Harvard UP.

1962/1970, *The Structure of Scientific Revolutions*, rev. ed., U Chicago P.

1977, *The Essential Tension*, U Chicago P.

2000, *The Road Since Structure* Conant and Haugeland, eds., U Chicago P.

Lakatos, Imre. 1978, *The Methodology of Scientific Research Programmes*, Cambridge UP.

Lane, Robert. 2018, *Peirce on Idealism and Realism*, Cambridge UP.

Laudan, Larry. 1973, 'C.S. Peirce and the Trivialization of the Self-Corrective Thesis', in *Foundations of Scientific Method in the 19th Century*, Giere and Westfall, eds., Indiana UP.

Lefebvre, Martin. 2007, 'Peirce's Esthetics: A Taste for Signs in Art', TCSPS.

Legg, Catherine. 2014, '"Things Unreasonably Compulsory": A Peircean Challenge to a Humean Theory of Perception, Particularly with Respect to Perceiving Necessary Truths', *Cognitio* (Sao Paulo).

Lenzen, Victor F. 1964, '*Charles S. Peirce as Astronomer*', in Moore and Robin, eds., 1964.

Levinas, Emmanuel. 1991, *Otherwise than Being: Or Beyond Essence*, Lingus, trans., Kluver.

Levi, Isaac. 1980, 'Induction as Self-correcting According to Peirce', in *Science, Belief, and Behavior: Essays in Honor of R.B. Braithwaite*, Mellor, ed., Cambridge UP.

2004, '*Beware of Syllogism: Statistical Reasoning and Conjecturing According to Peirce*', in Misak, ed., 2004.

Liszka, James. 2012, '*Charles Peirce on Ethics*', in de Waal and Skowroński, eds., 2012.

2014, 'Peirce's Idea of Ethics as a Normative Science', TCSPS.

2021, *Charles Peirce on Ethics, Esthetics and the Normative Sciences*, Routledge.

Maier, Anneliese. 1982, *On the Threshold of Exact Science: Selected Writings of Anneliese Maier on Late Medieval Natural Philosophy*, Sargent, ed. and trans., U Pennsylvania P.

Mayorga, Rosa Maria. 2012, '*Peirce's Moral "Realism"*', in de Waal and Skowroński, eds., 2012.

Merchant, Carolyn. 1980, *The Death of Nature: Women, Ecology, and the Scientific Revolution*, Harper & Row.

Migotti, Mark. 2004, 'Critical Notice: Christopher Hookway, Truth, Rationality and Pragmatism', *Canadian Journal of Philosophy* 34(2), 287–310.

2005, 'The Key to Peirce's View of the Role of Belief in Scientific Inquiry', *Cognitio* 6(1), 446–68.

Misak, Cheryl. 1991, *Truth and the End of Inquiry: A Peircean Account of Truth*, Oxford UP.

1994, 'A Peircean Account of Moral Judgments', in Parret, ed., 1994, 39–48.

1995, *Verificationism: Its History and Prospects*, Routledge.

2000, *Truth, Politics, and Morality: Pragmatism and Deliberation*, Routledge.

2004, '*C.S. Peirce on Vital Matters*', in Misak, ed., 2004, 150–74.

2008, 'Experience, Narrative, and Ethical Deliberation', *Ethics* 118(4), 614–32.

2013, *The American Pragmatists*, Oxford UP.

Misak, Cheryl, ed. 2004, *The Cambridge Companion to Peirce*, Cambridge UP.

Moore, Edward C. and Richard S. Robin, eds. 1964, *Studies in the Philosophy of Charles Sanders Peirce*, Second Series, U Massachusetts P.

Moore, Edward C., ed. 1993, *Charles S. Peirce and the Philosophy of Science: Papers from the Harvard Sesquicentennial Congress*, U Alabama P.

Moore, Matthew E., ed. 2010, *New Essays on Peirce's Mathematical Philosophy*, Open Court.

Murphey, Murray G. 1961, *The Development of Peirce's Philosophy*, Harvard UP.

1968, 'Kant's Children: The Cambridge Pragmatists', TCSPS.

Nagel, Ernest. 1961, *The Structure of Science*, Harcourt, Brace, & World.

Neugebauer, O. 1969, *The Exact Sciences in Antiquity*, 2nd ed., Dover.

Newton, Isaac. 1687/1962, *Mathematical Principles of Natural Philosophy* (Motte's 1729 translation of the 1687 *Principia*, revised by Florian Cajori), 2 vols., U California P.

Nowell-Smith, P. H. 1954, *Ethics*, Penguin.

Parker, Kelly. 1998, *The Continuity of Peirce's Thought*, Vanderbilt UP.

Parret, Herman, ed. 1994, *Peirce and Value Theory*, Benjamins.

Partington, J. R. 1957, *A Short History of Chemistry*, 3rd ed., Macmillan.

Peirce, Charles Sanders. 1931–58, *Collected Papers of Charles Sanders Peirce*, vols. 1–6, Hartshorne and Weiss, eds., vols. 7–8, Burks ed., Harvard UP.

1958, *Values in a Universe of Chance*, Wiener, ed., Doubleday.

1982–2010, *Writings of Charles S. Peirce: A Chronological Edition*, vols. 1–6, 8, various editors, Peirce Edition Project, Indiana UP.

1992, *Reasoning and the Logic of Things: The Cambridge Conferences Lectures of 1898*, Ketner, ed., Harvard UP.

1997, *Pragmatism as a Principle and Method of Right Thinking*, Turrisi, ed., SUNY P.

2010, *Philosophy of Mathematics: Selected Writings*, Moore, ed. Indiana UP.

Perry, Ralph Barton. 1935, *The Thought and Character of William James*, 2 vols., Little, Brown.

Popper, Karl. 1934/1959, *The Logic of Scientific Discovery*, Harper & Row.

1963, *Conjectures and Refutations*, Routledge & Kegan Paul.

1972, *Objective Knowledge*, Oxford UP.

Potter, Vincent G. 1967, *Charles S. Peirce on Norms and Ideals*, U Massachusetts P.

Potter, Vincent G. and Paul B. Shields, 1977, 'Peirce's Definitions of Continuity', TCSPS.

Putnam, Hilary. 1978, *Meaning and the Moral Sciences*, Routledge & Kegan Paul.

1981, *Reason, Truth, and History*, Cambridge UP.

1990, *Realism with a Human Face*, Harvard UP.

1995, '*Peirce's Continuum*', in Ketner 1995.

2002, *The Collapse of the Fact/Value Dichotomy*, Harvard UP.

2004, *Ethics without Ontology*, Harvard UP.

Quine, W. V. O. 1960, *Word and Object*, MIT P.

1961, *From a Logical Point of View*, rev. ed., Harvard UP.

1969, *Ontological Relativity and Other Essays*, Columbia UP.

1974, *The Roots of Reference*, Open Court.

1990, *Pursuit of Truth*, Harvard UP.

Raposa, Michael L. 1989, *Peirce's Philosophy of Religion*, Indiana UP.

Rawls, John. 1971, *A Theory of Justice*, Harvard UP.

1996, *Political Liberalism*, Columbia UP.

1999, *A Theory of Justice: Revised Edition*, Harvard UP.

Rescher, Nicholas. 1978, *Peirce's Philosophy of Science*, U Notre Dame P.

Reynolds, Andrew. 2002, *Peirce's Scientific Metaphysics: The Philosophy of Chance, Law, and Evolution*, Vanderbilt UP.

Roberts, Don D. 1973, *The Existential Graphs of Charles S. Peirce*, Mouton.

1978, 'An Introduction to Peirce's Proof of Pragmaticism', TCSPS.

Robin, Richard. 1964, 'Peirce's Doctrine of the Normative Sciences', in Moore and Robin, eds., 1964.

1967, *Annotated Catalogue of the Papers of Charles S. Peirce*, U Massachusetts P.

1997, 'Classical Pragmatism and Pragmatism's Proof', in Brunning and Forster, eds., 1997.

Rosensohn, William L. 1974, *The Phenomenology of C.S. Peirce: From the Doctrine of Categories to Phaneroscopy*, B. R. Grüner.

Salmon, Wesley. 1971, 'Statistical Explanation', in *Statistical Explanation and Statistical Relevance*, Salmon, ed., U Pittsburgh P.

1984, *Scientific Explanation and the Causal Structure of the World*, Princeton UP.

Sambursky, Shmuel. 1987, *The Physical World of the Greeks*, Princeton UP.

de Santillana, Giorgio. 1955, *The Crime of Galileo*, U Chicago P.

Savan, David. 1952, 'On the Origins of Peirce's Phenomenology', in Weiner and Young, eds., 1952.

Schiller, Friedrich. 1801/1967, *On the Aesthetic Education of Man: In a Series of Letters*, Wilkinson and Willoughby, trans., Oxford UP.

Sellars, Wilfrid. 1963, *Science, Perception, and Reality*, Routledge & Kegan Paul.

Sheriff, John K. 1994, *Charles Peirce's Guess at the Riddle*, Indiana UP.

Shin, Sun-Joo. 2002, *The Iconic Logic of Peirce's Graphs*, MIT Press.

Short, T. L. 1980a, 'An Analysis of Conceptual Change', *American Philosophical Quarterly*.

1980b, '*Peirce and the Incommensurability of Theories*', The Monist, Reprinted in Freeman, ed., 1983.

1983, 'Teleology in Nature', *American Philosophical Quarterly*.

1988, 'Hypostatic Abstraction in Empirical Science', *Grazer Philosophische Studien* (Graz, Austria).

1997, 'Hypostatic Abstraction in Self-Consciousness', in Brunning and Foster, eds., 1997.

2000a, 'Peirce on the Aim of Inquiry: Another Reading of 'Fixation', TCSPS.

2000b, 'Was Peirce a Weak Foundationalist?', TCSPS.

2002, 'Darwin's Concept of Final Cause: Neither New Nor Trivial', *Biology and Philosophy*.

2007, *Peirce's Theory of Signs*, Cambridge UP.

2010a, 'Did Peirce Have a Cosmology?', TCSPS.

2010b, 'What Was Peirce's Objective Idealism?', *Cognitio* (São Paulo, Brazil).

2012, 'Normative Science?', TCSPS.

2014, 'Questions Concerning Certain Claims Made for the "New List"', TCSPS.

2015, 'Empiricism Expanded', TCSPS.

2017, 'The 1903 Maxim', TCSPS.

2018, 'Peirce's Irony', TCSPS.

2021, 'On a Mistaken Emendation of Peirce's 1903 Harvard Lectures', TCSPS.

Sibley, Frank. 1959, 'Aesthetic Concepts', *Philosophical Review* 351–73.

Silber, John R. 1959, 'The Copernican Revolution in Ethics: The Good Reexamined', *Kant-Studien,* Band 51, Kölner Universitäts-Verlag.

1960, 'The Ethical Significance of Kant's Religion', Part II of the Introduction to the 2nd ed. of Kant, *Religion within the Limits of Reason Alone*, Greene and Hudson, trans., Harper Torchbooks.

Singer, Milton, 1980, 'Signs of the Self: An Exploration of Semiotic Anthropology', *American Anthropologist*, New Series, 82(3), 485–507.

Skagestad, Peter. 1981, *The Road of Inquiry: Charles Peirce's Pragmatic Realism*, Columbia UP.

Sowa, John F. 2007, 'Peirce's Contributions to the 21st Century', www.jfsowa.com/pubs/csp21st.pdf (accessed August 30, 2007).

Taylor, Richard. 1966, *Action and Purpose*, Prentice-Hall.

Thompson, Manley. 1953, *The Pragmatic Philosophy of C.S. Peirce*, Chicago UP.

Tiercelin, Claudine. 1993, 'Peirce's Realistic Approach to Mathematics: Or, Can One Be a Realist without Being a Platonist?' in Moore, ed., 1993.

2010, 'Peirce on Mathematical Objects and Mathematical Objectivity', in Moore, ed., 2010.

Toulmin, Stephen. 1953, *The Philosophy of Science*, Hutchinson.

1961, *Foresight and Understanding*, Hutchinson.

1972, *Human Understanding*, Princeton UP.

Turley, Peter T. 1977, *Peirce's Cosmology*, Philosophical Library.

Weinberg, Steven. 1992, *Dreams of a Final Theory*, Random House.

Weiner, Philip P. and Young, Frederick H., eds. 1952, *Studies in the Philosophy of Charles Sanders Peirce*, Harvard UP.

Weiss, Paul. 1965, 'Biography of Charles S. Peirce', in Bernstein 1965.

Wells, Rulon. 1964, 'The True Nature of Peirce's Evolutionism', in Moore and Robins, eds., 1964.

Whitehead, Alferd North. 1929, *Process and Reality*, Macmillan.

William of Ockham. 1957, *Ockham: Philosophical Writings*, Boehner, ed. and trans., Thomas Nelson and Sons.

Williams, Bernard. 1978, *Descartes: The Project of Pure Enquiry*, Penguin.

1985, *Ethics and the Limits of Philosophy*, Harvard UP.

Wilson, Aaron. 2012, 'The Perception of Generals', TCSPS.

Wilson, Curtis. 1956, *William Heytesbury: Medieval Logic and the Rise of Mathematical Physics*, U Wisconsin P.

Wittgenstein, Ludwig. 1953, *Philosophische Untersuchungen/ Philosophical Investigations*, Macmillan.

Woodward, James. 2003, *Making Things Happen: A Theory of Causal Explanation*, Oxford UP.

Wright, Larry. 1976, *Teleological Explanation*, U California P.

Index

For EU product safety concerns, contact us at Calle de José Abascal, 56–1°, 28003 Madrid, Spain or eugpsr@cambridge.org.

www.ingramcontent.com/pod-product-compliance
Ingram Content Group UK Ltd.
Pitfield, Milton Keynes, MK11 3LW, UK
UKHW020356140625
459647UK00020B/2503